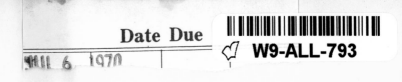

One Man Alone: RICHARD NIXON

Other Books by Ralph de Toledano

FRONTIERS OF JAZZ

SEEDS OF TREASON

SPIES, DUPES AND DIPLOMATS

DAY OF RECKONING

NIXON

LAMENT FOR A GENERATION

THE GREATEST PLOT IN HISTORY

THE WINNING SIDE

RFK: THE MAN WHO WOULD BE PRESIDENT

AMERICA, I-LOVE-YOU

One Man Alone:
RICHARD NIXON

RALPH DE TOLEDANO

Funk & Wagnalls   NEW YORK

Contents

1

A Beginning and An End

THE day was gray and cheerless, with the wind whipping the January dampness and chilling the feet, the spines, and the noses of the assembled crowd. The press stamped and gossiped before the white-painted abracadabra that is the Inaugural platform, a wooden temple standing before the imposing triptych of the Capitol. For the press it was a day of work, different from all other days only in degree of importance and the coverage their newspapers would give to the event. There was no telling when the red eye of the television cameras would swing their way, and so the reporters, correspondents, and scattering of columnists put on their show of above-the-battle interest, the bird-dog-and-cynic syndrome that is the mark of the nation's journalistic elite.

The more active and venturesome of the journalistic tribe were restively wondering what the Hippies and the Yippies were doing along Pennsylvania Avenue where it runs past the news-advantageous National Press Building. The wire service boys knew that trouble had already begun to brew, that arrests had been made, that the bearded and unkempt were already chanting their prefabricated slogans, tossing their paint cans on the wide ceremonial avenue, and sketching their graffiti—so they hoped—on the wall of history. But the main action was on Washington's high ground, on that knoll which Pierre L'Enfant had chosen as the hub of the nation, and perhaps the world. For here, in a grayness that threatened but never delivered the paralyzing snows of John Fitzgerald Kennedy's Inaugural day, Richard Milhous Nixon, the loser of 1960, would assume the world's most powerful office in the world's most critical hour.

With the lifting of a hand, those who over the years and through all the bright and dark hours had called him "Dick" would take a step back and address him as "Mr. President." The majesty of office would shut off this once-eager, once-accommodating boy from everyone but his wife, his children, and his valet. It had happened before, and it was about to happen on January 20, 1969—the chemical change that takes one man among 200 million and makes him the President of the United States. It was for this that the press had gathered—to see a man hated and beloved, attacked and defended, feared and trusted, transmogrified into a symbol that had little to do with his scope, his intellect, his dedication, or his genes.

The Inaugural ceremonies, for those who have seen them more than once, are bland though impressive—the swearing-in and the Inaugural Address that will be remembered for only a phrase or two, and then the long parade of foot troops and marching bands, satisfying the vanity of the participants and testing the patience of those whose major frame of reference is the Inaugural Ball, more plural with each passing Presidency. But in this instance, there were additional elements, promising drama or comedy but newsworthy. There on that lumber temple would be an outgoing President who had confounded his foes by laying aside his legendary pride and refusing to run for reelection in a magnificent gesture of self-denial—Lyndon Baines Johnson, out of the stellar role by his own choice. And there with him would stand the Vice President, Hubert Horatio Humphrey, defeated pretender to the Johnsonian throne. How would they act at this moment of divestiture? This, more than the ceremonial laying-on of hands that transfers the Presidential power, concerned the men who must write each day of humdrum events as if Washington were one round of ringing oratory and principled battle.

Lyndon Johnson, his sad, basset-hound face a complexity of enigmas, gave the reporters little to set their experienced fingers working over the typewriter keys. And Hubert Humphrey, whose tears and joyousness had for decades irritated and amused the press, was withdrawn behind a rigid mask that betrayed only his determination not to betray his deep but sportsmanlike disappointment. The outgoing President and Vice President, now citizens in a city that sets office above everything, were remote figures, yet tempting enough to move one reporter to say, "I'd give a thousand bucks to be able to know what's going on in their minds." As it happened it was another former Congressman, former Senator, and former Vice President who recaptured the moment and made the Inaugural his.

There is little in Richard Nixon's Inaugural Address that grade school children will recite in future decades. The cynics brushed it aside as the product of the speechwriting factory that every Presidential candidate, every President, assembles for the chore of putting words in his mouth. For better or worse, however, the Nixon Inaugural was the President's alone, whatever other hands and brains worked at its fashioning. Not once, in the many years and the many speeches of his public life, had he delivered what his writers had handed to him. Always there was the Nixon rephrasing, in the musical sense, the recasting of language to fit his speech patterns, the cadence of his voice, his manner of breaking down subject matter into explicatory sequences.* And so he had labored over the Inaugural Address, conscious that the world would examine it for "influences"—for modes of expression not truly his own, and for those hortatory elements that would be alien to him.

* In the years of his Vice Presidency, Richard Nixon asked me on several occasions to draft a speech for him. I was thanked for my efforts, and some of the ideas of my text would appear in his final version. But the language would always be his, and so would the loose rhetorical construction. "The speeches you write 'listen well,' " I would tell him, "but you need a body of speeches that read well." He would always agree, but that was not his style, and it still isn't. He is a speaker, not a writer.

What the Inaugural Address achieved, however, was far more important than the plaudits of the literary community. The affective symbolism of the swearing-in had been marred by the whispered comments of the reporters as they watched the tall, big-boned Chief Justice of the United States administering the oath, with Pat Nixon holding the family Bible. Everyone in the assemblage knew that Earl Warren had nursed an abiding dislike for Richard Nixon since that November day in 1946 when the voters had elected a callow and overeager Californian to the House of Representatives in defiance of the older man's wishes and to his undisguised pique. Yet there they were, face to face, the nation's Chief Justice and its new Chief Magistrate, locked in the solemnity of the moment, their antagonisms no longer relevant—the one with a scant five months of service to the courts left to him, the other stepping on a stage as broad as his talents, his energies, and his goodwill could make it.

And now, as the new President moved to the podium to speak in a voice more deliberate, more somber than usual, one era ended and another began. The stridencies of Lyndon Johnson's times, the pious vulgarities, the unabashed but sometimes stumbling uses of power, the iron fist in the Texas drawl, the puzzled misunderstanding of the national temper, the endless equivocation that tarnished decent purpose—all these disappeared so quietly that it was some time before anyone realized that Washington's decibel level had suddenly dropped. The new President was doing his thing, and precisely what it was neither friend nor foe knew exactly. But the change was there and the difference was palpable.

"Each moment in history is a fleeting time, precious and unique," said a man newly invested in the majesty that the Presidency offers and eventually bestows.

> But some stand out as moments of beginning, in which courses are set that shape decades or centuries. This can be such a moment. Forces now are converging that make possible for the first time the hope that many of man's deepest aspirations can at last be realized. . . .
> The greatest honor history can bestow is the title of peace-

4

maker. This honor now beckons America—the chance to help lead the world at last out of the valley of turmoil and on to that high ground of peace that man has dreamed of since the dawn of civilization. If we succeed, generations to come will say of us now living that we mastered our moment, that we helped make the world safe for mankind.

This is our summons to greatness.

I believe the American people are ready to answer this call.

Whatever the secret intent of the Inaugural Address, it was meant to tranquilize, not to set pulses racing. It was the prologue to the kind of Administration he had determined to put together—unpartisan, unpretentious, low key, earnest, eclectic, reasonable, high in tone but never self-righteous, moderate in its patriotism and its internationalism, tolerant of multiplicity, and as devoid of ideology as a polarized nation would permit it to be.

To those who watched him as he measured out his words, the changes in him were striking. He had ceased to be Richard Nixon, the officeholder, or Dick Nixon, the campaigner. In the few weeks between the election and the Inauguration he had become President Nixon in an osmotic process that filtered through his political tissues the newfound respect of public comment and the burdens and prerogatives of his unique office. There was also a bemused wonder that Nixon had made it. During the 1960 Republican Convention, when Republican hopes were high that he had locked up the election, a radical columnist remarked: "He's going to lose, and not for the reasons that people usually give. Nixon's unlucky, and that's why he can't win."

The course of that election campaign, and his later defeat in his attempt to win a California Governorship that should have fallen into his lap with little effort, bore out that prophecy. Nixon himself believed that he was finished, that he could play only an ancillary role in the nation's political life. He had retired to New York and to the business of making enough money to give his wife and family the kind of security—and luxury—that had passed them by during his years as Congressman, Senator, and even Vice President. Money had never been a major determinant in his life,

5

but it had its uses—and the Fifth Avenue look had its appeal. During the congressional years, the Nixons had lived in a pleasant but hardly pretentious house in Washington's Spring Valley. On his election to the Vice Presidency, he had moved to Wesley Heights, a neighborhood several cuts higher on the social scale. It was then that he came close to exhibiting pride in his possession, showing to friends the spacious rooms, a large study that never gave any signs of having been used for work, and a long view into the green of Glover Park.

But the New York years had been restless ones for Richard Nixon. The law was a challenge, but whatever stimulation it presented was circumscribed. In 1964 and 1966 he took to the campaign trail, driving himself and his staff headlong from airport to airport, from city to city as if his own political future were at stake—which, though few realized it, it was. He had promised Pat after the terrible California defeat that he would never again run for public office, a safe enough pledge at the time. It was the consensus of press, politicians, and public that Nixon had disqualified himself permanently.

In politics two strikes and you're out—and in the gubernatorial try Nixon had not even smelled the ball. Men running for office welcomed his help. He brought out the crowds and he gave party workers incentive. But his future was all in the past where politics were concerned, and none but the wide-eyed even mentioned the remote possibility that he would once again present himself to the public. From time to time there was talk of returning him to the Senate, but with New York as a base this was palpably impossible. Neither Senator Jacob Javits nor Governor Nelson Rockefeller, leaders of the anti-Nixon forces in the Republican Party and powers in the state, would have permitted it.

Riding from the Capitol to the White House in an Inaugural parade no duller or more listless than those that had quadrennially preceded it, the new President may have contemplated what the pundits had already proclaimed the greatest political comeback in the history of the Republic. He had achieved it by work and planning, by maneuver and guile, but mostly by making his availability the overriding factor. The other candidates were either weak or unacceptable to the Republican Party, particularly in the grass roots, where the choice was made. Those who might have counterpoised their candidacies to his were slow in their timing and meager in their institutional support.

Nixon had made it, and made it alone. True, he had called in the political debts that his many years of working for individuals and for the party machine had given him. Hardly a man, whether of small or large importance in the party, did not owe Nixon some sort of favor, some sort of gratitude for services rendered in the past. But the road was also strewn with friendships that had been dissolved, obligations that Nixon had ignored in the years of his rise and fall. Of these friendships and obligations there was much bitter talk, more from the sidelines than from those who might have felt the call to protest what was always misguidedly described as Nixon's lack of human feeling and personal loyalty.

Nixon, obviously, did not see it that way. Politics to him was more than a career or a profession. It was more than a way of life. It was life itself, and he had dedicated himself to it with a single-ness of purpose unmatched in the easygoing world of Washington or the boondock political scene. He had, from the start, been a loner. Those who considered themselves his friends were as much excluded from the sanctuary of his political dreams and his political motivations as the least "in" among his colleagues.

His major decisions were made in a solitude that was both physical and psychological. When he had to come to terms with the Hiss Case—to put it on the line or to withdraw, as his fellow Congressmen of the House Committee on Un-American Activities were disposed to do—Nixon took himself off to his parents' farm, where he thought through his position. But there were other times when, in conversation with a close friend, perhaps in the Vice President's Capitol Hill hideaway—a room reached by winding stairs and out of the mainstream of Senate communications—he would retreat into himself, pacing back and forth and, in reality, talking to himself and not to the ostensible recipient of his words. He also kept his life compartmentalized so that few if any of his "close" friends were aware of the degree of communication and intimacy he had with others. In time, he himself forgot.

In the early days of the journalistic quest for "the real Nixon" I had described him as "an introvert in an extrovert profession." The politician's back-slapping, anecdote-telling approach was not for him. He disliked the casual contact, the camaraderie over drinks, the barroom joke or obscenity. There were few who tried to tell him a dirty joke, but if exposed to one, he dutifully laughed. He had little small talk, and what there was of it might be witty but not especially humorous.

He was too single-minded to be quite at ease with people. Friends whose homes he had visited and whose wives and children he knew would, on seeing Nixon, find themselves plunged into a political dialogue. After a half-hour of this, Nixon would suddenly remember that it is customary to ask a few questions about a man's family. This embarrassing formality having been overcome, there would be a reversion to political matters. Nixon's fleeting awareness of these amenities betrayed his lack of interest in daily life apart from politics.

But for a President the ordinary rules of human discourse no longer obtain. The men who had given so much to his advancement would not necessarily be needed in the problems of governing. They could no longer loom large in the considerations of the nation or the White House palace guard. The power to affect the course of history was in temporary residence with the young men who had climbed the Nixon bandwagon at the strategic moment—before his ascendancy was completely certain, but after he had emerged from the shadows of despond.

There were shouts from the New Leftists and flying paint as the motorcade moved down Pennsylvania Avenue. But the police and the military units assigned to protect the parade route acted quickly and efficiently. The new President did not have to cope with the indignities that had been visited upon the Johnson Administration's Secretary of Defense, Robert Strange McNamara, or upon Secretary of State Dean Rusk. The new President may have thanked his stars that the sting had been taken out of the Vietnam war by the Paris negotiations. But he may also have mulled in his mind, as he smiled and waved at the crowds, the problems of any man who has just moved into a new house but still does not know where suits will hang or shoes be racked. For the Nixons, Richard and Thelma Patricia, this was the fifth major transfer of household gods in two decades. They could take it in their stride, even though locating a light switch in the dark might be a nuisance for several days.

Other questions, other problems were awaiting the new President as he rode down Pennsylvania Avenue. There were appointments to make, each weighed carefully against political needs and demands, and the threat of obstruction from a Congress dominated by the opposition. For all the soothing syrup that had been poured over the exacerbations of the Vietnamese war, it still presented problems and explosions that could upset plans for a renewal of his four-year lease on 1600 Pennsylvania Avenue. The system of alliances that had sustained Europe since the Second World War was in jeopardy. The economy, sound when seen only through the prism of the Gross National Product, was showing signs of fatigue. The nation's psyche was feeling the strain of too much permissiveness, too much tolerated crime, too much violence —and a superfluity of everything except restraint. Racial tensions, made taut by Supreme Court decisions, a national guilt-complex, and the hatreds and apathies of the body politic, found little relaxation. These, and a thousand other minor and major difficulties, confusions, and frustrations, were on the President's daily agenda.

Perhaps, as he spent his first night in the White House, the new President stared at the dark ceiling and asked himself what there was of the past that would be pertinent to the future. As a political figure he had consistently neutralized the efforts of friend or foe to mold him in a form alien to his nature. From time to time the Left and the Right each had attempted to re-create him in its own image. In the deadly shorthand of politics they sought to label him a reactionary or a liberal—as if it were obligatory to be either. Failing this, they had ascribed their own lack of insight to some flaw in Nixon's character, to "opportunism," to the emergence of a "new Nixon," or to a dozen other possible causes.

9

It had never come to them, simply, that Nixon was a Nixon Republican. In his Republicanism he was unabashed, but this was a party matter. In his personal formulation of the term he was a conservative. Speaking at a Republican luncheon in February 1959, he had said, "I don't think we could make a greater mistake than to say that because some people don't like being called conservative, the Republican Party should stop being conservative. We should be proud of what we believe."

But in the years of his troubled and dramatic rise, few had bothered to search for what *he* believed. Like Disraeli, he had argued that change was constant and necessary—that the great question was not whether change should be resisted but whether it should be carried out in relation to the laws and the traditions of the people, rather than to abstract principles and rigid doctrines. Like Disraeli, he felt that, in crisis, the human factor must override other considerations, that government must do what it can to minimize the privations and hardships of the poor and unemployed. But within the councils of government he had urged that the answer to unemployment was not merely to feed the unemployed. He had therefore advocated, along with direct aid to the unemployed, a revision of the tax structure that would cease to stifle the productive use of money and lead to the economic expansion that made for jobs rather than doles.

Through the years he had insisted that a free society was to a degree bound to ignore the act and the utterance of the vicious, the cantankerous, and the idiotic. But he also realized that in a behemoth state in which free forces become remote there was need for safeguards and impingements. Big business and big labor could not be allowed to fight freely if their conflict endangered those on the sidelines who could not cope with the mammoths, or if their battle imperiled the national interest. Minimal government was a dream in a nation organized by decades of New/Fair Deal encroachments and the coercion of the Johnson state, and then catapulted into a nuclear age of multibillion-dollar scientific projects. The individual corporation, the individual nuclear reactor, and the individual union loomed equally with government over the individual individual, inhibiting the interplay of social forces. Could single man redress the balance?

Nixon had called himself a conservative, but his definition had never rested on the belief that the color of a man's skin, the scuff marks on his shoes, or the religion of his birth or choice should create a hierarchy of rights. It was not only a question of human sensibilities. To Nixon, a lawyer, the language of the Fourteenth Amendment—forbidding the states to "make or enforce any law which shall abridge the privileges or immunities of citizens of the United States . . . [or] to deny to any person within its jurisdiction the equal protection of the laws"—had always remained crucial. "It's not a question of liberal or conservative," he would say.

Over the years Nixon had confused and irritated the intellectuals by his direct, undramatic, and unfashionable love of country—subjecting all action to the unfashionable criterion "What's best for America?" But he had refused to accept as an article of faith the perverse slogan "What's bad for General Motors is good for America." He had supported the United Nations as a faltering step in international order—thereby eliciting sharp criticism from doctrinaire conservatives. But he would not compromise that support by subscribing to a ritualistic belief in a supermechanistic world state—thereby earning the suspicion of the liberals. When, late in 1959, the steel industry and the Steelworkers Union had been deadlocked in their negotiations for a new contract, he had intervened to bring out a settlement that had forced both sides to consider the public interest, remaining consistent to the principle that government should not be the handmaiden of one interest or group—and the anti-statist conservatives had scolded him for not backing the steel companies. He had always respected the Bill of Rights as an instrument of the public weal, not as the fulcrum on which the lever of subversion could topple the Constitution—a concept that the liberals loudly deplored.

The issues, he had recognized, were not the test. The touchstone was a man's approach to the issues. He had lived through a period in which there was hardly a man who did not say he was against communism. But the measure of a legislator was not his

11

vote on specific anti-communist measures. The liberal mind, he had seen, could go along with any means proposed by its heroes, even as it was ready to accept Senator Humphrey's amendment to a communist control bill which provided for the mandatory setting-up of concentration camps in time of war. The *reductio ad absurdum* that made the communist problem a police matter, limited to the catching of spies, was not for him and it had brought him into conflict with the non-communist Left—as his assertion that "men become communists out of the best of motives" had upset the Right.

Looking back, Nixon could say that in what he had done and what he believed there had been a confluence of the theoretical and the practical. The current of the merged streams had borne his political boat. In the twenty-two years of his public life it had carried him past the shoals of dissension and distortion and along smoother waters of hope and achievement. There had been times of great discouragement in which he had envied those who drifted in the backwaters. At such times he had said to friends, "After this, no more. No more campaigns, no more speeches, no more battles." But he had continued. Understood or misunderstood, he had gone ahead. His course had never been decided by public opinion polls.

As President would he live up to what he had said a decade earlier: "It's the responsibility of a leader to lead public opinion, not just to follow it. Get the facts before making a decision, then develop support for that decision among the people by making the facts known to them. This was the way Abraham Lincoln, Theodore Roosevelt, and Woodrow Wilson worked—and it should be good enough for lesser men. If the public will not accept the facts as you see them—if you fail to convince people—then the failure is yours. You've lost and the failure is yours." Now that he was President, it would take courage and self-sufficiency to stand by them—and the kind of faith in himself that had sustained him in the long, troubled days of his comeback. History, chance, and his own capabilites had made him President. Would chance and history make him a good President?

There was a time for everything, Koheleth had preached. But

for the President of the United States that time is hedged in by the twenty-four hours between sunup and sunup. Even a man so adept at improving the shining moment as Richard Nixon, at utilizing the spaces between each tick of the clock, would find it hard to cope with time. And for the new President, thinking to the problems ahead, there was an additional stumbling-block. In his various capacities in government he had been able to handle each crisis as it came, alone and with no more than the mechanical help of his assistants. As President he would be compelled to accept the iron verdict that power, responsibility, and accountability must be delegated to others. This, for Richard Nixon—small-town boy from Whittier, eager Congressman, Senator, Vice President to a father image, man of all seasons in the political jungle—would be the test.

If the past is prologue, if the child is father to the man, the crystal ball of the new President's future would be the analysis of what had gone before, what had shaped him—as much as what he was. For a bothered and bewildered nation this was the great question mark. But for the new President, at that moment of his life, there was only one answer:

"For us, there is only the trying. The rest is not our business."*

---

* T. S. Eliot, from "East Coker," in *Four Quartets*.

2

Upward from Yorba Linda

HE was a determined boy, a hardworking boy, a lonely boy. Everything he had, he earned. He was respected and admired, sometimes envied, but the warmest and most spontaneous love came from his father. His mother loved him, too, but in her slight and gentle way Hannah Nixon was a woman of iron, annealed in a Quaker sense of duty. The love she gave helped make Richard Nixon what he is today; it gave him both drive and purpose. To many, considering the rise of Dick Nixon from penury in Yorba Linda to grandeur in the White House, the Horatio Alger analogy comes to mind—and it has been thoroughly plumbed by feature writers and Sunday supplement editors. But the comparison is forced, for there is little of the romantic hero in Nixon.

In another time and another place Richard Nixon would have been a farmer, living off the soil as his people before him had done for generations. Fate made him a product of a Los Angeles suburb, an aggressive student, a successful high school and collegiate politician, a lawyer, a Navy officer, a Congressman, a Senator, a Vice President, a political loser, and a President of the United States. In the years of his public life he became known as one of the most articulate men in America, yet he never broke loose from his introversion, never found the laughter that comes easily to some men, never learned to tell a dirty joke or to have one too many at the cocktail hour, never learned to give casually of his heart, never made a casual decision. From childhood he lived a disciplined life. Son, husband, father, he isolated himself from the day-to-day pleasures, the day-to-day relief that comes from wasting time. It was not only ambition that drove him, not the yearning for place and success, but the compulsion that drives the man alone to challenge history.

He would have been happier as a farmer, watching the quiet of twilight shrouding his fields.

How much was in his heredity, how much was passed on to him by a mother who both sustained him and leaned on him, how much was in his own unique alchemy? Historians will supply the answer when there is no one about to question their insights and their researches, when the chronicles of this time have become brittle and its *Weltanschauung* cold. For in his speeches, his writings, and his conversation Richard Nixon has said less about himself than any major public figure of the twentieth century. To this day those who probe in the kitchen middens of his life cannot say with certainty what his religion is or precisely where he stands on a hundred issues that his rhetoric has touched.

Those like myself who have known him, who have seen him in crisis and in triumph, can only approximate the nature and the meaning of this introvert who chose for himself the extrovert life of politics. The answer to the riddle—and Nixon has baffled arm-chair and professional psychologists—may be found in part in that strictly American heredity. Heredity is the operative word, for there have been Nixons and Milhouses in America almost as long as there has been a white man's America. And though Nixon has never made a fetish of it, the consciousness—and subconsciousness—of his antecedents as a fact of his life and character is with him at all times, as it should be.

On both his father's and mother's sides, Richard Nixon is of Scots-Irish extraction, the predominant strain of early American colonization—white, Anglo-Saxon, Protestant, if it does not offend his maternal Quaker forebears to be included in the WASP category.

Edward Nixon, the first of the family to reach the New World, landed in 1753, settling in Brandywine Hundred, Delaware. His two sons, John and George, fought in the War of Independence. John was Sheriff of Philadelphia and in that capacity gave the Declaration of Independence its first public reading. He rose to the rank of colonel in the Continental Army. George—private, ensign, and eventually lieutenant—crossed the Delaware with General Washington and fought in the Battle of Trenton. In time he followed the frontier to Ohio.

The records of the War Between the States show that George Nixon III of Clinton County enlisted with Company B, 73rd Ohio Voluntary Regiment. He is buried in Gettysburg, not far from the Eisenhower farm—one of the last to die in that bloody and decisive battle. His son, Samuel Brady Nixon, married Sally Ann Wadsworth. (According to amateur genealogists, the Wadsworths were descended from General "Mad Anthony" Wayne. The certified descendants of General Wayne have, however, denied this with bitterness, the idea of consanguinity with the Nixons causing them some pain.) Samuel and Sally Ann sired Francis Anthony Nixon, Richard's father, generally called Frank.

The Nixons were neither rich nor poor, humble nor proud. For the most part they were farmers who worked the soil and drew their living and their satisfaction from it. Some were preachers, some teachers, a few were merchants—but all were of yeoman stock. Strict in their religious observance, they were the kind of Methodists who took their Bible straight and rigorously. Francis Nixon was something else again, the characteristic American rolling stone. The death of his mother when he was seven may have been an element in his wanderlust. In any case, he left school when he was in the fourth grade to work as a farmhand, and from this followed his itinerancy.

"We farmhands usually had milk and bread for dinner," Frank Nixon would recall. "Fifty to seventy-five cents a day was just about tops in wages for a farmhand in those days." Restless by nature, extroverted, argumentative, gregarious, he could not stay in one place for long and set out to sample the world. The sampling was wide: glass worker, potter, house painter ("I even painted Pullmans at one time"), potato farmer, sheep rancher in Colorado, pioneer telephone linesman, motorman, roustabout in the oil fields, carpenter—a man of all work in all seasons in his working lifetime.

At one time he was even a labor agitator. The Ohio winters were bitter cold, and the motormen on streetcars stood in open vestibules. Frank Nixon literally froze his feet. Organizing the other motormen, he beat at the door of the Ohio State Legislature and demanded closed vestibules and improved working conditions. From this point on he was a dogmatist in politics, and his opinions echoed in the Nixon home.

California was the last frontier, and Frank Nixon made his way there, seeking a better climate and more profitable employment. A Southern California as yet unscathed by the frenetic glamor of the movie industry was his destination. He became a motorman again, on the old red trolleys that linked Los Angeles and Whittier—a pleasant job. Living in Whittier, a Methodist among Friends, he was soothed by the placidity of the Quaker town, by its well-ordered streets and the quiet drone of its prosperity. The Quaker settlers had chosen this site because it was well away from the hubbub of Los Angeles and off the main railroad line. Its citrus and avocado groves would not succumb to the developer's "progress" for another generation, and the spirit of the men who had founded it in 1887 was still abroad—the men who, naming it after the New England Quaker poet, may have had in mind his simple verse:

We cross the prairies as of old
The pilgrims crossed the sea,
To make the West, as they the East,
The homestead of the free.

For the first time the rolling stone came to rest. Then, on February 15, 1908—a date Frank Nixon remembered all his life— he met Hannah Milhous. The Milhouses were Irish Quakers, a rare breed. A family Bible records that Thomas Milhous came from the Dublin Meeting to Chester County, Pennsylvania, in 1729. Like the Nixons, the Milhouses followed the frontier. In Indiana the gentleness of their Quaker faith was tempered by a resolute awareness of man's inhumanity to man, and the Milhous family was long remembered for the help they gave runaway slaves subject to the cruelties of the Fugitive Slave Law. Descendants of these fleeing Negroes still live in Columbus, Indiana, witnesses to the efficiency of the underground railroad run by the Milhouses and their fellow Quakers who endangered their own lives to bring freedom to others.

In 1897 Franklin Milhous pulled up stakes in Indiana, leaving a home as four-square as his sturdy Quaker faith, and settled in Whittier. He brought his wife, Almira, his nine children, and his mother, Elizabeth, with him. (When she died at age ninety-six, the firm-willed matriarchal influence of Mrs. Milhous had spread over the town.) Four months and ten days after Frank Nixon and Hannah Milhous met, they were married and moved into the Milhous home. For a time, long enough to let their first son, Harold, be born, Frank worked as a foreman on the Milhous ranch. Then he struck out for himself.

Details of the Nixon family fortunes during this period are meager. The Nixons set up in the San Joaquin Valley briefly and then moved back to Southern California, to Yorba Linda, where on the side of a barren hill Frank planted a lemon orchard. It proved to be a failure from the start, and eventually Frank Nixon gave it up to return to Whittier. According to family legend, oil was later discovered under that piece of land, but the story may be apochryphal. Another legend has it that he turned down property in Whittier which also proved to be oil rich—but every family has its tales of regret over millions missed. Yorba Linda is important, however, because on January 9, 1913, Richard Milhous Nixon was born. Two years later he was followed by Donald; Arthur was born in 1918, Edward in 1930.

Give me the child and I will form the man, the Jesuits say. Richard Nixon was formed by a home life in which work and struggle were always present, in which parents and children shared the daily burdens, in which there was little time to play, in which self-reliance was expected of all. Even when the economic pressures eased slightly, the Nixons continued to live as if poverty lurked beyond every payday. The idea of work as a way of life was impressed on young Dick—his mother always called him "Richard" —by others in his environment. Lewis Cox, his seventh-grade teacher and a major influence in the making of the future President, stressed "the importance of fighting hard all the time and working hard all the time."

Life was more expansive at the home of Grandmother Milhous. Describing his childhood to Earl Mazo, Nixon recalled that his grandmother "had a big house on the boulevard and every year at Christmas and usually once in the summer we had a family reunion. She kept the family together through the years. She was a prolific letter writer. On birthdays, she composed rhymes and couplets and sent them to us. She used the 'plain speech' (thee and thou) exclusively. My mother used the plain speech in talking with her and her sisters, but never with the children. So with us, the children, we don't use it at all."

This grandmother set the standards for the whole family, Nixon said, and they were stern: "Honesty, hard work, do your best at all times—humanitarian ideals. She was always taking care of every tramp that came along the road, just like my own mother too. She had strong feelings about pacifism and civil liberties. She probably affected me in that respect. At her house, no servant ate at a separate table. They always ate with the family. There were Negroes, Indians, and people from Mexico—she was always taking somebody in."

In later years, when the complexity of his public life alienated him from much that had been real in his nature, his grandmother's concern for the persecuted of the world remained with Richard Nixon. But from the start, the young Dick Nixon was a creature unto himself.

Of all the reminiscences about him, none describes him as an outgoing child, a personally involved child. The novelist Jessamyn West, a cousin of the Nixons, comes closest to this in her report that Dick liked to swim in Anaheim Ditch, dangerous for its steep sides and fast currents, in violation of the law and his mother's vigorous admonitions. This Tom Sawyer view of Nixon stands alone. The record is more austere as it delineates a Dick Nixon who was never tardy during his elementary school years, who cut his reading teeth not on children's books but on the daily newspapers, who covered four years of grade school work in three, and who did his chores faithfully and without fuss. The Yorba Linda Nixon was in no way different from the Whittier College Nixon or the Nixon of the Vice Presidency. For him work always came first, the give-and-take of human relationships second.

In 1922, when Dick was nine, the Nixons returned to Whittier, where Frank opened a country store. The town had been off the main thrust of urban growth, but the automobile followed the highways, not the railroad line. To profit from the ubiquity of cars, Frank Nixon added a gas station to his store—one of the first in the area and perhaps his first stroke of sound business enterprise. The Nixons settled down, and though they continued to work as unremittingly, money ceased to be the forgotten commodity it had been in Yorba Linda. The store became a kind of neighborhood club, with Frank debating his customers on the political issues of the day and Hannah Nixon soothing them.

Dick Nixon admired his father's argumentativeness, and Jessamyn West attests to the richly complex nature from which it stemmed. Her Cousin Frank, she recalls, taught Sunday School and "related his lessons to the life about us, to politics, local and national. His class was so popular it overflowed the space allotted to it and if I could have attended it a few more years I think I might have become a fair stateswoman myself." Dick Nixon never stood up in argument to his father, often counseling his brothers never to challenge Frank Nixon in debate. In later years he drew heavily on the genuine and unreconstructed liberalism of his father's thinking. But he never found in himself that open approach to controversy which enjoyed the challenge without demanding the victory.

Dick Nixon was a "serious" boy, as the feature writers noted when his early life was at issue. Frank Nixon could hold forth in the family store, but Hannah drove herself and her family. Her day would begin at the first morning light, and the boys rose with her. The family ate breakfast together, saying their prayers and reciting Bible verses. The chores fell most heavily to Dick when his older brother, Harold, was invalided by tuberculosis. For Richard, then, there was school, there were Quaker services at midweek and three times on Sunday, there was work at the store, there were violin and piano lessons. Years later Donald Nixon would say, "None of us had too much time to play. Dick has had a lot to make him serious."

Perhaps the roughest period of Richard Nixon's boyhood came when his mother took Harold to Arizona in the hope of curing his tuberculosis. For two years she remained with her ailing son, paying for their board at the nursing home by being a maid of all work, a cook, a furnace hand. At home her husband sold half of the acre on which his store stood in order to pay medical bills that seemed astronomical to him. Richard and the other sons took on Mrs. Nixon's household tasks, cooking and cleaning and helping with the store. Meals consisted of hamburgers, fried eggs, canned chili, pork and beans, or spaghetti. "There were many mornings," Nixon said years later, "when I had nothing for breakfast but a candy bar."

Harold and Mrs. Nixon returned from Arizona, but the dry climate had not cured the boy. His death came suddenly. Early one morning Harold had asked Dick to drive him to town in order to buy a birthday present for their mother. He chose an electric mixer, which pleased Richard, the family's champion potato masher—"He never leaves lumps," Mrs. Nixon would say. Both boys were pleased that it would save their mother hours of work in the kitchen. They returned home and Dick headed for school. When he arrived, he found a message waiting for him: "Come home. Your brother has died." "It is difficult to understand the ways of the Lord," Mrs. Nixon said. "But the best happens for every person."

In those boyhood days two aspects of what his associates would later call the "Nixon method" were already apparent. The first was his passion for facts. In the seventh grade he was chosen to take the affirmative part in a debate whose momentous subject was: "Resolved—That insects are more beneficial than harmful." This maiden effort in public speaking frightened Nixon, but he sought out an etymologist uncle, stuffed himself with information, snowed under his opponents, and won the debate—the first of many such victories. The second aspect of the "Nixon method" was summed up by one of his debating opponents, Merton G. Wray: "Since high school, Nixon has had an uncommon ability to take advantage of a situation before and after it develops. His success is due to knowing what to do and when to do it, perfect timing in everything."

Nixon had another characteristic even as a boy. His brother Donald, in a reminiscent mood, touched on it: "Dick always planned things out. He didn't do things accidentally. He had more of Mother's traits than any of us. He wouldn't argue much with me, but once, when he had just about as much of me as he could take, he cut loose and kept at it for a half hour. He went back a year listing things I had done. He didn't leave out a thing. I've had a lot of respect ever since for the way he can keep things on his mind." Twenty-five years later this capacity for keeping things on his mind would make him one of the best-informed members of Congress.

The young Nixon did not grub for high marks and extracurricular success, but neither did they come easily to him. His rule was to work and to achieve, singlemindedly, with no thought of the casual satisfactions of the bull session or the high school flirtation with sex and romance. If this set him apart, Nixon might have chafed as he did many years later when the hail-fellow approach of other politicians eluded him. But on the surface he seemed to move serenely, doing what came naturally and accepting without rancor the wry envy of his contemporaries.

The excellent marks of grade school continued in high school, and so did Dick Nixon's prowess as a debater. Though his two years at Fullerton High School were relatively uneventful, he did win the Constitutional Oratorical Contest as a sophomore and was lauded in the 1928 yearbook for his "excellent work" as representative of West Coast high schools in the National Oratorical Contest.

His subject, interestingly, was the United States Constitution, which had begun to fascinate him in the seventh grade and was to be the topic of many later speeches. The text of one of those speeches still exists, and for all its schoolboy rhetoric, it expresses a Constitutionalist faith that to this day is his. "It is our duty," he said in earnest peroration, "to protect this precious document, to obey its laws, to hold sacred its mighty principles, that our descendants may have that priceless heritage—our privileges under the Constitution."

In his junior year Dick Nixon transferred to Whittier High School. It was at this time that Hannah Nixon was with Harold in Prescott, Arizona. But though he was driving to the Los Angeles public market before sunrise to do the purchasing for his father's store, running the fruit and vegetable department, and waiting on customers in the afternoon, his academic work did not suffer and he was able to maintain the equivalent of an A average. In both his junior and senior years Nixon won the Constitutional Oratorical Contest again. And in an intelligence test on which the norm was 35 Nixon scored 59. O. C. Albertson, the Principal of Whittier High, remarked many years later that "Dick was a marked man when he transferred to us. He was a leader in scholastic and student activities—a self-starter." And, irrelevantly, "I think of Dick as a 'fighting Quaker.' "

When at seventeen Richard Nixon was graduated, he received the California Interscholastic Federation Gold Seal Award for scholarship and the Harvard Award as "best all-around student." He might have gone on to Cambridge and a Harvard education. But he turned down the opportunity to apply for the scholarship that could have been his because he felt he could not afford the expense of an Eastern school. Had he left California, history might have been different, with Nixon one more of those who in those years moved into important Federal legal dead ends on the strength of the Ivy League patina. Instead, he chose Whittier College, a quiet school of high academic standards, dedicated to Quaker ideals and George Fox's dream of a "Christian democracy." It was also the kind of determinedly unsophisticated institution that leaves its imprint on all who are exposed to its simple view of life and success.

At Whittier, Nixon's prodigious energy, his capacity to learn, to assimilate, and to cut through to essentials was already strikingly apparent. Paul Smith, then a professor and subsequently President of Whittier, in 1956 still remembered Nixon's brief examination papers. "At first you thought that he couldn't answer the question in that short a space," he said. "But, by golly, he had gone to the heart of the problem and put it down simply."

At commencement Nixon was second in his class, and he had also piled up an extracurricular record of sizable proportions. The tribute of Whittier's football coach for a man who won his freshman numeral and then sat on the varsity bench for the rest of his college career is well known, but it bears repeating:

"He was a second-string man. He played tackle and he played it well, but the kid was too light. Weeks would go by and he wouldn't even play a minute, but he'd hardly ever miss practice, and he worked hard. He was wonderful for morale, because he'd sit there and cheer the rest of the guys, and tell them how well they'd played. To sit on a bench for four years isn't easy. I always figure, especially in the case of Dick, who excelled in everything else, that kids like that have more guts than the first-string heroes."

Another kind of tribute came from one of Nixon's teammates: "Dick had two left feet. He couldn't coordinate. But, boy, was he an inspiration. He was always talking it up. That's why the coach let him hang around, I guess." This is what others saw. But life on the bench is lonely—"lonely as hell," as one friend put it—and it could not help but force him to rely on his inner resources. It also drove him to compensate in other fields, other activities, in which he could be "one of the gang" and in which he could excel with almost monotonous regularity.

And excel he did. He was president of the freshman class. As the freshman star on the debating team he helped defeat the University of Southern California, defending the proposition that "All Nations Should Adopt a Policy of Free Trade"—a philosophy that, with modifications, he still holds. He won the *Reader's Digest* Southern Conference Extemporaneous Speaking Contest, and in his senior year became the Southern California Intercollegiate Extemporaneous Speaking champion. He was red-faced about a yearbook quip that he "left a trail blazed with fluttering feminine hearts." He traveled thousands of miles to represent Whittier in debates as a member of the champion team of his college conference.

One episode has an ironic relevance to Nixon's later life. At the end of his sophomore year he ran for vice president of the student body and won on a platform of "impartial cooperation with the president." He became president in his senior year after a hard-fought campaign. In that office he embarked on a program for training underclassmen to prepare them for student leadership. The student newspaper, of which he was an associate editor, found that during his term of office "President Nixon" was "always progressive and with a liberal attitude," leading the school "through the year with flying colors."

Unlike the great secular universities, Whittier College had no fraternities, no sororities, no drinking clubs, not even a chapter of Phi Beta Kappa. But it did have the Franklins, a snobbish and highbrow society, whose members wore black ties and dinner jackets to school functions, and which included the town's richer families and wielded considerable influence on campus. With a group of other students Nixon set out to break its monopoly of Whittier's social life by organizing the Orthogonians, a name from a composite Greek word meaning "square-shooters." The Orthogonians affected loose sweaters and open collars. Their symbol was the square, the four corners standing for "Beans, Brawn, Brains, and Bowels." Nixon wrote its song, a bravura tune entitled "Ecrasons l'infame," and became its first president. He also collaborated in the writing of its first play, *The Trysting Place*, a mock heroic melodrama which he directed.

One of Nixon's fellow Orthogonians, William Brock, Negro and a Whittier football star, added a footnote to this phase of Nixon's college life. A democrat who voted the ticket except when Nixon was a candidate, Brock said, "I really get mad when I hear Democrats or anybody accuse Dick of bigotry. That sort of thing is fantastic. Dick was my buddy in college many years before he or anybody else figured him to become a politician. He was one of the fellows who got me into the Orthogonians."

Richard Nixon made his mark on the social life of Whittier College in two other ways. Seeking as always to be with it, he used the muscle of his student body presidency to convince Whittier's faculty and trustees that the Quaker prohibition against dancing was counter-productive. If students were not allowed to dance on the wholesome precincts of the campus, then they would fall prey to "the dens of iniquity in Los Angeles." The powers-that-be capitulated.

In his junior year, as chairman of a traditional ritual—the annual bonfire on Fire Hill—he exceeded all others. The bonfire followed a set pattern. Students would pile the burning materials on Fire Hill for days. It was the duty and privilege of the chairman to top the heap with as large and gaudy a privy as he could steal from the neighboring countryside. It was honor enough to cast a one-holer on the pyre. A few chairmen had shown their mettle by showing up with a two-holer. Richard Milhous Nixon, destined to the Presidency of the United States, set the record with a four-holer.

But as it must to all Big Men on Campus, the four years ended. Dick Nixon could not graduate with honors—Whittier then considered such ostentation unseemly for a Quaker institution—but he stood second in his class and his extracurricular record was of the sort valued by American institutions of learning. He was therefore easily qualified for any graduate school in any of the disciplines. But he had his eye on the law. His mother once said that this ambition was expressed when Nixon, then nine years old, read a newspaper account of the Teapot Dome scandal, which rocked the post-Harding era. "When I get big," he remarked, "I'll be a lawyer they can't bribe."

"The boy with the intellectual look above the eyebrows"—as the Whittier paper had referred to him—might have set his sights on Harvard or Yale, then the two most desirable law schools. He chose instead the Duke University Law School—attracted by the possibility of a tuition scholarship. In those Depression years Duke, heavily endowed by tobacco millions, was able to award scholarships to the very bright young college graduates.

A warm letter of recommendation accompanied Nixon's bid for entrance and a scholarship to Duke Law School. His faculty adviser wrote: "At Whittier, Richard Nixon displayed a rich sense of humor, human understanding, personal eloquence, and a marked ability to lead. He is intellectually honest, modest, and youthfully enthusiastic. If he has any handicap, it is his lack of sophistication." President Walter F. Dexter of Whittier introduced Nixon to Dean H. Claude Horack in even warmer terms. "I believe that Nixon will become one of America's important, if not greatest, leaders," he wrote.

In September 1934 Richard Nixon, a young man of twenty-one, thin, serious-faced, the jowls that so delight political cartoonists not yet upon him, determined, hopeful, and worried, looked at the lovely and luxurious campus that the Duke millions had created. Years later a classmate named Hoover Taft, Jr. (no kin, no Republican), said, "Dick was there for only one purpose, and that was to train himself to be the best lawyer in the country."

The law as it is taught in America, however, is more an ordeal by grind than an indoctrination in jurisprudence. For Dick Nixon the difficulties were multiplied. To hold his full-tuition scholarship, he was required to maintain an average of B or better. His family could send him only $35 a month toward rent, food, clothing, books, and incidental expenses. Even at Depression prices he could not afford the relative luxury of a dormitory room, and the thirty-five cents an hour he made doing research for Dean Horack on a National Youth Administration grant made his lot only slightly less penurious.

He solved the problem by sharing a room in an old farmhouse with three economy-minded law students—William R. Perdue, who became an executive of the Ethyl Corporation; Fred S. Albrink, who made a career of the Navy; and Lyman Brownfield, who has a prosperous law practice in Columbus, Ohio. The ramshackle farmhouse was a mile through the woods to the Duke campus, a mile that was muddy or dusty as the weather dictated, and the four students paid about fifty dollars a year for the back room.

It was, as Brownfield describes it, "a pretty crude place with no running water and no heat other than an old laundry stove." They called it Whippoorwill Manor to make up for some of its drawbacks. "It was cold on some of those winter nights," Brownfield says. "Those old laundry stoves were made of thin metal that would heat up fast and cool off just as quickly. At bedtime we'd stuff the

27

thing with papers and get it going while we undressed and hopped into bed. But it had its pleasant side, too. A good part of the year was mild and those woods are lovely in the fall and spring."

They worked hard—Perdue, Brownfield, and Nixon were graduated the top men of the class in that order—and there was little time for recreation. Now and then Nixon would take time out to listen to the music of Johnny Long and Les Brown, two undergraduates who led orchestras at Duke which had made the big time. "Old Nixon used to like to hear them play," Albrink recalls, "but he'd only hang around fifteen minutes and then he'd hit the books again." There was handball, the occasional luxury of a football game, and a very few dates. "Dick wasn't allergic to girls," Brownfield has said. "He liked them, as all of us did. But we just didn't have the money, and the dates were few and far between."

The pressures of a law school education closed the door to any real social life. There were forty-four students in Nixon's first-year law class, most of them on scholarship. It was Duke's policy to reduce the number of these scholarships in the second and third years, and those who wanted to hold on to theirs were ruggedly competitive. "Richard Nixon demonstrated his superior legal ability by maintaining his scholarship for his entire three years," says one of his teachers. Work, worry, and his iron butt were the prescription for academic success.

This was the first time Nixon had been away from home. One night, in the first month of his freshman law year, he sat studying—working, worrying, and trying to shuck off his homesickness. William Adelson, an upperclassman, noticed the look of distress on Nixon's face. "What's bothering you?" he asked.

"I'm scared," Nixon said. "I counted thirty-two Phi Beta Kappas in my class. I don't believe I can stay up in that group."

"You needn't worry," Adelson told him. "The fact that you are studying so late shows that you're not afraid of hard work. You've got an iron butt and that's the secret of becoming a lawyer."

His contemporaries had no worries about his future success. "Nixon was not outward," one of his classmates says. "He was friendly, but in a shy way. He was no smiler, quite the contrary. Like most others, I figured he would wind up doing a wonderful job in a big law firm, handling securities or other matters that needed the attention of a scholar, not a politician."

In his second year at Duke, Nixon had relaxed enough to show his political side. He ran for the presidency of the Duke Bar Association, an organization of the school's students and the most sought-after office. He won. He was on the *Law Review* staff, and between his second and third years he remained at Duke to write a full length article for *Law and Contemporary Problems*—one of the two members of the entire Law School student body chosen to write articles that year. As a senior he was elected to the Order of the Coif, a national honorary society to which only the top 10 per cent of the country's law students are qualified for membership. Most important for Nixon, however, was the warm friendship that resulted from the research work he had done for Dean Horack. Nixon specialized in taxation, but his main interest was Constitutional law—his classmates considered him a "conservative liberal" —and the respect for the Constitution that he had demonstrated in his high school days was nourished and matured in long conversations with his teacher.

To his classmates at Duke, Nixon was known as a "Gloomy Gus." "I'll never learn the law," he would complain constantly. "There's just too much of it." Then he would come up with high marks. In 1937 his pessimistic predictions notwithstanding, he received his law degree and prepared to face maturity. The years at Duke had been tough, but they had been rewarding. They had opened for him a door that gave out on a world he had never known, different in every way from the provincialisms of Whittier. For the first time—and as a civilian, the only time—in his life, he had been alone, away from family and family influence.

Now he had a choice to make. He could pass through that door into the life of the East, with its great law firms, its sophistication, its wealth. Or he could return to the comfort and safety of the small town he had left. His classmates all believed he would take the former course. They foresaw a career for the quiet, friendly, yet unsmiling young man which would sweep him upward in the less combative aspects of the legal profession—an expert in securities, perhaps, or a delver into precedent. The thought that Nixon might choose politics never entered their minds—though it had his. But his classmates were doubly mistaken. Nixon returned to Whittier—and set in motion those forces that would project him into the most remarkable political career of his time.

3

The Law, The War

J UNE of 1937 was not an auspicious time to begin a career. Officially, the Depression had ended, to be replaced by the Recession. The difference between the two was academic.

Convinced that the nation was cured of its economic ills, Franklin Delano Roosevelt had, months earlier, cut off the outpouring of vast funds to the Works Progress Administration (WPA), the Public Works Administration (PWA), and some of the other alphabet agencies—in effect closing the books on the New Deal. But his own Bureau of Labor Statistics was reporting that well over 11 million Americans were out of work—roughly a million less than the number of unemployed of 1933, when he had taken office. Industrial production had nosedived, and the stock market was following it down. Looking about him, the great liberal historian Charles A. Beard could remark that the "economic collapse was startling to President Roosevelt and his advisers." It would remain so until war had erupted in Europe and rearmament replaced relief as the great Rooseveltian pump-primer.

To a young man embarking on his career, the prospect ahead seemed one of perpetual economic crisis, although like most of his generation Richard Nixon had become inured to this. Only a

prophet could have foreseen President Roosevelt's shift from isolationism to interventionism—a policy about-face that set the
wheels of heavy industry rolling again. For young lawyers, however, there was one obvious solution—government service, which
seemed to have an unlimited capacity for absorbing junior legal
talent. The huge exodus from Harvard and Yale, which had peopled the New Deal agencies, had slowed down, but there were still
openings. Dick Nixon was aware of this and he discussed the possibility of taking a government job with his friend and adviser,
Dean Horack, who volunteered his good offices to get him a position with the Justice Department.

But Horack also had some advice to offer. He and Nixon had
frequently discussed politics as a career, and Nixon had given that
possibility more than casual thought. Horack told him, "Dick, if
you're really interested in politics, go back to your home town and
establish yourself in a law firm." Having lived for three years in
the East, Nixon demurred. Service with the Federal Bureau of Investigation, then in its gangbusters period, appealed to him more
than the quiet of Whittier—"the FBI looked very good to a young
lawyer that year," he says—and Horack wrote a letter of recommendation to FBI Director J. Edgar Hoover, calling to his attention "one of the finest young men, both in character and ability,
that I have ever had the opportunity of having in my classes. He
is a superior student, alert, aggressive, a fine speaker, and one who
can do an exceptionally good piece of research."

Nixon took and passed the FBI examination, then waited for an
appointment. A cut in the Bureau's appropriation, however, destroyed his chances, though he later learned that a form notifying
him to report for duty had already been prepared. But by this time
the glamor of the FBI had dimmed for Nixon.

His efforts to find work with one of the major law firms in New
York had been rewarded by no more than an "iffy" response from
Donovan, Leisure, Newton, and Lombard—"Wild Bill" Donovan's law firm—and Nixon decided that Horack's advice to return
to Whittier was sound. He therefore wrote to Horack that the FBI
had been "investigating my character. . . . But unless my present
prospects fall through, I shall not accept the job even if it is offered

to me." There was one obstacle to a legal career in California. He had not made application to take the California Bar Examination, scheduled for that summer. Once more Dean Horack came to the rescue. Through the intervention of one of Horack's friends in California, Nixon's name was added to the list of candidates.

Faced with the task of cramming five months of work into two, Nixon again became the "Gloomy Gus" of his law school days. On July 3, 1937, he wrote to a friend at Duke: "I seriously doubt that I can get up the stuff in good enough shape in two months but I'm going to try. Tell Dean Horack, therefore, that the first Duke graduate to take the California Bar Exam has a darn good chance to fail it the first time." Horack answered: "Don't worry . . . they will have to flunk all of them if they don't let you by." In spite of an attack of influenza, Nixon made it. He was one of the 46 per cent who passed the examination, and on November 9, 1937, Richard Milhous Nixon became a member of the California Bar, sworn in before the State Supreme Court in San Francisco.

Strait-laced and in a neatly pressed blue serge suit, Dick Nixon began work immediately with Whittier's oldest law firm, Wingert & Bewley. They had been looking for a young lawyer to handle the routine trial work, and Nixon's reputation as a skillful debater had won him the job. His first chore was self-assigned—dusting and arranging the hundreds of books in the firm's library, after varnishing the shelves. His first assignments were hardly the kind that Nixon wanted. As the most junior lawyer on the staff he was given the divorce cases to handle. Quaker-born and Quaker-bred and living a life in which the temptations of the flesh played little part, Dick Nixon was acutely embarrassed by the details of marital discord, adultery, and personal complications that lead to the breakup of marriages. The intimacies of the bedroom confided by his female clients frequently made him blush—and to this day he frowns on those of his friends who become involved in litigation before the Domestic Relations courts.

The seamier side of man's inhumanity to woman—and vice versa—was not for Dick Nixon. As a trial lawyer he was neither flashy nor dramatic, carefully building up his cross-examination of witnesses, never badgering and always detached. After one year with the firm, Nixon became a partner. Tom Bewley said of Nixon, "He always seemed to be way ahead of the witness and to anticipate what answers the witness would make." His strong point with juries was cool logic, the arguments set up like duck pins to fall one after the other. His briefs were the joy of the firm, not only because they were cogent but because he turned them out with computerlike speed. "Give Dick a problem at noon," Bewley would say, "and he could pull down the books and dictate a brief. He was ready to approve the final draft, meticulous as he was, before I could have looked up the books."

Successful in Whittier, Nixon set up a branch office of Wingert, Bewley & Nixon in La Habra, a nearby town whose thousands of population could be counted on the fingers of one hand. From a desk in a real estate office he conducted business so well that he was chosen to be Town Attorney. His next step up was to Assistant City Attorney and police prosecutor in Whittier. It was a dry town, and not until the Fifties did it relax its ban on hard liquor, permitting the opening of a single cocktail lounge. When one "café" sold too much wine to its customers, Nixon called out the police force, picked up the drunks as they staggered away, and eventually shut it down.

His sixteen-hour day as a lawyer was apparently not enough to keep Nixon busy, and he looked for some business enterprise to occupy the remaining hours. He found it when Whittier and its environs began producing too many oranges. With a group of local people he set up the Citra-Frost Company—Richard Nixon, President—with a capitalization of $10,000. The problem was not in finding buyers for frozen orange juice but in processing and packaging it. Present-day methods were unknown, and while Nixon and his associates experimented, picking and squeezing the oranges themselves, the company failed—somewhat like Harry Truman's haberdashery shop.

It was not all work, not all career, for Richard Nixon in those years. He was active in civic organizations, becoming President of the Whittier 20-30 Club, a kind of Junior Chamber of Commerce. His alma mater beckoned, and he happily accepted a post on Whittier's Board of Trustees—the youngest member. When he was twenty-nine, there was an abortive move to draft him for the college presidency. Perhaps searching for a wife—the girls thought he was "too intelligent to be much fun"—he joined Whittier's "little theater" group.

At rehearsals for a production of the George S. Kaufman-Alexander Woollcott play *The Dark Tower* he met Thelma Ryan, nicknamed "Pat" by her father—a tall, redheaded girl, quiet, unassuming, and friendly.

There had been few girls in Nixon's life—the daughter of the local police chief whom he had dated before going to Duke, the girls he met when he attended law school dances as a stag. A friend of Dick's had told him that at the tryout for *The Dark Tower* there would be a glamorous schoolteacher, and he had gone down to take a look. That same night he proposed to Pat Ryan. "I thought he was nuts or something," she has told reporters. "I guess I just looked at him. I couldn't imagine anyone saying anything like that so suddenly. Now that I know Dick much better, I can't imagine that he would ever propose like that, because he's very much the opposite; he's more reserved."

Pat Ryan was not bowled over. Two months older than Dick, she was cut from a similar pattern of workaday American life. She was Connecticut Irish on her father's side, German on her mother's. Like many Californians, she had been born out of state—in Ely, Nevada, where her father had been a miner—and she had been brought to the Pacific Coast as a baby. The Ryans settled in Artesia, on a small farm some eighteen miles from Los Angeles.

"Both my parents died before I had grown up," Pat Nixon wrote in an as-told-to magazine piece when Nixon was nominated for the Vice Presidency in 1952, "and when I finished high school I went to work in a bank at Artesia to earn enough money to complete my education." Sharing the driving with friends who were going East, Pat Ryan remained there, getting a job in the laboratory of a hospital near New York. Two years later she returned to the West to attend the University of Southern California. "I had a research fellowship. I graded papers, and I worked weekends and holidays in a department store until I was graduated. I had studied merchandising, but after graduation I went to Whittier to teach school."

While still in college, Pat Ryan had ventured into the Hollywood jungle, as an extra and a bit player. "I was in quite a number of movies," she told Earl Mazo, "but mostly in just mob scenes. You would have to hunt real hard to find me, but I made quite a bit of money. I was in *Small Town Girl*. In *Becky Sharp*, I had a little walk-on part and got twenty-five dollars. I just walked on, but at least I could be seen. I did have a line. I can't remember what it was though, because it was cut before it reached the screen. What I do remember about that movie is that I got twenty-five dollars for it, rather than the usual seven dollars."

When she met Dick, she was teaching commercial subjects, typing and shorthand, at Whittier. But if it was "destiny," as she later said, to meet Dick Nixon, she was not aware of it at that time. Nixon pursued her, but she continued to go out with other men. He was, as she told reporters during campaign trips, "dutiful" even when she had other dates. "He would drive me to meet other beaux," she said, "and wait around to take me home." Dick was not a dancer, but he tried hard in order to please Pat. Skating at a newly opened artificial ice rink was a fad, and Pat got Dick to try it. "But it was awful for him," she said. "He almost broke his head two or three times, but he still kept going."

It was not until the spring of 1940 that Pat consented to marry Dick Nixon. But it was not until June 21, 1940, that they had saved enough money to "pool our savings to buy a wedding ring." The ceremony was performed at the Mission Inn in Riverside, and then Pat and Dick took off on perhaps the only unplanned trip of their lives, driving in their car "generally for Mexico City," Pat recalls, "but without any particular destination. . . . We felt real splurgy." On their return the Nixons rented an apartment over a garage and became part of Whittier's young marrieds. Dick continued his practice of law and Pat kept her teaching job. Their best friends at the time were Jack and Helene Drown, later to be among Nixon's major supporters in California politics.

His political life in pre-marriage and post-marriage days was nominal. He had registered as a Republican in 1938—Whittier was conservative—but Nixon had "no grandiose ambitions" for political advancement. "I wasn't a youngster who wanted to be President of the United States," he would say. Pat Nixon corroborates this. "There was no talk of political life at all in the beginning." In 1940, as Assistant City Attorney of Whittier, he made a few speeches for the Republican Presidential nominee, Wendell Willkie, but it was strictly a *pro forma* performance. The passions of that campaign did not cut deeply into the pattern of his daily life. Actually, he was still under the law school spell of the great progressives of the Supreme Court, Justices Louis Brandeis, Benjamin Cardozo, and Charles Evans Hughes. There was, of course, a war in Europe, and Great Britain faced extinction in the daily raids of Hermann Goering's *Luftwaffe*, but in the Quaker quiet of Whittier it must have seemed very remote. President Roosevelt had promised "again and again and again" that American boys would not be sent overseas, and that was sufficient guarantee.

December 7 was a peaceful Sunday and Pearl Harbor was no more than a geographical cipher to most Americans. The excited and shocked voices of the announcers who interrupted radio programs caught Richard Nixon in the upsurge of national feeling. As a Quaker he could have sat out the war, exempted from military service. But he felt a need to participate in the war effort and satisfied it by moving to Washington and seeking employment in the beehive of bureaucratic activity on the Potomac. It is ironic that he applied for a job with the Office of Price Administration (OPA), later to become the target of vitriolic Republican attacks in which Nixon joined.

There was a second, richer irony. The man in charge of the tire-rationing section, where Nixon found a job, was Thomas I. Emerson, a member of the Yale Law School faculty. Emerson belonged, along with Alger Hiss, to the International Juridical Association. He subsequently became President of the National Lawyers Guild, later to be cited as the "legal bulwark of the Communist Party" by the House Committee on Un-American Activities (HUAC). He was a chronic joiner of organizations that eventually found themselves on the Attorney General's subversive list, and an articulate spokesman for left-wing views. When Nixon became a national figure and one of the country's leading anti-communists, Emerson told a correspondent for the Boston *Globe,* "Dick Nixon came into my office without warning. My secretary had been making appointments for applicants. I don't recall that Nixon had any letter of introduction. He just walked in and said he had come to Washington to get in the war effort. I found he had a very good record at Duke and a good law practice in Whittier. He gave that up to enter the war effort. He was a nice-looking boy, seemed intelligent, and . . . he was obviously a person we could use. I gave him the job right then and there."

Starting at a salary of $61 a week, Nixon worked his way up to $90 before he quit to join the Navy, a considerable cut from the $6,000 he was making as a lawyer in California. But his government service was an important experience. "In OPA," he said fourteen years later, "I learned respect for the thousands of hard-working government employees and an equal contempt for most of the political appointees at the top. I saw government overlapping and government empire-building at first hand. I was startled by the mediocrity of many of my fellow civil servants. But most important, I became more conservative as I realized that what I thought it was possible for government to do, government could not do. In OPA, too, I saw that there were people who weren't interested in carrying out the regulations, but who had a real passion for *getting* business and used the authority they had to that end. There were the remnants of the old, diehard New Deal."

Six months of OPA was enough for Richard Nixon. He was young and vigorous, in excellent health, and consumed by the feeling that he was wasting his time. Like many of his generation, he wanted a more direct part in the war. As a lawyer he was entitled to a direct commission, so he waived his religious exemption and joined the Navy. On September 2, 1942, Lieutenant (j.g.) Richard Nixon reported for active duty. After training at Quonset, Rhode Island, he made the mistake of applying for sea duty and was sent forthwith to an unfinished base at Ottumwa, Iowa, where Pat joined him. In May 1943, after again applying for sea duty, Nixon was assigned to the South Pacific Combat Air Transport Command (SCAT), serving at Guadalcanal, Bougainville, and eventually at Green Island—no Bali H'ai. He was an operations officer, but at Bougainville he got his share of passive action when he was under bombardment for twenty-eight nights out of thirty.

Edward J. McCaffrey, a fellow Navy officer and in the Fifties a Democratic postmaster in Concord, Massachusetts, has given a thumbnail of Nixon in action: "If you saw Henry Fonda in *Mister Roberts*, you know how Lieutenant Dick Nixon looked the first time I met him on a coral atoll off Bougainville in 1943. Dick was a Navy orphan, officer in charge of a unit without precedent, but with a mission. Dick, a full lieutenant, and a j.g. named Jim Stewart, with a dozen enlisted men, radio operators, and flight operations rates, would be given transportation to an island completely unequipped except for a few hand tools. Left to their own resources, they were expected to establish a makeshift base for the DC-3s in a matter of days. And they did just that. How they did it I'll never know, though I saw them operate on several different islands over a period of months.

"To set up their operation, Dick's outfit needed matériel, and the most basic building supplies were precious. Some of the stuff they procured was 'liberated,' but most of it Dick wangled out of units better equipped than his. A single sheet of plywood would set in motion for him a chain reaction of swaps that in a couple of days would have his unit housed and operating.

"Dick was a worker. He was tireless. But when he spoke, he made an awful lot of sense. He had no more rank than most of us, he was our age generally speaking, but he commanded a lot of respect from the guys with whom he came in contact. When things got a bit hectic, he never lost his head. No matter how badly things got fouled up, Dick got his part of the operation straightened out and he did it without a lot of hullaballoo."

But Nixon's job in the South Pacific did not merely consist of setting up DC-3 operations bases. He was, in fact, something of a glorified Seabee—and he acted like one. Planes had to be loaded and unloaded, always under pressure, always in a rush. On January 24, 1944, for example, he received a message from Guadalcanal that 30 planes carrying 135,000 pounds of a new type of rocket would arrive at his Bougainville base. He and a crew of nine men were ordered to unload those planes, and to "bomb up" combat planes that were taking part in the great strike against Rabaul. On their return the bombers were to be sent back to Guadalcanal loaded with litter cases, casualties of a Japanese attack on Bougainville the night before. Beyond the organization of this operation, it was enlisted man's work, but Lieutenant Nixon stripped off his shirt and pitched in on the grueling physical labor. The job was done as ordered.

Officers and men who served with Nixon on Green Island remember him more for his less heroic but more relevant attentions. Hard liquor was precious and rare, but he was able to promote it from visiting Navy vessels and from Navy fliers, and he distributed it even-handedly. Service rations were frequently not of gourmet class, but he was able to supplement them by setting up the only hamburger stand in the South Pacific. Known throughout the area as "Nixon's Snack Shack," it was located right near the airstrip, and there tired fliers could get coffee, sandwiches, and fruit juice— all free. He got the makings from a Navy supply depot on the other end of the island "by trading everything from captured Japanese rifles to introductions to the Army nurses who arrived to take care of the casualties." He also looked to the inner man by organizing a school for enlisted personnel—a typical cross-section of farm, slum, and rich boys from California, Nebraska, New York, New Mexico, or Indiana—to whom he taught a course in business law.

For himself the war was a broadening influence. Until he joined the Navy tobacco was a dirty weed and lips that touched liquor had never touched his. In the South Pacific he took a very occasional drink, and in moments of relaxation he would even puff a cigar. To fill the long pauses between frenetic action—on board a Navy transport, on Green Island, or wherever there was a hiatus —Nixon began to play poker. "I didn't know what poker was until then," Nixon has said, "and the only card game I had ever played was bridge, a little of it, during law school." The games at Green Island were for high stakes, with pots sometimes running to more than $1,000.

Nixon played a cold and cautious game. If he did not have the cards, he folded. If he did, he carefully pushed his luck. One of his fellow officers has said of Nixon's poker game, "He never lost, but he was never a big winner. He always played it close to the belt. He always seemed to end up a game somewhere between thirty and sixty dollars ahead. That didn't look like showy winnings, but when you multiplied it day after day, I'd say he did all right." By the time he shipped back to the states, according to report, he had squirreled away at least $10,000. Pat, working as a bank teller in San Francisco, had also been saving money.

After fifteen months in the South Pacific, Nixon was transferred back to the states, to Fleet Air Wing 8 at Alameda, California, and from there he was assigned on special orders to the Navy Bureau of Aeronautics. The war was over now, and the Navy finally took cognizance of his legal background. He was assignd to winding up and renegotiating contracts with aircraft firms such as Bell and Glenn Martin. He pushed hard enough to save the government millions of dollars, and to receive a letter of commendation for his efforts.

In November 1945 Lieutenant Commander Nixon waited impatiently in Baltimore to get his Navy discharge. Like the preponderance of men in his position, he saw no need for further service. And like millions of other Americans marking time before they were released from the military, Nixon asked himself the big question: "Where do I go from here?" He could return to the Office of Price Administration, but that seemed like a barren future. There was his law firm in Whittier, and a career of minor cases and major profits. This did not really appeal. Following the dictates of his ambition, he could find a new career, but this course was fraught with many uncertainties, many question marks. Events and circumstances decided the question for him. The instrument of fate was a telegram.

4

1946 — The First Campaign

To this point, the Nixon story had been unexceptionable and uncontroversial. He had lived by the storybook precepts—he was honest, hard-working, helpful to those who needed his help, kind to his parents, loyal to his friends. Few had penetrated his reserve, and the claims of this or that biographer that this or that man was his "closest" friend were justified only by the propinquity of the relationship. In later years those who accepted the title of "intimate" usually qualified it in private.

But this lack of the more human juices, this tendency to remain uncommitted on the personal plane, was not a handicap in the days of his boyhood, adolescence, and young manhood. It was accepted that Dick Nixon was a "loner." Those who dabbled in armchair psychoanalysis called him introverted—describing a trait of psyche that later endeared him to Washington hostesses like Alice Roosevelt Longworth, whose living room was always cluttered by the more common type of self-propelled conversationalist.

In 1946, however, he made a conscious decision to enter politics, thus becoming a public figure. "If you can't stand the heat," Harry Truman has said to those who seek political office, "then stay out of the kitchen." Nixon stood the heat very well, much better than those who over the years have been subjected to the flames of the front burner. This is not unusual. Like many inner-directed people, Nixon was able to sustain the acute pain that public attack inflicts, spared by the kind of insulation that the extroverted sometimes lack. He also had the aggressiveness that often goes with introversion, and these two traits conditioned his public manner as a campaigner. He could never understand why, in the clash of political battle when charge and counter-charge filled the air like flak, his own animadversions against the opposition should not have been accepted with the same kind of tolerance that Truman's "Give 'em hell" received from press and public.

It should be noted here that the so-called "Nixon style of campaign"—a style he employed with great effectiveness until 1960—was hardly his own invention. It had grown with the Republic and was far gentler than what had been commonplace when candidates horsewhipped each other in the service of truth. And it had been suggested to him in 1946 by the most astute and able of campaign managers, Murray Chotiner, a veteran of Earl Warren's gubernatorial battles, who accepted a $500 fee to serve as a consultant to Nixon though he was more than occupied by managing William F. Knowland's Senate race that year.

Chotiner's method, later codified in a fourteen-thousand-word speech that he delivered in 1955 to Republican workers, was characterized by William Costello, a Nixon antagonist, as "a catalogue of political mayhem." When a transcript fell into the hands of the Democrats, they assailed it as "probably one of the most cynical political documents since Machiavelli's *The Prince* or Hitler's *Mein Kampf*"—which shows that they had themselves taken its precepts seriously.

Costello summed it up more precisely in an anti-Nixon campaign tract published in 1960: "With professional thoroughness Chotiner developed his subject topically, discussing in turn such practical problems as timing, starting the campaign, cataloguing volunteer workers and contributors, how to pick a candidate, how to select a campaign theme, how to deflate the opposition, how to limit the issues, campaign ethics, smears, attacks and counterattacks, and the details of organization."

42

Singled out for particular disapproval by the Democrats were Chotiner's insistence on the use of professionals in campaigning, on leaving nothing to chance, and on starting early, "one full year ahead" if necessary. "You need that time to deflate your opposition. . . . I say to you in all sincerity that, if you do not deflate the opposition candidate before your own candidate gets started, the odds are that you are going to be doomed to defeat." It was also important to create the illusion, Chotiner said, that the candidate had really been drafted by the people, a device he had used to obtain the nomination and election of Earl Warren as Governor of California. Somewhat wryly he would ask his audiences of campaign workers, "What is the difference between legitimate attack and smear?" With a smile he would answer, "It is not a smear, if you please, if you point out the record of your opponent. . . . Of course it is always a smear, naturally, when it is directed to our own candidate."

"Make sure," Chotiner told Republicans, "that you have a separate organization that is set up of Democrats or independents or whatever you may want to call them. . . . We never put out the complete voting record for our candidate, vote by vote, in spite of the demands from people within our organization. The reason is, even if your candidate has voted 99 per cent right according to the person who reads the record, that 1 per cent will often turn the prospect away from you." If the candidate is attacked, hold your fire until the opponent has run out of steam. "But if you find the attack has reached such proportion that it can no longer be avoided in any way, when you answer it, do so with an attack of your own against the opposition for having launched it in the first place." And, he stressed, "I cannot overemphasize the fact that the truth is the best weapon we can use."

In this highly pragmatic analysis of campaign techniques, reprehensible to some only because he said candidly what others practiced covertly, Chotiner left out one prime rule that he abided by: Never tell the candidate everything that is going on in his behalf.

To these propositions, from which Nixon developed his campaign style, he added a few of his own: "Whenever possible, do away with the written text and use your fireside chat, a straightforward, sincere type of presentation. . . . A good off-the-cuff speech takes more preparation than a speech you read, and the candidate must realize that he can't just get up there and talk off the cuff without having spent hours in preparation."

Long speeches on radio and television were counterproductive, he warned. "People will say that spot announcements do not give an audience a chance to know the candidate. Sometimes that is a good thing for the candidate. Spot announcements at least get your name and face in the minds of the average people, and you will find in analyzing election contests that a great number of voters vote only names. . . . Consequently, using the television medium as a billboard for spot announcements is very effective. It is very hard to get up and tune the television station off before the one-minute spot announcement goes off."

To this he added these political aphorisms: "There is no public relations gimmick that will take the place of hard work." "In a political campaign, you've got to dramatize your case." "You should fight the battle on the ground on which you are strongest. Avoid the tactical error of fighting on your opponent's strongest ground." "Whenever anybody attacks, the way to answer is not to defend but to take the offensive."

Again there was an undeclared codicil—one that most Americans believe in their hearts but deny with their lips: The important thing is to win.

Neither Nixon nor Chotiner had, in 1946, thought through to an explicit statement of these rules of political organization and political warfare. But they were implicit in their thinking and in their character, and they became clearer in the minds of these two moody men as they assessed the advances and setbacks after each battle.

When Nixon received the telegram in 1945 which launched him on his political career, his knowledge of campaigning was instinctive. That instinct had, of course, been sharpened by his experiences in running for office as a high school, college, and law school student. In other ways, he was naïveté personified, lacking sophistication, as noted by his teachers, in spite of his period in the Navy. That he won over Horace Jeremiah Voorhis, a five-term Congressman, shocked the professionals. How he won has been shrouded in a fog of irrelevancies, false charges, and misemphasis on the part of friend and foe alike.

The 1946 campaign in California's Twelfth District began fifteen months before election day. In August 1945 twenty-six newspapers in the district carried on page one what amounted to an announcement. It had come in the mail as a publicity handout, and the papers had printed it as a curiosity:

> WANTED: Congressman candidate with no previous political experience to defeat a man who has represented the district in House for ten years. Any young man resident of district, preferably a veteran, fair education, no political strings or obligations and possessed of a few ideas for betterment of country at large, may apply for the job. Applicants will be reviewed by 100 interested citizens who will guarantee support but will not obligate the candidate in any way.

The "advertisement"—as unorthodox a way to find a candidate as California could produce—was in reality a cry for help. Since 1936, a year in which Franklin Delano Roosevelt's coattails carried almost every Democratic candidate to victory with the exception of those in Maine and Vermont, the strongly Republican Twelfth District had been represented in Congress by Jerry Voorhis. Strongly entrenched even among Republicans, he seemed to be a permanent fixture. His tenure had given him a national reputation, he was well liked by his fellow Congressmen and popular with the press. He was, moreover, conscientious and hard-working—tending to the mail from his constituents and handling their problems with dispatch. And, as Earl Mazo has noted, "when Congress was not in session he seldom passed by opportunities to be guest teacher of Sunday-school classes or to address church and civic groups. Furthermore, the Congressman faithfully remembered births, anniversaries, and other happy occasions in his district. . . . In short, Jerry Voorhis was a smart politician."

The Republican legislature had tried to dislodge him by gerrymandering his district, lopping off two communities that usually gave him a five-to-one edge in the vote. This reduced the size of his majorities, but it failed to defeat him. The Republican Party washed its hands of the Twelfth District, leaving it up to interested citizens to continue the losing battle.

The Committee of One Hundred was formed—"a political and economic cross-section of the area which sprawls from the southern border of Los Angeles to the foothills of the San Gabriel Mountains," *The Saturday Evening Post* would report—representing small businessmen, farmers, citrus ranchers, professional men, commuters, laborers, housewives, and career women. Murray Chotiner, then a successful Beverly Hills lawyer and public relations consultant, with a growing reputation as the manager of political campaigns, agreed to help them. The advertisement, however, turned out to be a dud. There were applicants, eight in number, but not the type that the Committee of One Hundred was seeking. In short order they turned down an ex-Democrat-ex-socialist who offered to turn Republican, a smog expert, a politician who talked of keeping "the Jews and the niggers" out of the district, and five other hopeless young hopefuls.

The committee then sought out Walter Dexter, former President of Whittier College, who was serving as California's Superintendent of Education. But Dexter demurred. To run, he pointed out, would mean that he would have to resign his state office, and he could not afford the risk of financial loss should he be defeated. Dexter, however, suggested that one of his former students, Richard Nixon, would meet the committee's requirements. A deputation visited the Nixon grocery store to sound out Frank and Hannah Nixon. They mentioned that Herman L. Perry, manager of Whittier's Bank of America branch, had spoken of their son as a possible candidate. When approached, Perry agreed to act as the intermediary and sent a telegram to Nixon in Baltimore, asking him to call long distance. On the telephone he put the questions to Dick: Was he available and was he interested? The answer to both was in the affirmative, and Nixon was urged to "fly out here right away."

Seventy-seven members of the Committee were assembled when Dick Nixon arrived. In ten minutes he stated his case. He stood for "a return to individual freedoms and all that private initiative can produce," he said, and he promised "an aggressive campaign on the platform of progressive liberalism designed to return our district to the Republican Party." As he spoke the committee looked him over. They saw a young, pleasant-faced, intense young man whose slightly mumpy cheeks and thrust-out nose took the curse off what would have been collar-ad good looks. They liked his directness of speech, and they were impressed by that indescribable quality which promises success in politics. By a vote of 55–22 they approved Nixon, and on the second ballot made it unanimous. On December 4, 1945, Nixon accepted the committee's endorsement.

Discussing it many years later, Dick Nixon remarked, "Voorhis looked impossible to defeat. He was intelligent, experienced, had a national reputation, and came from a well-known California family. Why did I take it? I'm a pessimist, but if I figure I've got a chance, I'll fight for it. And I thought this was as good a time as any to get into politics."

In 1945, however, Nixon was far more enthusiastic. In his letter of acceptance to Roy O. Day, Republican District Chairman, Nixon showed that he was off and running. "I am going to see Joe Martin and John Phillips and try to get what dope I can on Mr. Voorhis' record," he wrote. "His 'conservative' reputation must be blasted. But my main efforts are being directed toward building up a positive, progressive group of speeches which will tell what *we* want to do, not what the Democrats have failed to do." And he urged Day to "bring in the liberal fringe Republicans. We need *every* Republican and a few Democrats to win. I'm really hopped up over this deal, and I believe we can win."

Before making his final decision, Dick talked it over with Pat. She had worked at various jobs throughout the war, saving what she could. To this they added what he had been able to put aside from his service pay, as well as his Green Island poker winnings. They had earmarked these savings for a payment on a house, and for his start in civilian life. "We'll gamble half of it on the election," they decided. And gamble it they did. The Nixon campaign was run on a shoestring, leaning heavily on volunteer help when

47

the big contributions they expected never materialized.* Indeed, Pat Nixon recalls the time she wept because they had no campaign funds for stamps to mail their campaign literature. Even the Republican County Finance Committee maintained a hands-off attitude, arguing that financial assistance to Nixon would be a waste of money since he couldn't possibly win.

Nixon was released from active duty in January 1946 and returned immediately to California to begin campaigning. Shortly thereafter the Nixons' first child, Patricia, was born. But three weeks later Pat was back at work, having left Tricia with Hannah Nixon.

On March 19, 1946, Richard Nixon filed in both the Democratic and the Republican primaries, as did Jerry Voorhis. This, in California, was standard operating procedure. Under the state's system of cross-filing, candidates tried to knock out their opponents by capturing both nominations. Failing this, they were able to get some idea of their strength in the opposition party. The Nixons rented a small office in a dusty old building in Whittier's downtown section. They borrowed desks, chairs, tables, office equipment, and Hannah Nixon gave them an old leather sofa, which Dick's brother Don hauled to the office in his grocery truck. Pat Nixon and her high school friend Marion Budlong ran the office and handed out the campaign literature that Nixon had had printed at his own expense. They were elated by the demand for this literature until they learned that the opposition had pulled one of the oldest tricks in politics and sent in "volunteers" who asked for bunches of pamphlets and then destroyed them.

At first Nixon planned to campaign in his Navy uniform, and he had brought pictures of himself in the service to use on Lieutenant Commander Richard Nixon's literature. But he learned pretty quickly that there had been more Indians than chiefs in the Army and Navy, and that many enlisted men had left the service with a grudge against all officers. Nixon immediately bought a gray suit

---

* After the election Jerry Voorhis charged that a heavy Nixon newspaper advertising campaign was financed by a large New York financial house. A check of the Alhambra *Post-Advocate*, the newspaper of the largest city in the Twelfth District, shows that Voorhis had 269 inches of paid space, Nixon 162.

of somewhat dubious fit. He bought a second suit, this time of the conventional blue, and sold the gray one, putting the money into the campaign kitty.

The primary campaign failed to set the Twelfth District on fire. Nixon campaigned energetically, but Voorhis remained in Washington, announcing to his constituents that his Congressional duties prevented him from taking time out to solicit their votes in person. This strategy succeeds against an unknown who needs something solid to punch, and it worked perfectly for Voorhis. He walked off with the Democratic nomination and polled enough votes on the Republican line to hold a seven thousand-vote overall lead. "The election is in the bag for Voorhis," professionals said—and the Committee of One Hundred shrugged its collective shoulders, convinced that they had picked a loser. But Nixon was not dismayed. In a letter to Roy Day he cited "keen political observers" who "thought we ran a darn fine race, and this was the best Republican primary showing in years. Frankly, Roy, I really believe that is true, and it is time some of the rest of the people began to realize it. All we need is a win complex and we'll take Voorhis in November."

The "keen political observers" were, in fact, a Los Angeles political writer who had carefully studied the returns and noted that the Voorhis vote had dropped from 60 per cent of the total in 1944 to 53.5, thus making the Twelfth District what the professionals call "marginal." The "sure" victory for Voorhis that some predicted was not that certain—an illusion created by the Voorhis form sheet of past elections and not by 1946 performance. What Nixon needed was an exciting issue, some demonstration of his capabilities or potential. With this in mind, Nixon tucked his pessimism away and set out on a door-to-door campaign of the district's two hundred thousand voters, hoping for a break.

That break came, oddly enough, because Voorhis was a methodical politician. When Tricia was born, Voorhis had sent the Nixons a government pamphlet, "Baby Care," as he did to all new parents in his district. The one he sent to Pat and Dick, however, had a note attached. "Congratulations," it read. "I look forward to meeting you soon in public." Dick Nixon politely thanked Voorhis, then grasped the opportunity by challenging him to a series of debates on the issues—as, fourteen years later, an underdog named John F. Kennedy did, and with the same effect.

The professional politicians shrieked in anguish. Didn't Nixon know that Voorhis had won his first election by challenging his opponent to debate and then taking him? "I'll risk it," Nixon answered. "If I don't carry the fight to Voorhis, this campaign will never get off the ground."

Nixon, of course, was right. For Voorhis, as he later admitted, had lost touch with the thinking of his district—a failing common to all legislators who get so immersed in the national picture that they lose sight of what their constituents feel. In Washington, Voorhis was a big name, but in California the voters no longer knew where he stood. Nixon prepared for his debates with Voorhis by immersing himself in the record, in every speech his opponent had delivered, and in a Voorhis book on monetary theory which he quoted back at its author with devastating effect. Good or bad, the Voorhis record was one of which few in the Twelfth District were aware.

Jerry Voorhis was an earnest, pleasant, somewhat humorless man, given to soul-searchings and admissions of error, a doctrinaire thinker primarily interested in issues. He considered himself a "Christian socialist," and he had in fact been a registered member of the Socialist Party before it had blended into the New Deal. He had entered politics as part of EPIC—End Poverty In California—a share-the-wealth movement launched by the idealist and muckraker Upton Sinclair, and he had never shaken loose from some of the "funny money" programs of that frenetic group. Voorhis, however, had taken the brunt of communist attack by serving on the House Committee on Un-American Activities and by sponsoring the Foreign Agents Registration Act, one of the most effective and least used pieces of antisubversive legislation. He had also won the plaudits of the Extreme Left by resigning from the committee with a blast at Red-hunters.

There were other entries on his confused record which even a middle-of-the-road war veteran could attack. He had advocated the socialization of the Federal Reserve System and the nationalization of the oil industry. He was closely associated with the National Citizens and the CIO Political Action Committees. In a year when the Republican slogan of "Had enough?" was meeting with widespread response, he called for even more of the same, angering the housewives who were fed up with meat rationing and OPA controls. He had failed, at a time when the veterans were returning in force, to vote against a bill cutting veterans' compensation and had introduced a bill of his own which sought to make veterans' disability payments loans instead of grants. He favored restrictions on grain for use in the manufacture of liquor. For comic relief, one of the bills he sired transferred control of the rabbit industry from the Interior to the Agriculture Department.

This is the record that Nixon attacked in his speeches. "Had enough?" he would ask, and then stress the socialist aspects of the Voorhis program and its left-wing character. Nixon's aim was to drive a wedge between the district's right-of-center voters and a left-of-center incumbent, as well as to capitalize on the deep dissatisfaction of the constituency for the Federal controls that grated increasingly as the war and its needs receded. The Nixon forces also launched a word-of-mouth campaign that Voorhis hadn't done anything for the district, and in the election post mortem Voorhis complained of this tactic.

In the Fifties, when Nixon became a national figure, there were stories that he had used against Voorhis tactics that had by then come to be known as "McCarthyism"—a charge he energetically denied. "Communism," Nixon complained, "was not the issue at any time in the 1946 campaign. Few people knew about communism then, and even fewer cared." This assertion was accepted by Nixon supporters at the time, but it was true only to the extent that the communist issue was not controlling in the campaign. By November of 1946 the Cold War was upon the country and resentment was building over the cavalier actions of the Kremlin vis-à-vis the United States. Voorhis might have weathered this, in spite of his somewhat naïve and careless association with Stalinist front groups. What hurt him was his attempt to deny these associations against an opponent who was ready to offer documentation for every charge. The forum for this charge and denial was the first of the debates between the two men.

In the debates the candidates spoke before packed houses. Voorhis, as he says of himself, was "dull" and weighed down by a sense that the public would never understand what he was talking about, and Nixon was persuasive, carrying the attack to his opponent and showing the ease that years on the debate platform had given him. The first confrontation sparked the Nixon campaign, and Voorhis left the platform feeling bewildered, discouraged, and tired. "How did it go?" he asked Chet Holifield, his campaign manager and now a member of Congress. "Jerry," Holifield hold him, "he cut you to pieces. He had you on the defensive all the way. He picked the battleground and you let him fight on his own terms."

"What do you suggest?" Voorhis asked.

"You have two choices," Holifield answered. "You can go in there, no holds barred, and slug it out. Or you can cancel the rest of the debates, saying he's using dirty tactics."

Voorhis slumped. "I can't do that," he said. "I agreed to five debates and I can't back down now."

Holifield's assessment of the first debate had been accurate. Nixon had planted Voorhis right in the middle of the controversy over the two Political Action Committees, one National and the other CIO, but with interlocking directorates, openly manipulated by communists and fellow travelers, and Voorhis bumbled. There has been much controversy over what happened, but the account in *The Saturday Evening Post*, written shortly after the campaign, warrants serious attention.

Nixon, the magazine reported, "kicked off the debate by asking Voorhis if he was endorsed by the PAC. Voorhis denied this categorically. In long strides the challenger crossed the stage and thrust a paper bearing the list of candidates endorsed by the National Citizens Political Action Committee under Voorhis' nose, commanding him to read it aloud. After an understandable pause, he replied that he didn't know Nixon meant *that* PAC list. Voorhis said he meant that the CIO-PAC had not endorsed him, but Nixon then pointed out—by reading off the names of officers of CIO-PAC and NC-PAC—that in many cases the leaders of the two organizations were the same. Not only was Voorhis doing some fancy hairsplitting, Nixon observed, but this was the first time Voorhis had mentioned in his denials the CIO-PAC, which indeed had not endorsed him, as opposed to the NC-PAC, which had."

At the last of the Nixon-Voorhis debates, at the San Gabriel Mission, the crowds overflowed the hall and amplifiers were needed to carry the speakers' voices to several hundred people who stood outside. Contributions had begun to flow in, often in the form of a crumpled bill or two pressed into the hands of a volunteer worker after a speech. Very few contributions were as high as $100. The professionals were elbowed aside and the amateur politicians handled everything, dreaming up slogans ("Put the Pin in PAC"), writing handouts for the newspapers, mailing out literature, canvassing from door to door. An apathetic district came to life. And the PAC issue continued to be used.

"In the last four years," Nixon would say, "out of forty-six issues sponsored by the CIO and PAC, my opponent has voted against the CIO and PAC only three times. Whether he wants it now or not, my opponent has the PAC endorsement and he has certainly earned it. It's not how a man talks, but how he votes that counts." He pressed this line against "lip-service Americans" who fronted for "un-American elements, wittingly or otherwise, by advocating increasing Federal controls over the lives of people." And three days before the election Republican headquarters was accusing Voorhis of "consistently voting the Moscow-PAC-Henry Wallace line in Congress." Against this Voorhis wasted his political substance denying, and telling the voters that if he were defeated, the Twelfth District would have a Congressman without seniority.

Richard Nixon's victory was overwhelming, 65,586 to 49,994, and Voorhis did not even carry his own home town. The victor had proved one of his favorite maxims: The greater the risk, the greater the opportunity. Nixon was one of seven Republicans to defeat incumbent Democrats in California. Nationally, the Republicans picked up fifty-five seats in the House of Representatives and took control of the Eightieth Congress. It was their year.

Years later Nixon summed it up. "Voorhis lost because the district was not a New Deal district. Our campaign was a very honest debate on the issues." At the time he said, "I do not consider this a personal triumph." Looking back, Voorhis would remark, "I'm frank to say that I felt a little bit this way: I had been a Congressman for ten years. I'd done the best I could. And I really felt if the voters wanted to throw me out, by golly, okay. I'm afraid this was on my mind the whole time, to some extent. I hated a fight like that."

Late in 1946 Voorhis returned to Washington to wind up his affairs and, in a valedictory mood, to write to the man who had defeated him a long and generous letter:

> ... I remember most poignantly the time in late December of 1939 when I first came to Washington as a new Congressman. Little did I realize then all that the job entailed, the long hours of very hard and frequently thankless work, the many periods of frustration when one was unable to get the thing done which he believed most necessary for the country, as well as those times of encouragement when something worthwhile seemed to have been accomplished.
>
> During the ten years of my service I came to have a profound respect for the Congress of the United States and to realize the critical importance of its work, not only for the future of our country, but for the future of the whole world. . . . It becomes more and more evident that the one essential bulwark of the people's liberties in such a nation is the vigor and effectiveness of the national legislature.
>
> If that national legislature occupies a proper place as a co-equal branch of government, and especially if it puts forth and enacts into law a program calculated to meet the nation's present and future problems, the future of freedom will be safe. . . .
>
> The long and short of this letter is simply to say, as I said in my newspaper release after the election at home, that I sincerely wish you well as you undertake the tremendous responsibilities which will soon be yours.

. . . I want you to know that I will be glad to be of any help that you believe I can render. . . .

I have refrained, for reasons which you will understand, from making any reference in this letter to the circumstances of the campaign.

The "circumstances of the campaign" for Jerry Voorhis could not have been very horrendous or long-lasting. In a book he wrote in 1947 Voorhis published the full text of his letter to Nixon, followed by this paragraph:

A couple of weeks passed and I had received no answer. I began to wonder whether Mr. Nixon had received my letter. Then one day when I came back from lunch he was standing there in the outer office. He smiled and so did I. We shook hands and went into the inner office, which by that time was pretty bleak and bare. We talked for more than an hour and parted, I hope and believe, as personal friends. Mr. Nixon will be a Republican congressman. He will, I imagine, be a conservative one. But I believe he will be a conscientious one. And I know I appreciated his coming to see me very sincerely indeed.

5

Mr. Nixon Goes to Washington

IN mid-December of 1946 Representative-elect Richard M. Nixon arrived in Washington, one of the fifty-five victors in an election that had given the Republican Party its first control of the House since the Depression. He had $10,000 in government bonds, a GI life insurance policy, a fairly new Ford car, $14,000 in life insurance, two suits of clothes, a wife, a ten-month-old daughter—and no place to live.

The corridors of the Old House Office Building and of the Capitol echoed emptily to his footsteps, subduing his excitement. He knew the city from his OPA days, but there is a wide chasm between the legislative acres of the Hill and the downtown bureaucracy. For him and for Pat, neither of them gregarious, there was little but the letdown that followed a hard-fought campaign. He himself confessed to "the same lost feeling that I had when I first went into the military service." And his start was not auspicious. It would change, of course, when he bought a house in Spring Valley—modest but pleasant—with a screened porch looking out on the well-groomed order of Washington's North West limits.

It did not take long for the Washington *Post* to pin a label on Nixon: "The greenest congressman in town." The superlative may have been invidiously meant, but it was accurate. Though Nixon was no hayseed, there was a wide-eyed quality about his early meanderings on Capitol Hill. Photographs taken of him then betray it. His eagerness to do the right thing showed in his eyes and in his manner. His clothes were provincial, as former legislative colleagues still recall, but the externals were surely deceiving. For Nixon could feel, as he did, that the Quaker boy from Whittier was now moving in fast company. But he was shrewd enough to understand that Congress could be his oyster if he applied to himself the same rules that had brought him success in high school, college, law school, and the Navy.

The freshman Congressman reacts in a variety of ways to the heady atmosphere into which he has been thrust. He can become simply a vote to his party whip, finding fulfillment in the cocktail parties and the free-and-easy life Washington can offer. He can don the toga and pretend to statesmanship. Or he can become that very unusual specimen, the Congressman who "does his homework." Nixon's background and self-discipline made the determination. In very short order he became known as the man who attended all the committee sessions, who carried a briefcaseful of work home every night, who took his apprenticeship seriously.

From the very start he invited the suspicions or the sarcastic amusement of the more experienced Congressmen by doing what they considered a Boy Scout act. When Representative Adolph Sabath, a veteran New Dealer and octogenarian "dean" of the House, pushed for legislation that would provide housing for homeless Congressmen, Nixon objected. Millions of Americans were caught in the postwar housing squeeze, he argued, and it would not be proper for Congress to grab what the average citizen could not get. Ironically, some of those who knew little of Nixon's circumstances and judged him only by his brashness in opposing the Establishment accused him of opposing the Sabath proposal because he himself lived in luxury. In fact, he was then living in a small hotel room with Pat and Tricia.

It was Nixon's good fortune to be assigned to the House Education and Labor Committee and the House Committee on Un-

American Activities. The first of these had never been considered one of the politically glamorous committee appointments. The second, while it gave a young Congressman a chance to earn headlines, could be the graveyard of his career. Yet these assignments propelled him into the thick of what were to be among the most controversial measures proposed by the Eightieth Congress—"do nothing" to President Truman because it enacted so much legislation that he did not like. Nixon's membership in HUAC, moreover, dropped into his lap the Hiss Case, which made him a national figure and was to propel him ultimately into the Presidency.

Many years after his freshman days in Congress the apocrypha mills ground out a story that Nixon had grandiosely announced to a reporter, on the day he was sworn in, "I was elected to smash the labor bosses." This statement has lived to plague Richard Nixon. There are some who wish he had said it—and done it. Others use it to justify their dislike of Nixon. Those who know him well find it impossible to believe. He was new to the Congress and cautiously learning its ways, and that statement reflected neither his thinking about labor nor that of those who sponsored him in the Twelfth District. He was against the CIO Political Action Committee because it represented a pro-communist line at the time, and, naturally, because it had fought him in the election campaign. But it would have been completely out of character for Nixon to voice or accept a vulgar and blanket condemnation of organized labor. In fact, there were times when those diehard elements that tried to dominate his career expressed considerable concern over what they considered a "softness" on the issue.

Nixon consistently held that it was equally wrong to consider labor a sacred cow or one of the Devil's offspring. "Labor is a legitimate force, serving a legitimate function in the nation's economic life," he said. "In every situation its demands and its grievances must be judged strictly on the merits of the case. No Congressman can do his job properly if he is dogmatically for or against labor. This same applies to business—big or little. I know this is an unpopular position on labor-management relations, because you catch it from both sides. But it's the only one I can take." Stressing a distinction, Nixon added, "When you talk about labor, what do you mean? There is often a big difference between the interests of the labor leader and the man who pays the dues."

These were strong views from a freshman Congressman. But very early in the session Nixon had joined with other freshmen to organize the Chowder and Marching Society—fifteen young Republicans who met once a week to work out their position on pending bills and other House business. Among its members were John Byrnes of Wisconsin, now ranking Republican on the powerful House Ways and Means Committee; Gerald Ford of Michigan, now Minority Leader of the House; John Lodge of Connecticut; and others whose fortunes rose with those of the Chowder and Marching Society. It was not long before Nixon became the acknowledged leader of the group, and this gave him a solid foundation on which to build his career in the House.

Without the prestige he gained from the collective strength of the Society Nixon would have wasted months asserting himself as a voice in the first Republican Congress since the early Thirties. It was not necessary for him to take to the floor in those seldom-reported speeches of young Congressmen. He could deliver votes, and though the seniority system relegated him to one of those shabby and cheerless offices on the fifth floor of the Old House Office Building, he was welcome in the Victorian dignity of the suites that housed Congressmen who made daily headlines.

When the House Education and Labor Committee began to write its version of what became known as the Taft-Hartley Act, Nixon had already become more than the cipher indicated by his brief tenure. Having done his homework, Nixon was convinced that the nation's labor statutes, the Wagner and the Norris-LaGuardia Acts, badly needed revision. They had been written when organized labor was small in numbers and weak against management, and they were drawn up specifically to favor the unions in their struggle to establish equitable collective bargaining with big management. But since those days of struggle, the unions had become rich and powerful. Some, in fact, had more money in their treasuries than the individual employers they had unionized—the International Ladies Garment Workers Union being a case in point. In the early Forties, moreover, the unions had shocked many people by the way they wielded political power. Two strikes, at Allis Chalmers and at Vultee, had dangerously slowed down defense production during the period when Molotov was saying that "fascism is a matter of taste" and pro-communist American labor leaders were intoning that "the Yanks aren't coming."

There were other abuses. Labor unions could make charges against an employer, but if he attempted to answer them, it was by legal definition an "unfair labor practice." The First Amendment right of free association had, in effect, been abrogated by the existing labor statutes, and a worker who did not belong to a union was barred from employment in a closed shop and could be hired by a union shop only if he agreed to sign up with the union.

The time had come, Congress felt, to restore the balance. The question was how. Representative Fred Hartley, who headed the Education and Labor Committee, took an extreme view of the Wagner Act. He hoped not only to junk most of its provisions but to apply restrictions on unions which would sharply whittle away their power. Nixon took a considerably more moderate view. He was interested in the individual rights of unionists, and the justice of his stand became evident after passage of the bill, when the National Labor Relations Board was flooded with cases brought not by management but by members against their own unions. Nixon was also worried about the widespread communist infiltration in a group of CIO unions. (Two years later the CIO availed itself fully of the "non-communist affidavit" provision of Taft-Hartley to rid itself of the communist monkey on its back.)

The testimony taken by the House Education and Labor Committee was voluminous and the paperwork deadly. Nixon, his fellow committee members recall, plowed through all of it, assimilating the complexities of a law that Emil Schlesinger, counsel for the ILGWU, described as "a full employment act for lawyers." If Nixon contributed little to the drafting of the new statute, he was among those who led the fight for its enactment. On April 16,

1947, Nixon took the floor of the House to defend the new labor measure against charges by labor and the Truman Administration that it would be "a slave labor law." "The issue on this particular legislation," he said, "is that this Congress must recognize that this is the time to enact a labor bill which is not class legislation but which is in the best interests of all the people of America." Current assaults on Taft-Hartley give Nixon's arguments continuing significance:

The suggestion has been made that [this bill] was introduced because a few greedy monopolists . . . ordered a bill which would allow them to wring the last dollar out of the laboring men of this country. But what are the facts? When this Congress convened in January of this year it looked back on a record of labor management strife. . . . We know that in the year after V-J Day we had lost $6 billion in the standard of living in America, due to industrial strife. We had seen unprecedented force and violence in labor disputes. . . . We had seen . . . how a few persons . . . could paralyze the entire country by ordering a strike by stroke of a pen. . . .

[President Truman] recommended that machinery should be set up providing for peaceful settlement of jurisdictional disputes, secondary boycotts arising out of jurisdictional disputes, and disputes over the interpretation of contracts. . . . I wish to point out that if this Congress were to limit its action to carrying out the President's recommendations, we would be acting only on disputes which caused less than five percent of the days lost in strikes in the United States in the past two years. . . .

Are the workers of this country, the members of its unions, objecting to this bill? Or are the objections coming only from a few entrenched leaders of union labor . . . ? Do [the workers] object to the fact that [it] gives them the right to vote freely in democratic elections for their officers and to organize and bargain collectively? Do they object to the fact that it protects their right to strike over fundamental issues involving wages, hours, and working conditions? Do they object to the fact that this bill provides that where two union leaders are fighting between themselves . . . such a dispute shall not be a basis for a strike depriving innocent workers of their jobs . . . ?

The workers of America have a great stake in the passage of this bill. It has been said that management suffers from strikes, but we must remember that the man who suffers most, the man who has the greatest stake in industrial peace, is not the public, it is not management, but it is the man who goes out on strike. [That man] should make the determination as to whether he should go out. So we have provided that the decision to strike will be made . . . by secret ballot of a majority of all employees in the plant affected.

"We passed Taft-Hartley," Nixon says, "in spite of all the charges by labor leaders that it would usher in an era of 'slave labor.' It's not a perfect act, and I've always said I'd vote to amend it. But it hasn't been repealed because the average union leader knows it hasn't hurt his union. And he knows, too, that labor has made great gains in wages and hours under it—and without paying the terrible price of striking."

Two years later, when the Democrats had regained control of the House of Representatives, efforts were made to repeal the Taft-Hartley Act. Among the Republicans there were some who felt that whatever virtues the 1947 statute might have had, it hurt their party and should be repealed. Nixon, however, continued to defend it. He was willing to accept amendments that would improve its legal machinery and clarify some of its provisions. But he was also ready to tell the House in 1949 that it protected "the fundamental rights of the sixty million people in America who work for a living."

"Whether you consider yourself to be in the so-called pro-labor group or in the group of those who are attempting to retain what we think are the good features of the present law," he told his fellow Congressmen, "I think all of us will recognize that there should be some provision in the law making both unions and management responsible for their contracts." Labor's fears of Taft-Hartley, he pointed out, had been thoroughly groundless. Since its passage, he said, "wages have increased, pensions have improved, there have been fewer strikes and work stoppages, and labor and the general public have benefited by the law."

The debate over Taft-Hartley degenerated into a series of parliamentary maneuvers in which amendments to the 1947 act were adopted by a narrow margin on one day and then killed the following day. Nixon rose in the House to charge the Democrats with a "deliberate campaign of distortion and misinformation" against the defeated amendments, which, he contended, were "pro-labor." William Costello—one of Nixon's more unfriendly biographers, and later appointed to a diplomatic post by President Lyndon Johnson—would write that Nixon's "contention was not without validity."

Nixon's other assignment was the House Un-American Activities Committee. The decision to accept or reject was a difficult one. Though he knew little about the workings of the communist apparatus, he shared the concern of many Americans over the increasing belligerency of the Soviet Union, reflected in the strident communist and fellow-traveling movement in America. But the vehicle for action against this danger to American institutions was tainted. Though sincere and selfless men had served on HUAC, the headlines were made by political mountebanks like Representative John Rankin, whose racist vulgarities dotted the record. Time and again the careful accumulation of data by the committee staff was compromised by undignified political squabbles. Valid material was sometimes put to invalid use—and this opened the door to a distortion of the committee's efforts so systematic that to this day many otherwise well-informed Americans believe that it accused Shirley Temple, then a small child, of being a communist.* Nixon's opinion of the committee, he

---

* The Facts: It was common practice for the communists, in setting up "front" groups, to list famous people without bothering to get their permission. In exposing this practice, the committee's then research director, Dr. J. B. Matthews, pointed out that so careless and arrogant had the communists become that they had even misused the name of Shirley Temple, then a tot, in a list of sponsors to a Hollywood committee they had organized. Matthews' purpose, as the record clearly shows, was to expose the mendacity of this technique —but ignoring fact and record, the press accused him of having called Shirley Temple a communist.

says, was "not particularly friendly." To his friend Representative
Donald Jackson, a member of the Chowder and Marching Society,
Nixon said, "Politically, it can be the kiss of death."

Pacing up and down in Jackson's office, Nixon debated the
problem. "He felt," Jackson would recall, "the moral obligation
to accept, but he asked himself repeatedly if the condemnation
of the committee by the liberals was sound; if there were the in-
justices and irresponsibilities complained of; if the committee
could do a sound job." In the end his decision to accept what he
knew was "probably the most unpleasant and thankless assignment in the Congress" was based on the belief that he might be
a brake on possible committee excesses and on the realization
that as the communist problem became ever more vexing to the
nation, he would be on the scene of the action.

Nixon's timing was right. Between 1947 and 1950 the committee had some of its most productive years. The social condemnation of anti-communists, so prevalent during the wartime
years of American-Soviet co-belligerency, eased markedly. Toward
the end of that period, in fact, the term "anti-communist" assumed
a respectability it never had before or since. Public opinion had
been stirred by Stalin's brutalities in Eastern Europe, by the
Gouzenko spy case in Canada with its leads into the United
States, and by the shift in party line among the American com-
rades from advocacy of "Twentieth-Century Americanism" to
overt anti-American hostility. Former communists found the courage to step forward, and wavering party members found the
strength to break. HUAC still had its hair shirt in the person of
Rankin, who wandered in and out of hearings asking irrelevant
and viciously inflammatory questions. But Representative Karl E.
Mundt and Nixon were there to bring stability and direction to
committee procedures.

The first witness to appear when the committee began its 1947
hearings was Gerhart Eisler, a notorious and high-ranking operative of the Communist International in the United States, who
had operated here with impunity while living off tax-exempt funds.

"This was really the first time I had brought home to me the character of the Communist Party and the threat which it presented to the country," Nixon said to me. "The Civil Rights Congress, on the very morning that the hearing was held, had circulated all the members of Congress with a petition violently criticizing the chairman for having Eisler subpoenaed. I, of course, at the time did not know that the Civil Rights Congress was a communist front. I read the petition and was so concerned about it that I went to talk to Bob Stripling [the committee's chief investigator] and asked him if we were justified in calling Eisler. He gave me a half-hour lesson in communist activities. I wasn't convinced immediately, but that was the beginning of my education in this field."

At the time he testified Eisler was in the custody of the Immigration Service, charged with passport fraud. (Eventually, he jumped bail and turned up as a Red *Gauleiter* in East Germany. He has since died.) The party had not yet developed the strategy of pleading the Fifth Amendment to all questions asked by House and Senate investigating committees. But Eisler was determined not to divulge any information about his underground activities. He avoided this by deliberately courting a contempt of Congress citation. The colloquy is interesting:

STRIPLING: Mr. Gerhart Eisler, take the stand.

EISLER: I am not going to take the stand. . . .

THE CHAIRMAN: Mr. Eisler, will you raise your right hand?

EISLER: No, before I take the oath—

STRIPLING: Mr. Chairman—

EISLER: I have the floor now. . . .

THE CHAIRMAN: Just a minute. Will you please be sworn in?

EISLER: You will not swear me in before you hear a few remarks.

THE CHAIRMAN: No, there will be no remarks.

EISLER: Then there will be no hearing from me.

The committee made several more attempts to persuade Eisler to follow orderly procedure, then voted to cite him for contempt. By today's standards of protest and contemptuous action, Eisler's demonstration seems mild. But in 1947 it shocked the committee and many of those who had filled the hearing room. Before the guards had removed the witness Richard Nixon took a long look at the small, balding man, almost mousy in appearance yet arrogant in his concealed power. This was Nixon's first view of a professional communist revolutionary—a man who had plotted in Germany and China, who had ordered murders, who had practiced every form of deceit and participated in sabotage, and yet had the temerity to act the injured party before a Congressional committee.

It was Nixon who represented the committee several days later in its formal request for a contempt of Congress citation. It was his maiden speech in the House, and *Newsweek* described him as "youthful and intensely sincere," and speaking in "calm, measured tones." Two Congressmen, both from New York, spoke against the contempt citation—Adam Clayton Powell, who abstained from voting, and the openly pro-communist Vito Marcantonio, who cast the only opposing vote.

In the weeks and months that followed, the committee piled up mountains of evidence and millions of words on the Communist Party—basic research on a situation that has since become all too familiar to the country. And Nixon got a thorough grounding on the subject at first hand from committee witnesses, as well as from former communists like Benjamin Mandel, the committee's research director.

Fred Beal, a onetime party member who had fled to the Soviet Union after being convicted of complicity in the shooting of a police chief during a strike in Gastonia, North Carolina, told the committee why he preferred an American penitentiary to "freedom" in Russia, and then gave cogent evidence on the workings of the communist forged-passport ring.

Ruth Fischer, Eisler's sister, who had been a charter member of the Austrian Communist Party and played a leading role in the post-World War I German Communist movement, testified in detail on conspiratorial and murderous activities of which she had personal knowledge. These experiences and insights she later put into her scholarly work, *Stalin and German Communism*, which was published by Harvard University.

Victor Kravchenko, author of *I Chose Freedom*, testified to the illegal and subversive work of the wartime Soviet Purchasing

Commission, of which he had been a part before his defection.

FBI Director J. Edgar Hoover reported in close detail on the aims, methods, activities, and strength of the American communist movement.

At the stormy "Hollywood hearings" in the fall of 1947—which could have meant death at the polls for a Californian like Nixon— the extent of communist infiltration and influence in the movie industry and its staggering financial contributions to the party were sketched in.

The investigation of communist infiltration of labor unions brought agonized howls from union leaders that Nixon and the committee were attempting to smear the American workingman and destroy the labor movement. But Nixon, questioning friendly witnesses as stringently as hostile ones, continued to draw out information that the CIO used two years later in expelling eleven unions as communist-dominated.

Early in 1948 Nixon was appointed chairman of a special subcommittee on legislation. After studying HUAC's voluminous files, holding hearings, and issuing two definitive monographs ("The Communist Party as an Agent of a Foreign Power" and "The Communist Party as an Advocate of Force and Violence"), Nixon's subcommittee issued a report proposing legislation that was later embodied in the Mundt-Nixon bill of that session. The report, written by Nixon himself, ended with these words:

The subcommittee has not attempted to recommend legislation which will deal with so-called theoretical communists in the United States. We are seeking rather to strike a body blow at the American cadre of the Soviet-directed communist conspiracy. We believe that if its criminal activities are prosecuted, its false fronts exposed, and its foreign assistance and direction cut away, the movement in the United States, standing alone for what it is, will be overwhelmingly defeated. We are willing to permit the theories of communism and democracy to clash in the open market place of political ideas in America, but we insist that communism not be allowed to have the unfair advantages in this conflict of the unrestricted use of illegal means, the cloak of secrecy and fraud, and the assistance and direction of a foreign communist dictatorship.

The legislation that followed, written by Mundt and Nixon, was based on proposals made by a heterogeneous group of liberals and conservatives which included A. A. Berle, Jr. (later to become Chairman of the Liberal Party in New York), Donald Richberg, socialist leader Louis Waldman, Felix Cohen, former Ambassador to Russia Admiral William H. Standley, Professor William Yandell Elliott of Harvard, and John Foster Dulles. It had the distinction of being the first piece of legislation proposed by the committee in the ten years of its existence.

The Mundt-Nixon bill was a serious effort at coping with an ambiguous situation. In 1920 Lenin had drawn a "mandatory" blueprint for the world communist movement. "For all countries, even the most free 'legal' and 'peaceful' ones," he had written, "it has become absolutely necessary for every communist party to combine systematically all legal and illegal work" carried on by a well-organized illegal apparatus. Twenty-eight years later, as *Newsweek* would point out, "operating with impunity behind a camouflage of 'legitimate' communist parties and multitudinous 'front' groups, the worldwide conspiratorial network was a testament to Leninist vision." Along with other thoughtful men, Nixon and Mundt realized that the communist movement was not covered by Magna Carta, the Bill of Rights, or by a sentimental reading of Anglo-Saxon jurisprudence. Resisting pressure to ban the party outright or to make the belief in a communist society a crime, the two Congressmen sought to draw up a statute that would apply the force of law and the weight of public opinion to the gray areas of Leninist illegality.

The Mundt-Nixon bill, therefore, provided that the Communist Party annually must file with the Justice Department the names of all officials and members; that organizations designated by the Attorney General as communist fronts must file the names of all officers, plainly stating their communist origin in all literature, broadcasts, etc.—but with the right to appeal their classification in the Federal courts; that the party and its front groups must keep accurate records of all moneys received and expended, including the sources of all such funds; that party officers and members be denied passport privileges; that party officers be barred from seeking or accepting any Federal office without disclosing their communist affiliation. Penalties for violations ranged from heavy fines and jail sentences to loss of citizenship and expatriation.

There was criticism of the bill from both the Left and the Right. The communist *Daily Worker* cried that it was "a step to fascism." Governor Thomas E. Dewey, preparing for his last lunge at the Presidency, dismissed it as "an attempt to beat down ideas with clubs." *The New York Times* editorialized that it "could be used to impose restraints on freedom such as the American people have not known for one hundred and fifty years." *The Christian Science Monitor* argued that it would create "precedents and a machinery for the kind of political proscription which could be turned by any party in power against any minority."

Nixon, who led the floor debate in the House, answered the critics by analyzing in detail the controversial provisions of the bill. "There is too much loose talk and confusion on the communist issue," he charged. "By passing this bill, the Congress of the United States will go on record as to just what is subversive about communism." Then, using some body English, he added, "It will once and for all spike many of the loose charges about organizations' being communist fronts because they happen to advocate some of the same policies which the communists support."

The House of Representatives passed the Mundt-Nixon bill overwhelmingly—319 to 56. The Senate, intimidated by press attacks on the measure, let it die in committee. But when the Democrats regained control of the Eighty-first Congress in 1949, the national temper had changed. The disclosures of Whittaker Chambers and the indictment of Alger Hiss had rocked the country. Judith Coplon, a Justice Department employee, was arrested for espionage in a case that combined sex and subversion, including assignations in a Philadelphia hotel. Western European communists were bluntly announcing that in case of war between their own countries and the Soviet Union, they would side with

Moscow. Those who opposed the bill in the past tripped over themselves to support it. Senator Hubert H. Humphrey, sensing the public mood, threw in an amendment that would permit the setting up of concentration camps for communists in times of national emergencies. Other amendments cluttered up the House and Senate hoppers. The bill that finally went to the Senate floor, now bearing the name of the tough and powerful Senator Pat McCarran, reflected the popular mood.

The debate, both in and out of Congress, was acrimonious. The San Francisco *Chronicle*, a major voice of Pacific Coast liberalism, charged with some justice that the new bill was "subversive of the spirit and the letter of the Constitution." Leon Henderson, then Chairman of Americans for Democratic Action, asserted in all seriousness that the communists secretly favored passage. And Congress was pelted with mail from every quarter. Examining a large batch of angry letters addressed to him, Nixon discovered that though they bore different names, many signatures were in the same handwriting. His public disclosure of this fact led others in Congress to examine the bushels of mail they were receiving, and they too began turning up forged communications. Irate men and women descended on Washington, invaded the offices of Congressmen, riffled mail and other papers on congressional desks, and screamed invective. The American Slav Congress gave itself away by sending a passionate denunciation to Congress which was being broadcast from Moscow at the very moment when it arrived in Washington. These tactics were, however, counterproductive. The bill, officially tagged the Subversive Activities Control Act, sailed through Congress, which then overrode President Truman's veto. By this time it was no longer Nixon's and would be attached to him only in later years when anti-communism ceased to be respectable in some quarters.

In this period of his development Nixon's foreign policy positions were emerging fairly rapidly—in scope and perception a far cry from the naïve formulations of his 1946 campaign. He believed that the United States had imperative responsibilities abroad and that those responsibilities were as much to itself as to the rest of the world. He introduced a resolution to commit this country to defensive military alliances and to military aid for any

non-communist country threatened by Kremlin-directed infiltration. He appealed for American protection of Trieste, then
receiving Marshal Tito's tender treatment, and spoke against
Secretary of State Dean Acheson's bifurcated policies that re-
treated in the Far East while fighting the communists in Europe.
He favored, in short, a unified American foreign policy on a global
scale and a national cognizance that the communist universal state
was the enemy. He did not oppose the United Nations, but he
stressed the older American internationalism, which relied on
temporary alliances with like-minded nations for specific purposes
rather than permanent ties to a body already showing its basic
weaknesses.

During the Eightieth Congress, when Senator Joseph Martin
named the eighteen members of a Select Committee to study the
Marshall Plan proposal and to recommend enabling legislation,
Nixon was among the ten Republicans chosen. This appointment,
which he learned about by reading of it in the papers, was both
taxing and rewarding. "It was one of the biggest thrills of my
lief," he told me, "because I had never been to Europe, and I
had never dreamed that I might be going that year."

The group, headed by Representative Christian A. Herter,
embarked on a strenuous tour of Europe, paced by an indefatigable
Nixon. No dinner clothes were taken and Nixon, with pre-emptive
virtue, announced at the start that "this will be no junket . . .
no cross-Atlantic cocktail party." In that month of travel Nixon
talked to government officials, directly to the people, and to
communist leaders like Arthur Horner in Great Britain, and De
Vittoria, second-in-command of the Italian Communist Party.
From a Veronese woman he learned what poverty was like when
she told him that when she and her people were without heat, "we
go to bed." In Greece he flew to the front where Greek troops
and communist guerrillas were still fighting and talked to soldiers
and prisoners.

Speaking in 1952 of his Greek visit, Nixon enunciated a principle that he probably would find valid today. "There was no
more corrupt or unstable government in the world than the government of Greece," he said. "But we recognized that it was not
a question of the Greek government or something better, but a

question of the Greek government or something worse, and we gave the Greek government the assistance which enabled it to defeat the communists." As Nixon stressed, this lesson was one that a State Department, splitting hairs over Nationalist "corruption" in mainland China, ignored until it was too late and the communists had taken over.

Nixon returned to Washington that much less the unsophisticated Whittier boy who had been brushed aside as the "greenest" Congressman to be elected in 1946. He had done no violence to the ideas he brought with him, but he had gained a broader view of world affairs, and he had seen at first hand what foreign economic and military aid could mean to a Western Europe digging out from under the physical and psychological rubble of World War II. The Herter Committee was lauded for the volume and intensity of its work—a report running to thousands of pages, to which Nixon made a major contribution. It became the encyclopedic source from which much of the Marshall Plan, as enacted by Congress, would derive.

Looking back in later years at his foreign policy votes during that period, Nixon remarked to me that perhaps "my record here may be too consistent." He went down the line on measures for relief assistance to the people of war-devastated countries, for aid to Greece and Turkey, for the Reciprocal Trade Agreements Act —to the dismay of protectionists, Nixon has always been a free trader—for the Marshall Plan, and for Selective Service. This happened to be all of the foreign policy legislation that came up in that session.

In domestic policy he confounded many who expected him to be a doctrinaire conservative. His voting record, in fact, was completely eclectic, much to the annoyance of those who claimed him as theirs, as well as those who tried hard to banish him to the outer darkness of reaction. It was hard then, as it is now, for Left and Right to understand how he could vote for continuation of wartime excise tax rates, reduction of individual income tax rates, removal of disloyal persons from the Executive Branch, abolition of the poll tax, extension of housing and rent controls, the return of rent control powers to local authorities, return of the tidelands and their oil to the states, and admission of displaced persons.

On all of these issues, he made his own alliances and remained his own man, compromising on particulars but hewing to a line that left him isolated—as perhaps he wanted to be. He never believed in repealing the entire New Deal. It had been woven too closely into the fabric of American life, and to discard it would have meant the kind of dislocation that Nixon instinctively rejected. But he felt too that much of the New Deal was crisis legislation and should be concluded, that some of it needed revision. By conviction and temperament he was a free enterpriser, but by temperament and conviction he was always ready to consider alternatives and to arrive at moderate solutions which, though they sometimes pleased no one, made economic and political sense.

Like many other Congressmen, Nixon did not always vote as his district would have liked. But like only a few, he let his district know when he differed with its thinking. He made this clear in the newsletter he sent his constituents, and in the broadcasts he recorded at the Capitol for use at home. In the polls he mounted Nixon tried to reach every voter in his district, and his returns usually averaged about 30 per cent, causing considerable comment in the local press. When a poll showed that his district was generally opposed to the Marshall Plan, he returned home to take part in its defense. His vote on rent control was highly unpopular —most voters were small property owners—but as more than one newspaperman would later discover, the district was ready to allow him to disagree. "Dick's thinking of the country again instead of us," an apartment house owner said with wry resignation.

All of this would have made him a better-than-average Congressman, working hard and looking to the day when he might run for the Senate. What made all the difference for this man alone was not his record on legislation, not his service with the Herter Committee, and not the machine he had made of the Chowder and Marching Society. The catalyst was the testimony of a single man on a hot third day of August in 1948, in a crowded hearing room in Washington.

6

The Hiss Case

RICHARD Nixon has called the Hiss Case his "first crisis." It was more than that. He had arrived in Washington a year and a half before the hot and muggy day when the case broke—testing his powers, overeager, determined to be more than the usual run of Congressmen. His earnestness was almost amusing to Capitol Hill sophisticates, who nonetheless admired his abilities. He was a superb technician who made use of the world of politics without really penetrating to its fascinating and human side.

The Hiss Case changed all of this. For the first and perhaps the only time in his life he was not the canny poker player, watching the unfolding of the game. He was completely committed, taking risks that no prudent politician would have taken.

In the lexicon of the cliché experts, Nixon was ready and willing to cast the die, to cross the Rubicon, to be counted. He may not have known it, but on the third day of August, 1948, Richard Nixon had taken the measure of his decision in the half-empty but tense hearing room of the Ways and Means Committee of the Old House Office Building. Those who knew him in those trying, dangerous, and exciting days—who stood by his side against an angry and taunting Establishment—can never forget it, in spite of whatever trespasses they profess to see in his later career.

Many years afterward, as he recounts in *Six Crises*, when he had lost the Presidency by one of the closest votes in American history— with rumors of Democratic fraud filling the air—one of his friends told Nixon, "If it hadn't been for the Hiss Case, you would have been elected President of the United States." Another friend, perhaps more perceptive, said, "If it hadn't been for the Hiss Case, you never would have been Vice President of the United States or candidate for President." At the time thoughts of the Presidency were not on Nixon's mind. In the postlude of the Hiss trial I said to him, "Dick, if you play your cards right, you can be President of the United States." His genuinely deprecating laugh told the story, and it was not until years later that he conceded the possibility to himself.

That was not what Nixon's commitment in the Hiss Case was about. In the atmosphere of the early hearings—the first when Whittaker Chambers took the stand, the second when Alger Hiss called Chambers a liar—it would have been infinitely easier and, as it looked then, smarter to side with the Establishment, tossing the case into a political dung heap and clothing himself in the outrage of those who came to the aid of Hiss. Instead Nixon followed his instincts and took up a cause that he knew was right. Because he was a lawyer, with a lawyer's eye and an ear for evidence, he approached the case with cool rationality. Instinct and conscience, however, had spoken first. To the man alone, this was important— and Nixon was young enough then to accept what he might later have rejected. Of him, as of everyone who had an intimate connection with that tragic episode in American history, it can be said that he was never the same again.

In public comments on the case, Nixon has said that it began for him "personally" on the day in August when Chambers testified. Only reading of the word "personally" makes that statement accurate. But in private conversation years later he would admit that like so many whose work or interest touched on communist activity, he had heard the story of Hiss's involvement long before it became a matter of national attention. In February of 1947, during a discussion of communist infiltration, the name of Alger Hiss had been mentioned to him by Father John F. Cronin, who had put aside his work with labor unions to probe into a murky world of subversion and espionage. Father Cronin was not the first to come upon the name of Alger Hiss in his researches into the communist apparatus, but he had taken his information to Nixon. Nixon, in turn, was not the first to hear the tale and brush it aside. (President Roosevelt had angrily rejected it in 1938, John Foster Dulles in 1946.) It seemed all too unbelievable, and there was the more important business of getting acclimated to the new world of Congress.*

The House Un-American Activities Committee, of which Nixon was one of the more solid members, came upon the Hiss Case almost inadvertently. Through channels it had developed into various government agencies, the committee learned that a former courier for a major communist spy ring in the Federal government was willing to testify publicly. Leaks to the New York *World-Telegram* had depicted Elizabeth Bentley—"Mary" in its veiled stories— as a "blonde spy queen." In reality Elizabeth Bentley hardly fitted a Mata Hari role. She was a big, plain woman whose idealistic concern for sharecroppers and the victims of Hitler's terror had been skillfully exploited by the communists. She had little or no understanding of Marxism, Leninism, or Stalinism—and whatever New England repugnance she might have felt for participating in espionage operations against her country was dulled by the joys of a love affair with a high-ranking Soviet agent in New York.

The Bentley testimony made very big headlines when she appeared before HUAC on July 31, 1948, as she recounted with

---

* In retrospect it should be noted that President Truman was far more astute politically than Nixon or his other critics in understanding the significance of the Hiss disclosures. His persistent attempts to downgrade the investigation of Hiss as a "red herring" were motivated by his conviction that the Republicans who pressed it were after him, rather than Hiss—and this was his visceral response. Had he been another kind of man, he would have taken hold of the investigation and made political capital of it. But the true test of his thoughts and feelings came when he sanctioned the Justice Department action that led to Hiss's trial and conviction.

the trained recall of an agent the names, dates, and places of her prior perfidy. But those she incriminated appeared before the committee and blandly denied everything except that they had known her casually. To bolster her stories, the committee staff dug into the files and came up with the name of Whittaker Chambers, then a $30,000-a-year senior editor of *Time*, who reluctantly and under subpoena agreed to take the stand.

Though Chambers had left the spy apparatus before Elizabeth Bentley entered it, there were enough overlapping alumni from his Washington cell and hers to give corroboration to part of the Bentley story. The major thrust of his account was not espionage, though he mentioned it, but on the policy-muddling and related subversion by a communist group within the State and Treasury Departments. Among those he named were Alger Hiss, who had risen to the important State Department post of Director of the Office of Special Political Affairs and then, under fire, moved on to the even more prestigious presidency of the Carnegie Endowment for International Peace, an office that paid $20,000 a year—or $5,000 more than a Cabinet member's salary at the time.

This is how Nixon, almost a dozen years later, would describe his first view of Whittaker Chambers during the brief executive session that preceded the public hearing: "Both in appearance and in what he had to say, he made very little impression on me or the other members. He was short and pudgy. His clothes were unpressed. His shirt collar was curled up over his jacket. He spoke in a rather bored monotone. At first he seemed an indifferent if not a reluctant witness. But his answers to the few questions we asked him convinced us that he was no crackpot. And we decided to save time by going at once into public session. None of us thought his testimony was going to be especially important. I remember that I considered for a moment the possibility of skipping the public hearing altogether, so that I could return to my office and get out some mail."

Nixon sat in the hearing room, listening to the prepared statement Chambers was reading, at first not particularly impressed. "As he droned on," Nixon has written, "I found my thoughts wandering to other subjects. He was halfway through the statement before I realized that he had some extraordinary quality which raised him far above the witnesses who had appeared before our committee. It was not how he spoke, it was, rather, the sheer, almost stark eloquence of phrases that needed no histrionic embellishment. . . . And then, speaking with what seemed to me almost a sense of sadness and resignation, he said: 'Yet so strong is the hold which the insidious evil of communism secures upon its disciples that I could still say to [my wife] at the time—"I know that I am leaving the winning side for the losing side but it is better to die on the losing side than to live under communism." ' From that moment on, I came more and more to realize that despite his unpretentious appearance, Chambers was a man of extraordinary intellectual gifts and one who had inner strength and depth. Here was no headline seeker but rather a thoughtful, introspective man, careful with his words, speaking with what sounded like the ring of truth."

The Chambers testimony made its own headlines, but they did not compare with those that Elizabeth Bentley had prompted. What he said might have been forgotten—one more hearing in the long record of the committee—but for the intervention of Alger Hiss. The next day Robert Stripling, HUAC's chief investigator, phoned Nixon to tell him that Hiss had sent the committee a telegram demanding that he be heard to deny in open session the charges made by Chambers. Of all the men named by Chambers, Hiss was the only one to seek this chance of rebuttal. The committee scheduled his appearance for the following day, August 5.

There had, however, been a curtain-raiser for Hiss's appearance. Though the committee had been impressed by the testimony of Whittaker Chambers, major newspapers were launching a counterattack even before all the facts were in. *The New York Times*, long an enemy of HUAC, thundered that "we have a precious heritage in this country of protection of the innocent against false accusation. . . . What price a few headlines if those rights are compromised . . . ?" And even the Washington *Star*, less prone to this kind of prejudgment, published a cartoon depicting an open sewer manhole labeled "The House Un-American Activities Committee."

This set the stage. The Washington press corps, largely antagonistic to the committee, turned out in force to hear Alger Hiss.

Here was a man, many reporters felt, who could demolish the committee by his unqualified denials and by the prestige of his past and present. Smiling pleasantly but distantly, Hiss took the stand to lay the groundwork for the case that would eventually destroy him. In the glare of kleig lights and the flash of photographers' bulbs, he began his testimony:

"I am here at my own request," he said, "to deny unqualifiedly various statements about me which were made before this committee by one Whittaker Chambers. . . . I welcome the opportunity to answer to the best of my ability any inquiries the members of this committee may wish to ask me. I am not and never have been a member of the Communist Party. I do not and have never adhered to the tenets of the Communist Party. . . . I have never followed the Communist Party line, directly or indirectly. . . . The statements made about me by Mr. Chambers are complete fabrications. I think my record in the government speaks for itself."

Under the committee's questioning Hiss became very precise. He had never, he said carefully, "known *a man named Whittaker Chambers*" (author's emphasis). As a lawyer Nixon realized that this could be an evasion. Had he been more experienced in the ways of communist espionage, he would have known that Chambers, as head of the cell and its liaison man with the underground in New York, would have been known to his "contacts" by a cover name.*

Not long after this, Nixon said to me: "I felt that Hiss was much too careful a witness in his testimony for one who purported to be telling the whole truth without qualification. I noted that throughout his testimony he never once said, 'I have never known Whittaker Chambers.' He always used the qualifying phrase, 'I have never known a man by the name of Whittaker Chambers.'

---

* The underground alias used by Chambers had been "Carl" and this was the name he used with Hiss. This technique of exact but limited truth adding up to a complete falsehood was later employed by John Sherman, another witness in the case, who was asked if he had ever been introduced to Hiss by Chambers. His answer was, "I wouldn't know Alger Hiss from Adam"—true enough since they had, in fact, been introduced at the time when Hiss was using the cover name of "Adam."

Could Hiss have known Chambers under another name? I also felt that Hiss seemed to be putting on a show when he was shown a picture of Chambers. His statement to Karl Mundt that 'this might look like you, Mr. Chairman,' and his elaborate explanation all combined to make me think that he actually did recognize the picture and was attempting to give a disarming statement concerning it. All in all, I felt that Hiss was a very smooth witness, but between him and Chambers, Chambers had been the more convincing witness. But I could only offer this as a personal suspicion on my part."

By the time Hiss had completed his testimony the committee was ready to capitulate to him. Mundt, the acting chairman, thanked him for his "forthright statements." John Rankin offered his congratulations. There was a general rush of newspapermen to shake his hand. "He had won the day completely," Nixon would write in 1962. "It would not be an exaggeration to say that probably 90 percent of the reporters at the press table and most of the committee members were convinced that a terrible mistake had been made . . . and that the committee owed an apology to Hiss for having allowed Chambers to testify without checking the possibility of such a mistake. Most of the news stories the next day and the editorials during the week were to express the same opinion . . . completely overlooking the possibility that Chambers rather than Hiss might have been telling the truth."

A veteran of committee hearings approached Nixon and asked, "How are you going to dig yourself out of this hole?" Ed Lahey of the Chicago *News*, a respected reporter with no ax to grind, confronted Nixon. He was shaking with anger as he declared, "The Committee on Un-American Activities stands convicted, guilty of calumny."

"It would have been easy then," Nixon told me, "to have dropped the case, patted Hiss on the back, and become a hero to his many friends and admirers. I recall that Mary Spargo, who had the unusual distinction of being friendly to the committee even though a reporter for the Washington *Post*, came up to me after Hiss concluded his testimony and warned that both the committee and I personally would be destroyed if we didn't get ourselves off the hook. She said to me, 'Here's a chance to win some liberal support by repudiating Chambers and clearing Hiss.'. . . I told her we had an obligation to conduct further investigation in view of the very serious nature of the Chambers charges. 'Well, go ahead,' she said. 'But I warn you, you'd better be right or you're a dead duck.' "

To make matters worse, the President of the United States jumped into the battle on Hiss's side. Nixon was eating lunch after what seemed like a catastrophic hearing when he learned that Harry Truman had attacked the Hiss investigation as a "red herring" being dragged across the trail by Republicans eager to forestall legislation on price controls, the postwar inflation, and other matters that he considered important to the nation. The President's remark added a new dimension to Nixon's—and the committee's—problems. What had been a controversial espionage case had, by Truman's intervention, become a bitterly partisan issue. The question would echo: "Who is lying, Hiss or Chambers?" But in counterpoint, there would be another theme: "Are the Republicans wrong, or the Democrats?"

In those first hours of worry and confusion, Nixon realized that he could still play it either way, as prosecutor or impartial judge. If he washed his hands of the case, HUAC would bear the brunt of press attacks, whereas his reputation for "fairness" would go up. His predecessor, Jerry Voorhis, had withdrawn from the committee at a time when it was under similar attack, to the applause of press and Administration. But if Nixon pressed the case and failed to prove it completely, he would be marked for the rest of his political life as Red-baiter and witch-hunter. A career that had begun with so much promise—just a year earlier Speaker Joe Martin had said of him, "Mr. Nixon is one of the ablest young men to come to Congress in many years"—could peter out dismally in partisan recrimination.

Having seen the two protagonists of the case on the stand, he could not say with certainty that Chambers was telling the truth. But he was sure that Hiss was lying about something, and to Nixon's legal mind, this cast doubt on his entire testimony. As he joined the committee in executive session that afternoon, he came to the conclusion that it would have to stall long enough to give its investigators a chance to probe more deeply into the conflicting evidence before it.

But a majority of the committee, in panic, wanted to shut the books on the Hiss Case. "Let's wash out hands of the whole mess," said Representative F. Edward Hébert. "Let's turn the record over to the Justice Department and let them decide who's lying." Nixon's public relations sense told him that this was no solution. It would be, he argued, a public confession that the committee was inept and reckless, that it had no business investigating subversion. Having gone this far, he argued, the committee would have to continue down the road it had taken, unpleasant though it might be.

It was at this point that Nixon devised the strategy that eventually helped to crack the case. "I knew enough about the communist movement to realize that with the committee's resources it would be impossible to determine whether or not Hiss had ever been a member of the party," he told me. "But if Hiss and Chambers had known each other, as Chambers testified, then we had a fighting chance to prove it." He had discovered for himself what every experienced investigator knows: no matter what care they may take, conspirators always leave tracks.

The telling argument may have been Bob Stripling's. He told the committee that from the moment Chambers had left the stand, he had been the butt of a calculated whispering campaign in Washington and in New York. Wherever the case was discussed, the rumors would be heard: Chambers was an alcoholic, he had been in a mental institution, he had paranoid delusions. (These charges would later be made before the committee by Hiss, in the form of questions, and conclusively proved false.) This, Stripling pointed out, was the standard technique employed to destroy a committee witness, particularly a former communist.

Nixon and Stripling prevailed. Mundt, as acting chairman, appointed Nixon to head a subcommittee that would cross-examine Chambers. As a cover-up the committee announced that Nixon was going to New York to follow up some of the leads in Elizabeth Bentley's testimony. That night, however, Nixon's doubts returned.

82

How could Hiss, a man of sound middle-class background, and a record of achievement that included attendance as a trusted aide to President Roosevelt at Yalta, the post of Director of the Office of Special Political Affairs in the State Department, and the post of Secretary-General to the San Francisco Conference at which the United Nations was born, have been a member of a communist espionage ring? And how could this record be challenged by a man who was admittedly a former spy, who had been an editor of *The Daily Worker* and the party's magazine, *The New Masses?* To find his answers, he jotted down a long list of questions bearing on Hiss's personal life to put to Chambers when the subcommittee examined him again.

On August 7, in the portentous atmosphere of a walnut-paneled courtroom in New York's Federal Building, the three members of the subcommittee and several members of the staff went into executive session with Chambers. For some three hours Nixon examined and cross-examined his witness exhaustively. Chambers told the subcommittee the nicknames Hiss and his wife called each other, described the homes they had lived in and their hobbies, recalled the location of the kennel to which they took their dog, recalled Hiss's excitement when he had seen a prothonotary warbler, a rare bird, on one of the birdwatching walks he and his wife, Priscilla Hiss, took along the Potomac, and most important of all, the history of an old Ford car. When Hiss had bought a 1936 Plymouth, Chambers said, he had insisted on giving his old Ford to the Communist Party, and the transfer had been effected through a communist employee of a reputable motor company.

At the end of Chambers' testimony, Nixon asked him, "Would you be willing to submit to a lie detector test?"

"Yes, if necessary," Chambers answered—the first of many times that he agreed to this suggestion.

"You have that much confidence?"

"I am telling the truth," Chambers said.

Nixon returned to Washington convinced that he had struck paydirt, but still needing reassurance. Working on a round-the-clock basis, the committee staff set out to verify or disprove the statements made by Chambers. "The story checked out in every detail where corroborative evidence was available," Nixon recounted later. "We then concluded that we had enough evidence to call Hiss before us again and ask him to explain how Mr. Chambers could know these things about him." But before it did the committee suffered another setback.

Among those named by both Whittaker Chambers and Elizabeth Bentley as a member of the communist apparatus in the Federal government was Harry Dexter White, a former Assistant Secretary of the Treasury and author of the Morgenthau Plan for the industrial destruction of postwar Germany. Had HUAC done its homework, it would have known that since 1942, Civil Service records had listed Harry White as "a known communist," that he had colonized the Treasury Department with identifiable communists and fellow travelers, that his division was known for the way in which it brusquely transferred out anyone with anti-communist sympathies. It would have discovered that White was responsible for turning over to the Soviet Union the plates for printing occupation money in Germany, a gesture that cost the American taxpayer millions of dollars when it became necessary for the Treasury to redeem the bills that Russian presses had rolled out.

But when White took the stand, the committee was just as unprepared as it had been at the time of the first Chambers and Hiss appearances. An assured and plausible Harry Dexter White quickly took the initiative and proceeded to lecture the committee on Americanism, to insult the members, to make witty remarks, and to "explain" airily why he had been the biggest single employer of Soviet agents in the Washington wartime bureaucracy. When he stepped down, having denied the Bentley-Chambers charges, he was a hero to the press, which turned on the committee savagely. Several days later White died of what the death certificate recorded as a heart attack. (He was cremated before an autopsy could be performed, and there is still some doubt as to the cause of his death.) HUAC was accused of having brought on the heart attack, which was cited illogically as proof positive of White's innocence. (Ironically, when Nixon was Vice President, the case was reopened by Attorney General Herbert Brownell, who placed J. Edgar Hoover on the stand and opened the voluminous FBI record to senatorial and public scrutiny.)

In the period between the second Chambers examination and August 16, when Hiss was to be questioned again, Richard Nixon conducted a soul-searching of his own, seeking advice and counsel from men who would be disposed to side with Hiss. First he called Bert Andrews, chief Washington correspondent of the New York *Herald Tribune,* asking him to visit his office. Andrews had recently won a Pulitzer Prize for *Washington Witch Hunt,* an attack on the State Department's loyalty program based on a book-length memorandum presented to him by Abe Fortas, then counsel for a number of security-risk defendants. With James Reston of *The New York Times,* Andrews had recommended Hiss to John Foster Dulles for the Carnegie Endowment post, and at the time he was highly regarded in Washington for his switch to a soft line on security matters. Nixon asked Andrews to study the transcript of the Chambers testimony on the private life of Alger Hiss. "I wouldn't have believed it after hearing Hiss the other day," Andrews said. "But there's no doubt about it. Chambers knew Hiss."

Nixon consulted William P. Rogers, then counsel for the Senate committee that had also heard Elizabeth Bentley's testimony. Rogers agreed with Andrews that, on the face of it, Chambers was telling the truth and Hiss was lying. Then, on August 11, Nixon journeyed to New York for a consultation with John Foster Dulles. Since Dulles had defended Hiss against charges of communism in 1946, he could be counted on to bring no bias to the discussion. Nixon and Dulles met that evening in Nixon's suite at the Hotel Roosevelt. Allen Dulles, former head of the Bern operation of the Office of Strategic Services and later Director of the Central Intelligence Agency, was also present.

"Both men read the [Hiss and Chambers] testimony," Nixon would write in *Six Crises.* "When they had finished, Foster Dulles paced the floor, his hands crossed behind him. It was a characteristic I was to see many times in the years ahead when we discussed important issues. He stopped finally and said, 'There's no question about it. It's almost impossible to believe, but Chambers knows

Hiss.' Allen Dulles reached the same conclusion. I asked Foster Dulles whether he thought I was justified in going ahead with the investigation. He replied without hesitation. 'In view of the facts Chambers has testified to, you'd be derelict in your duty as a congressman if you did not see the case through to a conclusion.' "

This should have settled it. Nixon had asked four men to read the testimony—an experienced newspaperman, an investigative lawyer, a defender of Hiss, and an expert on espionage—and all had agreed that his only course was to press the case before the committee and the country. But almost compulsively, Richard Nixon arrives at his decisions alone, as if the presence of another person, no matter how intimate, intrudes on his thought processes. Between the night of his meeting with the Dulles brothers and August 16, when Hiss was scheduled to testify again, Nixon drove to a small farm near York, Pennsylvania, where his parents had been living since his election to Congress. Among the outbuildings was a reconverted washhouse, and Nixon sat there for hours, slumped on an ancient couch and staring into the empty fireplace. When his mother called him for meals, he called back, "Go ahead and eat— I'm not hungry." From time to time he wandered out for long, brooding walks.

"Why don't you drop the case, Richard," his mother said to him. "No one else thinks Hiss is guilty."

"I've got a feeling Hiss is lying," Nixon answered. "I've got to stick to it until I prove whether I'm right or not."

"Don't give in then," she said. "Do what you think is right."

Braving possible criticism from his colleagues, Nixon set out to put that decision to its final test. To avoid publicity, he made the two-hour car trip alone to the Chambers farm in Westminster, Maryland:

"We sat on some dilapidated rocking chairs on his front porch overlooking the rolling Maryland countryside. It was the first of many long and rewarding conversations I was to have with him . . . through the years until his death in 1961. Like most men of quality, he made a deeper impression personally than he did in public. Within minutes, the caricature of him drawn by the rumormongers of the drunkard, the unstable and unsavory character, faded away.

Here was a man of extraordinary intelligence, speaking from a great depth of understanding; a sensitive, shy man who had turned from complete dedication to communism to a new religious faith and a kind of fatalism about the future. One thing that especially impressed me was his almost absolute passion for privacy.

"Why then was he willing to sacrifice this privacy and risk his own financial security by testifying against Hiss? I told him bluntly that many of those who questioned his credibility believed he must have some personal motive for doing what he had to Hiss. Chambers replied, 'Certainly I wouldn't have a motive which would involve destroying my own career.' He had come forward out of necessity, he said, as a kind of duty to warn his country of the scope, strength and danger of the communist conspiracy in the United States. It would be a great pity if the nation continued to look upon this case simply as a clash of personalities between Hiss and himself. Much more was at stake than what happened to either of them as individuals. Turning to me, he said with great feeling, 'This is what you must get the country to realize.'"

The relationship between Nixon and Whittaker Chambers that began then was a poignant one. At times of stress, even when he was Vice President, Nixon would drive to Westminster for a visit, informing only friends such as myself and the most reliable members of his staff. It was not only counsel that he sought from the older man, but a kind of intellectual replenishment and emotional stability. Chambers' knowledge of history and of the political movements of the past hundred years was encyclopedic, and he could place in proper context events and problems that were new to Nixon in those days of his apprenticeship. Chambers was also a man of great insight, and he quickly assessed Nixon's abilities and limitations. Nixon, never one to open his heart or his mind unstintingly, came as close to this with Chambers as he has with any man. Chambers had great affection for Nixon and considerable respect for him as political being. But he had one reservation. To him, Nixon was a part of the state machinery and therefore the state police power. His experiences in the communist underground and as one of the protagonists in the Hiss Case made him cautious. To Nixon's credit, he never allowed his rapid rise in the world of affairs to interfere with his friendship and loyalty to Chambers, and it was at the Chambers farm that he remarked, "If the American people understood the real character of Alger, they would boil him in oil."

On August 16 the committee met in executive session to question Hiss. In this hearing a confident Nixon, his mind finally made up, carried most of the questioning—as indeed he did throughout the rest of the inquiry. Taking Hiss over the ground that had been covered by Chambers—the small and mundane facts of a long association—Nixon found a far different man from the poised and slightly condescending witness of the August 5 hearing.

"Now he was twisting, turning, evading and changing his story to fit the evidence he knew we had," Nixon has said. There had been leaks, and Hiss knew that blanket denials would no longer work. He still insisted that he could not recognize the pictures of Chambers that had been shown him during the first hearing, but he began to shift ground. There was "a certain familiarity" about the face, he said, and as Nixon pressed him, Hiss "recalled a man named 'George Crosley,' a freelance writer to whom in the Thirties, he said, he had sublet his apartment. This Crosley, Hiss told the committee, was a "deadbeat" but he had lent him money, put him up in his home for several nights, driven him to New York, and finally given him his old Ford ("I just turned it over"). All of this had occurred in 1935—a date that assumed tremendous importance. But Hiss did not think, he said, that Crosley was Chambers.

"The obvious thing to do then was to confront these two men," Nixon described it later, "since it was apparent that both men must know each other in view of the testimony we had. The confrontation took place in Room 1400 of the Commodore Hotel in New York."

We brought Hiss into the room first and seated him at a chair. We then had a committee investigator bring Chambers into the room and had him sit on a sofa opposite Hiss. During the time Chambers was entering the room, Hiss, who had said he would like to see this man who had made the charges against him, stared straight ahead. He did not turn around once to look at Chambers as he entered the room. Then we had the two men rise.

I said "Mr. Hiss, can you identify this man as anybody you have ever known?"

Mr. Hiss said: "I wonder if you could have him speak?"

Chambers spoke. But this did not satisfy Hiss. He insisted that Chambers speak some more. Then he asked to look inside Chambers' mouth while he was speaking. George Crosley, he said, had bad teeth. Nixon asked Chambers if he ever had work done on his teeth. Chambers said that he had.

We thought certainly that Hiss would admit then he had known Chambers as Crosley. But no. He said: "I wonder if you could give me the name of the dentist who did the work."

I said: "Do you mean you would have to have a man's dentist tell you just what he did to his teeth in order to identify him as somebody you once knew?" At that point, Hiss changed the subject. . . .

For half an hour Hiss fenced with Nixon. Then he admitted that he had known Chambers—as George Crosley but not as a communist. The veneer had begun to crack. At one point he started toward Chambers as if to strike him. He made impossible and illogical accusations against the committee and Nixon. He implied what he had said more baldly to a committee staff member when he was not under oath—that Chambers had been in a mental institution. In the first hearing Hiss had built his case on the issue of whether or not Chambers had known him. Now he reversed himself. "The issue is not whether this man knew me and I don't remember him. The issue is whether we had a particular conversation that he said he had with me, and which I have denied, and whether I am a member of the Communist Party or ever was, which he has said and which I have denied."

The private confrontation was followed by a public repetition in Washington. The impact of Hiss's belated admission that he had

89

known Chambers had been tremendous, and an hour before the hearing began a capacity crowd of a thousand had pushed its way into the big caucus room of the House. A line of spectators, four abreast, circled the Capitol Rotunda and stretched far down a corridor. The doors were closed by Capitol police fifteen minutes before the hearing was to begin, but three hundred people remained outside, pouring in during the luncheon recess when those in the caucus room left.

The drama of the case had been high, but it rose in intensity when the true story of Hiss's old Ford was put on the record, with documentary proof to back it. For it was shown that one year after the time Hiss had said he forever parted company with the "deadbeat" Crosley, the car was still in his possession, that it had never been turned over to Chambers, Crosley, or any freelance writer, and that in fact—as Chambers had sworn—it had been turned over to a communist organizer. Hiss's reaction to this evidence hardly helped him: he denied saying what was in the black-and-white of the hearing transcript. This was the beginning of the end. And it had been brought about, as the hearing record shows, by Nixon's persistence, by his penetrating questions, and by his ability to stick to the subject despite the artful dodging of Alger Hiss.

In the six hours in which Hiss was on stage he showed no sign of nervousness. He was quick in his answers, although they were now prefixed by "to the best of my recollection," in marked contrast to the seeming forthrightness of his first public hearing. While Chambers testified, Hiss scribbled notes, smiled wryly at what Chambers was saying, and played to the crowd. When it was all over, however, the audience registered a difference. After his first appearance many people had pushed forward to shake Hiss's hand and to congratulate him. After the public confrontation Hiss and his lawyer walked out of the hearing room alone.

From that point on the unfolding of the Hiss Case should have been a Justice Department matter. The Chambers and Hiss testimony, all given under oath, was there in cold type. Nixon had shown that in every instance in which proof was adducible, Chambers had told the truth and Hiss had lied. The law of perjury is complex and weighted in favor of the defendant, as any lawyer will attest. But there were enough points that were material, one of the tests in perjury, to warrant an indictment. Two witnesses to each count, or one witness and corroborative evidence, are required —and here again the Hiss Case met the test. Nixon was aware of this, and though he knew that President Truman continued to see the case as a personal attack on himself, he believed that the Administration could not ignore facts that had so captured the public imagination.

In the aftermath of the second confrontation, Nixon looked back with much satisfaction and some chagrin at what his efforts had wrought. He had worked hard on the case, sometimes putting in a twenty-hour day. He had neglected wife and children and, out of fatigue and tension, been short to his office staff. He had made one serious miscalculation when questioning Priscilla Hiss, Alger's wife, compassionately refusing to press her when she gave vague and evasive answers during her one executive session appearance. Since Nixon was the only member of the committee present, his failure to probe had lost him—and the committee—an opportunity to clarify other aspects of the case.

Thirteen years later he would write: "I thought that after our major break-through with Hiss . . . Mrs. Hiss's testimony was not too important. I felt, in other words, that the battle was won, that I could afford to relax. . . . She succeeded completely in convincing me that she was nervous and frightened. . . . I should have remembered that Chambers had described her as, if anything, a more fanatical communist than Hiss. I could have made a devastating record . . . but I dropped the ball. . . ."

There was still one undotted "i" as far as the committee phase of the case was concerned. In his first confrontation, Hiss had gotten out of his chair, stormed over to Chambers, and shaking his fist had said, "May I say for the record at this point that I would like to invite Mr. Whittaker Chambers to make those same statements out of the presence of this committee, without their being privileged for suit for libel. I challenge you to do it, and I hope you will do it damned quickly." He had repeated this statement, though with less passion, at the second confrontation. On August 27, 1948, Chambers complied. On *Meet the Press*, in answer to a question by Edward Folliard of the Washington *Post*, he said, "Alger Hiss was a communist and may be now." When, three weeks later, Hiss had still not taken legal action, even the strongly sympathetic *Post* said editorially, "Mr. Hiss himself has created a situation in which he is obliged to put up or shut up." It took Hiss another week to make up his mind—and then he filed a defamation of character suit in the Baltimore courts, asking $75,000 in damages.

For Nixon that wrapped it up. The case was now before the courts, and he was confident that Chambers would be vindicated. Nixon turned to other matters. It was an election year and though he did not have to campaign—he had won both the Democratic and Republican nominations in his district—he was much sought-after by other candidates. When the Hiss Case began, he had been one Congressman among many. Now he was a national figure, with audiences eager to hear his account of the dramatic events.

He was jolted, however, when the expected Republican victory of 1948 turned into the defeat of Governor Thomas E. Dewey, the party's Presidential candidate, and the loss of control of the Congress to the Democrats. President Truman, having confounded the experts by his victory, could be expected to do his utmost to liquidate the Hiss Case—along with Grand Jury proceedings in New York which had been going into the whole field of communist infiltration and subversion. "There was nothing at all I could do about the election results," Nixon has written. He decided that now was the time to take a long postponed vacation with his wife—the first since their honeymoon. They booked passage on the S.S. *Panama* for a cruise through the Caribbean and the Panama Canal. Sailing date was December 2, from New York.

"This time," he told Pat, "nothing is going to interfere with our vacation."

"I hope you're right," she answered, "but I still have to be shown."

On December 1, however, Nixon saw a small item in the newspapers, a United Press story: "The Justice Department is about ready to drop its investigation of the celebrated Alger Hiss-Whittaker Chambers controversy, it was learned today. Department officials still have under study the question of possible perjury proceedings. But officials said privately that unless additional evidence is forthcoming they are inclined to forget the whole thing. One Department source said that on the basis of available evidence, officials in charge of the case believe it would be unwise to take it before a grand jury."

Though he was preparing to go to New York, Nixon felt that it was imperative to talk to Chambers. He and Chief Investigator Stripling drove out that same afternoon to Westminster, where Nixon showed the UP story to Chambers. "This is what I was afraid of," Chambers said. "In a deposition hearing two weeks ago I produced new evidence in the case—documentary evidence. It was so important that Hiss's attorneys and mine called the Justice Department. Alex Campbell, chief of the Criminal Division, came to Baltimore and took the documents back to Washington. Before he left he warned everybody present to say nothing whatever about these documents, and that if we did divulge any information we would be in contempt of court. So I can't tell you what was in the documents. I will only say that they were a real bombshell." Beyond that, he would say no more.

"Do you mean that Campbell has these documents in his possession and it is completely up to him if anything is done about them?" Nixon asked.

"No, I wouldn't be that foolish," Chambers said. "My attorney has photostatic copies, and also I didn't turn over everything I had. I have another bombshell in case they try to suppress this one."

"You keep that second bombshell," Nixon told him. "Don't give it to anybody except the committee."

The word "bombshell" brought Nixon up short. It was not the kind of word Chambers used, yet he had stressed it, as if trying to impart some meaning or nuance. But what shook Nixon up the most was that the Justice Department had swept the case under the carpet after it had gotten the documentary proof that the UP story, planted with a reporter by an official, claimed did not exist. Nixon thought of postponing his vacation. Then he thought of Pat's reaction and how disappointed she would be. Signing a *subpoena duces tecum* on Chambers for any documents relative to the case, he instructed Bob Stripling to serve it the next day. And then he took off for New York, the S.S. *Panama*, and the warm waters of the Caribbean.

But it was not to be. On December 3, the Nixons' first full day at sea, a radiogram arrived from Bert Andrews:

INFORMATION HERE IS THAT HISS-CHAMBERS HAS PRODUCED NEW BOMBSHELL STOP INDICATIONS ARE THAT CHAMBERS HAS OFFERED NEW EVIDENCE STOP ALL CONCERNED SILENT STOP HOWEVER JUSTICE DEPARTMENT PARTIALLY CONFIRMS BY SAYING IT IS TOO HOT FOR COMMENT STOP

That evening a second radiogram was delivered to Nixon as he was at dinner. This one was from Stripling:

SECOND BOMBSHELL OBTAINED BY SUBPOENA 1 AYEM FRIDAY STOP CASE CLINCHED STOP INFORMATION AMAZING STOP HEAT IS ON FROM PRESS AND OTHER PLACES STOP IMMEDIATE ACTION APPEARS NECESSARY STOP CAN YOU POSSIBLY GET BACK QUERY

The following morning, Andrews sent still another radiogram:

DOCUMENTS INCREDIBLY HOT STOP LINK TO HISS SEEMS CERTAIN STOP LINK TO OTHERS INEVITABLE STOP RESULTS SHOULD RESTORE FAITH IN NEED FOR COMMITTEE IF NOT IN SOME MEMBERS STOP NEW YORK JURY MEETS WEDNESDAY STOP COULD YOU ARRIVE TUESDAY AND GET DAY'S JUMP ON GRAND JURY STOP IF NOT HOLDING EARLY HEARING WEDNESDAY STOP MY LIBERAL FRIENDS DON'T LOVE ME NO MORE STOP BUT FACTS ARE FACTS AND THESE FACTS ARE DYNAMITE STOP HISS'S WRITING IDENTIFIED ON THREE DOCUMENTS STOP NOT PROOF HE GAVE THEM TO CHAMBERS BUT HIGHLY SIGNIFICANT STOP STRIPLING SAYS CAN PROVE WHO GAVE THEM TO CHAMBERS STOP LOVE TO PAT STOP VACATION-WRECKER ANDREWS

It took a special order from Defense Secretary James V. Forrestal to get Nixon off the ship. A Coast Guard amphibian plane met the S.S. *Panama*, Nixon was lowered to the water in a lifeboat, and members of the ship's crew rowed him to the PBY, which flew him to Miami. In Washington he learned what Chambers' two "bombshells" had been. They were papers, some in Hiss's handwriting, some typed on Hiss's old Woodstock typewriter—copies of State Department classified documents so secret that to this day one of them cannot be published. There were other incriminating documents in the handwriting of Harry Dexter White.

Behind the documents was another dramatic story. During the pre-trial deposition in the Hiss libel suit, Chambers had been pressed by Hiss's lawyers to produce any documents, correspondence, or other papers that would establish his relationship with the plaintiff. Chambers did have such documentary evidence, hidden away in New York. He had turned over some of it to Hiss's lawyers and these had been delivered to the Justice Department. He had held back some microfilmed records, which he had given to Stripling under subpoena. And with this the Hiss Case had assumed a new proportion. It was no longer a question of subversion, of Communist Party membership. The Hiss affair had become a spy case. This was, for Nixon, the first time he had seen tangible proof—proof beyond the unsupported testimony of former communists—that the communists had been plundering the United States of its precious military and diplomatic secrets.

With Nixon back, the committee sprang into action. On December 6 Nixon's subcommittee rushed to New York to question Chambers. It was intercepted at the station by representatives of the Justice Department who pleaded with Nixon at a stormy session in a Hotel Commodore suite that no public action be taken. So violent was the debate that at one point a staff member interrupted the shouting by throwing open a window and saying, "Let's let the whole world know." The committee finally agreed to hold off, but Nixon warned that new hearings would be scheduled unless the Justice Department acted expeditiously and with probity. That same day the Federal Grand Jury in New York resumed its hearings. But Nixon was not satisfied. "On the record to date," he would write, "we simply did not have confidence that the Justice Department would resist the political pressures being brought to bear in behalf of Hiss and against Chambers."

There was another factor, summed up by Nixon: "We also faced an acute problem of time. The term of the blue-ribbon grand jury in New York was to expire . . . on December 15. If it failed to return an indictment against Hiss, it would probably be months before the case could be presented to a new grand jury." President Truman still continued to dismiss the case as a "red herring." The committee, of course, had an ace-in-the-hole—the microfilmed documents that it had taken from Chambers under subpoena. At Nixon's urging it was agreed that this material would not be turned over to the Justice Department until the committee had "absolute assurance" that the case would be properly prosecuted.

The following day, December 7, the committee questioned Under Secretary of State Sumner Welles and Assistant Secretary John Peurifoy. Both men forthrightly assessed the importance of the documents and destroyed Hiss's contention that he had prepared the handwritten memos as part of his work. They also agreed that the verbatim copies of State Department cables, part of the Hiss-Chambers material, certainly allowed the Russians to break the United States diplomatic code. At the same session former Assistant Secretary Francis Sayre, a good friend and former employer of Hiss, and subsequently a character witness in the first trial, admitted that three of the documents could have been taken out of his office only by Hiss.

"Did Mr. Hiss [as he claimed] have as one of his duties the paraphrasing of these documents and bringing them back to you in this way?" Nixon asked.

"The answer is 'No,' " Sayre replied.

"Do you agree [with press reports quoting 'State Department sources'] there was nothing important or nothing wrong with turning this stuff over [to a Soviet apparatus]?"

"I violently disagree," said Sayre, "not only because of the substance of these cables, but because some of them were in highly confidential codes. . . . [They also] reveal sources from which information was obtained, sources planted in foreign countries. . . . You kill off what you have been working on for years."

But when it seemed that all the pieces were falling into place, Nixon received what seemed for a while like the *coup de grâce* against the committee's case. Staff investigators had asked the Eastman Kodak Company to examine the microfilm received from Chambers. On December 7 Stripling received a call from Rochester, informing him *that the microfilm could not have been manu-*

factured before 1945, though Chambers had testified that it had been used in 1938.

"Well, we've had it," Stripling told Nixon. If the microfilm had been manufactured after 1945, it meant that Chambers was a liar—and the whole case against Hiss was dead. Nixon got Chambers on the phone in New York. "Am I correct in understanding that these papers were put on microfilm in 1938?" he asked.

"Yes," said Chambers.

"We have just had a report from the Eastman Kodak Company that film of that type you turned over to us was not made by the company until 1945," Nixon said angrily. "What is your answer to that?"

"I can't understand it," Chambers said. "God must be against me."

Almost shouting, Nixon said, "You'd better have a better answer than that. The subcommittee's coming to New York tonight and we want to see you at the Commodore Hotel at nine—and you'd better be there!" Then he slammed the receiver on the hook.

"What'll we do now?" Stripling asked.

Without hesitation Nixon told him, "There's only one thing we can do. Have the staff call the reporters who cover the committee and ask them to come to my office in thirty minutes for a statement from me."

But five minutes before the reporters were to arrive there was another call from Rochester for Stripling. As he listened the expression on his face changed and he shouted, "You mean you were wrong? You did manufacture that film through 1938 but then discontinued it during the war?" And he let out a war whoop. "Chambers' story has stood up again," he said. "Each time we check into something which sounds questionable, he comes through."

There was one more major battle. On December 8 Nixon interrupted a committee hearing to state: "We have learned from unimpeachable sources that the Justice Department intends to indict Chambers for perjury before any other of the people named by Chambers in this conspiracy are indicted.* . . . Chambers has

---

* In his first appearance before the Grand Jury, Chambers denied that the communist cell in Washington had been involved in espionage.

confessed. He is in the open. He is no longer a danger to our security. If Chambers is indicted first, Hiss and the others will go free because the witness against them will have been discredited. . . ." This would have meant the end of the case—and Nixon prepared to mount an assault on the Justice Department.

But other forces were at work. Even as the Grand Jury prepared to drop its inquiry and to issue an attack on HUAC, the Federal Bureau of Investigation, in a classic of crime detection, came up with evidence of Hiss's guilt so conclusive that it could not be ignored: proof that the documents had been typed on Hiss's Woodstock typewriter. Every typewriter is unique and distinct. A study of blow-ups of letters admittedly typed by Mrs. Hiss on the Woodstock were identical in all characteristics with the copied documents.

On December 15, 1948, Alger Hiss was indicted for perjury. The jury disagreed, eight to four, on a verdict of guilty in a trial marked by defense flamboyance and what many believed was conduct by the trial judge, Samuel Kaufman, prejudicial to the defense.* On January 21, 1950, the second trial jury convicted Hiss on two counts of perjury, for denying that he had committed espionage. The verdict and sentence were upheld by the U.S. Court of Appeals, and the Supreme Court, finding no issue of fact or law, refused to review. Hiss served his sentence and then retired into semi-obscurity, openly moving among the communists whom he had denied, still protesting his innocence.

Chambers, who had resigned from *Time* when he presented evidence of espionage, returned to his farm in Westminster, where he wrote *Witness*, a moving and eloquent account of the Hiss Case

---

* After the first trial Nixon sharply criticized Judge Kaufman and asked for an investigation of his behavior by the House Judiciary Committee. In a letter dated July 15, 1949, Nixon wrote to me: "I am glad you liked our statement concerning Kaufman. I agree with you that Kaufman should be the target and not Hiss. Incidentally, I was glad to note that *Newsweek* got the facts right although *Time* did not in their report of the incident. [We] had requested that the Judiciary Committee investigate Kaufman's conduct of the trial. Our friendly enemies on the other side attempted to create the impression that we had asked that the Un-American Activities Committee do the investigating. *Time* so reported it; *Newsweek* did not. *Newsweek* was right!"

and its ramifications. It is a book that bids fair to become a classic of autobiography.

For Nixon the Hiss Case brought great rewards and great penalties. From that time forth he was marked—doubly marked.

To most Americans, he was a hero, the Congressman who had by sheer determination forced the Truman Administration to prosecute Hiss. In less than three years he was catapulted from the relative obscurity of the House of Representatives to great prominence—a man to be watched, with a future as great as his own capabilities could make it.

But the case also earned him the enduring enmity of powerful men in high place, and lesser men—in government, in journalism, among the liberal intelligentsia—whose aggregate influence is immense. These were the men who had been proved monumentally and catastrophically wrong. They turned on him not only because of Hiss, but because he had proved the dangerous error of their belief that communists were merely "liberals in a hurry."

In a sense the Hiss Case put these men on trial, and they could never accept the circumstances that made them look at best foolish, at worst sinister. After the conviction and imprisonment they could no longer openly defend Hiss (though more than a few did, and do to this day), but they could take out their chagrin on Nixon. In this they were joined by important segments of the press which, from that time to this, devoted themselves to an unceasing search for clay feet and sticky fingers in the man responsible for their discomfiture—and to the kind of zealous scrutiny that few men in politics can survive.

The Hiss Case won for Richard Nixon the Vice Presidential nomination in 1952, the Presidential nomination in 1960. But in all other ways it cost him dear.

7

The Nixon-
Douglas "Debate"

"**D**OMESTIC communism," Richard Nixon would say in 1959, "is no longer a political issue. The danger has receded a great deal in the last few years, domestically, mainly because we have become increasingly aware of it. The communists used to fool an awful lot of well-meaning people who were not communists. There is still a group, a small group, that can be fooled."

This statement was widely quoted to show either that Nixon had undergone a change of heart, or that he was paying his respects to political expediency and the changed mood of the United States. Forgotten completely were his words, uttered in the fall of 1949, at the start of his campaign for the Senate: "Believe me, I am well aware of the communist threat and I do not discount it. But I am convinced that an even greater threat to our free institutions is presented by that group of hypocritical and cynical men who, under the guise of providing political panaceas for certain social and economic problems in our society, are selling the American birthright for a mess of pottage."

Yet given these two statements, the first made in conversation and the other in a political speech, the fact remains that communism has always been an issue for Richard Nixon—sometimes out of choice and at other times because it has been thrust upon him. In the 1950 Senatorial campaign it was a little of both. Because that campaign has been used as a litmus test of Nixon's character, soul, and approach to political and human problems, it warrants some discussion. In his 1959 biography of Nixon, Earl Mazo astutely led his chapter on 1950 with the sentence, "Nothing in the litany of reprehensible conduct charged against Nixon, the campaigner, has been cited more often than the tactics by which he defeated Congresswoman Helen Gahagan Douglas for senator." The tactics employed by Nixon's Democratic opponents in describing that campaign have received somewhat less attention.

To begin with, it should be noted that Nixon's soul aside, it was inevitable that he should have been chosen by the Republican Party to be its candidate for the Senate that year. The Hiss Case had, in show business terms, made him the hottest Republican property. It is forgotten today that the Hiss Case was not an isolated event that captured the imagination of the country. It was the culmination of many small and large events—the Cold War, the Berlin Airlift, the loss of mainland China to the communists, and a series of cases in which known communist spies had been allowed to ply their trade without even a by-your-leave to a casual Truman Administration. Because the Hiss Case was reduced to the dramatic confrontation of two men, it had been easy to assimilate. It polarized feelings and, because for reasons best known to themselves many liberals continued to encase Hiss in martyrdom, it inspired suspicions among many whose anti-communism was at best amorphous.

As the man who "got Hiss," therefore, Richard Nixon was widely assumed to know more about communism and how to cope with it than any other living American—a reputation he neither deserved nor claimed. There were other factors that made Nixon the logical candidate in the 1950 Senate race. He had proved himself to be a gut fighter—his repeated use until 1958 of the phrase "a rocking, socking campaign" bears this out—which Americans admire in a politician until, of course, he has been badly bloodied. And he came from California, a state strongly Democratic in registration but given to voting for the man, not the label.

Nixon fitted in with the temper of his state. He called himself "a liberal in foreign policy and a conservative in domestic policy" —a useful oversimplification in terms, but one which did him no justice. In fact, as his voting record showed, he was a loner who made his own decisions regardless of party stand—consistent only in that he never voted with the dead-end extremists of Right or Left. Though he consistently supported foreign aid, both economic and military, he believed that Congress should retain control of this spending and not allow it to become an indiscriminate outpouring of the nation's wealth or a political stick to implement American policy. In domestic affairs he took a view that more often than not was moderate. On Taft-Hartley, for example, he listened carefully to labor's criticisms and voted to amend the act—but he refused to go along with one minority that hoped to make it punitive or another that sought to kill it outright.

The 1950 election year was auspicious for Nixon in other ways. A Republican Governor, Earl Warren, sat in Sacramento and was coming up for re-election. Republican professionals enjoyed Warren's vote-getting powers but resented his refusal to allow the use of his coattails to lesser candidates. The party, therefore, needed a candidate on the Senate line to strengthen the rest of the ticket— and Nixon seemed to be the only man available. The Democratic incumbent, under fire at home, was known to be considering the possibility of dropping out of the race, which would make the job of a Republican challenger that much less difficult.

On November 3, 1949, Nixon made known his intentions. In a speech in Pomona, where he had launched his 1946 congressional campaign, he said, "I am convinced beyond question that the election of 1950 will be the most crucial election in our nation's history. I realize that this has been said before—about other elections—but we have only to survey the situation here and abroad to confirm this conviction. . . . There is only one way we can win. We will put on a fighting, rocking, socking campaign. . . ." He appealed to the Democrats for support, though berating the national party, and raised "a banner of freedom which all people, regardless of party, can follow."

The only opposition to Nixon's candidacy came from several

of the original supporters in his district. They felt that by attempting a Senate race, Nixon would give up a safe seat in the House of Representatives. But there was ample support from all other quarters. Former President Herbert Hoover, whose moral and personal influence in the state was very great, urged Nixon to go ahead. Senator William F. Knowland gave Nixon the "unqualified support" of his own political machine in northern California and of the Oakland *Tribune*, the family newspaper. Most important of all was the decision of Murray Chotiner to throw in his lot with Nixon. He was then at the peak of his reputation as a political wizard—having managed Earl Warren's highly successful gubernatorial campaign, and being credited with Knowland's stand-up victory over Will Rogers, Jr. Chotiner had been only an adviser in Nixon's first political race, but now he took on the assignment of campaign coordinator and manager.

It was during the 1950 campaign that Nixon and Chotiner developed a close relationship, both political and personal. Chotiner, a quiet-spoken man, understood the mechanics of politics as few men in these times have done. In his self-effacing way he had the capacity to make tough decisions and to carry out tougher assignments. Then as now, Nixon felt that Chotiner was the ablest campaign director of his time. Chotiner, in turn, considered Nixon an excellent candidate. If there were any differences between them, they stemmed from Nixon's insistence on absolute precision in every operation, and from the fact that he tried to be his own campaign manager, the most serious error in politics. An irritated Chotiner told Nixon in the nearest thing to an angry exchange between them: "Dick, you can be the candidate or you can be the manager. But you can't be both. A candidate's job is to speak and to reach the voters. You go out and make speeches and get votes, and let *us* make the other mistakes."

Chotiner also realized that though a campaign manager should not lie to the candidate, there were things he should keep to himself on the theory that "it's better for the candidate not to know in so many words." In the 1950 campaign Nixon was not informed of many tactical moves made by Chotiner and his aides—but it is unrealistic to argue, as some of his supporters have done, that he was ignorant of what was going on. If questioned, he could say with precise truth that he did not know directly, the "directly" never being stated.

In the pre-primary period Nixon's campaigning was low key and low budget. He traveled the state in a borrowed station wagon, talking mostly at street meetings, where he could get voter reaction by asking for questions. The Hiss Case and his role in it figured largely in his speeches. With token opposition he could afford not to enter into controversy that would be damaging in the regular election. The Democrats, on the other hand, were engaged in a bitter primary battle. In the early stages the antagonists were Senator Sheridan Downey and Representative Helen Gahagan Douglas, one of the first of the Broadway-Hollywood contingent to enter politics. She accused Downey of being a stooge for big business. He answered by linking her with the "extremists" of the Left. Then, two months before the primary, Downey withdrew with a blast at Mrs. Douglas, contending that he was physically unable to wage "a personal and militant campaign against [Mrs. Douglas'] vicious and unethical propaganda." In rebuttal Mrs. Douglas brushed aside Downey's claim of illness as a "gimmick."

The Senator's replacement in the primaries was Manchester Boddy, publisher of the Los Angeles *Daily News*, the city's only Democratic newspaper. Boddy looked about him and decided that in the atmosphere of the times Mrs. Douglas would be most vulnerable on the communist issue. Senator Joseph R. McCarthy had been drawing blood with his attacks on the Truman Administration. Secretary of State Dean Acheson had remarked that South Korea was "outside the defense perimeter" of the United States, and when the North Koreans invaded the south, there was an outcry that he had invited the attack by his unfortunate statement. The Korean war had brought about the first military confrontation between the communists and the United States. If the communist tag could be successfully pinned to Helen Douglas, Boddy reasoned, he could win the nomination. In his kickoff speech, therefore, Boddy set the line for his primary battle.

"There is indisputable evidence of a statewide conspiracy on the part of this small subversive clique of red-hots to capture through stealth and cunning the nerve centers of our Democratic Party—and by so doing to capture the votes of real Democratic citizens," he said. A "blueprint of subversive dictatorship" had been drawn up, Boddy added, to make the Democratic Party serve the "twisted purposes" of these "red-hots"—and he left no doubt that he considered Mrs. Douglas one of them. Though he was out of the race, Downey then joined the fray. He charged that Mrs. Douglas had the longest absentee record of any California Congressman, and then took up the Boddy theme.

"Mrs. Douglas gave comfort to the Soviet tyranny by voting against aid to both Greece and Turkey," Downey said in a state-wide radio address. "She voted against the President in a crisis when he most needed her support and most fully deserved her confidence. . . . She was one of a small but determined band which fought to the bitter end to keep Henry A. Wallace on the Democratic ticket at the 1944 Democratic convention and . . . she wept in total collapse when Harry Truman was finally nominated over Wallace." And then he made a statement that was to echo throughout the campaign and was to be mistakenly ascribed to Nixon or to his campaign aides—that Mrs. Douglas, on votes against the investigation of communism, had "joined Representative Vito Marcantonio, an admitted friend of the Communist Party."*

What Senator Downey had said was true, but its implications were as false as later attempts to paint Mrs. Douglas as a fighting anti-communist. Helen Douglas' politics represented the confused ideology of her environment—a Hollywood that had succumbed to a love affair with the Soviet Union in the prewar years and during the period of its co-belligerency. That ideology was condi-

---

* Had she known, Mrs. Douglas might have made capital of a cocktail party at the Essex House in New York to which Nixon and Representative Donald Jackson, both members of HUAC, had invited Marcantonio. Marcantonio appeared with several friends, had a few drinks, and chatted amiably with Nixon and Jackson. There was no political significance to this. The invitation was considered by both men as something of a joke, but it could have been made the basis of charges that Nixon was "close" to Marcantonio.

tioned by the large and noisy group of Hollywood communists and fellow travelers, by the confused "liberalism" of those whose knowledge of international affairs began and ended with the declaration that Russia must be good because it had fought the Nazis, and by an amorphous suspicion of the United States. It was in Hollywood that Henry Wallace's communist-run Progressive Party got its most enthusiastic support in 1948—and it must be pointed out that Mrs. Douglas had resisted this Wallaceite enthusiasm and remained loyal to Mr. Truman and to the party on whose ticket she was running.

The Democratic primary campaign—six candidates vying for the senatorial nomination, with Mrs. Douglas and Manchester Boddy leading the field—devoted itself almost exclusively to the style of party self-destruction that the Republicans had long since perfected. There was only a passing shot fired at Nixon, as when Mrs. Douglas expressed her "utter scorn for such pipsqueaks as Nixon and McCarthy." When Nixon proposed to counterattack, his wrath was turned away by Chotiner's soft answers. As long as the Democrats were cutting one another up, Chotiner said, it would be foolish to divert their attention from an endeavor so laudable to Republicans. To attack Helen Douglas would be doubly foolish. "We wanted her to win the Democratic nomination," he has explained. "I knew that it would be easier to defeat her than a conservative Democrat, who would cut into Nixon's vote among Republicans and make it difficult for him to get the Democratic votes he needed to win. If you look at the record, you'll see that Dick said nothing about Helen Douglas until after the primary."

The primary results reflected the opposition of many Democrats to Helen Gahagan Douglas. For though she won the nomination handily with 734,842 votes, close to 830,000 votes were cast against her for the other candidates on the Democratic line. Nixon polled 22 per cent of the Democratic vote and 64 per cent of the Republican vote. His total in both primaries was more than 170,000 above the combined Douglas vote—she had polled 13 per cent of the Republican total—but short of a clear majority of the 3 million cast for all six candidates. Nixon's showing had been encouraging, but he viewed it with his usual strategic pessimism. The outcome of the election obviously hinged on how the Democrats who voted against Mrs. Douglas in the primary would swing. It was her feeling that they would remain in the party, in which case the election would be hers.

Nixon suffered a setback at the start. He had hoped that Governor Warren, who had tacitly supported Jerry Voorhis against Nixon in the 1946 congressional campaign, would endorse him. But Warren refused, remaining so aloof from Nixon that the Douglas camp was able to whisper gleefully that the Governor really wanted the Democrats to win the Senate seat. In order to keep Warren friendly, Mrs. Douglas said nothing in support of James Roosevelt, Warren's Democratic opponent.

Nixon and Chotiner realized that if they could force Mrs. Douglas to speak up for Roosevelt, Warren might break his silence on Nixon. They therefore assigned campaign workers to attend Douglas meetings and to ask for a clarification of her position on the gubernatorial contest. Less than a week before the election, Mrs. Douglas succumbed. "I hope and pray Jimmy Roosevelt will be the next Governor," she said, "and he will be if Democrats vote the Democratic ticket." When Warren was told of this, he rose angrily to the bait. "In view of her statement," he told reporters, "I might ask her how she expects I will vote when I mark my ballot for United States Senator next Tuesday." It was not very much of an endorsement, and some Californians felt that he would vote for neither candidate, but it hurt Mrs. Douglas.

Nixon, moreover, did not have the endorsement of labor, which went to Mrs. Douglas—although a number of union leaders, particularly those from the Hollywood studio unions, privately gave him their blessing. He did not have union money at his disposal, or the assistance of United Auto Workers (CIO) campaign workers from Michigan and Washington who did for his opponent the hundreds of necessary campaign chores. He was so limited in funds, particularly in the early stages of the election campaign, that he continued to do most of his campaigning from his station wagon (when necessary making a few long hops in a small plane piloted by a wartime buddy), whereas Mrs. Douglas ranged the state in a helicopter. To add to his difficulties, Nixon had the un-wanted help of one Leo Casey, on the payroll of a lobbyist named David Charnay, who set up the Independent Voters Committee for Nixon, representing no one and contributing to Nixon's efforts by issuing press releases. Casey was firmly pushed aside by Chotiner when he tried to inject himself into the private councils of the Nixon campaign, and he spent much of his time doing nothing in his suite at the Beverly Hills Hotel. (After the election Casey helpfully announced that he had been the pawn of the so-called China Lobby, but had not known it.) Also an embarrass-ment were the dead-end extremists of the Right who always fasten themselves to anti-communist candidates.

Among his assets, however, Nixon had the organizational genius of Chotiner; the embattled anti-communists of Hollywood—indefatigable campaign activists like Morrie Ryskind, Irene Dunne, Adolphe Menjou, and Ward Bond—and, of great strategic importance, the Democrats for Nixon. George Creel, President Wilson's wartime information chief and an honored citizen of San Francisco, lent his name and prestige to the Nixon cause. Ruth Turner, former President of the San Francisco League of Women Voters and member of the Community Chest, worked as zealously for Nixon as she had in past years for President Roose-velt. In a strongly worded statement addressed to Mrs. Douglas, Miss Turner summarized the arguments of Democrats for Nixon: "You, and you can't deny it, have earned the praise of communist and pro-communist newspapers for opposing the very things Nixon has stood for. And you have done this, as I and so many of my Democratic friends are well aware, against the judgment and the votes of the majority of Democrats in Congress."

Democrats for Nixon went far beyond this. In answer to Mrs. Douglas' claim that she was being Red-baited, it prepared and issued a list of her communist-front affiliations, culled from the primary campaign literature of her Democratic enemies:

> . . . speaker before the International Workers Order, cited by two Democratic U.S. Attorneys General as "Communist and subversive." . . . sponsor of the Win the Peace Conference . . .

cited as "Communist and subversive" by a Democratic Attorney General. . . . On October 17, 1947 . . . speaker at a dinner meeting of the Civil Rights Congress, cited as "Communist and subversive" by the Democratic Attorney General. . . . speaker at a political meeting . . . sponsored by the California Labor School, cited as "subversive and Communist" by a Democratic U. S. Attorney General . . . etc.

As Nixon had said, it was a "rocking, socking campaign" on both sides, with no holds barred. Nixon's original intention of playing down the communist issue and battling it out on other questions of policy had been taken from his hands, first by the advantage thrust at him by the Democrats during the primary war, second, by the sudden popular outburst of anti-communism, and third, by the tactics Murray Chotiner devised. For her part Mrs. Douglas traded blow for blow, beginning with a characterization of Nixon and his supporters as "a backwash of young men in dark shirts"—in other words, fascists—and then by open charges that he and not she was pro-communist. "On every key vote," she said, "Nixon stood with party-liner Marcantonio against America in its fight to defeat communism."

The Nixon forces issued what became known as the "pink sheet"—a flyer that made statistical the Downey-Boddy charges that Mrs. Douglas had voted with Marcantonio by stating specifically that those votes totaled 345 and that they were frequently cast against the Democratic majority—and distributed half a million copies. The Nixon campaigners, moreover, never let it be forgotten that *The Daily Worker* had lauded both Mrs. Douglas and Vito Marcantonio as "heroes of the Eightieth Congress" while marking Nixon as "the man to beat."

Nixon pounded away at the fact that Mrs. Douglas had voted against Greek-Turkish aid, a Truman measure that helped defeat the communist takeover of these countries; against Selective Service in 1948; against bills to weed out communists from the Atomic Energy Commission, the State Department, and other sensitive agencies; and against citing recalcitrant communists for contempt of Congress. (This last charge wildly overstated the case; Mrs.

Douglas had voted for some contempt citations, against others.)

When Douglas campaign literature listed among her achievements that she "exposed communist propaganda in her famous speech, 'My Democrat Credo,' " Nixon quoted from it and stressed its opening sentence: "I think we all know that communism is no real threat to the democratic institutions of this country"—a statement hardly appealing at a time when liberal California Democrats like Edmund (Pat) Brown, running for Attorney General of the state, and James Roosevelt were vying with each other and with the Republicans in warning of the communist threat to the United States and in proclaiming their support for anti-communist measures passed by the State Legislature. There was widespread anger at the time when communist-dominated countries were using American foreign relief for political purposes, and Nixon pointed out that Mrs. Douglas had voted against a bill to prevent this practice.

A "yellow sheet" issued by the Douglas forces—presumably an analysis of Nixon's voting record—accused him of having "joined Marcantonio in voting against aid to Korea." This might have been explosive had it been true. It wasn't. In 1949 Nixon had voted for military aid to Korea. In 1950 he had joined a majority of the House in voting down a bill that granted economic aid to Korea but none to Formosa. When the bill had been rewritten to include both countries, Nixon was among those who helped to pass it. The "yellow sheet" accused Nixon of having voted to cut foreign aid in half. In fact, he had voted against a two-year foreign aid bill and in favor of a one-year bill with renewal clause so that Congress could control the purse strings. The money to be spent over the one-year period was, naturally, one half of what the two-year bill called for.

While Nixon and his campaign aides beat away at the "soft on communism" theme, the Douglas side launched a whispering campaign aimed at totally destroying Nixon in Southern California, an area with a large Jewish vote, and in the movie colony. People would ask indignantly, "How can you be for Nixon? Don't you know he's anti-Semitic?" Or "Don't you know he's Jim Crow?" That his close friend and campaign manager was a Jew, that Jack Warner of Warner Brothers had contributed to the Nixon campaign, or that the Anti-Defamation League of B'nai B'rith denied these racist charges did not interfere with the rumors. Neither, for that matter, did the fact that he was enthusiastically endorsed by the Los Angeles *Sentinel*, a Negro newspaper. Nixon's stand on the anti-poll-tax bill and on a measure to create a Federal Fair Employment Practices Commission were ignored or minimized with, "He just did that to look good." So prevalent did these rumors of racism become that Nixon was forced to issue a formal statement refuting them.

"I have never sought, accepted, or would accept the support of any fascist or communist organization," he said. "I have been informed of attempts by my political opponents to create the impression that I have received and accepted the support of Gerald L. K. Smith—the notorious racist agitator—and his organization. I want to make it clear that I do not want that support and that I repudiate it." Nixon also repudiated Republican State Senator Jack Tenney, chairman of a joint committee of the State Legislature, because he accepted the support of Gerald L. K. Smith.

It was during this campaign that Mrs. Douglas' followers coined the "Tricky Dick" pejorative, a strange enough label coming as it did from those who were spreading the fantastic intimations of Nixon's "anti-Semitism." Mrs. Douglas herself linked Nixon and Senator Joseph McCarthy whenever possible. "Do you want a good story?" she asked me. "Joe McCarthy is going up and down this state campaigning secretly for Nixon. But the Republican press is so ashamed of McCarthy that they don't publish a word about it." When I asked how anyone could campaign "secretly," she answered, "You just check and you'll see I'm right." The check showed that McCarthy had been in California during the campaign just once, to deliver an anti-communist speech before the Military Order of the Purple Heart, and had left immediately.

As the campaign progressed Mrs. Douglas grew increasingly bitter. On several occasions she antagonized labor votes by being acidulous when only a driblet of workers attended her lunch-hour speeches outside the huge industrial plants that fringe Los Angeles. "Why aren't there more people here?" she scolded a half dozen girls who had turned out for her at the gates of the Douglas air-craft plant. And she tried to avoid foreign policy questions, insist-ing that the key isues were Social Security, unemployment insur-ance, defeat of Taft-Hartley, and low-cost housing. "Why," she asked, "won't Nixon debate me on these important things?"

This Nixon was both willing and anxious to do, and he let his sentiments be known. The Fresno *Guide* described Mrs. Douglas' reaction. "More than a month ago," it reported, "the Junior Cham-ber of Commerce invited senatorial candidates to debate the cam-paign issues at one of their meetings. Richard Nixon, the GOP nominee, accepted by return mail. But today, three registered let-ters later, the Jaycees haven't heard a line from Mrs. Douglas. 'The only thing I can conclude,' concluded President Jack Erbes, 'is that she isn't interested in debating here—but doesn't want to say so publicly.' "

Other organizations, prodded by Nixon campaign aides, issued similar invitations with the same result. Toward the end of the campaign, however, the League of Women Voters offered its platform jointly to Nixon and to Mrs. Douglas. At Murray Cho-tiner's suggestion Nixon announced that he could not be present because he was scheduled to speak in Sacramento on the night set by the League, and he declined the invitation with regret. Mrs. Douglas promptly accepted. But actually Nixon had no intention of going to Sacramento. As Mrs. Douglas was addressing the League, Nixon walked in unannounced. Mrs. Douglas cut short her remarks and abruptly departed, leaving Nixon to "debate the issues" alone.

Nixon's campaign was strenuous enough to tire the reporters who merely had to cover him. Sometimes he delivered as many as fourteen speeches a day—on streetcorners, at clubhouses, auditor-iums, meeting houses, ranging the state from one end to the other. Late at night he would meet with Chotiner and other assistants to discuss the day's campaigning and to plan for the following day. Once, at a big meeting in Los Angeles, Pat Nixon brought Tricia, then four and a half years old. She listened with interest as Nixon spoke, then began to grow restive. Finally, during one of his rhe-torical pauses, her child's voice rang out loud and clear, "My goodness, Daddy talks a long time, doesn't he?" On another occasion, when the whole family was on television, Julie Nixon expressed similar detachment by probing her little nose contentedly, and the camera spotted her. Nixon later remarked philosophically, "Julie, honey, you've either just won or just lost me the election."

It wasn't always so cozy. Sometimes the crowds were small, sometimes hostile. In the industrial sections there were usually hecklers who followed the Nixon station wagon from meeting to meeting. Once, outside a factory, he got the silent treatment from workers eating their lunch. He launched into a discussion of Taft-Hartley, and the men began to drift toward the platform to hear him. Pat Nixon, who was handing out campaign literature as she usually did, recalls that "he must have impressed them because that locality, usually Democratic, went two to one for Dick."

In San Francisco a Douglas sound truck followed the Nixon party, trying to drown him out. It was a cold day and few stopped to listen. But at one corner, as Nixon spoke, the sound truck began throwing questions and heckling. The crowd started to grow, attracted by the clamor, and Nixon answered the amplified questions as fast as they came. Pretty soon there were cheers of approval from the audience, and then mutterings of anger at the heckling, turning to shouts of "Don't answer them, Dick. Pay no attention."

"I can answer them and I will," said Nixon—and the crowd cheered.

"That sound truck won us a lot of votes in San Francisco," Pat Nixon says. The Douglas forces must have realized this, because from then on the heckling tactics, the pickets, and the attempts to drown out Nixon ceased.

When he spoke of foreign policy, Nixon stressed the fact that America won wars and lost the peace that followed. He contrasted the Truman Administration's strong stand against communism in Europe and its appeasement in Asia, though he gave energetic support to President Truman's intervention in Korea. He contended that appeasement in Asia and the loss of mainland China to the communists had led directly to the bloody Korean war, and he drew his biggest applause when he called for the ouster of Secretary of State Dean Acheson. He spoke of the Hiss Case, of

Harry Dexter White, and of Truman's repeated charge that the investigation of communists in government was a "red herring." And, of course, he never let up on Mrs. Douglas and on her record.

When he touched on communism, he would point out that there was opposition in his ranks to the use of this subject in the campaign. This was a shrewd tactic out of the Chotiner book, but it was also true. From time to time campaign workers in all echelons would urge him to play down the subject and to desist from further attacks on Mrs. Douglas. But Nixon and Chotiner felt that it was an effective tactic. When Mrs. Douglas took it up, trying to outdo Nixon, they realized that they had been correct. I was present at a discussion between Chotiner and novelist Adela Rogers St. John, active in Democrats for Nixon, over a leaflet that stressed the "soft on communism" theme and emphasized Mrs. Douglas' record. Mrs. St. John fought hard to tone down the leaflet and to delete much of its tougher material. Chotiner mollified her and got her out of the room. Then he took off his jacket, rolled up his sleeves, and said, "Let's get to work." The leaflet appeared as originally planned.

Mrs. Douglas herself handed Nixon one readymade issue. The Veterans Administration had closed the Birmingham, California, hospital for paraplegics. For disabled veterans this meant transfer to other hospitals far from their families. There was considerable clamor for a rescinding of the order. In the closing days of the Eighty-first Congress, Nixon had called on the VA to reopen the hospital and had introduced a bill calling for an investigation. Mrs. Douglas, however, promised that she could do better. She was a friend of the President, she said, and she would ask him personally to reopen Birmingham. Not long after making this promise, she had a conference with Truman at the White House. Asked by reporters if she had taken up the question of the paraplegics with him, she said, "No, I didn't." That "No" resounded throughout the campaign.

---

* This led Chotiner to remark, "She made the mistake of attacking our strength instead of sticking to an attack of our weaknesses."

In mid-October, as part of her attempt to prove that she was more anti-communist than Nixon,* Mrs. Douglas called in Truman's Attorney General, J. Howard McGrath, to belittle Nixon's role in the Hiss Case. In Los Angeles to campaign for the Democratic slate, McGrath told a press conference that "Alger Hiss would have been prosecuted by the Department of Justice" without "prodding" from Nixon. In California to cover the campaign for *Newsweek*, I was asked to comment on McGrath's statement—not as a newspaperman but as the author of a book on the case. Making it clear that I was "not intruding in a political fight but merely attempting to set the record straight," I prepared an analysis of the Justice Department's actions in the case—the record of delays and obstacles I have outlined in an earlier chapter. The wide publicity given this rebuttal further hurt the Douglas candidacy.

The McGrath ploy was a forlorn hope for Mrs. Douglas, although no one knew it then. Through the final days of the campaign political writers for the major California newspapers continued to write that it would be a tight race—tight enough to make predictions of victory dangerous—and Nixon sustained an attitude of pessimism to the very end. On Election Day he firmly refused to spend the day listening to early and inconclusive returns. He decided on a family picnic. But the beach was cold and miserable, and Pat Nixon ruled that they should go home. Dick Nixon said he wanted to go to a movie—but what he really sought was solitude in this time of personal crisis. Driving home that night, he passed through the Long Beach industrial area. Everywhere he could hear the Douglas sound trucks exhorting the people to vote against him. "He got home in a despondent mood," Pat recalls, "sure that we were licked."

Nixon was wrong by more than 680,000 votes, the largest plurality to go to any senatorial candidate that year. Swinging from despondency to tremendous elation, he spent the rest of the night going from party to victory party, rattling off his own stiff piano rendition of "Happy Days Are Here Again."

It was not all that simple, however. The Nixon-Douglas campaign was over, but again he had made enemies. The electioneering methods had been hard-swinging on both sides, and certainly there had been nothing more "tricky" in the Nixon camp than in the Douglas. Yet the "Tricky Dick" label stuck. The major difference between the two candidates had been in the effectiveness and efficiency Nixon brought to the battle. His adversary had bumbled badly, had shifted her position on domestic communism, and had seriously misrepresented Nixon's record. From an ethical point of view, who was the greater sinner? All this was forgotten, however, and from the anger and disappointment of Mrs. Douglas' supporters the anti-Nixon myth of that campaign grew.

This myth would harden in later years into "fact," repeated in books, articles, and news stories written by people who had not been present, people who echoed the litanies of complaint by Mrs. Douglas and her friends but neglected to check the facts.

In 1956 I appeared on the Tex McCrary program to discuss Vice President Nixon. The 1950 campaign came up, and during a break for commercials, Mrs. Douglas called up to protest what I had said. "Will you come on this program tomorrow night with Toledano?" McCrary asked her. "No," she said, "the subject is closed." McCrary pointed out that this was an excellent opportunity to state her case, but she remained adamant. The case, however, is not closed—for her or for other Nixon critics—to this day.

8

Lull Before the Battle

WHEN the Senate of the United States convened in January of 1951, eyes hostile and friendly were focused on Richard Nixon. He was thirty-eight, the youngest member of that greatest of deliberative bodies, yet he made more headlines and generated more controversy than many of the veterans who watched him being sworn in.

He had challenged the Truman Administration and rocked it to the heels. He had braved the wrath of the Liberal Establishment and forced it to the grudging admission that the charge of "communism in government" was not the exclusive property of crackpots and bigots. In a bitterly contested election he had demonstrated that he could give even better than he received, and his victory over the massed might of the Democratic Party had made him the darling of Republican professionals. The naïve quality that had brought smiles to some faces four years before when he arrived in Washington was proving to be a considerable electoral asset. The Right, which understood him as little as the Left, was ready to follow him down any road he chose to take. Anti-communists looked forward to his making an alliance with Senator Joseph R. McCarthy, still basking in the glory of a routine speech on communist infiltration which, for reasons unknown, had caught the national imagination and lifted him out of the obscurity of congressional business.

Senator Nixon's friends, therefore, expected to see him hold front and center in a Republican Party revived by its electoral victories of 1950 and scenting victory in the quadrennial pageant when 1952 rolled around. Those with some experience of Senate traditions knew that for a brief period he would be required to act the "freshman" in a body jealous of its prerogatives and suspicious of newcomers. Nixon confirmed this when he confided to friendly newspapermen that he would spend some time "learning the ropes" and practicing the circumspection that was expected of him. The only question seemed to be: "In what direction would he move?" Those who had rallied round during the Hiss Case hoped that he would continue the work of exposing communists and security risks in government. But Nixon made it plain, almost from the start, that this was not what he had in mind. "I'm not going to compete with Joe McCarthy," he said to me. "And I'm not going to be a 'Johnny One-Note' in politics." Public opinion is fickle, and Nixon may have foreseen that in time conspicuous anti-communism would become a liability to those in public office.

His major interest was foreign policy, but the Foreign Relations Committee was a prestige appointment, open only to Senators with considerable seniority. The same was true of the Judiciary Committee, even though it was entrusted with the enforcement of a law Nixon had helped to write. He was offered and accepted assignment to the Senate Labor Committee, though he felt little enthusiasm for the post. "I'll be sniped at, and worse," he said. "But my work with the House Labor Committee gives me the background for it. Let them snipe away." He need not have worried. During Nixon's two years in the Senate, there was little activity there. His really important assignment, ironically, came from Joe McCarthy, and Nixon accepted it even though he was attempting to keep his distance from the controversy that the Junior Senator from Wisconsin generated with every breath.

The Republican leadership had placed Nixon on the Executive Expenditures Committee, a watchdog operation since renamed the

Government Operations Committee. The ranking Republican member of its powerful Permanent Investigations Subcommittee was McCarthy—and he was feuding with Senator Margaret Chase Smith of Maine who had signed a "Declaration of Conscience" aimed at him. Invoking his seniority rights, McCarthy forced Mrs. Smith off the subcommittee and gave her place to Nixon.

McCarthy was motivated by more than animosity toward Mrs. Smith and respect for Nixon. Scandals were cropping up almost daily, the subcommittee had virtually unlimited powers to inquire into the actions of the Executive Branch, and McCarthy had real need of one member who did his homework. There were cases to be studied, committee sessions to be attended with regularity, complex detail to be absorbed, and meticulous cross-examination to be employed if the investigations then being scheduled were to get off the ground. McCarthy was realistic enough to know that this kind of legislative labor was not his forte. Only by the kind of preparation that Nixon was known to make could the Republican minority overcome the natural reluctance of Democrats to embarrass their own President. It was according to McCarthy's plan that he throw the fireballs and let Nixon do the spadework.

There was much to investigate and much to debate in 1951. The country was prosperous, but economic gains lagged behind a runaway inflation. President Truman's own party had for the two years of the Eighty-first Congress blocked the legislation sent up by the White House. It was the questionable truism of the day that the Truman foreign policy had failed, that his "government by crony" was destroying America's prestige. And the first enthusiasm over Truman's courageous action in Korea had been soured by disclosures that the United States was unprepared for war despite the vast outlays of money for defense.

On the national scene "natural royal pastel mink" and "deep freezer" had become symbols of widespread "influence peddling" in the Administration. The President had stuck too loyally to those in his official family whose activities were suspect, but the long green herring continued to flap on the White House lawn. When outright fraud and corruption in the Internal Revenue Bureau and the Reconstruction Finance Corporation were spread across the nation's front pages, tax-scarred Americans could not take them lightly—and Republicans lost no time in reminding the public of the Kansas City vote frauds and Truman's persistent loyalty to Michael Prendergast's political machine, which had perpetrated them.

In a speech before the Women's National Republican Club on February 27, 1951, Nixon wove these threads together into a strong indictment of the Truman Administration. Attacking policies that had contributed to the onset of war in the Far East, Nixon pointed out that even after the communist invasion of South Korea the State Department was still reluctant to bolster the defenses of Formosa or to encourage anti-communist guerrilla activities on the Asian mainland. He called for full participation in the conflict by the United Nations, for a UN resolution branding Red China the aggressor, and for a UN embargo of trade with the Chinese communists, amounting then to more than $1 billion a year. "We are fighting communists in Korea," he said, "and feeding them through Hong Kong."

When, less than two weeks later, President Truman answered his critics by firing General Douglas MacArthur, Commander-in-Chief of the UN forces, the national reaction was immediate and spontaneous. Congress was swamped by more than a hundred thousand telegrams—Nixon alone received seven thousand—and the number of letters seemed beyond count. Truman was burned in effigy in California, and New York longshoremen walked off their jobs. Nixon was shocked by MacArthur's recall, but he never questioned the President's authority to fire a general. Though he was not a member of the Joint Senate committee that investigated the firing *in camera*, he attended many of the MacArthur hearings and gave himself the task of describing and explaining what the public knew about only through carefully censored transcripts. Millions of words of the expurgated testimony were published faithfully by *The New York Times*, but few other newspapers had the space or the inclination to follow suit.

In a series of speeches Nixon gave the picture of MacArthur and his own views on the issues involved. It was an excellent job of interpretive reporting, used to expound Nixon's political line:

. . . The members of the Senate who sat and heard him for those three days were impressed by the sheer physical endurance of the man. Anyone who for seven, eight, and nine hours a day could sit there and answer questions as he did would be a remarkable man. And General MacArthur is seventy-one years old. In addition . . . it was a tremendous intellectual performance. Even General MacArthur's critics will agree that he is one of the ablest men of our times, a man with rare intellectual ability. Throughout the three-day period, not once did General Mac-Arthur come into the hearing room with a file full of papers; not once did he ask to refer to documents before answering a question. . . .

Then Nixon gave his audiences some of the color of the hearings:

. . . A considerable amount of tension had built up in the hearing room. Senator [J. William] Fulbright, with that soft Arkansas drawl of his, started his questions along this line: "General, I want to make the record clear on one point. Certain misinformed representatives of the Senate and the Congress have referred to Wisconsin as your native state. Now, General, for the record, I want you to state here in a positive manner where you were born."

General MacArthur smiled and said, "Well, Senator, I was born in Little Rock barracks in Arkansas, and I remember that one of the early jokes with which I was twitted was the comment that I was born when my parents were away." You can see that the tension which had been built up by the previous questioners was completely dissipated.

Having described the scene and outlined the testimony, Nixon used them to make his political argument:

At the conclusion of the most costly war in the world's history, we were the most powerful nation on the face of the globe and had a monopoly on the atomic bomb. Five years have passed since then, five years of conferences and little wars. Today we no longer are stronger than the enemy on the ground, we are stronger in strategic air, but not as strong in tactical air. We are stronger on the sea, but weaker under the sea. And they have the atomic bomb. Five years ago the odds in people were nine to one in our favor. Today they are five to three against us.

In the context of today's Vietnam war Nixon's comments on the Korean "police action" are of some importance. The conduct of the Korean war, he argued, was another step in the nation's five-year retreat. Only immediate and energetic action could bring victory in a conflict that had been compromised by political tinkering. He predicted that a continuing stalemate would force the United States to accept half-victory, which meant total defeat in the propaganda war. As of 1951 Nixon could see three possible ways to end the war—the three ways that confronted him when he took over the reins of government during the Vietnamese struggle: (1) an abject withdrawal, (2) a political settlement with the communists, or (3) a complete victory on the battlefield. The first way, he said, was out of the question; the second would mean a "compromise," which would give the communists what they had not won by force of arms. "This means that the only way we can end the war in Korea is to win it on the battlefield. . . . The Administration policy adds up to this: They will continue the war as it is until the communists somehow, some time in the future, see the light and quit."

The parallels between the Korean situation and its Vietnamese successor are obvious. Nixon hoped for a change of heart in the Truman Administration. But once the Great Debate over the Mac-Arthur dismissal had petered out in political bickering, the nation moved on to other, newer topics of interest. In July 1951 the spotlight shifted to another scandal in the Truman Administration. It began with a charge by the St. Louis *Post-Dispatch*, a pro-Truman newspaper that had nevertheless devoted itself tenaciously to exposing corruption in the Administration, that the Democratic National Chairman, William M. Boyle, Jr., and Internal Revenue Collector James P. Finnegan had used political pressure to squeeze out a loan from the Reconstruction Finance Corporation, a Federal agency, for the American Lithofold Corporation of St. Louis. Boyle denied the accusation, but it could not stop there. Boyle was one of Truman's oldest friends, the top strategist of the 1948 Presidential campaign, and a key man in the Democratic hierarchy. The Senate Permanent Investigations Subcommittee was compelled to institute hearings.

The case developed rapidly and sensationally, with Nixon bearing down with the same tenacity that had marked his cross-examination in the Hiss Case. Early testimony disclosed that the Lithofold Corporation had been turned down for loans three times by the RFC's Board of Review. Then Boyle had been retained at $500 a month, although he was already Acting Chairman of the Democratic National Committee. Boyle phoned an RFC official, made an appointment for two members of Lithofold—and a loan of $565,000 was quickly granted. The subcommittee subsequently discovered that Max Siskind, Boyle's former legal associate, had given Boyle more than $100,000 as payment for turning over a number of lucrative cases involving government contracts. Under sharp questioning by Nixon, it was further discovered that 40 per cent of these cases had been handled by Boyle while he was Democratic Acting Chairman. On the stand Siskind could not explain why payments to Boyle and to himself had been carried on Lithofold's books as "salesmen's commissions." When Nixon was able to show that an RFC employee had simultaneously been on Boyle's payroll and that this employee had arranged for at least one appointment in the Lithofold case, Boyle was forced to resign.

The RFC investigation cut both ways, however. A study of the agency disclosed that Guy G. Gabrielson, the Republican National Chairman, had applied for and received loans for a company in which he had a financial interest. Republican Senators argued heatedly that Gabrielson could exert no influence in a Democratic Administration, but Nixon pressed for his resignation because "his effectiveness as chairman of the minority party has been irreparably damaged." This angered many Republicans, but it gave Nixon a position of impartiality which allowed him to press forward. The investigating subcommittee discovered that Mrs. Flo Bratton, Vice President Alben Barkley's secretary for more than twenty-five years, had presented herself to RFC officials to intercede for a $1.1 million loan that a friend wanted in order to build a hotel in Miami. That loan had been rejected four times, but after her intercession the RFC reversed itself. This case, coming so close to the White House, led to a promise by President Truman that he would take "drastic action"—the appointment by Attorney General McGrath of Newbold Morris, a liberal Republican, to clean up the "mess in Washington."

"He's too little and McGrath is too late," Nixon remarked, but there was no need to worry. Morris was blown out of the water by the Executive Expenditures Subcommittee. One of its investigations showed that he was innocently and tenuously involved in a dubious oil-tanker deal. Called to testify, Morris lashed out at the "diseased minds" and the "mental brutality" of his questioners. His performance, and what Nixon called his "violent, childish outbursts" and "basic emotional instability," destroyed his effectiveness and McGrath fired him, only to be fired in turn by the President.

But though scandals continued to pop up until well into 1952, the national attention had begun to shift. The preliminary jockeying for position in the 1952 Presidential campaign began to command page-one space. The average voter, now convinced that a "mess" existed in Washington, was more interested in the primary fights, the National Conventions, and the ordeal by ballot that would seize the candidates. As a member of the Senate—and, with Senator Knowland and Governor Warren, one of the triumvirate governing the California party—Nixon had a stake in the quadrennial game of choosing up sides. He had, since the 1950 election, continued to build up his personal machine in his home state, as all Senators must if they are to protect their flanks while serving in Washington.

But he had also grown personally remote, maintaining what some considered an aloof attitude to those who had been close to him in his years of crisis and growth. In his public utterances he seemed to be mending fences more among those who had opposed him in the past than among those who had been his front-line troops. There was annoyance and bewilderment in some Republican quarters over this, as there had been resentment among anti-communists over his withdrawal from the ideological battle. Those who cared, and it was not a matter of widespread popular interest, began to express doubts as to his precise political position. The liberal New York *Herald Tribune* classified him among Republican liberals. The supporters of Senator Robert A. Taft claimed Nixon as their own—ideologically speaking—and praised his commitment to the free enterprise system. Who was right?

Nixon's voting record during his Senate tenure covers issues and areas no longer of interest to the political world. But they do show how difficult it is to pigeonhole Richard Nixon or to label him by conventional standards. This is how he was recorded on measures then of significance:

Against an amendment to the Universal Military Training bill barring ground forces in Europe without certification by the Joint Chiefs of Staff that there was available air power to secure their effectiveness.

For a McCarthy amendment that the resources of West Germany, Spain, Turkey, and Greece be utilized on a voluntary basis in the defense of Europe.

Against a Wayne Morse amendment to the Defense Production bill suspending price supports on agricultural products.

Against a Republican amendment raising ceiling prices.

Against a Paul Douglas amendment that sought to cut down funds for the Bureau of Reclamation.

Against a Douglas attempt to cut down Foreign Service allowances and reduce funds for the acquisition of buildings abroad by the State Department.

For a Mundt amendment that increased funds for informational and educational activities abroad—the Voice of America and the U.S. information libraries.

Against attempts by Everett M. Dirksen to cut $500 million from foreign aid funds and to cut $250 million from military aid; *for* an amendment to discourage cartel practices and encourage the growth of free labor unions in other countries; *for* a compromise token cut of $39 million in foreign aid, and for passage of the bill.

Against a Douglas measure to make it a felony knowingly to employ illegal aliens.

In these votes Nixon had thus been with the so-called liberals as often as he was against them. To those who demanded an all-or-nothing-at-all commitment in their public figures, Nixon's flexibility was thought to be an indication of lack of character and conviction. They accused him of placating his enemies and ignoring his friends—a charge that still echoes among those who do not understand his record. But the simple explanation evaded them—that whereas Nixon believed in party responsibility and party unity, he was basically a maverick, a man who went his own way ideologically and personally, who judged issues and their impact by standards of his own, and who seldom bothered to explain.

He could, therefore, caution members of both camps of the Republican Party, as the 1952 convention showdown approached, not to let pre-convention passions run too high. On February 19, 1952, he repeated earlier warnings in specific and urgent terms. "The greatest threat to the Republican victory in November," he said, "is being created by what the Republicans themselves, rather than the Democrats, are doing and saying. Though the major candidates have themselves avoided personalities in their campaign to date, their supporters are saying things now which will be used to defeat the man who may be selected as the Republican candidate in July. Too many people today are declaring that if their candidate fails to get the nomination, they are going to 'take a walk.' What all of us must bear in mind is that our major objective is to defeat the present Administration."

His objectivity was genuine, even though he had already begun to make the moves that would put him solidly in the Eisenhower camp. Had Senator Robert A. Taft won the nomination, Nixon would have campaigned for him as energetically as he did for Dwight David Eisenhower—and himself—in the summer of 1952. But he was putting first things first—tidily, as he always did. He realized that he had a role and a stake in the coming political battle. He had no way of knowing, however, how big that stake would be.

9

1952 — By Work to the Stars

THE 1952 Presidential campaign began for Richard Nixon on February 27, 1951—though he may not have known it. As the most exciting of that year's new crop of Senators, and as the most poligenic, he had been invited to address the Women's National Republican Club in New York—the distaff side of the powerful Eastern Establishment. Corollary to that appearance was an invitation to a dinner at the River Club. His dinner hosts were Mrs. Theodore Roosevelt, Jr., the gallant daughter-in-law of the first Roosevelt, and Mrs. Preston Davie, a power in New York politics. The guests included the Chase National Bank's Winthrop Aldrich, Mrs. Clare Boothe Luce, doyenne of the *Time-Life-Fortune* interests, Peter Grimm, luminaries of the Wall Street branch of the GOP, and a scattering of newspapermen who were on close personal terms with the Very Important Persons there. Few realized that this gathering at one of New York's more exclusive clubs was a nominating convention in microcosm. Even fewer knew that Nixon was not there by the accident of his luncheon speech before the Republican women, that already he was being weighed and watched by the kingmakers of his party.

Over coffee Mrs. Davie suggested that those sitting at the large oblong table indicate their choice for the Republican Presidential nomination. A few spoke up for Senator Robert A. Taft. Some, like myself, pleaded journalistic detachment. But the preponderant majority voted for General Dwight David Eisenhower. The query direct was never put to Senator Nixon; this would have been a political gaucherie. But when he rose to speak, there was little doubt where he stood. He spoke warmly and generously of Bob Taft, but it was obvious that his choice for 1952 was Eisenhower.

His reasons, as he explained some months later in a discussion at my home with columnist George Sokolsky and other dedicated pro-Taft Republicans, were these: "I have tremendous respect for Bob Taft. I like him personally and I think he would make a fine President. I've met Eisenhower and I found him to be tremendously impressive. But I think it narrows down to this. I don't say that Taft can't win, but I do say that I'm not *sure* he can win. And I'm sure Eisenhower can win. If I thought General Eisenhower was the wrong man for the job, none of this would make any difference. But I think he will make a fine President—and I think the Republican Party has to win, if only to clean up the mess in Washington."

Between the River Club dinner and the discussion with Sokolsky, Nixon had visited Eisenhower in Europe, at the Supreme Headquarters of the NATO command. Eisenhower had asked for a full briefing on the Hiss Case and on the nature and dangers of communist subversion. They had discussed the NATO Alliance and the Republican Party's search for a Presidential candidate. Nixon had tried to determine where Eisenhower stood on the issues and whether, in fact, he was a Republican. At parting the two men were impressed by each other—Nixon by the General's tremendous charm and his ability to win over people, Eisenhower by Nixon's articulateness, by his ability to marshal facts in a discussion, and by the earnestness of his manner. There was another bond, though both men would have denied it. Each in his own way was a "country boy"—up from America's grass roots, of hard-working stock, disciplined to sophistication but still slightly uneasy in the world of cities.

By the fall of 1951 whatever reservations Nixon may have had about Eisenhower were dispelled and he was working for the General's candidacy, though indirectly. At a Los Angeles press conference in November of 1951, for example, he had named Taft and Eisenhower as the front runners. But Eisenhower, he told reporters, though "hard to beat," was hurting himself by not declaring his candidacy. He could not and should not expect a draft. "He will have to make a move before the first major primary," Nixon said, hoping thereby to prod the General into action. At the time this was the big question—did Eisenhower really intend to run?—and there were others engaged in the great game of prying loose an answer from the man they were supporting, Governor Thomas E. Dewey and his political henchman, Herbert Brownell, Jr., among them. They had almost decided that, barring opposition from Eisenhower, Nixon would be the best running mate available.

Brownell would later recall that "Nixon seemed an almost ideal candidate for Vice President. He was young, geographically right, had experience both in the House and Senate, with a good voting record, and was an excellent speaker. Our concept of the team was to have a President who was experienced on the world scene, and a Vice Presidential candidate who knew the domestic side and went along with General Eisenhower's policies." When Brownell mentioned this to Nixon, early in 1952, it was accepted as flattery but not taken too seriously. There were other Presidential hopefuls who dangled the Vice Presidency before Nixon, but it was his feeling that they were really angling for California's delegate vote at the coming Chicago convention, not for him.

How the California delegation would go was a major question. Governor Earl Warren had suddenly decided to make a try for the nomination. He had been unable to carry his home state when he ran with Dewey in the ill-fated 1948 Presidential election, but he nevertheless declared himself a "favorite son." Though he publicly announced in April of 1952, when entering the Wisconsin primary, that he would release his delegates to Eisenhower if he saw that he had no chance at the convention, he stubbornly remained in the race after being soundly defeated by Senator Taft. The Wisconsin vote had put him out of the running, but Warren clung tenaciously to the hope that the convention would deadlock, at which point he could enter triumphantly from the wings. He therefore ran in the California primary, winning the state's seventy-six delegate votes. Under California law, these delegates were bound to him until he released them.

As one of the California delegation, Nixon's hands were tied. But he opposed the Warren candidacy, first, because he thought it divisive and futile, and second, because he had little use for Earl Warren.*

To strengthen his hand against Warren, Nixon sent out twenty-five thousand letters to constituents. "As a result of the primary election of June 3," he wrote, "I am to be one of the delegates to the Republican National Convention. This delegation is pledged to support Governor Warren for President." Reminding his constituents of Warren's promise to step down should he fail to make it, Nixon asked them to fill in the blank in the following statement: "From my conversations with other voters and my analysis of all the factors involved, I believe that ————— is the strongest candidate that Republicans could nominate for President." The vote was overwhelmingly for General Eisenhower, a fact that infuriated Warren and his aides.

Prior to this Nixon had been under the scrutiny of Governor Dewey, the major architect of the Eisenhower candidacy. "I had heard a lot of very fine things about him," Dewey later told Earl Mazo. "I checked with a lot of people who worked with him in both the House and the Senate. Everybody whose opinion I respected said he was an absolute star, a man of enormous capacity. They liked and admired him. So I pretty much made up my mind that this was the fellow." He had, however, never seen how Nixon would do before a big Eastern audience, and so he invited him to address a $100-a-plate dinner on May 8 in New York. "He made a very fine speech, from notes, not a prepared text. He demonstrated that he does not speak from what someone else writes and also had a very fine understanding of the world situation."

---

* The lack of affinity was mutual. In 1957, when the American Bar Association met in London, there were a number of requests from British lawyers and jurists that Vice President Nixon be invited. When Chief Justice Warren, who had already accepted an invitation, was informed of this, he told an ABA official, "If you let that fellow in, count me out."

Dewey then invited Nixon to his suite in the Roosevelt Hotel. "The two of us sat around for about an hour and a half before he took his train," Dewey said. "That was the occasion on which I discussed with him briefly the possibility of his becoming the Vice President." But it was general talk, with no firm commitments, a sounding-out. Nixon was pleased, but he insists that he did not take the conversation seriously. After the California primary, moreover, he felt that he could do little for the Eisenhower team. Not only was he bound to vote for Warren until released, but with the other delegates he was under instructions from Senator Knowland, the delegation chairman, not even to discuss another candidate.

Whatever other role of importance he might play at the convention was precluded when twenty-one Republican Congressmen petitioned the Republican National Chairman to make Nixon the convention's presumably impartial keynote speaker. The chairman, however, was the same Guy Gabrielson whose resignation Nixon had demanded—so the choice went to General Douglas MacArthur, then sitting on the veranda of politics but still hopeful that somehow the convention would turn to him. Nixon, however, was able to perform one service that, seen in retrospect, may be said to have clinched the nomination for Eisenhower.

The first real test of strength between Taft and Eisenhower came before the convention began. There were two sets of delegations from Texas and Georgia—one for Taft, the other for Eisenhower. The Taft forces controlled the Credentials Committee and voted to seat their own people. Had the convention sustained this decision, it would have been a crippling blow to Eisenhower, for with the Georgia and Texas delegations on his side Taft would have been able to show challenging strength. The California delegation was pivotal in this struggle. A worried Eisenhower was likening the Credential Committee's actions to cattle rustling. Nixon was publicly charging the Republican National Committee with dishonesty and warning that if the Credentials Committee vote were sustained, it would destroy the party. And Senator Henry Cabot Lodge, a leader in the Eisenhower movement, was composing a leaflet that would be slipped under every delegate's door before the crucial vote. It was headed "Thou Shalt Not Steal."

This was all rhetoric. The Eisenhower forces, pushing for a reversal, invoked what they called the "Fair Play" rule. But the votes were still necessary. It was Nixon who supplied Eisenhower with the margin of victory. When the California delegation caucused on the "Fair Play" rule, there was widespread dissension. To restore peace, Knowland urged that the state's seventy-six votes split fifty-fifty. Then Nixon entered the battle, calling on the delegates to vote their consciences and not accept a compromise. Since a majority of the delegates were for Eisenhower, they sustained Nixon. On the convention floor the delegation's votes carried the day, giving the Eisenhower bandwagon the push it needed and conclusively preventing the deadlock on which Earl Warren counted.

On the morning of July 11 the Republican National Convention nominated Dwight David Eisenhower its candidate for President on the first ballot. There were rumors that the second spot on the ticket had already been reserved for Nixon, and John S. Knight, the highly knowledgeable publisher of the Chicago *News*, stated flatly that Nixon was the man. Nixon has always steadfastly denied that he had any foreknowledge of this. But the thought was sufficiently in his mind that he had presented the possibility to his wife. She was firmly against his acceptance. Politics had never been for her, though she had done faithful service at Dick's side during his House and Senate races, and she was satisfied with the life of a Senator's wife in Washington.

Murray Chotiner knocks down Nixon's contention of innocence. "At the convention," he says, "Brownell had taken me aside to ask me who'd be the best campaigner, Nixon or Knowland. I had worked with both men, and I gave him my best opinion that Nixon had it over Knowland as a campaigner and also had a wider appeal. He wanted to know what Knowland's reaction would be. I told him that Dick was willing to stand down for Knowland, if the choice narrowed down to the two of them, but that Helen Knowland, Bill's wife, had said to me, 'You tell Dick to go ahead and not think of Bill.' That seemed to convince Brownell."

The official Nixon account is that he gave no credence to the stories that he was being seriously considered for the Vice Presidential nomination—and that, in fact, on July 11 he had lent his car to a reporter and gone to his room in the Stockyards Inn, taking off his clothes and trying to catch up on sleep. The Chotiner account is somewhat different. In interviews since then he has given a different sequence of events. At 4 in the morning before the Presidential nomination, Chotiner says, he received a call from Nixon asking him to come to his room.

When Chotiner walked in, he could tell that there was some constraint between Dick and Pat. This was hardly a comfortable situation for him, but Chotiner is a blunt man. When Nixon asked him, "If this Vice Presidential thing is offered to me, do you think I should take it?" Chotiner said, "Yes, I do." Nixon asked, "Why?" Chotiner knew that Pat hated the limelight of politics and that she resented the time away from her children that campaigning with Dick entailed. He also knew that she had been trying to talk Nixon out of accepting the nomination, if it were offered. Nevertheless, he said, "Dick, you're the Junior Senator from California, and that's all you'll ever be unless something happens to Bill Knowland. He's young, he's healthy, and he's a real power in the state—so you'll never amount to much in politics as Junior Senator. For you, it's a question of going up or out—there are no other alternatives. If you run for Vice President and Ike loses, what have *you* lost? You're still Junior Senator from California. But if the ticket wins and at the end of four years you find yourself out of office, you've still been Vice President of the United States. You can still go back into the law and be successful at it."

At 5 A.M., when Chotiner left, Nixon was still wrestling with himself. He had listened intently to what his wife and Chotiner had said, but his decisions did not derive from what others said or urged. Chicago in 1952 gave him no hiding place in which to come to his lonely conclusions. Though he had been sounded out, there had been no firm commitments. What he did not know until later was that Dewey and Brownell had already decided that Nixon was the man for the nomination, and that only he could add the kind of drive to the campaign that Eisenhower, a political novice who read politics in terms of a civics textbook, lacked.

After General Eisenhower had been nominated, Nixon left the

convention hall with Chotiner and Bernard Brennan, an old friend and political associate, lending his car to Earl Behrens, the "Squire" of California political reporters. At the Stockyards Inn, he thought, he would be able to rest. He shucked off his clothes and tried to catch some sleep. But at the Blackstone Hotel, Eisenhower leaders were gathering to select a nominee for Vice President. This should have been the Presidential nominee's job, but Eisenhower was surprised that he had "any great influence in the choice," so he left the matter to a group of twenty Senators, Governors, National Committeemen, and political musclemen who withdrew to the Conrad Hilton. Brownell and Dewey had gotten this much of a commitment from the President-to-be: a list of seven names, "any one of which will be acceptable to me." Like Abou ben Adhem's, Nixon's name led all the rest. The other six included Henry Cabot Lodge, William F. Knowland, and Harold Stassen.

There was some pro forma discussion of other candidates. One participant recalls that the "first person to be discussed was Taft, but in this pro-Eisenhower group little enthusiasm could be generated for him." The phone rang. It was Senator Taft saying that he had a commitment to Senator Everett Dirksen and that he wanted to suggest the name. Dewey made a sour face. He had been the target of a violent *ad hominem* attack by the pro-Taft Dirksen the day before on the convention floor. During the desultory consideration of other names, Dewey bided his time. Then, in his own words, "I named Nixon as the logical candidate." The committee thereupon dutifully voted unanimously for Nixon. Brownell picked up two phones to give the news to Eisenhower and Nixon.

At the Stockyards Inn, Nixon drowsily reached for the receiver. A secretary told him that Brownell wanted to speak to him. There was a brief lull, and Nixon could hear Brownell talking. "Hello," he was saying, "I wanted to tell you that the committee met and unanimously agreed on Nixon." He waited for an answer, then said to Nixon, "Can you get to the Blackstone right away? The General would like to see you." Nixon got dressed in a hurry. He needed a shave, but there was no time for that.

Without his car, in a city short of taxis, Nixon had no transportation. But Chotiner, now at Nixon's side, was able to get a car and a motorcycle escort from the convention motor pool. Sirens screaming, they were rushed to the Blackstone.

Nixon, according to Chotiner, was calm but in-turned. Just before they arrived at General Eisenhower's hotel Nixon said to Chotiner, "Murray, when you get a chance, will you call the folks? I want them to know before they hear it on television that I'm being nominated for Vice President." The only one who was really surprised that Nixon had accepted was Pat, who was eating a sandwich in a restaurant. "An old movie was being shown on television," she recalls. "But just as I took a bite, the movie was interrupted for a news bulletin that General Eisenhower wanted Dick as his running mate. That bite of sandwich popped right out of my mouth." She paid the check and made a dash for the convention hall.

When Nixon and Chotiner got off the elevator at the Blackstone, they were surrounded by newspapermen—more, Chotiner says, than he had ever before seen in his life. Flashbulbs were popping and reporters were trying to get a statement from Nixon. "Boy," he said, "they know the news." Chotiner looked for a telephone while Nixon went into the General's suite. Chotiner called Whittier, but this was an unnecessary courtesy. "I got Dick's sister-in-law," he remembers, " 'We know about it,' she said. 'We got it on television.' "

In the suite, Nixon was warmly greeted by Eisenhower. A brief formality, introducing Dick to Mamie Eisenhower, and then the General made the ritual offer. "I want to make this campaign a 'crusade,' " he said. "Will you join me in such a campaign?" he asked.

"I'd be proud and happy to," said Nixon. His first act after this was a conciliatory one. He asked Bill Knowland to make the actual nomination—and Knowland agreed.

At 5:25 P.M. Nixon appeared at the convention, badly needing a shave and with his clothes rumpled. When the crowd spotted him, it stood up and cheered. Delegates pushed down the aisles to surround him and to offer congratulations. One reporter wrote: "Nixon, tall and husky, looking more like a college crew man than like a senator, smiled and waved happily." After Knowland's nominating speech Governor Alfred E. Driscoll of New Jersey was the first to second. In Nixon, he said, the Republicans would have a man as well aware of "the internal dangers to this country as General Eisenhower is aware of the dangers from abroad." Governor John S. Fine of Pennsylvania moved to discard the roll call and to nominate Nixon by acclamation—and the convention roared its approval. The delegates almost catapulted their Vice Presidential candidate to the platform. He stood there, with Pat at his side, raising his hands to the cheers of the delegates, smiling and laughing.

This was the greatest moment of his life to that time—and perhaps the greatest ever, since it was untinged by the bitterness of what he would go through in the 1952 campaign, in 1960, and in 1962, when he ran into the buzz-saw of California politics. Six years after his entrance into national politics he was the running mate of a loved and admired American and within reach of the Vice Presidency. He was moved deeply by the warm and spontaneous acclaim of all factions of a party that, hours before, had seemed irrevocably divided, and he was conscious that it is seldom given to a Vice Presidential candidate to evoke such an outburst of enthusiasm. "Here by the grace of God go I," he thought. To add to the glory of those first hours as the running mate, he had the assurance of Eisenhower that, if elected, he would make the Vice Presidency a meaningful office with an important role in the councils of government.

Richard Nixon's acceptance speech began with the somewhat mawkish question, "Haven't we got a wonderful candidate for President of the United States?"—an honest expression, but one that reflected the lack of sophistication that embarrassed many of his followers. But it reached the hinterland, the people who shared his country-boy attitude. Once beyond this, he called for Republican unity. Lauding Taft as "one of the great Senators," he pointed out that his party's victory would make Taft the Majority Leader of the Senate and give him a place in the nation's highest councils.

The next day Nixon became known as the busiest man in Chicago. He held two long conferences with Eisenhower; he had a private talk with Robert Taft; he met with Republican congressional leaders and with the Republican National Committee; he went into a huddle with Arthur Summerfield, the new National Chairman; and he talked to reporters who lurked behind every potted palm in convention hotel lobbies, waiting to pounce on him for an exclusive.

For reporters he sketched in what he thought would be the two big issues to place before the voters—the Truman record and "communism at home and abroad." "Any Democratic candidate can be defeated on those issues," he said. "Regardless of who the [Democratic] Presidential candidate is, he'll be Truman-named and Truman-controlled." As to the Republican platform, which he had helped to draft, he was not entirely satisfied. It lacked directness, he pointed out—as if platforms meant very much in the electoral process—and should have been "much shorter, with less adjectives, more direct and simpler to read." It did not go far enough on civil rights, nor was it sufficiently explicit. When a reporter asked him about Eisenhower's lack of political experience, Nixon grinned. "I've been in politics a little longer myself," he said, aware perhaps of the years of Army politics that the General had survived. "And there isn't much he needs to learn about politics that he doesn't already know."

Two weeks later, when Nixon visited Eisenhower in the Colorado mountains, he was accompanied by five carloads of reporters. The General asked him, "Are you going to have a press conference? I'm out of touch. I'll go inside and do the cooking." But the running mate quickly found himself on K.P., peeling potatoes while photographers snapped pictures. Then Nixon pulled on fishing boots and tried his hand at trout fishing—an exercise of all candidates who know that they usually look better than the fish they catch. Despite the instructions Eisenhower gave him, Nixon caught nothing and managed only to look very self-conscious.

After dinner Eisenhower and Nixon got down to business. It was at this meeting that the two men worked out the one-two campaign technique that was to prove to be so effective. It was agreed that, whenever possible, Eisenhower would stress the "moral" campaign issues, appealing to the voters' "militant faith and hope" in his crusade. Nixon, on the other hand, would pound away at the specifics of the Democratic record and at the flaws and weaknesses of the Democratic Presidential candidate, Adlai E. Stevenson. In short, as the Democrats would later charge, Eisenhower would take the high road, safe from the antiaircraft fire, while Nixon was to go in and slug, on the low road. Neither man quite saw it that way, but that was what it added up to—and Nixon was willing, if need be, to make himself the whipping boy of the campaign.

The polls gave the Eisenhower-Nixon ticket a commanding lead, but Nixon did not believe in letting the pollsters decide. What was more, he had seen them guess wrong too many times to take their predictions seriously. Before the 1952 campaign had been officially opened Nixon told reporters, "I don't intend to take anything for granted. We're going to win, but only if we fight to win. It will be my job to cover as much of the country as possible, to tell the voters what's been going on in Washington and the Far East. I'll talk about corruption and communism. I'll explain what the Republican Party stands for—and what Stevenson and the Democrats stand for. That's how elections are won—not by sitting around to see what Mr. Gallup has to say. The great weakness in polls is that they cannot take into account the effect of an intensive, hard-hitting campaign."

In the days that followed, Nixon was the first to draw blood. The Korean fighting was dragging on, with no sign of ending. Responsible military leaders were complaining that the State Department would not let them wind up the war in all-out victory. In the opening day of the campaign, moreover, Stevenson opened himself to attack on the Korean question. The specific instance was reported in *Newsweek*. "Stevenson claims to have a plan for bringing the war to a successful conclusion," the magazine disclosed, "but he says that revealing it would give the Reds vital military information." This, ironically, was the precise line that Nixon took on the Vietnam war in the 1968 campaign. In 1952 his reaction was almost identical to that of his critics in 1968.

In a formal statement Nixon said: "Mr. Stevenson is putting out bait for voters and working a cruel hoax on the men fighting and dying in Korea . . . if he continues to leave the impression in the public mind that he has some magic formula which could bring the Korean war to an end on an honorable basis. . . . If he has had such a plan, he should have disclosed it to the Joint Chiefs of Staff. . . . Certainly he cannot contend that the Joint Chiefs would give his plan to the communists. . . . The time for ending the Korean war should not be selected on the basis of the effect it may have on an election."

It was a sanguinary thrust, and one that the Democrats should have remembered in 1968 when Nixon announced that he had a plan for ending the Vietnam war quickly. In 1952 the effect was dramatic. For Stevenson neither conferred with the Joint Chiefs nor repudiated the widely quoted *Newsweek* story. Instead, he tried to look mysterious while Democratic spokesmen complained that Nixon was "unfair." But Nixon remained on the attack, swinging across the country and into the Northwest, bombarding the Truman Administration with ammunition collected by committees of the Democratic-controlled Eighty-first and Eighty-second Congresses. The crowds he drew were not as big as those turning out for Eisenhower. But they were outsize for a Vice Presidential candidate, and commensurately enthusiastic. Republican strategists were delighted, convinced that they had chosen the right running mate for the staid and paternalistic Presidential candidate.

It would have been bad politics, the Democrats realized, to make a frontal attack on General Eisenhower. Too many of them had tried desperately in 1948 to get him to run as a Democrat, and to turn on him now would have smacked too much of opportunism. The Achilles' heel of the Republican ticket was Richard Nixon, they believed. If they could demolish him, the Republicans would suffer at the polls. The question remained: How? Calling him "anti-Semitic" and "anti-Negro" had died as an issue when the Anti-Defamation League, dedicated to fighting racial prejudice, had said, "The record of Senator Nixon is clear on the question of the hatemongers. There is nothing in that record which in any way would indicate that he had anti-Semitic tendencies or had participated in anti-minority activities." *The New York Times*, never friendly to Nixon, blunted another issue when it editorialized that "he has shown interest in the problem of protecting witnesses before congressional committees. He has proved himself quite unafraid of leaving the party reservation when the occasion demanded" —those occasions being votes on civil rights and civil liberties. His personal life was above reproach. The only area not yet protected, because there had seemed to be no need for that protection, was political corruption.

On September 18, 1952, as the election campaign was warming up, the New York *Post*, a tabloid with violent anti-Nixon biases, found an answer to the Democratic dilemma. It devoted its entire page one to a block-type head: SECRET NIXON FUND. In a story that it incorrectly tagged "Exclusive," the *Post* charged that a "millionaire's club" had collected an $18,000 "slush fund for Nixon's financial comfort." The story, by Leo Katcher, a screen writer who doubled as the paper's Hollywood correspondent, was, as *Look* magazine later said, the beginning of "a smear campaign without parallel." In a sense Nixon had inspired it by his insistence on sitting in judgment of the Truman Administration. "What corruption means to all of us is that every time we pick up our paper, every day, we read about a scandal," he had said. The statement was fundamentally true, though overstated, but it infuriated the Democrats.

The story of the fund would have fizzled out except for the clever use of the word "secret," which added moral stigma to the widely known facts. Politicians without large incomes have always needed financial help to run their campaigns—and Dick Nixon was no exception. When those funds are collected openly, no stigma is attached. As a Senator, Nixon's salary was $12,500 a year, with other moneys for staff and office expenses, and one annual free round-trip home. Just to mail Christmas cards to his constituents cost him $4,237. In his first year in office he had made twenty-nine political trips, three of them to the West Coast. Murray Chotiner, Bernard Brennan—his two political lieutenants—and Dana Smith, treasurer of the 1950 Nixon campaign, had all agreed that if Nixon's political future were to be assured, it would require twelve-month-a-year campaigning, to be financed by supporters. The subject was discussed with Nixon who agreed to it, just so long as the money raised for him was clearly identified as being for campaign purposes, which even the most moralistic reading of the law allows.

Dana Smith became the manager of the Nixon fund-to-be, projected at $16,000 a year. A letter spelling out the purpose of the fund was sent to campaign contributors.

"A group of us here," Smith wrote, "after the dust of battle had settled and we found that Dick was safely elected, began to realize that electing him was only part of what we really wanted to accomplish. We not only wanted a good man in the Senate from this state, but we wanted him to continue to sell effectively to the people of California the economic and political systems which we all believe in. It was immediately apparent to us that this would take money and that Dick himself was not in a position financially to provide it. We have therefore set up a pool, to which a considerable number of us here are contributing on an annual basis. . . . We have limited contributions to a minimum of $100 a year and a maximum of $500 . . . so that it can never be charged that anyone is contributing so much as to think that he is entitled to special favors."

When this appeal failed to raise the money needed, Chotiner, Brennan, and Smith ranged California for three days in June of 1951, speaking to Republican groups from the south to the north, seeking contributions at open meetings. There was a second appeal by letter in September of 1951, but the results were not very encouraging. By that time thousands of people had been approached by direct mail or by the speeches of the Chotiner-Brennan-Smith team, making the "secret" descriptive not only cruel but ridiculous. Hardly any professional or contributor in California did not know about it, and even in Washington liberal Republicans like Paul G. Hoffman were aware of its existence. (Hoffman, in fact, said after the *Post* story had created a sensation that he would have contributed to the fund had he been asked.) At the Republican Convention, a number of conservatives, angry because Nixon had supported Eisenhower instead of Bob Taft, had tried to peddle the story to newspapermen, but they had found no takers. And after the nomination Nixon had entertained a group of high-ranking newspapermen at New York's Pen & Pencil restaurant. When the check was presented, Nixon had passed it to Representative Pat Hillings, remarking that the money to pay it would come from a fund collected for his political expenses in California.

As the campaign progressed the original nature of the fund and its size were transmogrified into a story that Nixon was collecting a "supplementary salary" from the special interests in his state— the money to be used for his own purposes. This was the story that Peter Edson, a columnist for the Newspaper Enterprise Alliance, picked up. On September 14, 1952, Edson interviewed Nixon on *Meet the Press*. After the telecast he asked, "Dick, what about this fund we hear about?" "Without a moment's hesitation," Edson later wrote, "he told me that the rumor [of a supplementary salary] was all wrong. But there was a story there and it would be all right for me to use it. He didn't attempt to duck the question in any way." In fact, Nixon told Edson that if he wanted any details, he should call Dana Smith in Los Angeles. This Edson did, getting a full account of how and why the "fund" operated. Smith also urged Edson to suggest that a plan be adopted whereby political figures in every state be similarly endowed so that they would not be subject to pressures from special interest groups.

Edson wrote a straightforward news account that was in the mails to newspapers twenty-four hours before the *Post* began to move. His story written, Edson mentioned it to Katcher, the *Post* man on the Coast, to Ernest Brashear of the anti-Nixon Los Angeles *Daily News*, and to other reporters. Brashear's story was so distorted that Robert Smith, General Manager of his paper, refused to publish it. "I did some checking on my own," he said later, "and I was convinced Nixon had not used the money for personal living expenses. I'm not proud of the New York *Post* in this matter. I'm not running that kind of newspaper." James A. Wechsler, then Editor of the *Post*, was.

When the *Post* broke the "exclusive," it was carefully examined by newspaper and newsmagazine editors in New York, and rejected as a campaign stunt. At *Newsweek*, for example, the consensus was that it added up to nothing more than a sensational piece that would either be ignored by the general press or backfire badly. In the Nixon camp, which heard of the *Post* story second hand, there was no flurry of apprehension. The facts were known and, it was felt, no harm could come of them. But the word "secret" had captured the imagination of a substantial portion of the national press, much of it antagonistic to Nixon, the rest looking for something to add controversy to a campaign not yet marked by any real drama. The United Press and the Associated Press included both the straight Edson story and the *Post* story—"Rich Men's Secret Fund Keeps Nixon in Style Far Beyond His Salary"—in their daily budget, with the sensational account getting the major play.

When Democratic National Chairman Stephen Mitchell took to television to demand that Nixon be thrown off the Republican ticket, the "fund" story became major news. Eisenhower, in his political inexperience, was as he privately put it "hit between the wind and the water." And the Republican leadership began to panic. Only Robert Humphreys, then public relations director of the Republican National Committee and a man who had lived through the political wars—as a newspaperman, as Alfred Landon's publicity director in 1936, and as National Affairs Editor for *Newsweek*—realized that anything short of "down the line support for Dick Nixon" could well destroy Republican chances. He had support from National Chairman Arthur Summerfield and from Senator Karl Mundt, but there were others who immediately wanted to jettison Nixon.

On Eisenhower's campaign train the Presidential candidate found himself subject to pressure from the sensationalizing reporters to speak out against Nixon—and to dump him. The Washington *Post* thundered that Nixon must be dropped from the ticket. In the Northwest, as the Nixon campaign train moved from town to town, huge crowds were listening to the Vice Presidential candidate's explanation of the fund—and cheering—but this news was not reaching the Eastern press or Eisenhower's campaign train.

In the midst of the furor one Democratic voice spoke out with restraint—for reasons that later became apparent. "I am sure the great Republican Party will ascertain the facts, will make them public, and act in accordance with our best traditions," said Adlai Stevenson. Then, ignoring the fact that the editor of the newspaper that had initiated the charges was a member of his braintrust,

Stevenson added, "Condemnation without all evidence, a practice too familiar among us, would be wrong. . . . I hope you will forgive me if I don't cut the enemy to ribbons."

To make matters worse for the Republicans, there was no communication between Nixon and Eisenhower for a full two days after the story broke. Nixon, imprudently angry, waited to hear from the Presidential candidate. Eisenhower did not call because his staff had withheld the facts from him.

When they did speak, Nixon said, "General, I'm only interested in seeing that you win. If you think that my remaining on the ticket jeopardizes your chances, I'll turn in my resignation right now." "Let's wait and see what the facts are," Eisenhower said. As James A. Farley, Franklin D. Roosevelt's wise old campaign manager, would point out later, an experienced politician would have decided then and there—one way or another. But Eisenhower's "wait-and-see" attitude, inexperienced though it was, took considerable courage. He was beset on almost every side to fire Nixon— and the press corps on the Eisenhower train let it be known that in a private poll they had voted overwhelmingly against his running mate. This was immediately conveyed to the General by James Hagerty, his press secretary, who concurred.

The pressure from the press was so great that Eisenhower was forced to call an off-the-record press conference. "I don't care if you fellows are forty to two against me," he said, visibly annoyed at their extracurricular meddling. "I'm taking my time on this. Nothing's decided, contrary to your idea that this is all a set-up for a whitewash of Nixon. Nixon has got to be clean as a hound's tooth." Republican National Chairman Summerfield, however, had been looking into the procedure for dumping one Vice Presidential candidate and substituting another. He discovered that this was not up to the Presidential candidate but to the Republican National Committee, and he realized that any attempt to utilize this machinery would split the party from Genesis to Revelations. To him, this meant that no matter what the public reaction might be, Nixon would have to stay.

On September 19 the California Franchise Tax Board officially announced that it would investigate the Nixon fund. On the same day the Democratic National Committee invoked criminal law against "bribery and graft" by members of Congress, implying an illegal act. This was the first and most serious of Democratic mistakes. The second was a decision by Democratic headquarters in Sacramento to send out hecklers to meet the Nixon train at every whistle stop. This allowed Nixon to counterattack and to use the still-potent communist issue against his enemies.

The first confrontation came in Marysville, California. The Nixon train was slowly pulling out when a carload of young Democrats arrived. "Tell them about the fund," they shouted. "Hold the train, hold the train," Nixon called out. Controlling his anger as best he could, he pointed to one of the hecklers and said:

"You folks know the work that I did investigating communists in the United States. Ever since I have done that work, the communists, the left-wingers, have been fighting me with every smear that they have been able to. Even when I received the nomination for the Vice Presidency . . . I was warned that if I continued to fight the communists and the crooks in this government they would continue to smear me. . . . They started it yesterday—you saw it in the morning papers. . . . What they didn't point out is that what I was doing was saving you money, rather than charging the expenses of my office, which were in excess of the amounts which were allowed by the taxpayers and allowed under the law, rather than taking that money.

". . . What did I do? What I did was have those expenses paid by the people back home who were interested in seeing that the information concerning what was going on in Washington was spread among the people of their state." There was applause. "I'll tell you what some of them do. They put their wives on the payroll"—Senator John Sparkman, the Democratic Vice Presidential candidate, had his wife on the Senate payroll—"taking your money and using it for that purpose. And Pat Nixon has worked in my office night after night after night, and I can say this, and I say it proudly, she has never been on the government payroll since I have been in Washington. (More applause.)

"Point two. What else would you do? Do you want me to go on and do what some of these people are doing? Take fat legal fees on the side? During the time I've been in Washington—and I'm proud of this—I've never taken a legal fee, although as a lawyer I could have legally but not ethically done so. And I'm never going to in the future, because I think it's a violation of a trust which my office has. . . ."

The crowd cheered and the hecklers departed. Had the Democratic high command been astute enough, it would have realized that leaving the Nixon fund issue up in the air would have been smart politics. But it decided to force General Eisenhower and the Republican Party to the wall. And so the attacks grew louder. The Republicans writhed, not understanding the nature of political and psychological warfare. In Los Angeles, Dana Smith released a complete list of the contributors to the fund. It read like a *Who's Who* of Southern California—men of sufficient sagacity who, had they needed a piece of a Senator's integrity, would certainly have made the purchase in a less public manner.

Meanwhile, on the Eisenhower train, there was talk of replacing Nixon with Senator Knowland or with Governor Earl Warren. Harold Stassen was wiring Nixon to step down—a suggestion also made by the New York *Herald Tribune,* one of the few newspapers that Eisenhower read. Herbert Hoover came to Nixon's unqualified defense, and Senator George Aiken of Vermont told the press that he knew that "no senator can maintain a family in Washington and stay in the Senate on his present salary unless he has outside financial help." The CIO charged that Nixon was in the pay of "the real estate interests," and Democratic Chairman Mitchell called Nixon a "Holy Joe that's been talking pretty big."

Three days after the story broke, a strategy meeting was held at the Hotel Statler in St. Louis. It was Sunday midnight when the meeting began. Present were Summerfield, Karl Mundt, Representative Leonard Hill, and Bob Humphreys. Along with Knowland, they represented the backbone of the pro-Nixon movement. They discussed plans to put Nixon on a coast-to-coast radio hookup, and Mundt insisted that television be included. Summerfield complained that the Republican Party could not afford it. Perhaps, it was suggested, some commercial sponsor would contribute the time.

"Get somebody out of bed in New York and arrange for that show as soon as possible," Summerfield told Humphreys. The Westinghouse Company offered to sponsor the Nixon appearance, but when Humphreys called to tell Chotiner about it, he refused to allow Nixon to go on a commercially sponsored show. "If Dick is off the ticket," Chotiner said, "all the printing you'll have to throw away and do over again will cost lots more money than a television program." At 2 A.M. Monday Humphreys called Chotiner to tell him that a nationwide radio-TV hookup had been arranged, to be financed by the Republican Party, for that Tuesday night. Eisenhower had agreed that it was important to "put the whole works on the record."

That night Nixon was ready to walk out of the campaign. "It took some of my toughest arguments to hold him back," Chotiner says. At a strategy meeting, Bill Rogers, later to be Eisenhower's Attorney General and Nixon's Secretary of State, urged that Nixon would have to resign if Eisenhower suggested it. Chotiner disagreed, arguing that if Nixon dropped out it would spell defeat for the national Republican ticket. Nixon said almost nothing, but muttered once, "I will not crawl."

At 10:05 P.M. Eisenhower called from St. Louis. After some inconsequential chitchat Eisenhower said that Dewey agreed that a television presentation by Nixon would be good. "I want you to know that if you reach the conclusion that I should get off the ticket, I will immediately respect your judgment," Nixon said. But Eisenhower demurred. He did not think that the decision was up to him. Nixon reddened. There comes a time in a man's life, General, he answered, when he has to fish or cut bait. By the next morning Nixon was in Los Angeles, working on a speech to be carried by 64 TV and 754 radio stations, on a time spot right after the Milton Berle show.

At 5:30 P.M. that Tuesday, Nixon drove from the Ambassador Hotel in Los Angeles to Hollywood's El Capitan Theater, an NBC television studio. He had arrived in town that morning, relaxed briefly in the hotel pool, and taken a walk with Bill Rogers. Then, after conferring briefly with Chotiner, Rogers, and other advisers, he had made the technical arrangements for the broadcast, vetoing the suggestion that a set representing his Senate office be built and insisting on a stock "library" set. He also turned down insistent demands from his TV adviser, Ted Rogers, that he rehearse the speech. (Rogers was forced to get a stand-in of Nixon's height and general coloring, so that the technicians could set up the lights properly. This gave rise to a widely publicized rumor that Nixon spent the afternoon rehearsing the "effects" of his speech.)

The rest of the day Nixon remained alone, sending Pat to visit a friend, preparing his speech—filling legal-size sheets with the scribbled notes from which he finally spoke. The night before, on his flight from Portland to Los Angeles, he had pulled out some airline postcards from the souvenir packet in front of him and made a general outline. "That was when the idea came to me to mention Checkers, Pat's cloth coat, and Lincoln's reference to the common people," he said later. Two hours before air time he received the accounting of fund receipts and disbursements made by the firm of Price, Waterhouse. It tallied exactly with the figures that Dana Smith had released.

An hour before leaving for the studio Nixon had received the worst blow of all. There had been a call from "Mr. Chapman" in New York—the code name used by Governor Dewey. He had asked to speak to Nixon, but had been told that he was not available. "Don't give me that," Dewey had said. "It's essential that I talk to him." When he was not put through to Nixon, he said, "I'm not going to get off this phone until I speak to him. It's essential." Chotiner was summoned and tried to put Dewey off. "He's out someplace and I can't reach him," he said. "Well," Dewey said, "I'll hold the phone." When Nixon finally took the call, he was told that Dewey had polled the campaign leaders and that most of them felt he should resign. "I am reporting that the group feels you should," Dewey said. "I regret this very much."

"I sat alone for at least thirty minutes, debating what I ought to do," Nixon says. "The question I had to decide was whether I was justified in putting my judgment above his—and maybe General Eisenhower's—by not announcing my resignation from the ticket."

He still had not made up his mind, but just before departure time, as he was shaving, Chotiner walked into the bathroom. "Dick," he said, "a campaign manager mustn't be seen or heard. But if they kick you off the ticket, I'm going to call the biggest damn press conference in history. I'm going to break every rule in the book, and I'm going to tell everybody who called you, what was said, names, dates, places, everything." Nixon asked why. Chotiner told him: "Hell, we'd be through in politics anyway. What difference would it make?" That, Nixon says, broke the tension. By the time he left for the studio he had decided to ignore Dewey's advice—and by extension Eisenhower's—and to leave the decision to the people.

Nixon arrived at El Capitan some fifteen minutes before airtime. The technicians were still clamoring for a rehearsal, but he flatly refused. "I don't want this to look like an act," he said. Like all experienced speakers, moreover, he knew that much of the spontaneity would be gone if he had to repeat himself before the cameras. His only suggestion was that Pat Nixon sit on stage with him. "Will you get up or remain seated?" a technician pressed. "I don't know," Nixon replied. "Just keep the camera on me. I want to be completely free in my movements." Had he timed his speech? "I'm talking from notes," Nixon said, holding out five sheets of paper. "But don't worry about that."

Nixon's lack of a prepared text bothered many others. Earlier in the day Sherman Adams, the "chief of staff" of the Eisenhower campaign, had called Chotiner to ask what Nixon would say. Chotiner replied that he did not know.

"Come on, Murray, you must know. He has a script, doesn't he?"

"No," Chotiner told him.

"Look, we've just got to know what he's going to say," Adams pressed.

"If you want to know, Sherm," Chotiner said, "you do what we're all going to do. Sit down in front of the television set and listen."

Just before the small red eye of the television camera flashed on,

Nixon turned to his wife and said, "Pat, I don't think I can go through with it." Then, facing an empty theater, he looked out at an unseen audience of 55 million people. He was on the air.

"My fellow Americans," he began. "I come before you tonight as a candidate for the Vice Presidency and as a man whose honesty and integrity have been questioned. The usual thing to do when charges have been made against you is either to ignore them or to deny them without giving details. I believe we've had enough of that in the United States. . . . I have a theory, too, that the best and only answer to a smear or to an honest misunderstanding of the facts is to tell the truth. And that's why I am here tonight. I want to tell you my side of the case."

And he told it—directly and without frills—in a voice charged with emotion, leading his critics to call it "soap opera." In retrospect much can be said about the naïveté of manner, the appeal to the nation's sentiment. But that night it was high drama, affecting all but the most cynical, the most partisan. And as Cabell Phillips of *The New York Times* would point out much later, the cynics "are heavily outnumbered" by the uncynical.

One by one, in his speech, Nixon ticked off the points that showed the accusations against him to be false. The fund was no secret, every penny had been spent for purely political purposes, thereby making the fund both legally and morally legitimate. He reminded his audience that members of Congress had to supplement their incomes in order to serve their constituents properly. Some were rich, "but I don't happen to be a rich man." Some put their wives on the payroll and others kept up their law business —a practice that often led to dangerous conflicts of interest. Then he cited the Price, Waterhouse accounting statement of fund expenditures and receipts and asked himself rhetorically: "Is there a possibility that maybe you got some sums in cash?" To answer that question, he detailed all of his personal finances and his net worth, what he and Pat had inherited, what they owed on their mortgage, his earnings from nonpolitical speaking engagements. It did not come to very much.

"Pat doesn't have a mink coat," he said—a poke at Democrat scandals. "But she does have a respectable Republican cloth coat."

Harking back to Franklin D. Roosevelt's speech about his dog, Fala, Nixon remarked that his children had received a dog, Checkers, which they were not going to give back.

"It isn't easy to come before a nationwide audience and air your life as I have done. But I want to say some things, before I conclude, that I think you will agree on. Mr. Mitchell, the Chairman of the Democratic National Committee, made a statement that if a man couldn't afford to be in the United States Senate, he should not run for the Senate. . . . I don't believe that represents the thinking of the Democratic Party, and I know it doesn't represent the thinking of the Republican Party. I believe that it's fine that a man like Governor Stevenson, who inherited a fortune from his father, can run for President." But a man of modest means, he added, should not be excluded.

"I don't believe I ought to quit. . . . But the decision, my friends, is not mine. I would do nothing that would harm the possibilities of Dwight Eisenhower to become President. And for that reason I am submitting to the Republican National Committee tonight through this television broadcast the decision which is theirs to make. Let them decide whether my position on the ticket will help or hurt. And I am going to ask you to help them decide. Wire and write the committee whether you think I should stay on or get off. And whatever their decision is, I will abide by it."

The camera's red eye blinked off before Nixon could give the Republican National Committee's address. He realized he was off the air and stopped. "I'm terribly sorry I ran over," he said to Ted Rogers. "I loused it up and I'm sorry." To Pat he said, "I couldn't do it, I wasn't any good." "Dick, you did a terrific job," Chotiner said, but Nixon was not consoled. "No, it was a flop." He thanked the technicians, gathered up his notes neatly and dropped them on the floor. Then he made his way to the dressing room, where he cried. But outside his hotel there was a cheering crowd. The telephones at TV stations and Republican headquarters throughout the country were lighting up like Christmas trees, and Darryl Zanuck called to say that it was the "most tremendous performance I have ever seen."

More than 2 million letters were received by the Republican

National Committee—350 to 1 in Nixon's favor. Western Union officials declared that they had never seen so great a volume of telegrams in one night. Contributions poured in to more than make up the $75,000 spent for the broadcast.

In Cleveland, Eisenhower and his party had been watching the broadcast from the manager's office in the Public Auditorium, where the General was scheduled to speak that night. A crowd of seventeen thousand was in the auditorium, hearing Nixon's explanation. By the time Nixon had finished, Mamie Eisenhower was weeping. The General, whose eyes had never left the screen, turned to Arthur Summerfield and said, "You surely got your seventy-five thousand dollars' worth." "General," his press secretary said, "you'll have to throw your speech away. Those people out there want to hear about Nixon."

While Eisenhower scrawled notes for a new speech, the auditorium crowd was chanting, "We want Nixon. We want Nixon." Representative George Bender, who was presiding, asked rhetorically, "Are you for Nixon?" and the crowd went wild.

Thirty minutes later Eisenhower faced the crowd. "I have been a warrior and I like courage," he said. "I have seen many brave men in tough situations. I have never seen any come through in better fashion than Senator Nixon did tonight." But he himself did not have the courage to decide right then and there in Nixon's favor. Though he deplored the "pussyfooters," he could not get himself to tell the audience that Nixon's ordeal was over. He had, in fact, already sent a telegram congratulating Nixon but adding that he felt "the need for talking to you and would be most appreciative if you could fly and see me" the following night at Wheeling, West Virginia.

But the telegraph lines were clogged by messages of congratulation and so were the telephones. Nixon was celebrating the reaction to his speech at his hotel suite when a reporter brought him the news that Eisenhower wanted still another explanation. Nixon thought for a few minutes, then dictated a telegram to Summerfield, resigning his candidacy. Chotiner followed Nixon's secretary, Rose Mary Woods, out of the room and tore up the telegram. She hadn't intended to send it anyway. Meanwhile, Summerfield was frantically trying to reach Nixon by phone. He missed him at the studio and at the hotel—Nixon had left for the airport to fly to Missoula, Montana—but he was able to pass on the summons to go to Wheeling. "What more can I explain?" Nixon asked. And he dispatched a telegram to Eisenhower, notifying the General that he was resuming his campaign tour, which would terminate in a week: "WILL BE DELIGHTED TO CONFER WITH YOU AT YOUR CONVENIENCE ANY TIME THEREAFTER." As Chotiner put it, "Dick isn't going to be placed in the position of a kid going somewhere to beg for forgiveness."

When Nixon reached the hotel in Missoula, there were many messages from the Eisenhower camp. But the one that meant most to him was a telegram from the Republican National Committee stating that 107 of its 138 members had been polled and that all had voted "with enthusiasm" to keep him on the ticket. There was also a call from Summerfield to Chotiner, assuring him that all was well and that Nixon should proceed to Wheeling.

When the Nixon plane put down at Wheeling's mountaintop airport, Nixon was prepared to receive a hand-signal from Chotiner, directing him where to meet Eisenhower. A raised arm would mean that Nixon should go to the hall where Eisenhower was to speak. Both arms would mean a meeting at the hotel. "And if I raise both hands and feet," Chotiner said, "that means we are flat on our ass."

But Eisenhower was waiting at the airport, and was the first to dash up the boarding ramp. "Where's the boss of this outfit?" he asked.

Frank Kuest, a correspondent for the Copley papers, pointed forward. "Up there, General," he said. Eisenhower pushed through to Nixon, who was with Pat.

"General, you didn't have to do this," Nixon said.

"You're my boy," Eisenhower answered.

The Eisenhower accolade settled it. The "secret fund" episode had badly backfired on the Democrats by giving new life to the Republican campaign. Many voters were indignant and became increasingly so when it became known that Stevenson had an $18,000 fund of his own—money left over from his gubernatorial campaign—which he had distributed to "deserving" state employees. The Democratic candidate, his earlier "charity to Nixon" now explained, attempted to ignore this disclosure, when up popped a second. This one was brought to light by William J. McKinney, head of the Illinois Department of Purchases under Stevenson. The second fund, McKinney reported, was of $100,000 or more—made up of contributions from individuals and companies doing $35 million worth of business with the state. Stevenson never denied the existence of the fund—or its purposes. Silence was his only answer.

That should have ended it—but there was more to come. General Eisenhower, who had remarked when the "secret fund" story broke that "all this campaigning is hard enough without getting into a jam like this," believed that the opposition would now return to the issues of the campaign. Nixon, shaken by the ferocity of the onslaught and showing a humbleness toward Eisenhower that Chotiner and other aides resented, braced for new attacks. "This is not the last of the smears," he said in his televised defense, and he was right.

The St. Louis *Post-Dispatch* front-paged a story that a refugee for whom Nixon had introduced a private bill to prevent his deportation was really a communist. Twenty-three professors at Columbia, one of whom had contributed evidence to the Alger Hiss defense and nineteen who had signed a paid advertisement for Stevenson, issued what they called a "nonpartisan" statement, branding the Nixon fund "vicious." On October 30, the St. Louis *Post-Dispatch* published a page-one story that in April of 1952 Nixon had spent a vacation in Miami with the fund trustee, Dana Smith, and then had gone with him to Havana for a gambling spree—still as Smith's guest—on which $4,200 had been lost. The point of the story was obscure, but it implied an improper relationship between Nixon and those who contributed to the fund—and subliminally suggested that the fund money had been spent for high living rather than political activity. Nixon said flatly that the story was a lie, and subsequent investigation bore him out. Between mid-March and May 1 Nixon's movements could be completely accounted for. Yet two days before the election Drew Pearson repeated the fabrication.

Pearson, moreover, also broadcast to the country that Mr. and Mrs. Richard Nixon had signed a pauper's oath in California in 1951, several months before they made a $20,000 down payment on their Washington house. "If Nixon lacked [the money] in March of 1951," Pearson asked, "where did he get it in July? This is a question the public has a right to ask of any candidate for office." Nixon demanded an immediate retraction, which he got —two weeks after the election, buried at the end of a Pearson column.

An attempt was made to create a "second fund." The charge was made by Democratic Party spokesmen who gilded that lily by also charging that Nixon and his family owned real estate "conservatively valued at a quarter of a million dollars." How that false figure was arrived at was a mystery that no one bothered to clear up. But in San Francisco to campaign for Stevenson, President Truman picked up the first charge, telling a group of Democratic leaders: "Documentary evidence has been dug up, linking Nixon with another fund. He won't get off the hook this time." Nothing concrete was said beyond that, but there were hints and rumors that Nixon was the recipient of $52,000 from oil interests.

The basis of these rumors was a forged letter that had been offered by a public relations man, Roy de Groot, to Drew Pearson and to the New York *Post*. It was such a palpable fraud that even James Wechsler, the *Post's* bitterly antagonistic Editor, would have no part of it. The letter, purportedly written by H. W. Sanders, Vice President of the Union Oil Company, to Franklyn Waldman, Publicity Director of Sun Oil, said:

"To be certain that there is no misunderstanding in our conversation, let me explain that when I said we would be paying Dick Nixon more than $52,000 in the course of this year, I did not mean that all of it would come from our side. . . . The remainder comes from our business friends in the area and from other sections of the oil industry. . . . Feel free to call on him for anything you need in Washington.

"He regards himself as serving our whole industry."

After the election Pearson decided to make oblique reference to the whispered charges. He wrote that if a letter in the possession of

Sun Oil were published, it would destroy Dick Nixon. A "copy" was produced and the FBI was called in to investigate. Meanwhile, a Democratic-controlled Senate committee, headed by the strongly anti-Republican Thomas Hennings, conducted its own inquiry, proving that Sanders had not written the letter—and Waldman had not received it. Handwriting experts demonstrated that the signature was forged. Roy de Groot testified that he had not offered the letter to Pearson and Wechsler until it had been declared authentic by the Democratic National Committee. This was violently but unconvincingly denied. There was talk of prosecution, but no newspaper was sufficiently outraged to make an editorial crusade of it.

One charge went back to Nixon's Navy days, when he was working on the termination of wartime contracts, and he was now accused of having shaken down one company for a loan. This, as Nixon's most antagonistic biographer would later write, "collapsed under investigation." The New York *Post* tried once more to revive the "secret fund" story. Dana Smith, reporting to the Clerk of the House of Representatives that $25,056.63 had poured into the fund after the Nixon telecast, stated that it had been distributed to various Republican campaign groups, which he listed. The *Post* added that figure to the original $18,235 and charged "exclusively" that there was "a Nixon fund" of $43,291.63. It was a good try, but no one took it seriously.*

To the world, Nixon remained outwardly serene. He was hurt by what the false accusations did to his family and he suffered personally, but he allowed himself few outbursts of indignation even among those whose discretion he trusted. He could not know, after the "secret fund" broadcast, that, as Stewart Alsop remarked, the furor that followed it would promote him "from a youthful would-be Throttlebottom into the really major political figure he has been ever since." But he could see that his campaign tour had become a triumphal procession, with crowds almost as large as

---

* For those obsessed with Nixon's finances it can be added that he resigned his Senate seat two days before he would have become eligible for a $250-a-month pension in order to give Thomas Kuchel, the successor appointed by Governor Warren, seniority.

those turning out for the Presidential candidates. To the chagrin of the opposition, his utterances were now widely reported, and those who came out to hear him were more attentive and enthusiastic. He had become a personality in his own right. Years later it would be said that the broadcast, referred to as the "Checkers speech," had damaged him by its emotional intensity and its tone of pleading. To an extent this was true. Newspapermen, the pundits, the intellectuals, and even some of his friends had been upset by the tone of the presentation—but for the public as a whole it became ancient history in very short order.

In the heat of the 1952 campaign, however, the crowds, the cheers, and the immediate effect of the speech were what mattered. On Boston Common ten thousand persons in the Democratic stronghold cheered him as he asked them to vote for Eisenhower, "not as Republicans, not as independents, not as Democrats, but as Americans." In the industrial areas of Massachusetts, where he had drawn but a scattering of voters before his TV appearance, he was speaking to between fifteen hundred and two thousand people at whistle stops. Downtown Boston lined up two and three deep along the sidewalks to wave to him.

The test of his drawing power came in South Boston—"Little Southie"—a section so overwhelmingly Irish and Democratic that GOP campaigners had always passed it by completely. The Nixon motorcade pulled up in Perkins Square and was immediately engulfed by a quiet, palpably hostile crowd. A small boy shied a tomato at Nixon, but missed. Within minutes after Nixon began speaking the atmosphere had changed. By the time he had finished, half an hour later, the crowd was applauding in approval of his attack on communism and on the State Department, as well as his praise of General Eisenhower. There was laughter as the tomato-throwing boy was chased into a saloon by his father, dragged out, and spanked.

As the Truman-Stevenson attacks on Eisenhower increased in intensity Nixon was assigned the task of striking back—and he did with the kind of bite that to this day infuriates his opponents. By spending his time on the campaign circuit, Nixon said, the "Commander-in-Chief is AWOL . . . when the United States is facing serious problems with Russia" and in Korea. To Stevenson's quip that General Eisenhower was "a khaki-colored package being sold by the political hucksters," Nixon replied with a little flag-waving: "If we're going to have color in this campaign, I'd rather have good old U.S. Army khaki than State Department pink. . . ."

Reporters covering him before and after the "fund" episode noted a difference in Senator Nixon. The quality of earnestness that had made him such a good vote-getter in California was intensified, but the boyishness in manner and gesture was less pronounced. He was friendly to the press, though in an abstracted way, and he emerged less and less from the candidate's private car on his special train. He was more guarded in his off-the-record remarks, less willing to chat informally with the first-string correspondents who were now assigned to him. He was working on a murderous schedule, of course, shifting from train to plane and back to train, making as many as twelve speeches a day, and it might have been said that he was conserving his energies. If this was a factor, it was also true that he had withdrawn into himself— a withdrawal from which he never fully returned.

In mid-October, Nixon returned to nationwide television to discuss the Hiss Case, its aftermath, red herrings, and Adlai Stevenson. He accused the Democratic candidate of having disqualified himself for the Presidency by giving Alger Hiss a favorable character deposition for the first espionage-perjury trial in 1949. And he also criticized Stevenson for attempting to give the impression that this had not been a voluntary act—that he had been ordered by the court to do so. This may now seem like an inconsequential point, but in 1952 the Hiss Case was still alive. "Let me emphasize that there is no question in my mind as to the loyalty of Mr. Stevenson," Nixon said in that speech. "But the question is one as to his judgment, and it is a very grave question. He has failed to recognize the threat of communism as many have failed to recognize it around him."

The 1952 campaign wound up with a big radio-TV rally in Boston at which Eisenhower and Nixon spoke. There had been a brief period in the closing days when General Eisenhower seemed to falter, when the Scripps-Howard newspapers were saying that he was "running like a dry creek," but the Eisenhower pledge of "I will go to Korea" had been a shot in the arm for the Republicans. Victory was in the air on that election eve, and Nixon seemed to be carried away by its spirit. Privately, he was as always wary, and he warned his friends not to take anything for granted.

On November 4, the voters went to the polls to give the Eisenhower-Nixon ticket a landslide: 33,938,000 popular votes, 442 electoral votes, 39 states. For Richard Nixon it was a summit. In six years the obscure Navy officer and small-town lawyer had risen from "greenest Congressman" to Vice President.

10

The Vice Presidency

THE election of Richard Nixon to the Vice Presidency was seen by some as a promotion, by others as a rest cure. In his first days of office all the deprecatory remarks of other Vice Presidents were dusted off—as they are whenever a new incumbent enters the scene. Theodore Roosevelt called it "taking the veil." John Adams complained that his was "the most insignificant office that ever the invention of man contrived or his imagination conceived," and Harry Truman, in the sun-blotting shadow of Franklin Delano Roosevelt, saw himself being "about as useful as a cow's fifth teat." But for Nixon it meant the penetration into a new world of status —a world in which white tie and tails were not the rented gear of a wedding's best man but a uniform, which, if not donned nightly, at least did not gather dust in the closet.

The change in him, though not apparent to the newspapermen who gathered around with less than friendly concern, was visible to friends who had seen him come up from the eager and determined young politician from a Los Angeles middle-class suburb to a position one heartbeat away from the world's most significant office. In the eight years that he carried the title he was subjected to the terrors and pleasures of working for Dwight David Eisenhower. In the tired phrase, he hobnobbed with kings and presidents; he moved in that level of place, limousines, and Secret Service protection. To put it vulgarly, he had moved from one side of the political tracks to the other.

By that concatenation of circumstances which lifted him to the ambiguities of the Vice Presidency, he had been offered a stake in the Establishment, and he had accepted it. His pleasant house in the Spring Valley section of Washington, furnished by Pat, no longer measured up, and he moved into a mansion on Wesley Heights, contrived by an interior decorator, in which he never seemed quite comfortable, for it deprived him of shirtsleeve informality. His style of dressing changed, more somber and anonymous now, and he took up golf. At Burning Tree, where the President played, Nixon could be seen with men who had driven down for eighteen holes in their private railroad cars—board chairmen, like Elmer Bobst, the talkative head of Warner-Lambert.

Yet the effect of this was not to make him more expansive, more man of the world. He still nursed a martini long past its natural life. He suffered if there was too much cigarette smoke in the room. And he began separating his friends into two categories—those of intrinsic value to him and those of extrinsic importance. The first were invited to Sunday afternoon drinks for brain-picking sessions or to his office for long chats valuable to him and to them; the second to what, for want of a better term, were state dinners in the correct and sterile ambience of his new life.

In these relationships he was two different people. And in his public posture he also split in two—a phenomenon that puzzled and angered many in the press. On the one hand, he was the statesman who had been told, on the day that General Eisenhower knighted him at the Blackstone Hotel in Chicago, "Dick, I don't want a Vice President who will be a figurehead. I want a man who will be a member of the team. And I want him to be able to step into the Presidency smoothly in case anything happens to me." On the other hand, he was the political figure who had to take over the onerous tasks of winning elections, of holding the Republican Party together, of hitting the campaign trail with that instinct for the jugular which wins elections but makes implacable enemies.

In retrospect what President Eisenhower wanted of Nixon—and what may have contributed to Nixon's receding hairline—was a combination of Jekyll-Hyde and whipping boy. The new President may not have had any firm knowledge of the workings of White House politics and of the interplay between 1600 Pennsylvania Avenue and Capitol Hill. He certainly lacked the in-depth understanding of the functioning of Presidential power and its effect on the electorate. But those who saw him as nothing more than a bumbling refugee from the military life seriously underestimated and misunderstood him. As the New York columnist Murray Kempton repeatedly noted, though in a hostile context, Eisenhower was a consummate politician who had earned his service stripes in his taxing relationships with the Washington military bureaucracy, headed by George Catlett Marshall, and the touchiest of British generals. From the start he respected Nixon's ability to grasp and synthesize issues—and he used that ability to the maximum. He was keenly conscious of Nixon's expertise, his knowledge of the nitty-gritty of day-to-day politics in the jungles of Washington. And he took what those in Washington who could peer over the transom of White House deliberations considered then and now a sardonic advantage of Nixon's awe of those who had wielded great power at a time when he was still a fledgling in the world of affairs.

It is not telling tales out of school to report that Nixon would return from meetings of the National Security Council to his offices in the Senate Office Building as close to tears as any grown man can be. His pride was bruised, not because he had in any way failed the President but because Eisenhower seemed to take a particular pleasure in ignoring Nixon's tremendous services to the Administration, even though his Vice President was widely considered to be one of the ablest and perhaps best-informed man in all of official Washington.

All of this was a continuing process, and one that matured Nixon far beyond the demands of his responsibilities. It should be noted, however, that President Eisenhower kept his promise to give Nixon more than what Thomas Jefferson had called the "tranquil and unoffending" role of keeping a close watch on the

President's health. At the very start of his Administration, Eisenhower broke with tradition by announcing that in his absences from Washington, Nixon would preside over the National Security Council, the privilege previously assumed by the Secretary of State. This prerogative extended as well to meetings of the Cabinet.

These Presidential surrogations were of great importance to Nixon. The National Security Council was then, in effect, the real executive body of the United States, dealing with the most sensitive areas of domestic and foreign policy—creating and coordinating the plans governing all activity from the Cold War to atomic energy. Its members were privy to secrets so guarded that outside its membership and staff they were not known even to the most persistent and prying members of the press corps.

The ambivalent confidence that Eisenhower had in his Vice President gave Nixon a unique position. As President of the Senate —his one Constitutionally defined duty—he was the only member of the Congress to be a continuous participant in Executive policy-making and administration. But as Eisenhower's surrogate at the White House he could bring to the Senate more than the pounding of his gavel and the pleasure of his company. Nixon's status in the Eisenhower Administration was further enhanced by the nonpolitical background of many of the men brought by the President into his Cabinet. Secretary of the Treasury George Humphrey could advise the President on fiscal policy, but Nixon was the only man on the team who had been through the basic training of electoral battle and the advanced study of the congressional committee room and its devious maneuvers.

When, for example, extension of the unpopular excess-profits tax was being discussed at the White House, it was Nixon who could assert with assurance that it would get through the Congress and that its potency as a political issue was highly overrated. Again, when it was proposed that the military budget be cut—and Nixon argued against it—a few Cabinet members demurred on political grounds. But the Vice President maintained that Eisenhower's prestige as a military leader would quiet any opposition. Who in or out of Congress would try to set himself up as more informed than the nation's best-known and most-honored general?

In his first two years in office Nixon imposed a limited oath of silence on himself. He was available to a certain number of newspapermen—and they included some who had been through the wars with him, some like James Reston of *The New York Times* who were antagonistic but would not be ignored. His office door was open to Republican political leaders at every level, as well as to his unpaid and unofficial "staff" of friends and adherents who handled various chores that could not be added to the burdens of his single administrative assistant and the seven girls who slaved over the unending torrent of mail. This was less than half of what his senatorial staff had been. Offers of speaking engagements came in at the rate of about five hundred a month, with honoraria ranging as high as $5,000, but Nixon turned most of them down. When he did speak, he always refused payment. There were offers from magazines for articles, and these he might have written. But he was under an injunction from Eisenhower not to accept because it would appear that he was "making money out of his official duties." His phone, by actual count, rang every four minutes.

Vice President Nixon's workday was full. Arriving at the Senate Office Building before nine, he would put in nine hours—frequently meeting with Eisenhower, who wanted him fully briefed on everything that concerned the White House; attending Cabinet and National Security Council meetings; presiding over the President's Committee on Government Contracts as it pressed forward in its quiet but increasingly successful assignment of eliminating discrimination against Negroes among companies doing business with the government; and keeping up with the news by scanning eight daily papers. Frequently, he would end his day by shaving and changing into formal clothes in his offices in ten minutes flat and rushing out to an official dinner.

His relationship with President Eisenhower was, for the most part, cordial and on Nixon's side always correct. He was grateful that Eisenhower included him in the affairs of the Presidency to such extent that the President himself would publicly state that "no one in the history of America has had such careful preparation" as Nixon for assuming the nation's highest office should death or incapacitation remove the Chief Executive. Socially, there was little contact between Eisenhower and Nixon in those days. It was not until 1956, for example, that the Nixons were invited to make a quick tour of the Eisenhower farm in Gettysburg—and that only at the insistence of Mrs. Eisenhower.*

As the Administration's representative in the Senate, Nixon was faced with a touchy situation. The Senate of the Eighty-third Congress was equally divided between Republicans and the opposition. (Senator Wayne Morse, nominally a Republican, had resigned from the party and become an independent, an intermediate step to joining the Democrats.) Nixon had to be on hand or close by to break any tie votes—he established a Senate record by breaking two in one day—and to persuade recalcitrant Republicans and reluctant Democrats to vote with the Administration. This required time spent in learning how individual Senators felt about proposed legislation and Executive policy. Senator Lyndon Johnson, then Minority Leader, remarked on Nixon's efforts to be fair to the Democrats in his rulings and his special appointments, and to keep them informed of what was going on at 1600 Pennsylvania Avenue—the basis of their later friendship. When Nixon discovered that influential Democratic Senators like Richard Russell were resentful that Eisenhower did not consult them on foreign policy, he suggested that the President invite them to lunch, and a bad situation was avoided.

When legislation important to the Administration was up before the Senate, with passage a touch-and-go matter, Nixon would get to work. "I never ask a Congressman or a Senator to vote a certain way," he told me. "I'd feel that was bad manners, an unpleasant experience for both of us. And it's very, very few times I'd get tough. I've got a temper—I expect I got it from my father—but the only time I lose it in politics is when it's deliberate. The greatest error you can make in politics is to get mad—and that's something I learned when I was a kid on the debating

---

* Eisenhower was notoriously unthinking about his social obligations. In 1964, for example, Senator Barry Goldwater spent a morning going over the Gettysburg battlefield with General Eisenhower, to be recorded by the cameras for a campaign film. At lunchtime Eisenhower dropped Goldwater outside the farm, leaving an amused and chagrined Republican Presidential candidate to fend for himself.

team. I believe in discussion. If there's something I want to get across to a man, I talk it over with him. We look at both sides of the question. Maybe I indicate how the President feels about it. And then I let nature take its course. Usually, that works out fine."

Though the House of Representatives was no longer his bailiwick, Nixon continued to exert influence on Republican members. This came about partly by accident and partly because he had maintained contact with the Chowder and Marching Society, which he had helped to organize as a freshman in the Eightieth Congress. Representative Joe Holt, who had been aided by Nixon to win his seat against Jack Tenny in California, complained that after four months in Washington he still had to learn what was going on in the Administration from the newspapers. His situation was not unique, he told the Vice President. Would he meet with other Republican freshmen and explain the facts of life to them? Nixon agreed, and this first meeting was so successful that a newly reconstituted Chowder and Marching Society began meeting with him regularly.

In Congress only the leadership is regularly briefed, and it tends to use the information it gets as a status-maker, by dropping hints and feeding tidbits to the press. The average Congressman, remote from the center of power, welcomes any "inside information" he can get. Nixon supplied it within the bounds of security and discretion. And he made use of his regular sessions with House members to find out what was annoying the Congress, what reactions it was getting from the voters. He told the President of these meetings and received full approval and encouragement to continue. Eisenhower felt that the Republican Party did not do enough for its young people, and he hoped that through Nixon he would be able to groom some of the more personable and talented junior Congressmen for positions of leadership. The President also made use of these contacts by relying increasingly on Nixon for the political and legislative information on which to base Administration strategy, as a study of the notes taken at Cabinet meetings during this period discloses.

By midsummer of 1953 Arthur Krock could report in *The New York Times* that "persons familiar with the Vice President's helpful activities have told this correspondent that they consider them unique in the records of his high office." And *Life* quoted a member of the White House "team" in terms startling even to the Vice President's friends. "Nixon is a vital part of our leadership," said the member of Eisenhower's official family. "For all practical purposes he's running the government. . . . If you saw him at a Cabinet meeting, you would quickly recognize his stature vis-à-vis the other members of the Administration. He doesn't waste words. He gets right to the heart of the matter. He's realistic. From the political approach, he's very practical. But I think his judgment as well as his political acumen has impressed the Cabinet. . . . When a man produces, his reputation takes care of itself."

This reflected what Eisenhower was saying privately: "Dick is the most valuable member of my team."

His effectiveness, however, placed him in the line of fire. In September 1953, for example, the President called from Denver to ask Nixon to attend the American Federation of Labor Convention in St. Louis—an invitation to the lion's den. It was Nixon's assignment to read a Presidential message and then to speak informally to delegates furious at the Eisenhower Administration. Labor Secretary Martin Durkin, an obscure union official who had been raised to prominence by Eisenhower, had resigned in a huff, accusing the President of being a liar. The labor movement, moreover, had been violently antagonistic to Nixon ever since his defeat of Helen Gahagan Douglas in 1950. Under the circumstances Eisenhower's suggestion that Nixon make it plain to the AFL delegates that the Administration was not the captive of any segment of society, but instead represented all the citizens, was a rough and tough assignment.

By coincidence Nixon's appearance was scheduled for September 23, the first anniversary of his "fund" speech. He arrived in St. Louis and found no one from the AFL waiting to receive him. As he entered the convention hall there was dead silence, broken only by the whispered message from delegate to delegate: "The word is 'chilly.' " The audience stared coldly at him at he read the President's message. There was no applause when he finished and began his own remarks. But Nixon ignored the chill and the derisive laughter that met his first words. He went straight to the point, defending the President. "In forty years of service to his country, in the glare of publicity that men in public life must submit themselves to, Dwight Eisenhower has never been guilty of breaking his solemnly given word on anything," he said. Then he strongly endorsed the Administration's labor policies.

When he finished speaking, almost half the delegates rose and applauded, though many of them looked sheepishly over their shoulders as they did so. David Dubinsky, President of the International Ladies Garment Workers and a shrewd politician in his own right, grinned. "That clever son of a bitch," he said. "He spoke right over our heads to the people." And Eisenhower was satisfied. Speaking of Nixon to a friend, he said, "He's a good soldier."

It was during this period that Nixon's popularity with right-of-center voters and politicians began the ebb-and-flow that has been so conspicuous in his public life. (Those at left-of-center were too intransigently against him to shift in their basic feelings, although from time to time they were shaken by Nixon's stands on particular issues.) The conservative affection-disaffection syndrome was caused in part by Nixon's strict observance of the rule that the Vice President should reflect and sustain Presidential policy.

At all times there were unofficial and official advisers who urged him to "stand up to Ike"—to make his own position clear. Otherwise, he was told, he would antagonize the conservatives without ever winning over the liberals. The conservatives were his power base in the Republican Party, and without them he was exposed to the Venetian intrigues of Washington and the Republican National Committee. When Nixon spoke out in favor of legislation or policy that offended the conservatives, they would either mutter that he had "sold out" or commiserate over his anomalous position in the Administration. Two examples are illustrative.

Early in the first session of the Eighty-third Congress, Senator John Bricker of Ohio introduced an amendment to the Constitution which would limit the President's treaty-making powers and force him to rely more on the Senate's advice and consent.

Bricker was one of the leaders of Republican conservatism, in and out of Congress, and his amendment would have been reasonably certain of passage had Harry Truman still been in the White House. But at the time it seemed to be aimed at Eisenhower, then at the height of his popularity. The liberals, moreover, saw it as an invasion of Presidential prerogatives and an affront to the Roosevelt-Truman trend toward greater and greater Presidential control of foreign policy.* Nixon had favored the amendment during his Senate days. The question, then, was what his reaction would be now that he was on the Executive side.

Nixon's position was ambiguous, and infuriating to the Bricker forces. They expected his support and did not get it. Behind the scenes at the White House, however, Nixon reported to Eisenhower that the amendment had strong support among many Republicans and that a floor fight could bruise the Administration. He further reported what Senator Lyndon Johnson had told him privately—that many Democrats, remembering Yalta and Potsdam, supported some kind of restraint on Executive agreements that committed the nation to far-reaching decisions. As a result of this information Attorney General Herbert Brownell was ordered by the President to work out some compromise language on which Bricker and the Administration could agree. No substitute wording could be found, the floor fight ensued, and Eisenhower scored a tactical victory. For this Nixon received the blame from conservatives, who considered his advice and his actions in support of the Administration evasive.

The second example was more public—and more misunderstood. Involved was the Senate's traditional privilege of unlimited debate, and the filibuster, which implemented it. The filibuster had repeatedly been employed by Senate minorities to block legislation repugnant to them. Some of that legislation was good, some was bad. In the popular mind, however, the filibuster was seen as a tool of Southern reactionaries, although one of its most vocal

---

* Had the Bricker Amendment been passed, the liberals who defeated it would have found it of considerable use as a weapon against President Johnson and his almost unilateral moves to deepen further United States involvement in the Vietnam war.

practitioners was Senator Wayne Morse, the maverick liberal from Oregon. Students of Senate history could point out *ad infinitum* that the filibuster served a useful purpose by protecting minority rights from senatorial steamrollers in times of great national emotion, but with little impact.

Nixon's position was no secret. Even before his election to the Vice Presidency he had deplored the filibuster for the veto it imposed on civil rights legislation. "We have had promises but no performance," he said in October 1952. "Bills cannot pass the Senate of the United States as long as the filibuster exists." In 1957 an attempt was made by a group of Senators to put an end to the filibuster by amending Rule XXII of the Senate which permitted the termination of debate—or "cloture"—only after two-thirds of the Senate voted for it.

The question before the upper chamber boiled down to this: Could Rule XXII be amended by a simple majority or did it, too, require a two-thirds vote? The debate centered on one point: Was the Senate, only one-third of which is elected every two years, a continuing body, or was it like the House, all of whose members must stand biennially for reelection? On this issue hinged the fate of unlimited debate. If it was not a continuing body, then its rules could be established by a simple majority vote every two years, since precedent and the old rules were not applicable. When, on January 3, 1957, Senator Clinton Anderson moved for a change in the rules, it was up to Nixon to decide whether the motion was in order. Nixon, presiding over the Senate, ruled that the Anderson motion was in order. The traditionalists claimed that this was a betrayal of the Senate and the Constitution. Nixon was reversed the following day by a vote of 55 to 38, and he was again assailed by conservatives for "selling out" to the liberals.

All of this came later. In 1953, as the first summer of Nixon's Vice Presidency drew to a close, he was given an assignment that changed the whole pattern of his life. Secretary of State John Foster Dulles had just returned from a swing through the Near East. At a meeting of the National Security Council the President turned to Nixon and said, "Dick, I'd like you and Pat to take a trip to Asia after Congress adjourns." A goodwill trip, the President explained, would help dispel the false ideas about America prevalent in the Far East. The Asian nations had not been visited by anyone of high rank, and Eisenhower felt that a Vice Presidential tour would make American pledges of respect and interest more impressive.

Nixon accepted eagerly, and in his usual fashion began to prepare for the trip—a 45,539-mile jaunt covering 19 countries in 10 weeks—by learning all he could about the area he was to visit. The State Department supplied him with thick looseleaf notebooks, one for each country, crammed with data on geography and people, government, economic and social conditions, United States Embassy officers, biographical data on the leaders, and a breakdown of internal and external problems. To the horror of State Department briefing officers, Nixon informed them that he intended to mingle with the people wherever possible, instead of limiting himself to official functions and private meetings with heads of state.

Everywhere he went Nixon stopped his car, got out, and shook hands with people while security police hovered apprehensively and tried to get him to return to his car. The success of this phase of the trip has been hotly debated. Criticism ranged from the charge that it was a grandstand play to impress voters at home of his democratic instincts to the kinder admonition that it demonstrated a lack of sophistication and a failure to realize that in the Far East he would be going counter to local practices, thereby making himself look foolish. Against this, it was argued that by mingling with crowds, he was helping to destroy America's imperialist image. The usually cynical Washington press corps' stories supported the second argument.

Near Manila, for example, a shopkeeper exclaimed, "He is not afraid to shake my hand even if my face is dirty." In Hong Kong a plainclothesman said, "He's quite a bloke. He even talked to me." In Tokyo a small boy nudged a friend. "That's Nikushon," he said proudly. A correspondent wired: "THE COMMON TOUCH MAY BE OLD STUFF TO THE VOTERS BACK HOME BUT IT'S NEW STUFF TO THE PEOPLE OF ASIA. AND JUDGING BY THE REACTIONS, THEY LIKE IT. NO AMERICAN OF NIXON'S OFFICIAL STATURE HAS GOT OUT AMONG

THE ASIAN PEOPLE AS MUCH AS HE HAS." Another correspondent wrote: "The Nixons' Hong Kong accomplishments have cynical observers here shaking their heads in amazement."

Three years later Nixon was to receive evidence of the continuing impact of his trip. "I thought you might like to know," the manager of an Afghanistan business firm wrote in December 1955, "some of the reaction which the Afghans have shown in connection with the present visit of [Soviet leaders] Bulganin and Khrushchev. . . . The Afghans are saying, 'Why is it necessary for Bulganin to bring all of these secret police along with him? When Mr. Nixon paid us a visit, he did not bring secret police along with him. Mr. Nixon walked among the crowd of Afghans in Kabul and Kandahar shaking hands and never having any feeling that there was danger.' "

The crowds that turned out to see Nixon—smiling, shaking hands, asking questions, plucking flowers from his wife's bouquet to give to children—were tremendous. There were also the ever-present communist pickets and demonstrators. In Burma, at a ruined pagoda, a hundred communists carried placards emblazoned with the message "Go Back Warmonger, Valet of Wall Street," and a sound truck shrilled anti-American slogans. Nixon marched up to one of the communists. "I notice these cards addressed to Mr. Nixon," he said. "I'm Nixon, and I'm glad to know you. What's your name?" The communist ducked into the crowd. To an English-speaking Red leader Nixon said, "America doesn't want aggression. But what do you think of other aggressions such as Korea and Indo-China?"

"That's different," said the communist.

Nixon smiled and changed the subject. "Well, how many children have you got?"

"The closely-packed crowd roared with laughter," Time reported. "As Nixon pushed on, trying to shake hands with more demonstrators, they folded their signs and gave the whole thing up."

These were the outward manifestations. But Nixon was also in contact with the leaders of free Asia, with native and colonial officials, with the best-informed Americans in the area. He talked with Chiang Kai-shek, with the French generals fighting a losing war in Indo-China and the British generals holding their own in Malaya, and with Prime Minister Jawaharlal Nehru in India. He saw the Far East as a boiling mass of contradictions, threats, and aspirations. In its rawest and most violent form he surveyed communist aggression and subversion from the ringside seat of the Asian world. He realized that the uncommitted peoples of Asia held the balance of power, for the time being, between the American-British complex and the communist bloc—that they might be the key to the future.

Returning to Washington, Nixon reported the observations and conclusions of his trip in a two-hour speech to the National Security Council. According to an official who was present, the President and the entire Council stood up and applauded when he had finished speaking. The occasion was a landmark in Nixon's career. From that moment on he became a respected participant in Administration foreign policy discussions.

At the time the communists in Indo-China were beginning the great offensive that led to French defeat, to the partition of the country, and to the subsequent Vietnamese war. In his new role, Nixon warned the super-secret NSC that there was too much complacency among Americans about Indo-China. If Indo-China went to the communists, he reasoned, it would be followed by increased pressure on Laos, Cambodia, Malaya, Thailand, and the rest of Southeast Asia. If these countries were to go, then Japan would be forced to capitulate, at least economically, to the communists, since the bulk of her trading was with that area. The problem was both military and psychological. "Every time they talk negotiation with the Reds in the French Parliament," he quoted a high defense ministry official in Indo-China, "we lose ten percent of our Vietnamese effectives." These words may have echoed in his mind in the mid-Sixties, when a group of United States Senators began clamoring for negotiation and retreat in Vietnam.

Again in his new role, Nixon urged the creation of a military crescent—including Turkey, Iran, Pakistan, Indo-China, Formosa, and Japan—to close the ring around the Sino-Soviet empire. He called for the implementation of this defensive arrangement by some sort of Asian equivalent to the North Atlantic Treaty Or-

173

ganization. He argued for military aid to Pakistan, then under high-level consideration. After talking to Prime Minister Nehru, Nixon had returned from his trip convinced that India's neutralism was an outgrowth of Nehru's mistaken belief that India could be a dominant force only if the rest of non-communist Asia were weak and unarmed.

In the weeks that followed Nixon reported to television and other audiences, though stressing factual material and steering clear of observations that might seem to impinge on the foreign policy prerogatives of Secretary Dulles and the State Department. One of these reports, an off-the-record presentation, was to the annual meeting of the American Society of Newspaper Editors. Nixon was no more controversial than he had been in previous foreign policy speeches, but in the question-and-answer period he was asked by a South Carolina editor: "The government of France, if it should decide to withdraw French troops from Indo-China, do you think that the United States should send in American troops to replace them if that were necessary to prevent Indo-China being taken over by the communists?"

Nixon's reply, in the light of what has happened since, was a mild one. "The United States is the leader of the free world and the free world cannot afford in Asia a further retreat to the communists. . . . I think that with the proper leadership we can do it without putting American boys in. But under the circumstances, if in order to avoid further communist expansion in Asia and particularly in Indo-China, if in order to avoid it we must take the risk now by putting American boys in, I believe that the Executive Branch of the government has to take the politically unpopular position of facing up to it and doing it, and I personally would support such a decision." (Applause.)

Nixon was speaking strictly for himself, but within hours news stories appeared of a "trial balloon" by the Eisenhower Administration. Not long after, Nixon was identified as the balloonist and Washington echoed to rumors that he had proposed "another Korea" by means of a planted question. This was the signal for new *ad hominem* attacks on the Vice President. Had it been a "trial balloon," and had Eisenhower sent in American troops to bolster the collapsing French armies, history might have been written differently—and the bloodletting of more recent years might have been avoided.

But like all political flurries, those raised by Nixon's Indo-Chinese speculations were only momentary. Ahead for him, for the Republican Party, for the White House, and for the country at large was a longer, domestically more bitter controversy. Label it "McCarthy," and recall that 1954 was an election year.

11

Enter — and Exit — Joe McCarthy

"**I** do not mind lying, but I hate inaccuracy," Samuel Butler observed. It was Senator Joseph R. McCarthy's fate to generate, among both friends and foes, outrageous inaccuracies and some high-spirited lying. This was the tragedy of the McCarthy Era, and it left scars on the body politic which are still in evidence.

When the history of those years is written, its theme will be that otherwise decent and responsible men on both sides of the McCarthy controversy were so caught up in the passions of the times that they said and did unconscionable things. Some, again on both sides, were impelled by honest indignation and lack of knowledge. Others were pushed by less generous motives and they dragged the good men on both sides down to their level. In the end vindictiveness reigned, directed primarily against the Senator, and those who supported him found themselves marked, misrepresented, and therefore embittered.

It would be false to say that in the warfare of those dismal days Richard Nixon was an innocent bystander. It would be true to note that he was a reluctant participant, driven to action by his anomalous role in the Eisenhower Administration, by his concern for the country, by his self-imposed sense of responsibility for the

176

Republican Party, and especially by his knowledge that, whatever McCarthy's sins of exaggeration, there was a core of validity in most of what he charged and did. Nixon's reputation for anti-communist zeal, moreover, made it inevitable that regardless how he acted, his detractors would link his name with McCarthy's, as they did in the Nixon-Douglas campaign.

At the time the comfortable formulation among those who wanted simultaneously to approve and disapprove was that they "agreed with McCarthy's aims but disagreed with his methods." Vice President Nixon never took this way out, though it could be an accurate summation of his feelings. He was, to begin with, inhibited by the ambivalence of his gut reaction to the Wisconsin Senator. Like so many of those who knew McCarthy in person, and not in the press caricatures of him, Nixon was affected by his real charm, his Irish way of disarming those about him, his naïve emotionalism. Yet the two men were as far apart as two people can be—introvert versus extrovert; the man who took his own counsel and made his own decisions by ceaseless self-examination versus the ceaseless solicitor of advice he never took and the tool of those who knew how to manipulate him; the abstemious individual, ill-at-ease in the bluff, backslapping world of politics versus the drinker, the anecdote-teller, the brawler. Only the imperatives of politics could have brought them together.

The contrast between the two was discerned early in the story of the McCarthy Era and reported by *Newsweek* in what I converted into a two-act playlet. The setting was the executive Sulgrave Club in Washington on the night of December 12, 1950. The occasion was a small party at which Joe McCarthy, Drew Pearson (whose fictionalized reporting mightily exacerbated the nerves of an already touchy time), Senator-elect Nixon, and Representative Charles Bennett were among the guests.

Act One (*at dinner*)

MC CARTHY (*to* PEARSON)   I'm going to give a little talk about you on the Senate floor tomorrow. I'm going to say some things about you the country should know. I thought you'd be interested.

PEARSON   I have some things to say about you. My column has greater circulation than the *Congressional Record*.

MC CARTHY   There's nothing new you can say about me. I've been called everything in the world.

PEARSON   I haven't gone after a man yet I haven't gotten in the end.

MC CARTHY   Well, Drew, I just wanted to tip you off.

PEARSON   Why don't you give them a speech about your income tax? Tell them how you keep out of jail.

(MC CARTHY *stands up and seizes* PEARSON *by the neck.* BENNETT, *who is lame from polio, tries to separate the two men and slips to the floor. While* MC CARTHY *helps* BENNETT *to his feet,* PEARSON *exits left*)

Act Two (*later, in the cloakroom*)

MC CARTHY (*slapping* PEARSON *heavily on the back*)   It was a pleasant evening, wasn't it, Drew?

(PEARSON *flushes, then shoves his hand into his pocket*)

MC CARTHY   Don't you reach into your pocket like that!

(*He grabs* PEARSON'S *arms, moves forward. There is a brief struggle. Then* MC CARTHY *slaps* PEARSON *resoundingly.* NIXON *enters. He sees what is going on, and intervenes, separating the two men and pulling* MC CARTHY *away.*)

NIXON   Let's go, Joe.

MC CARTHY   I won't turn my back on that son of a bitch. He's got to go first.

(PEARSON *slips away*)
Curtain

Nixon later told friends, "I have never seen a man slapped so hard. If I hadn't pulled McCarthy away, he might have killed Pearson." The following day twenty-four Senators who had been smeared by Pearson called to congratulate McCarthy. And Senator Arthur Watkins, who four years later was to preside over the censure of McCarthy's rough methods, stopped him at the Capitol to add his own words of praise and commendation over the encounter.

Time and the clouds of politics have obscured the chronology of the McCarthy Era, and of Nixon's role in it. The great trauma began when Senator Joseph R. McCarthy, still two years from the completion of his first term, was asked to speak in Wheeling, West Virginia, in celebration of Abraham Lincoln's birthday. The date was February 9, 1950. McCarthy was then a relatively obscure Senator. His major claim to fame at the time was his participation in a Senate investigation of the Malmédy massacre— the killing by German troops of Americans in one of the late actions of World War II. Taking a minority, and civil liberties, position, he had shown conclusively that the Army's handling of the Germans accused of complicity in the "massacre" had been violative of the Geneva Convention on the treatment of war prisoners. His Wheeling speech, dealing with communist infiltration of the Federal government, had been no more than a compilation of what various Senate committees had already discovered and published—with no visible reaction from the Truman Administration. Neither McCarthy nor Willard Edwards, a veteran reporter for the Chicago News who gathered the material for the speech, had expected more than two or three sticks of copy in the metropolitan press.

To this day no one can prove conclusively just what McCarthy said. There are three separate versions of the "text," all contradictory, but since McCarthy spoke from notes, none of them is valid, as a Senate investigation later found. Did he say that there were 57 communists, 81 communists, or 205 security risks in the State Department? Of importance only was that the Truman Administration, bruised by the disclosures of the Hiss Case, decided to counterattack. Without that high-level intervention, the Wheeling episode would have been just one more anti-communist oration.

Now, suddenly, the obscure Senator found himself in the eye of a political hurricane. When a subcommittee of the Senate Foreign Relations Committee was formed to look into the McCarthy charges, such as they were, the issue was joined. Heading this subcommittee was Millard Tydings of Maryland, who made the second big mistake. If McCarthy could be destroyed, Tydings reasoned, the issue of communists in government would be forever put aside. But neither Tydings nor the Administration reckoned with the combative nature of McCarthy.

Irish by temperament, but with a broad streak of German stubbornness, Joe McCarthy chose to fight. In those early days, however, he had neither the facts nor the files to make his case. He therefore turned to Nixon, who offered him whatever materials were available to him. Nixon, still a Congressman, knew the pitfalls of communist-hunting. The mistakes of one anti-communist, he had learned, were often visited on all anti-communists. The slightest slip would be seized and blown up into a major transgression. Aware of this, he had attempted, during his tenure with the House Un-American Activities Committee, to impose a code of behavior that protected the rights of witnesses without allowing them to make a propaganda holiday of hearings.* In 1949, when the Democratic majority of the committee proposed a congressional investigation of textbooks, he had opposed it in a public statement, arguing that legislators were not competent to handle so technical and touchy a job, and it would lay the committee open to charges of "book burning." Unless handled by a qualified and non-political body, he argued, an investigation would badly hurt the struggle against communism and invite new attacks on the committee.

Shortly after the Wheeling speech Nixon met with McCarthy to discuss future tactics and behavior with him. He warned McCarthy that it would be a mistake to claim that the second-hand material he had used was the product of pioneer research. And he urged McCarthy not to overstate his case, but to allow the facts to speak for themselves without hyperbole. "Apparently," Nixon told me, "I did not make too much of an impression on

---

* The Nixon code: "Each witness should be allowed to present a statement in his own behalf where charges have been made against him before the committee. A witness should be allowed to submit the names of prospective witnesses who will testify in his behalf where charges have been made against him. A witness should be allowed to submit questions which he feels should be asked of individuals who have made charges against him. Televising of committee hearings should be prohibited because it places an unreasonable burden on the average witness."

him in this respect." McCarthy agreed with Nixon—but subtleties, distinctions, and motives were not to his liking, and he rejected Nixon's counsel as little more than the splitting of hairs. He could not curb his impulses or throw away his shillelagh. Nixon's files were gratefully accepted, but McCarthy refused to change his flamboyant approach.

He was, moreover, drinking the bubbling wine of his own successes. Mail by the sack filled his Senate office—large checks from worried Americans and contributions in pennies from little children who had been caught up in his crusade. Almost overnight McCarthy became the hero to millions of Americans, the villain to others. And in his onslaught on the communists and those who covered up for them he found himself surrounded by a group of admirers and advisers—intellectuals, place-seekers, reputable news-papermen, crackpots, experts in the field—all basking in the sudden respectability of anti-communism.

The clearly partisan nature of the Tydings "investigation"—in which Tydings flatly stated that he was not looking into the truth of McCarthy's charges but into McCarthy himself—added drama to what had become the biggest story of the year. The press did not like McCarthy, but it could not ignore him, and every headline added to his strength. Senate Democrats and Republicans sought to ally themselves with him. But few of them, in fact, rose to defend his sixty thousand-word attack on General George C. Marshall—a Senate speech that combined troubling fact with scandalous imputations of treason—and in the 1952 Presidential campaign General Eisenhower, who owed his rapid rise in the Army to Marshall, dared to stand up to McCarthy.

For the Eisenhower-Nixon ticket of 1952 what had already come to be called "McCarthyism"* was both an asset and a liability. The anti-McCarthy press, joined by liberal Democrats and Republicans, could plead with Eisenhower to take a stand against Joe, but the practical politicians in the General's camp were not convinced. They pointed out that McCarthy had the support of many of the ethnic groups that were defecting from Democratic

---

* The term, first used in the communist press, then picked up by the liberal journals, soon passed into general usage.

ranks because they believed charges of widespread communist infiltration of the government during the Democratic years. An open break with McCarthy would send them back to the party they had supported since Franklin Roosevelt's day, costing the Republicans the election.

More than most Nixon concurred, and he argued that once a Republican Administration was in office, McCarthy as a Republican would think in terms of his own self-interest, limiting himself to the Democratic record on subversion. The Republican platform promised a thorough housecleaning of Executive departments, and McCarthy had already endorsed it. "Whatever else you may say about Joe," Nixon said to me, "he's sincere. He believes in what he's doing." In public speeches, he put it this way: "The way to get rid of so-called 'McCarthyism' is to elect a new Administration which will deal honestly with the [communist issue], as has not been done up to this point." He did not take into account the maverick nature of McCarthy or the people who would dominate his thinking in the years ahead.

This was the situation in January of 1953, when a Republican President was ensconced in the White House, when the Republicans controlled House and Senate, and when Joe McCarthy became Chairman of the Government Operations Committee and its Permanent Investigations Subcommittee. Had McCarthy been a team player, he would have followed the original plan of appointing as his counsel the painstakingly careful Robert Morris, who had distinguished himself by his conduct of investigations such as those of the Red-tinged Institute of Pacific Relations. But there were others who had McCarthy's ear, and notable among them was George Sokolsky, an influential though capricious nationally syndicated columnist. It was Sokolsky who convinced McCarthy that the investigations subcommittee counsel should be Roy Cohn—twenty-six years old, spoiled, rich, undisciplined, and at times unscrupulous, a Democrat with no particular sense of loyalty to a Republican Administration. Sokolsky, bitter because Eisenhower had wrested the Republican nomination from Robert Taft, encouraged McCarthy to take on the Administration.

Nixon, on the other hand, was part of that new Administration and in the area of communism its spokesman. Continued Republican growth, he believed, depended on cooperation among the various elements of the party. To prevent an open rupture, he set about to bridge the gap between the Eisenhower Republicans and the conservative Republicans, most of whom had rallied to McCarthy since 1950. He was therefore compelled to labor on two fronts—to keep McCarthy in line and to counter those of the President's friends who had dedicated themselves to the destruction of McCarthy.

Nixon's view on McCarthy, which prevailed for a time, was that it would be "morally wrong and suicidal" to attack the Wisconsin Senator when he was right. He advised members of the Eisenhower team to examine each act of McCarthy's accusations and to support him when he was right, to criticize him when he was wrong. This position brought him into conflict with those in Congress and in the country at large who made it an article of faith that McCarthy was never wrong. It equally angered those whose own article it was that McCarthy was always wrong. Though he tried to prevent excesses in either camp, his was a losing battle. In the summer of 1953, he summed it up this way in a memorandum to me:

"My theory as far as relations with McCarthy are concerned is that while the President would undoubtedly win in any head-on clash with McCarthy, he could not help but be hurt in the process. A controversy would cause a very decided split among Republicans and could well lead to defeat for us in the 1954 elections. There may be a time when as a matter of principle the President may have to become involved in such a fight. But I think it is the responsibility of all of us to avoid it as long as we possibly can. It will give aid and comfort to no one but the Democrats. It is interesting to note that many of the columnists who have been taking the President to task for not attacking McCarthy are neither friends of McCarthy nor of the President."

When he said this, Nixon already had a long and wearying record of trying to avoid an open break. After the 1952 election he had brought McCarthy together with Jerry Persons of the

White House staff and Bill Rogers, much admired by McCarthy, to try to establish guidelines for the future. In an expansive mood McCarthy had conceded that perhaps he had been extreme or irresponsible in the past, but he defended his sincerity. He was reassured that the Eisenhower Administration did not want him to relax in his investigation of communists in government. But he was asked not to work at cross-purposes with the White House, and he agreed. Surprisingly, he stood by this agreement for a time.

When James Bryant Conant of Harvard was nominated High Commissioner for Germany, the President asked for speedy Senate confirmation. McCarthy had already indicated that he would make a public fight against Conant. "I talked to McCarthy," Nixon said, "and told him that I thought it would be unwise for him to do so for two reasons. One, because he was going to lose and therefore from his standpoint would suffer a defeat early in the session, thereby hurting himself immeasurably. Two, it would be detrimental from the standpoint of the country for Conant to go to Germany after being attacked on the Senate floor." At Nixon's suggestion. McCarthy wrote a letter to the President, stating his opposition but promising not to make an issue of it.

Again, when Ambassador to Russia Charles E. ("Chip") Bohlen's name was sent to the Senate, Nixon made it a point to find out what was in the FBI file. When he learned that there was no information derogatory to Bohlen, he tried to get McCarthy to hold off his attack. McCarthy refused, but the ground was cut out from under him, and many pro-McCarthy Senators who would have opposed the appointment voted in its favor. Nixon was able only to get McCarthy to tone down his attacks on Bohlen during the Senate debate. Later, McCarthy privately conceded that Nixon had been right.

The next Eisenhower-McCarthy crisis came when the McCarthy committee took up the question of East-West trade and the shipment of strategic goods to communist countries, an issue that is still explosive. There were loopholes in the law, and McCarthy had repeatedly clamored for some kind of Executive action. Finally, he called together a group of Greek shipowners who were doing business with Red China and got them to sign a "pact" that they would cease and desist. Most Americans applauded. But Harold Stassen, then Director of the Mutual Security Administration, took umbrage. He appeared before McCarthy's committee, and in a fine display of pique accused him of "undermining" United States foreign policy. Nixon acted quickly. He brought Secretary Dulles and McCarthy together to iron out the dispute. Dulles issued a statement that the agreement with the shipowners had been in the "national interest," and McCarthy assured him that he would keep the State Department informed if he made any other "foreign policy" moves.

The incident was not closed, however. Senators Stuart Symington and John McClellan, Democratic members of the Government Operations Committee, realized that Red trade had political possibilities that could embarrass the Administration. They suggested that McCarthy write a letter to the President, asking for a formal statement on Allied trade with the Reds. The Symington-McClellan booby trap was well conceived. It put Eisenhower in the position either of ducking the issue or of making a categorical statement that would irritate America's allies. When Nixon learned of the letter, he telephoned McCarthy that the only beneficiaries would be the Democrats. McCarthy agreed, and asked Nixon to withdraw the letter, then in White House staff hands, before it had officially come to the attention of the President.

On these issues Nixon was willing to act as the conciliator. But there were others on which he thought McCarthy was dead wrong —issues in which McCarthy was as much the victim of Roy Cohn's slapdash investigations as some of the Senate committee witnesses —or compromised a proper position by sloppy action. To investigate the Voice of America, for instance, was a legitimate function of the Congress. But Nixon did not believe that McCarthy's hearings—dramatic but full of factual bobbles and unwarranted conclusions—or the venture into Europe of Roy Cohn and his assistant, G. David Schine, was the way to go about it. Nixon also felt that McCarthy had played into the hands of the opposition by subpoenaing New York *Post* Editor James A. Wechsler. This again had been Cohn's doing, apparently to pay off a political debt to his nightclub crony, Walter Winchell. Though Nixon did not take seriously Wechsler's posture of martyrdom or consider it any threat to press freedom, he reasoned that it was a foolish move, striking at the integrity of all congressional investigations.

McCarthy, moreover, had begun to spread himself too thin. Investigations were begun and never brought to a conclusion. Conflicting testimony of witnesses was permitted to remain in the record unchecked. McCarthy was everywhere—speaking, attacking, defending, accusing. That some of his accusations proved to be true months, and in some cases years, later made little difference. The clean-up job was left for others. In time it became clear that Nixon's attempts to keep McCarthy in line were wasted effort. And when McCarthy set himself up as the arbiter of Republican policy, calling for the defeat of members of his own party who did not agree with him, the task became impossible.

Meanwhile, the President was under a ceaseless drumfire to come to a showdown with McCarthy. The Democratic National Committee, realizing that an open Eisenhower-McCarthy confrontation would return to its party millions of the voters who had deserted it in 1952, pressed hard for the coming battle. In mid-March of 1954 Adlai Stevenson, in a slashing political speech, characterized the GOP as "divided against itself, half McCarthy, half Eisenhower." The White House could no longer avoid the issue. At a meeting with the Presiednt—attended by Republican National Chairman Leonard Hall, White House Press Secretary James Hagerty, and Presidential "chief of staff" Sherman Adams—it was decided that Nixon should answer Stevenson.

This was one assignment Nixon did not want. He knew, as he said to me, that "this is one I can't win." If he answered Stevenson in kind, he would be accused of smear. If he attacked McCarthy as the White House team wanted him to, he would be the target of vilification from the Right. If he continued to be the mediator, his newfound respect among many who had previously derided him would be lost. But when Eisenhower personally called Nixon to tell him that he was to do the chore, Nixon bowed to his responsibility as a member of the Administration. He wrote his speech in a hideaway hotel suite and, as he later confessed, "it was the toughest speech I ever had to write." When he had finished it, he discussed it with the President for almost an hour to get full approval. Then he took himself to Washington's CBS television studios, while the President retired to Camp David, out of reach of the press.

Refusing to engage in a "rip-roaring political tirade"—his description of the Stevenson speech he was answering—Nixon devoted most of his time to measured criticism of McCarthy, without mentioning his name.

"Men who have in the past done effective work exposing communism in this country have, by reckless talk and questionable methods, made themselves the issue, rather than the cause they believe in so deeply," he said. "When they have done this, you see, they have not only diverted attention from the dangers of communism, but they have diverted that attention to themselves. Also, they have allowed those whose primary objective is to defeat the Eisenhower Administation to divert attention from its great programs to these individuals who have followed these methods. . . . [But] we must remember that the extremes of those who ignored the communist danger or who covered it up when it was exposed have led to the extremes of those who exaggerate it today."

Then, referring to McCarthy's frequent statement that fairness was not necessary when shooting rats, Nixon said, "I agree the communists are a bunch of rats. But just remember this, when you go out to shoot rats, you have to shoot straight because when you shoot wildly . . . you make it easier on the rats. Also, you might hit someone else who is trying to shoot rats, too."

But it was all wasted motion. Secure in the power his popularity gave him, McCarthy did not take the Nixon speech seriously—and when reporters braced him on it, he smilingly said that it did not refer to him. He was preparing then a major attack on the security practices of the Army, specifically the Signal Corps Center at Fort Monmouth, New Jersey—one of his soundest excursions into communist subversion. And he remembered, as he told me, a conversation with Nixon of the previous December at Key Biscayne in Florida. "Don't pull your punches at all on communists in government," Nixon had said. "It doesn't make any difference at all if they are in this Administration or in previous ones. If they are there, they should be out. On the other hand, remember that this is your Administration—that the people in this Administration, including [Army Secretary] Bob Stevens, are just as dedicated as you are to clean out people who are subversive. Go to the people you are now attacking. Discuss matters with them and give them a chance to do the job."

McCarthy did not guess, however, that time was running out for him. There is a rule in politics that you can't fight City Hall—and the City Hall he was up against was the biggest of them all, the White House. With every passing day, Eisenhower grew more receptive to the pleas of liberal Republicans to move against McCarthy. The opportunity came when Joe broadened his attack on "twenty years of treason" to include the Eisenhower Administration. This led to the defection of once pro-McCarthy Republicans in the Senate, not ready to take on the White House, who now found themselves subject to the implied criticism that their party was also "soft on communism." This defection left McCarthy's flank exposed for the first time.

The vehicle for his eventual destruction was a series of hearings into infiltration at Camp Kilmer in New Jersey and the Fort Monmouth Signal Corps Center. In its initial stages, the McCarthy committee's investigations were legitimate enough, turning up evidence that a communist cell connected with the atomic spies Ethel and Julius Rosenberg had operated with impunity in the Signal Corps during the Forties. Evidence of lax security in an installation doing highly secret work was also adduced. In this phase of the hearings McCarthy was getting tacit support from the Army, which wanted to clean house.

The blow-up came when McCarthy investigators discovered the curious record of one Irving Peress, a dentist at Camp Kilmer, who had been promoted from captain to major after Army Intelligence had discovered his membership in the Communist Party. Suddenly, "Who promoted Peress?" became the big question in Washington. General Ralph Zwicker, the commandant, appeared before the committee to give a confused account of the Peress promotion and subsequent honorable discharge from the service, and McCarthy charged him with being "unfit to wear the uniform." Summoned by the subcommittee to appear again, Zwicker was refused permission to testify by Army Secretary Stevens. A wrathful McCarthy thereupon unloaded on Stevens and the battle was joined.

This was precisely what Nixon had feared. On February 24, he tried again to mediate among the warring Republicans, bringing together Stevens and McCarthy at a luncheon in his Capitol hideaway. Unfortunately, chicken was on the menu of the Capitol kitchen that day, and when the press reported that Stevens had capitulated to McCarthy—an erroneous conclusion—the meeting became known as the Chicken Luncheon. This, of course, infuriated Stevens and inspired criticism of Nixon for being a party to the Army's "surrender." He was also roundly attacked by the pro-McCarthyites, who felt that he should have exacted even more cooperation from Stevens. "What could I do?" he said to me. "Let them tear the Republican Party to shreds? We tried until we were blue in the face to arrive at an agreement, a working arrangement which would prevent a suicidal bloodletting. And when Bob Stevens and Joe left my office, I thought we had made some progress. But Joe wouldn't let up."

Repeated references to the Chicken Luncheon and to McCarthy's ill-advised decision to take on the entire Administration—in which he was encouraged by Cohn and Sokolsky—led to renewed hostilities. Peace efforts by Nixon, Republican Chairman Hall, and Senator Knowland failed. Too many on both sides of the dispute were now clamoring for an open confrontation, and McCarthy was ready. He had, to that point, been able to withstand violent attack. And he now saw himself not as a man with an issue, but as the issue itself. There was some arrogance in this, and a great deal of innocence.

With the White House now openly committed to his downfall the chances for victory were relatively slim. But before the airing of spoiled linen began on April 22, 1954, in the undignified Army-McCarthy Hearings, a collateral issue was injected into the controversy. The special subcommittee had been set up to hear McCarthy's case against the Army and the Army's case against him. Now the Army counterattacked by claiming that the McCarthy investigation at Monmouth and Kilmer had been launched in reprisal for its refusal to grant G. David Schine, the committee's researcher, a draft deferment. Once in the Army, moreover, Schine had been repeatedly called from duty at the demand of Roy Cohn, who pleaded the committee's need. Few, if any, believed Cohn's excuse—but McCarthy was forced to defend it, thus compromising his own case.

For thirty-two days, the McCarthy case was in the headlines and filled the television screen. McCarthy's actions, in the sight of millions, weakened him so badly that a second committee, appointed by Nixon at the instigation of the Senate, held a new "trial," at which McCarthy was "condemned" by his peers for his actions. During this period, Nixon remained strictly aloof. Refusing to watch any of the proceedings on television, he said scornfully, "I prefer professionals to amateur actors." And he deplored the "tendency for both the witnesses and the committee members to play to the cameras" in all television hearings. When the hearings ended in mid-June, Nixon's prediction that a test of strength between McCarthy and the Administration could only bring lasting hurt to both had been abundantly proved, but by that time it was too late. McCarthy was finished as a force in American politics and the Administration had been soiled.

Months later Nixon summed up his views of the fiasco. "McCarthy and I broke when he attacked the Administration," he said. "I did my best to avoid this break, not only because I thought that it would be harmful to the party and the Administration, but because I felt it would be harmful to the cause of those who had been engaged for years in the anti-communist fight. To me, the greatest disservice McCarthy rendered was to that group of anti-communists. McCarthy's intentions were right, but his tactics were, frankly, so inept at times that he eventually did our cause more harm than good."

The timing of the McCarthy hearings, Nixon also knew, could not have been worse. The Republicans had won control of Congress in 1952 by a slim margin. Until the shattering confrontation they had hoped to widen that margin. After the "condemnation" of McCarthy the Republicans were divided and apathetic, the

Democrats exuberant. In the urban centers of the East, where the crucial Catholic vote had swung toward the Republicans as a result of the communist issue, the Democrats were regaining ground lost in 1950 and 1952. Gloomy Republicans predicted that a huge Democratic sweep was in the making. In September the Maine elections confirmed this when that traditionally Republican state elected a Democratic Governor.

On September 15, a "bone tired" and discouraged Nixon set out from Washington in a chartered Convair on an election tour of fantastic proportions. He had already decided that it would be his last campaign, that in 1956 he would retire from politics. He was also weary of having to carry the brunt of Republican campaigns against an unremitting Democratic opposition. "They have a 'murderers row' to come out at the drop of a hat and issue statements and fight for their party," he said with some bitterness. "We have practically nobody to stand up and fight back." He derived no pleasure from the admonitions of his fellow Republicans who were always there to urge, "Let's you and him fight." Others were aware of what Nixon's role would be. "He is not only the chief strategist of the campaign now being waged across the country," Cabell Phillips would write in *The New York Times*, "he is the main assault force." Less kindly newspapermen would refer to him as the "hatchetman" of the GOP.

In 48 days, nevertheless, Nixon visited 95 cities in 31 states, flew nearly 26,000 miles, delivered 204 speeches, and held more than 100 press, radio, and television conferences. He dictated a minimum of three press releases daily to his secretary, Rose Mary Woods, and substantial excerpts of forthcoming speeches for newspapermen who had to write their stories in advance of the actual addresses. In the last three weeks of the campaign he slept a maximum of four hours a night. "In the amount of effort expended, the distance covered, the words spoken and written, the hands that were shaken, the indigestible banquet lunches and dinners swallowed down," said *Newsweek* Washington correspondent Samuel Shaffer, "Nixon's performance was unmatched by anyone in the history of American politics in an off-year election."

This expenditure of effort was accomplished even though Nixon knew that his party was in trouble. He expected a loss of fifty in the House, unless other Republicans worked as hard as he, and he warned the party leadership—from Eisenhower down—that they were in bad trouble. A letter from the President, hoping that "we will be able to have a golf game" when they met to campaign in Denver and suggesting that "you pack your golf shoes," relaxed him, as did Eisenhower's thanks for his "intensive—and exhaustive—speaking tour." At every hand Republican leaders were calling on him to "Give 'em hell." Governor Dewey urged him to "hit harder . . . people like a fighter." Candidates who were in trouble pleaded for his help. And the Democrats responded by calling him a "gutter campaigner" and a "smear artist." Stevenson described Nixon's odyssey as an "ill-will tour."

Though Nixon ranged much of the country, his major efforts were concentrated to the west of the Mississippi. In California, where Thomas Kuchel, his successor in the Senate, was floundering, the Republican victory was directly attributable to Nixon. In the House elections the expected slaughter never developed. Despite the normal off-year trend against the party in power, the Republicans lost only twenty House seats—fewer than the number usual in the circumstances—and control as well. In the Senate only two seats were picked up by the Democrats.

Flying back to Washington with Murray Chotiner after his election-eve speech, Nixon handed his campaign manager his notes. "Here is my last campaign speech," he said. "You may like to keep it as a souvenir. I'm through with politics." Chotiner did not know that tucked in Nixon's wallet was a piece of paper on which he had written, at Pat's urging the previous February, that after his term expired in 1956, he would retire from public life. In those final hours of the 1954 campaign Nixon meant what he had written and what he said to Chotiner. But the decision was not his to make.

From the precinct level to the Congress, from the National Committee to the White House, there were strong expressions of gratitude for what Nixon had done in the campaign. He had been, in effect, the cement that held together the right and left wings of the Republican Party. The Democrats, robbed of the sweep they had expected, paid him another kind of compliment. "So far as we're concerned, his name is mud," said Speaker Sam Rayburn. Adlai Stevenson accused him of perpetrating "McCarthyism in a white collar." A Democrat, just elected to Congress, shouted at a party function, "It's open season on the Vice President." But when the Eighty-fourth Congress convened in January 1955, *U.S. News & World Report* would write:

"The man at the helm of the Republican Party, busily shaping policy and strategy for the 1956 Presidential contest, now turns out to be Vice President Richard M. Nixon. President Eisenhower wants it that way. In effect, he has made Mr. Nixon deputy leader of the party, virtually in charge of operations . . . a result of a newer, closer bond between President and Vice President."

Quitting, Nixon knew, would not be easy under any circumstances. He did not know that the old chestnut about being "a heartbeat from the Presidency" would acquire a new and agonizing pertinency for him. Long after the 1954 campaign, however, Earl Mazo asked Nixon why he changed his mind.

With typical fatalism Nixon answered: "Once you get into this great stream of history, you can't get out. You can drown. Or you can be pulled ashore by the tide. But it is awfully hard to get out when you are in the middle of the stream—if it is intended that you stay there."

12

Charting His Own Course

IN 1955 Richard Nixon still carried in his wallet the little slip of paper promising himself and Pat that he would never again run for public office. The 1954 campaign had seemed to foreclose forever the possibility of anything but the most bitter dialogue with the Democratic opposition—and Nixon found it harder with each passing day to contemplate the look of bewildered hurt on the faces of his daughters when they saw the slashing Herblock cartoons of their father in the Washington *Post*. Pat had decided long before that politics was no profession for civilized people. She longed for the day when they could return to a normal married life, far from the attacks, conjectures, and inferences of a press that for the most part carried on guerrilla operations against Nixon.

As a man sensible to the ways of political life, however, Nixon was aware that the decision to step aside was his only to a degree. He represented a grouping within the Republican Party, which needed him. If he were to retire, thousands of men for whom he was a hostage to fortune—from the grass roots up to the highest echelons of the GOP—would be left leaderless, as warring wings of the party pushed in to fill a political vacuum. He was aware, too, that politics was his life. He lived it morning, noon, and night, almost to the exclusion of everything else. Friends and associates who visited him in his Capitol hideaway or in the other two offices he occupied on the Hill remarked that he would immediately plunge into the business at hand and belatedly realize that he had forgotten the amenities—the questions about wives, children, and personal affairs. This was his way, and no one resented it. It was as much a part of his make-up as his lack of interest in small talk or the politician's exchange of gossip and off-color stories.

The decision to quit was compromised by the President's increasing reluctance to run again. Eisenhower's ambiguity about his future, his clearly manifested feeling that he had given enough of himself in the service of his country, and his open distaste for, and unease in, the role of professional politician, raised questions for Nixon which he never discussed publicly but which were understandably on his mind. If Eisenhower did not run, then Nixon, his "heir apparent," would be line for the Presidency. He would also become a target for every other Republican with Presidential ambitions. No man who approaches the Presidency can turn lightly aside. In the office of Vice President, Nixon had moved far beyond the standby role established by tradition. The President, out of respect and as a result of his own training, had imposed on Nixon an important, though painfully undefined, role in the affairs of government.

The rumors that eddied about the White House revived the hope among various Republican factions that the Presidency was "up for grabs." Followers of the late Robert Taft, who had found little in the Eisenhower Administration to please them, dreamed of a "really conservative" candidate who would sweep the country for them. The same group of disgruntled Californians who had touted the "secret fund" story to reporters in 1952 began to boom Chief Justice Warren, much to his honest embarrassment. His downright statement that he would not leave the Supreme Court, and that his decision was "irrevocable," stilled the clamor but slightly. Other coalitions, less forthright, worked quietly to capture the Republican Party machinery in anticipation of the President's withdrawal.

Nixon could do little but watch. As a member of the President's team he could make no overt moves to prepare for an eventuality that was by no means certain. There were men around Eisenhower who had never warmed to Nixon and others like Sherman Adams, the President's laconic "chief of staff," who were jealous of Nixon's importance and influence in the White House inner circle. Anything Nixon did to advance himself, to build up the machine necessary for winning the nomination, would have been reported immediately to Eisenhower and characterized as a subordinate's disloyalty.

Returning in March of 1955 from an extended trip to the Caribbean countries—another of the goodwill missions that Eisenhower had assigned him—Nixon immersed himself in the task of revitalizing a Republican Party that had grown sluggish under a nonpolitical President. Within a week of his return Nixon was warning a GOP meeting that "the Republican Party is not strong enough today to elect a President. We have to have a man who is strong enough to elect the party." This was sound strategy. For in giving the signal to Republicans that they would have to rally around Eisenhower, he was at once helping to overcome the President's reluctance and making it difficult for would-be candidates to press their cases too openly.

Nixon's insistence on an Eisenhower candidacy, however, was only partly motivated by personal considerations. It was also the expression of a deep conviction that the GOP needed a shaking-up in its higher echelons and a substantial infusion of that "new blood" which Eisenhower vaguely called for. Privately, Nixon went into greater detail. "It's not ideology that defeats the Republican Party," he told me at this time. "What we need are attractive candidates, young candidates, who are willing to go out and do battle for the party. One 'safe' Republican district after another falls to Democrats who are ready to work and fight for public office. The Democrats outnumber us, not because they've picked up voters, but because more and more Republican voters have lost interest in candidates who think of politics as an avocation."

Elections to come bore out his analysis. They saw old-line, fusty, and unattractive Republicans fall one after the other to young and attractive Democrats whose political philosophies ran counter to those of a majority of voters in their districts.

In the process of renovating the Republican Party, the President's support was essential, and Nixon continued to act as if he were certain that Eisenhower would run again in 1956. By the early fall of 1955 it was clear that Eisenhower had resolved his doubts and misgivings about a second term. The word became virtually official when, on September 5, 1955, Nixon emerged from an hour's talk with the President and told reporters, "The overwhelming majority of Republican leaders believe Mr. Eisenhower will run. They are basing their campaigns on this assumption." His pronouncement, coming as it did *ex cathedra*, foreclosed the possibility of a new Republican Presidential candidate. Four days later Nixon repeated his prediction in even more categorical terms.

It was at this juncture, ironically, that the first "dump Nixon" campaign began. A group of Eastern Republicans, now convinced that Eisenhower would be the candidate, set out on their own to find him another running mate. Working energetically behind the scenes in this drive to replace Nixon was Labor Secretary James Mitchell, his motives hardly obscure, with an assist from Senator Clifford Case, for whom Nixon had effectively campaigned in 1954. There were others equally active. Theodore Roosevelt McKeldin, then Governor of Maryland, was knee-slapping his way among Republican leaders, offering himself as a Nixon substitute. In California, Governor Goodwin Knight, whose anti-Nixon sentiments grew with every passing day, was also letting it be known that his hat twirled on the edge of the Vice Presidential ring.

There was, moreover, a very subtle push on behalf of Christian Herter, the gentle, gentlemanly, ailing Governor of Massachusetts. Herter, who had served in the House of Representatives with Nixon and counted himself a friend of the Vice President, was slightly embarrassed by these efforts, but for a brief period he did not discourage them. Sherman Adams looked pointedly in the other direction while these attempts on Nixon's political life were being made. But the careful plans to dislodge Nixon were themselves dislodged by an event that no one could have foreseen.

On Saturday evening, September 24, Nixon was casually reading the newspaper when the phone rang. The President's press secretary, Jim Hagerty, was calling long distance from Denver.

"Dick," he said, "brace yourself for a bad shock."

"What it is?" Nixon asked.

"The President has had a coronary," Hagerty told him. "We don't know yet how serious it is." There was silence at Nixon's end of the line. "Are you still on?" Hagerty asked. Nixon said he was. (Later he told me, "My heart just about stopped. I thought *I* was going to have a heart attack.") Were they sure that it was a heart attack? Nixon asked. They were sure, Hagerty replied. He informed Nixon that the press would be given the news in about half an hour. "Let me know where you can be reached at all times," he said, ending the conversation. Nixon returned to the living room and sat down.

"For fully ten minutes," he would write, "I sat alone in the room, and to this day I cannot remember the thoughts that flowed through my mind. The only accurate description is that I probably was momentarily in a state of shock."

And then he was seized by a complex of emotions—concern for a man whose life had come to be so closely involved with his, apprehension that he might be thrust into the Presidency so abruptly and under such circumstances, and, of more immediate importance, how to assume his new responsibilities with a minimum of damage to Eisenhower, to the Presidency, and to himself.

"With the President of the United States gravely ill," he would write, "the eye of the nation and the world would be focused upon me and what I did. Every word, every action of mine would be more important now than anything I had ever said or done before because of their effect upon the people of the United States, our allies, and our potential enemies." He would, what's more, have to walk a tightrope. His political rivals would be watching, ready to accuse him of a power grab if he took over too many of the President's duties, of timidity if he hung back. His first impulse, then, was to call on a friend known for coolness of judgment and caution, Acting Attorney General William P. Rogers.

Nixon dialed his number and without any explanation said, "I wonder if you could come right over." There was no need to be more explicit. Bill Rogers had already been informed, and he said he would be there as soon as possible. Next, Nixon informed Pat and asked her to break the news to the children. Pat also called Dorothy Cox, on Nixon's staff since his early congressional days, asking her to come and spend the night. Miss Woods, Nixon's personal secretary since the 1950 campaign, was at a wedding. The Vice President reached her there and told her to return to her apartment, where she could handle all incoming calls on the extension to his home phone.

When Rogers arrived, he and Nixon discussed the first of many pressing problems—what to do about the reporters who were already camping on his doorstep. Nixon and Rogers agreed that contact with the press must be strenuously avoided. No matter what Nixon might say, it would be subject to misinterpretation. While reporters clamored to see him, Nixon ducked out by the back door with Bill Rogers. At the Roger's home in Bethesda, Nixon met with Presidential Aide Jerry Persons. The first order of business was to find a tactful way to get Major General Howard Snyder, the President's physician, to call in a prominent heart specialist, Dr. Paul Dudley White, a pioneer in cardiology who had been recommended by Treasury Secretary George Humphrey.

But the main question had yet to be answered. What should the Vice President of the United States do? The Constitution offered no guidance. It provided only that the Vice President take over "in case of the removal of the President from office, or of his death, resignation or inability to discharge the powers and duties of said office." As Nixon noted in the discussions that night, carried on over the wall telephone in the Rogers' kitchen, with Humphrey, Secretary of State John Foster Dulles, and other important members of the Cabinet, the Constitution did not say who would decide if the President was disabled—or whether the Vice President assumes the "duties and powers" of the Presidency or the "office" itself. Eisenhower, however, was conscious and, in an emergency, could dictate actions to be taken, and this simplified the problem.

It was Richard Nixon, with the full concurrence of those with whom he consulted, who decided that a "business as usual" policy would be the best and wisest course. He himself would carry on as if the President were away on vacation, which indeed he had been at the time of the coronary. The "team" would work together, breaking no new policy ground and scrupulously avoiding "any semblance of a struggle for dominance." This was a good enough decision for the White House. But from Capitol Hill there were pressures on Nixon to assume the "duties and powers" of the Presidency. Senator Styles Bridges, Senate Minority Leader William Knowland, and House Minority Leader Joseph Martin urged Nixon that unless he asserted himself, the "White House clique" —which meant Jim Hagerty and Sherman Adams, then in Scotland on a fishing trip—would try to elbow him out, creating chaos and bad blood. Nixon rejected these suggestions and adopted a personal policy of "leaning with the wind," of seeming inaction. "I had to provide leadership without seeming to lead," he would say.

Though Nixon presided over the National Security Council and the Cabinet, it was from his usual seat, not the President's. If he had to confer with Cabinet members, he did so in their own offices or in his Capitol hideaway. He refused categorically to transact any business in the President's office. And he discouraged speculation as to his future role in the Administration should Eisenhower's illness be more protracted than the doctors anticipated.

The President was well satisfied with Nixon's handling of a delicate situation, one that could have led to a serious crisis in public confidence. During his first visit to Denver, where the President was in the hospital, two weeks after the heart attack, Nixon assured him that "the business of government is going forward in exactly the same manner that it would have proceeded had you been present." Should there be a sudden need for action, Nixon added—and he had in mind a possible international crisis —"the policies which you have laid down are so well defined that we can move without delay."

But for Nixon there were other problems. The realization that he was "a heartbeat from the Presidency" kept many cautious Republicans in line and brought the sycophants in numbers to pay him court. But as Eisenhower's recovery became less a matter for conjecture, the courtiers began drifting off. That Eisenhower would run, however, was no foregone conclusion. He himself swung back and forth in the moods of depression and exhilaration which follow a coronary. To intimates, the President referred to himself as an "old dodo" who had no right to hold on to his office.

In this mood he frequently said that he had intended from the start to serve only one term—long enough to strengthen the roots of free enterprise in the United States and thwart Democratic plans for substituting for the American system a socialist welfare state. Publicly, the "team" acted as if he had made the decision to run for reelection. Republican National Chairman Leonard Hall flatly told reporters that this was so, days after the heart attack. When asked what he would do if the President stepped down, Hall quipped, "When we come to that bridge, we'll jump off it." But the President's indecision, his heavy sense of mortality, were exploited by those who hoped that he could be dissuaded from having Nixon as his running mate in 1956.

On December 26, 1955, Nixon had a long, rambling talk with Eisenhower. Once again, the President wondered out loud whether he should run again, but this was merely an introduction to what he really had on his mind. It was "most disappointing," he said with the casual candor that had marked his relations with subalterns, that Nixon's great qualifications and his experience had failed to earn him the popularity necessary to run for the Presidency. Because of this, some of his advisers—unnamed—were arguing that he would be a liability on the ticket and that he should be dropped in favor of a Vice President less hated by the Democrats. Eisenhower was also disappointed because Chief Justice Warren had rebuffed those proposing his candidacy. "I don't see why he just couldn't have said nothing," the President said, adding that the Administration had "done pretty well by him."

Eisenhower cited a Gallup poll of Republicans which had shown Nixon running behind Warren, 11 per cent to 14 per cent, and he quoted from another poll that showed Nixon trailing Adlai Stevenson. "He apparently had not seen a later poll," Nixon would write, "taken after his heart attack, in which I had run ahead of Warren and in which Stevenson's lead over me had been greatly cut down. . . . It occurred to me that a pretty effective job had been done on him concerning my recent weak showing in the polls."

Then, almost casually, the President suggested that Nixon accept a Cabinet post in the new Administration, offering him any position he wanted with the exception of Attorney General (because of the Vice President's lack of practical legal experience) and Secretary of State (which he had felt should go to Under Secretary of State Herbert Hoover, Jr.). Secretary of Defense, the President said, would be an excellent Cabinet office for Nixon—and one from which he could prepare himself for the Presidential election of 1960. Obviously, it did not seem to enter Eisenhower's mind that his offer to Nixon would have value only if he intended to run again. Nixon quickly interjected that "in making your decision as to whether you should or shouldn't run, I don't want you to feel that I have to be the candidate for Vice President." Eisenhower answered that it would hurt the ticket if Nixon were "jettisoned." Perhaps realizing the implications of what he had been saying, the President added reassuringly, "There has never been a job I have given you that you haven't done to perfection as far as I'm concerned. The thing that concerns me is that the public does not realize adequately the job you have done. I just can't understand how any sane-minded person could choose Stevenson over you."

No decisions were made at that meeting. The President simply told Nixon that "I want you to come in from time to time to discuss the situation with regard to yourself. We might have to initiate a crash program for building you up." He also said that in the days to come he would be having conferences on the political situation to which Nixon would not be invited since he would be the subject under discussion.

Early in January of 1956, after a vacation in Florida during which he fished and talked politics with his brother Milton, Eisenhower finally made up his mind to run. He almost said as much to reporters at his second post-coronary press conference. During that period, the President reverted half a dozen times to his offer of a Cabinet post for Nixon, pointing out that no Vice President since Martin Van Buren had ever been elected President. Eisenhower was always casual—Nixon has said, in a non-pejorative way, that Eisenhower was "complex and devious"—and Nixon always answered, "You tell me what you want me to do and I'll do it. I want to do what is best for you." To which the President would demur: "No, I think we've got to do what's best for you."

This, said an understating John Foster Dulles, was "a very difficult time for Nixon." There were reports that Sherman Adams and the White House entourage, including Jim Hagerty, who had easy access to the President's ear, were attempting to convince Eisenhower that Nixon should be forced off the ticket. They could not attack Nixon frontally because the President would not permit it, and because Nixon had powerful allies in Republican leaders like Thomas Dewey and Senator Styles Bridges. Instead, they damned with faint praise or protested that they had Nixon's best interests at heart—sentiments they demonstrated by whispering to White House correspondents that the President was seriously thinking of dropping his Vice President.

On February 29 Eisenhower announced that he would seek a second term but refused to discuss Nixon's future. At his March 7 press conference the President converted an open secret into an open fact. He admitted, in answer to a reporter's question, that he had told Nixon to "chart his own course." The implication seemed obvious, and that was how Nixon saw it when he received the report of the President's statement.

"The impression I got," Nixon has written, "was that he was really trying to tell me that he wanted me off the ticket. I told Vic Johnston, chief of staff of the Senate Campaign Committee who was in my office at the time, that the only course I could properly take under the circumstances was to call a press conference the next day and announce that I would not be a candidate for Vice President. . . . It seemed to me that it was like the fund controversy all over again. But *then* Eisenhower had not known me well and had every justification for not making a decision . . . until all the facts were in. Now he had had an opportunity to evaluate my work over the past three years, and particularly during the period after the heart attack. If he still felt, under these circumstances, that he wanted me on the ticket only if I insisted on seeking the post, I concluded he should have someone else in whom he had more confidence as his running mate." (When I reproached him for even considering withdrawing from politics, Nixon answered, "But what would you do if you were told by the President of the United States that by running for the Vice Presidency, you would be hurting your country and your party?")

When Leonard Hall and Jerry Persons heard of Nixon's intention to bow out, they rushed to the Capitol. Nixon told them that he had been offered a partnership in a New York law firm that would give him an annual income of more than $100,000—and that he intended to take it. A Cabinet post was out of the question, he said. It would leave him with no influence, no political base. "I would have been like Henry Wallace if I had taken the Cabinet job," he later remarked. To me he said, "I know that as a member of the Cabinet, I'd be a sitting duck for every possible kind of attack. I would be in an appointive, rather than an elective, office and therefore completely vulnerable. It's a question of either/or—remain Vice President or get out of politics." To Persons and Hall he said bitterly of Eisenhower, "It's up to him if he wants me. I can only assume that if he puts it this way, this must be his way of saying he would prefer someone else."

"That's not what he meant at all," Hall answered. He and Persons pleaded that Nixon put off making any decision, at least until the air had cleared. They argued that the statement he planned to make would split the Republican Party down the middle and guarantee a Democratic victory in November. Nixon agreed to wait, though he knew that he would be in a political limbo until his future course had been settled.

Meanwhile other forces were at work. Within a Republican Party fed up by Sherman Adams and the manner in which he had shut party workers from all the benefits accruable in the Administration, there was an uproar. High-ranking Republicans wrote or called the Vice President, vowing to sit on their hands in November if he withdrew. Friends called him to assail Eisenhower and his "ingratitude" for Nixon's labors in the Administration vineyard, particularly during the trying period after the heart attack.

Sherman Adams, who had conceived of the Cabinet-post substitute, found himself on the defensive and barricaded himself in his office. When Nixon was not scheduled as a speaker before a conference of Republican women, they complained loudly. He was rushed up to New York, receiving a tremendous ovation that became even more vociferous when Helen Hayes introduced him as "that wonderful, attractive, honest, and good Dick Nixon." Len Hall publicly reiterated his support.

The clincher came in New Hampshire on March 13, 1956. To prove that Nixon would not be a drag on the ticket, Senator Bridges had passed the word in his home state of New Hampshire that a write-in vote was important. That night, Nixon was having dinner with Alice Longworth. She suggested that they turn on the radio to hear the returns. But Nixon, unaware of what was happening, said he was not interested. How could he know that 22,200 people in New Hampshire—the first state to hold its primary election—had written in his name. This was 500 more votes than the number received by Estes Kefauver, the Democratic Presidential aspirant, whose name was printed on the ballot. The following day the "dump Nixon" campaign should have ended when Eisenhower told his press conference, "I am very happy that Dick Nixon is my friend. I am very happy to have him as an associate in government. I would be very happy to be on any political ticket on which I was a candidate with him."

This was not categorical enough, however, and speculation still filled the air. On April 26 the President contributed to it by telling the press that Nixon "hasn't given me any authority to quote him, any answer that I would consider final and definite." It was clear to Republican leaders that if Eisenhower and Nixon continued to hold stubbornly to conditions previously taken—the President that he awaited Nixon's word, the Vice President that it was up to Eisenhower to decide—the Republican Party might be seriously hurt. Once again, Len Hall journeyed to Nixon's office. He pointed out that the President wanted him but that the first gesture would have to be made by Nixon. The President, after all, could not be expected to bend. When Hall left, Nixon—as in every crisis the man alone—shut himself off from phone calls, visitors, even his staff.

When he emerged, his decision had been made. He phoned the White House for an appointment with Eisenhower for that afternoon.

To the President, Nixon said that he had refrained from declaring his intentions because he did not wish to be on the ticket if Eisenhower did not want him. But since he had been assured that this was not the case, he had come to let the President know that he would be "delighted" to continue as Vice President.

"Fine," said the President, smiling, and he summoned his press secretary. "The Vice President was sitting there," Hagerty recalls. "The President and Dick had big grins on their faces. The President said, 'Jim, Dick just told me he would be happy to be on the ticket, and he has made up his mind that he would like to run with me.' Adams came in and we later saw Persons. We told them. The President said to me, 'What do you think we ought to do on the announcement?' I didn't have to think long about that. 'Why not let Dick go out and say it?' I replied. The President said, 'Jim, you go with him and after he finishes his announcement, you say to the press I was delighted to hear this news from the Vice President.'"

That was the end of it for Adams, Hagerty, and others of the Eisenhower team. The President had spoken and they bowed to his wishes. To do anything else would have smacked of presumption and disloyalty. But Harold Stassen, the Administration's "Secretary of Peace"—whose efforts at placing the crown on his own head were producing diminishing returns—decided to assume the role of kingmaker instead. After June 8, when the President's painful but not overly serious ileitis operation placed a moratorium on domestic politics, Stassen could do little. But with each passing hour Nixon's hold on the Vice Presidential nomination grew stronger, and Stassen became desperate.

On July 20, the day on which the President was to leave for a meeting in Panama of Inter-American Chiefs of State, Stassen visited Eisenhower to ask for permission to press the candidacy of Governor Christian Herter of Massachusetts. The President noncommittally told Stassen that he was free to do what he wanted and that he himself could not dictate to a convention that had not yet nominated him. Stassen assured the President that he would not openly push the Herter Vice Presidential candidacy before he had spoken to Nixon, Len Hall, and other party leaders—a promise he forthwith broke.

On July 23, Stassen called a press conference at which he made public a "poll" purporting to show that an Eisenhower-Nixon ticket would get only 45.7 per cent of the vote, whereas an Eisenhower-Herter ticket would receive 53 to 58 per cent of the national vote. (In rebuttal Senator Bridges released his own poll. It showed Eisenhower-Nixon with 54.3 per cent, Eisenhower-Herter with 25.7. In fact, the Eisenhower-Nixon ticket topped 57 per cent in November.) And Stassen assured the press and public that the President "will be pleased to have Chris Herter on the ticket." To the uninformed, this gave the Presidential imprimatur to the push. The story broke on the last day of the Panama meeting, taking the play away from Eisenhower and infuriating members of his staff. The "dump Nixon" movement came to life once more—and Nixon, not knowing what had transpired between Eisenhower and Stassen, was plunged into gloom and doubt.

For reasons never disclosed, Stassen persisted in his attempts at embarrassing the President, stating that he would drop the battle against Nixon if he were publicly asked to do so by Eisenhower. His support, small to begin with, was melting away rapidly, leaving only Governor Knight of California and New York's Attorney General Jacob Javits among the reasonably prominent sponsors. Four days before the Republican Convention, however, Herter announced that he would not allow his name to be placed in nomination. From that point on the Stassen *Putsch* ground slowly to a halt. Herter nominated Nixon, and Stassen—ordered to do so by the Republican leadership—delivered one of the seconding speeches.

But Nixon's time of triumph was short. He was in San Francisco, moving from delegation to delegation in the pre-convention jockeying, when he received word from La Habra, California, where his parents lived, that Frank Nixon, seventy-seven years old, had partially ruptured an abdominal artery and seemed near death. At his father's bedside Dick Nixon learned of Stassen's defeat and capitulation. The announcement that Nixon was still the one came from the President. "You heard that President Eisenhower opened his press conference by saying that everyone is praying for you," the Vice President said to his father. "Thank you, and thank him," Frank Nixon answered. When Nixon was unanimously nominated, his father urged him to return to San Francisco for his acceptance speech. Sure that his father was on the mend, Nixon agreed.

"We believe," he told a cheering convention, "that government should be a partner with business and labor, and not a partisan to encourage one to fight another. . . . We believe in human welfare but not the welfare state. We seek social gains, but we reject completely the well-intentioned but mistaken theories of those who would socialize, federalize, or nationalize basic American institutions." It was a philosophy he had expounded throughout his political career. Then a tired and worried Nixon, having faced the carnival uproar of the convention, returned to La Habra. On September 4, after a period of travail during which the Vice President remained at his side, Francis Anthony Nixon died.

Two weeks later, on September 18, the President, Nixon, and the leaders of the Republican Party met for a sendoff breakfast at National Airport in Washington. Eisenhower looked ruddy, fit, and untroubled—fully recovered from his ileitis operation—and he seemed really to enjoy the hoopla, the handshaking, and the applause. ("Look at him," said a reporter. "When he finishes out the next four years as President, he'll probably run for Governor of Pennsylvania.") In marked contrast was Richard Nixon. The death of his father had put the first real lines of age on his face. He looked worn and subdued. Behind him were five days spent at the Mayflower Hotel, days in which he slogged away at preparing basic speeches for a sixteen-day swing that would cover thirty-two states. There were tight schedules to work out, people to consult, hundreds of details to arrange.

Personal factors aside, Nixon was fully aware that in many respects the success or failure of the campaign ahead might depend on him. He was, after all, the Administration's only full-time campaigner. And he was bound by conflicting instructions from the President. Just a few days earlier, Eisenhower had told him to "lay

it on, Dick. The time has come to get rough with the opposition."
At the same time the President had given him explicit orders to
campaign on the Republican record and to avoid direct attacks on
the Democrats. Nixon's strategy, therefore, was to take a tough line
on the issues but to abstain from personal attack—if the Democrats
allowed him to do so. In this manner he hoped once more to wipe
out the picture that, accurate or not, the press had painted of him
since 1950. There was a sufficiency of reporters at hand to cover
him—twenty-five, or all that a chartered DC-6B could hold. The
rest of the space was occupied by Vice President and Pat Nixon,
press secretaries Herbert G. Klein and James Bassett, Rose Mary
Woods, Young Republican leader Charles McWhorter, a secre-
tarial staff, files, and a mimeograph machine.

Many of the reporters boarded the plane openly antagonistic,
ready to find fault. Some were as outspoken as Philip Potter of the
Baltimore *Sun*, who frankly stated his dislike of Nixon and swore
that he would make him lose his temper before the campaign was
over. Others had been sent not to report but to pontificate on the
sins and inadequacies of the Vice President, and Dick Nixon was
aware of this. He realized that because Eisenhower was politically
sacrosanct, he himself had to be the whipping boy. "They're afraid
to touch the President," Nixon said, "so they throw the custard
pies at me." Then he added, as if to reassure himself, "You make
friends and enemies in proportion to the energy you display."

With no false modesty Nixon was ready to concede that "Mr.
Eisenhower is the man the people are voting for—not me." His
major function was to revitalize a Republican Party still torn by
the dissensions of 1952 and 1954, seeking an identity less stultifying
than extreme conservative yet sharper than the "modern" Republicans would have, starved of attention by the Sherman Adams stran-
glehold on White House patronage, and bereft of encouragement.
With the possible exception of Len Hall, Nixon knew more Republican leaders, on every level, than anyone else in the country.
A party victory could be won only if precinct workers were spurred
into ringing doorbells and beating the bushes for those who would
ordinarily not vote. It was up to him to give them the impetus.

But the kind of bland campaigning expected of him by the President was hardly the way to stir up the faithful. At his first stop in Indianapolis he handed rhetorical posies to Adlai Stevenson, the Democratic standard-bearer, and had kind words for Mrs. Franklin D. Roosevelt, one of his more persistent critics. In Oregon, Senator Wayne Morse, running for reelection and in trouble with the voters, remained unscathed. Nixon admirers, many of whom had journeyed far to hear him pour it on, were baffled. Republican strategists and friendly reporters told him the campaign was not getting off the ground. The Republican National Committee, in a sweat over the reports it was receiving, put pressure on Nixon, but it refused to take the responsibility of getting Presidential approval for revised tactics. In the tail of the plane Nixon worked on his speeches or strode back and forth, his hands jammed into the pockets of the smoking jacket he wore when not in the public eye. "I'll switch when the President asks me to," he said.

Eventually Nixon felt that the time had come to counter the rising tempo of Democratic attacks. In Spokane, after working until past midnight, he turned and tossed until 5:30 A.M., then sprang out of bed. Writing in longhand on a pad of yellow legal-size paper, he blocked out new and harder-hitting statements. After handing them over to Rose Mary Woods for mimeographing, he sat down at the piano, playing a Brahms Rhapsody and "Rustle of Spring," transposing them to the key of G, in which he is most comfortable. Reporters in the hotel heard Nixon's playing and looked at their watches. It was 7:15 A.M.

Nixon later explained to me that he had no regrets about his early kid-glove approach. "You can't plot out a campaign," he said. "You've got to feel it as you go along." The Democratic opposition felt it, too. Nixon took up its favorite charge of "prosperity for a few" and rebutted it, asserting that the Democratic Party "talks a good game, but in twenty years they were never able to produce prosperity except during or as a result of war." In Minneapolis he jabbed at Stevenson for offering the "old Truman jalopy with a new paint job." In Colorado Springs he called on the voters to "wipe out bitterness and class struggle," which he described as the Democratic legacy. Though accentuating the negative, he did not overlook the positive, promising that with a Republican Congress the Eisenhower Administration would usher in a four-day week without loss of productivity. "We will do this," he said, "by unleashing the research facilities of our scientists and technicians. . . . Backbreaking toil and mind-wearying tension will be left to machines and electronic devices." For these words Nixon was accused of demagogy, and he left the four-day week alone after that.

In all, Nixon traveled forty-two thousand miles, covered thirty-six states, made close to two hundred speeches, and held innumerable public and private conferences. It was not unusual for him to campaign the clock around. For example, on one campaign swing he arose at 4:30 A.M. in St. Petersburg, Florida, flew to Grand Rapids, Michigan, for two meetings, on to Milwaukee for speeches, ceremonies, and an appearance at Marquette University, and ended up in Hartford, Connecticut, at 4:30 the following day.

In Salt Lake City, after a stop in Arizona's 140-degree heat, Nixon was hoarse and flushed. Dr. Michael Todd, the trip physician who had been treating members of the press for virus infections, warned the Vice President that he should not speak that night. Nixon insisted that he would appear at the Rainbow Randevu as scheduled. The official explanation of his condition at the time was that he had a slight cold. But when Nixon got up to speak—from a garish bandstand decorated with blow-up photos of Xavier Cugat, Cab Calloway, Gene Krupa, and other band leaders —it was clear that whatever ailed him was more than "slight." His eyes were fever bright, and he could speak only with great effort. After every few sentences he was forced to clear his throat painfully. His hands clutched the lectern as he swayed slightly. The next day he would say, "I guess I've made about five thousand speeches in my life. The one last night was probably the toughest. Halfway through I thought I couldn't make it."

As Nixon spoke, his inflamed throat sprayed with cortisone and pontocaine, Dr. Todd crouched just below the bandstand, surrounded by photographers and reporters, fearful that Nixon might collapse. Pat Nixon sat through the speech, a fixed smile on her face, never once taking her eyes off her husband. But after finishing his speech, Nixon remained on stage while "Ike girls" paraded, a quartet sang, and the interminable business of introducing local politicians went on. Returning to the hotel, he was put to bed by Todd, who intravenously administered achromycin and antihistamines. Nixon, however, refused to relax. Between 11 and 12, he dictated to his secretary, and he was up the next morning at 7:15.

Reporters by then were clamoring for a medical report, and Dr. Todd told a midnight press conference: "The Vice President has influenza with laryngitis. If he were a private patient, I would put him to bed for three or four days. But Mr. Nixon is insistent on carrying out the job. I advised him not to speak tonight. I guess he has what we used to call in the service the 'old crud.' " A reporter laughed and Todd grinned. "I don't mean what *you* would call the crud," he said. The following day, weak from antibiotics, Nixon appeared at a luncheon meeting in Oklahoma City. He was under strict orders not to say a word—and Pat had been coached to make her maiden political speech. (It lasted exactly one minute.) But when she had finished, the Vice President struggled to his feet and spoke for sixteen minutes. For several days, his voice was hoarse and he needed cortisone to make speaking possible. When asked how he felt, his stock answer was, "I frankly didn't know people were interested in the Vice President's health."

In Nashville, Nixon realized that he needed a haircut. He stopped the motorcade a few blocks from his hotel, near a small barbershop. As he approached it he was surrounded by police and reporters. The proprietor, who doubled as a bookmaker, saw the crowd and the police, and thought it was a raid. He grabbed his coat, running out the back way. The Chief of Police, knowing why the proprietor had ducked out, tried to prevent Nixon from going in. But there was one barber left, and he cut Nixon's hair.

In Houston, Nixon walked into what Southern Democrats had planned as a booby trap: the accusation that he was an honorary member of the National Association for the Advancement of Colored People. At a press conference at the Rice Hotel, a reporter popped the question: Was it true? Yes, said Nixon, he had been elected to honorary membership in 1947. He proceeded from there to a defense of desegregation. The booby trap failed to spring—and the Republicans carried Texas.

In the waning days of the campaign Nixon was called upon to

defend the Eisenhower-Dulles stand on the Suez crisis. Israel had invaded the Sinai Peninsula in a lightning attack, after continuous and brutal provocation, beating the Soviet-equipped Egyptian forces to the punch. The French had moved rapidly to aid the Israelis, but Britain had dragged her feet before entering the conflict to preserve world access to the Suez Canal. The laggard British policy had prolonged a situation that was critical in the extreme and that gave the Soviet Union a chance to mount a propaganda war against the West, taking the world's eyes off the spectacle of communist tanks mowing down workers in the streets of Budapest.

The President's counteraction had been to condemn the Anglo-French landings in Suez, to call on the United Nations for a cease-fire, and to demand the withdrawal of Israeli troops. Nixon's sympathies were with the Israelis. Had he been able to speak for himself, he would have tied the Soviet-inspired depradations of the Egyptians to the rape of Hungary. But as a member of the Eisenhower team he was bound to support its position and to act as its spokesman. Just before he was to speak in Hershey, Pennsylvania, on November 2, Nixon received a wire from the Secretary of State. In it Dulles spelled out in detail a paragraph to be inserted in Nixon's speech.

That night, Nixon read it as if it had been his own formulation: "In the past, the nations of Asia and Africa have always felt we would, when the pressure was on, side with the policies of the British and French governments in relation to the once colonial areas. For the first time in history, we have shown independence of Anglo-French policies toward Asia and Africa which seemed to us to reflect the colonial tradition. That declaration of independence has had an electrifying effect throughout the world." It was a lame explanation for a policy that saved Egypt from attack and ignored the colonialism of the Soviets—and it heralded a policy that planted the seeds of a new Middle East war that would erupt in June of 1967. But, as Eisenhower had said, Nixon was a "good soldier"— and after all, only the Vice President of the United States.

Before the November 6 day when Eisenhower received the greatest plurality in American history, Nixon was drawing larger crowds than the Democratic Presidential candidate—repeating his performance of 1952. Among the press corps he had won over reporters like Earl Mazo of the New York *Herald Tribune,* once highly critical, who could now say that "Mr. and Mrs. Nixon have been gracious, kind, and friendly. Leaving politics aside, they are a couple of decent human beings." Paul Healy of the New York *Daily News* praised the "tremendous guts Nixon is showing." And Ludwig Caminita, Jr., a Washington public relations counsel, polled 114 correspondents who covered the candidates, reporting that they "praised Nixon personally as cooperative and likable." This, Caminita said, was the consensus, even including those who "declared that they still do not like him politically and had (past tense) disliked him personally."

In the years ahead there would be a marked recidivism among some of those correspondents, of course, but for Nixon the feeling that the press liked him, however temporarily, meant a great deal. But of more importance to Nixon were the President's words to him: "Well done."

13

The Press and Nixon

THE 1956 campaign was for Richard Nixon no more, no less traumatic than those which preceded it. There was one difference. In 1950, with the liberal community still smarting from the Hiss Case, Nixon had expected the attacks against him. In 1952 and 1954 he could accept what was said of him—and how it was said— as a continuation of previous enmities. But in 1956 he had expected some carryover of the approbation he had enjoyed for his circumspection and good taste during President Eisenhower's heart attack. He could not understand why the press and the opposition continued to see him as a kind of Jekyll and Hyde—the enormously well-informed and conciliatory Vice President and the gouging political in-fighter. He could recognize that Nixon in his Capitol hideaway and Nixon on the campaign trail were not the same person. He could concede that his use of phrases in the heat of battle, like "the Acheson College of Cowardly Containment," transgressed the exact truth. But this was political hyperbole, for the most part less lethal than the shotgun blasts aimed at him.

His feeling, therefore, that he was more sinned against than sinning had an objective basis. The passions he aroused derived from a visceral reaction in those who had been proven wrong about

Alger Hiss, about his "secret fund," about communism, and about the double standard employed by his foes. But this did not explain it all, and it did not give him the explanation he sought. He was half aware that his flawless performance on the platform encouraged the suspicion that he was glib even when he was speaking from deep convictions. He had, to some degree, accepted what friends such as myself told him—that one segment of the American public could no more cotton to an introverted political man than another segment could warm to the superciliousness of an Adlai Stevenson.

In an effort to find the key to the reactions of otherwise sensible men, he commissioned me after the 1956 campaign to prepare an analysis of what Stevenson and Estes Kefauver, the Democratic Vice Presidential candidate, had said of him. This was a relatively simple task, requiring little more than the compilation of the Democratic candidates' more offensive quotations and a reasonably broad knowledge of Nixon's past. But it could not supply the answers he was seeking. It did not touch on the role of the press in creating the anti-Nixon mythology, and since he lacked any real knowledge of how reporters work, he remained a baffled and hurt man. A good social psychologist might have told him that Americans need a villain, even as they yearn for a hero, and that he had been cast as Mr. Hyde because few reporters bothered to understand him.

Even as a revolution devours its own children, so the press feeds off its own excesses. A good reporter, before he embarks on an assignment, usually digs back into the clips—and because the press has an almost reverential attitude toward almost anything in cold print, these journeys into the past are more often than not taken down the primrose path. Once a myth has been set down on paper, it crops up repeatedly in the writings of latecomers, who must demonstrate that they are well-informed and not to be taken in by anything in the actual man which runs counter to what is filed away in the newspaper morgue envelopes.

Smarting over past discomfitures and annoyed by its inability to fit Nixon into its own Procrustean bed, the press might have muttered darkly but unconvincingly. It had at hand, however, a document that supplied it the chapter and verse to substantiate amorphous prejudice—a two-part series for *The New Republic* that appeared in its issues of September 1 and 8, 1952, written by Ernest Brashear of the Los Angeles *Daily News*. If this seems like a simplistic explanation, a search of the record will give it weight. For the major false statements, misrepresentations, and destructive imputations found in the vast literature of the anti-Nixon press can be traced back directly or indirectly to *The New Republic* pieces.

The litany was all there for every harried reporter under pressure of a deadline. And with each repetition the picture of Nixon as political beast became more starkly delineated. The same allegations, quotations, and anecdotes, when repeated by the large-circulation periodicals, acquired a credibility that word-of-mouth rumor could never achieve. By that incestuous interaction which characterizes the press, the writer quoted would find authority in the words of the writer who had quoted him. This is sometimes cynically called "research," but it is in fact one of the major ills of the newspaper business, and one to which every participant in American journalism has at one time or another succumbed.

Brashear, of course, had his own reasons for writing as he did. He worked for an anti-Nixon newspaper, and if his own method were applied to him, it could be said that his bread and butter depended on it. This is, of course, as irrelevant as the motives that prompted a respectable liberal journal like *The New Republic* to publish Brashear's fictionalizing. More important is the substance of the pieces.

To make the point that Nixon was a political opportunist, Brashear wrote that when Nixon was approached by the Committee of One Hundred, which launched him into politics in 1946, he answered the question of political affiliation by saying that "he guessed he was a Republican because he voted for Tom Dewey in 1944." This made a good anecdote, but the easily ascertainable fact was that Nixon had registered in the Republican Party on his return to Whittier after getting his law degree at Duke, and that he had campaigned for Wendell Willkie in 1940.

Describing the 1946 congressional campaign, Brashear charged

that Jerry Voorhis had been "inveigled into a series of debates"—
a pretty shabby way of acting. But here again the facts spoke
somewhat differently. Nixon challenged Voorhis to debate and
Voorhis accepted. But more important than the debates in de-
feating Voorhis, according to the Brashear testament, was a telephone campaign: " 'This is a friend of yours, but I can't tell you
my name,' the unknown voice would say. 'I just wanted you to
know that Jerry Voorhis is a communist.' Sometimes the caller
would hang up, at other times a quotation or misquotation would
be given to support the claim. It worked."

This fable of reprehensible conduct was born in 1952, six years
after the fact. The authority for this charge was "many observers"
—none named—all of whom had waited for years in utter silence
before telling their horrendous tale. The fullest and most authori-
tative source of information on the 1946 campaign had been a book
by Jerry Voorhis. In it he had mentioned telephone calls, though
not anonymous ones, in which the caller argued that Voorhis had
done little for his district—a fact that the defeated candidate freely
acknowledged.

The theme that Richard Nixon was not a sincere anti-communist
but a cynical manipulator of people's fears got its first extended
treatment in *The New Republic* series. To make it stick, Brashear
had to create a new image for Helen Douglas, Nixon's 1950 opponent, whom he transmogrified into "one of the most effective
enemies of the Communist Party." Researching newspapermen,
reading this, had no way of knowing that Mrs. Douglas' "effective"
fight had nevertheless won her the endorsement of *The Daily
Worker*. She had voted 354 times with the party-lining Vito Marcantonio, but to the chronicler, this was an indication that she
merely followed in the footsteps of other Congressmen "who
fought Hitler abroad and inflation at home." The point was driven
home with the sentence: "That, said Nixon, made her a Stalinist
at heart"—something Nixon had never said.

Certain charges concerning Nixon's voting record had been
thoroughly laid to rest during the campaign, but *The New Republic*
exhumed them as obvious "fact." Mrs. Douglas, Brashear wrote,
"even pointed out that Nixon voted with Marcantonio against

financial aid to Korea on January 19, 1950, just six months before the North Korean aggression, a vote interpreted in Moscow as confirmation that Congress would allow the Republic of Korea to be invaded and overrun." As a Los Angeles labor reporter, Brashear might not have known that the Korean aid bill was defeated because it did not include help to the Chinese government on Taiwan, or that passage of a more inclusive bill shortly thereafter would certainly have disabused the Moscow whose mind he was so easily reading.

To introduce and sustain a thesis that Nixon had millions to spend in 1950, Brashear, presumably the reporter on the scene, cited as authority that Ananias among columnists, Drew Pearson. "Nixon," Pearson had written just before the 1950 election, "has so much money that he even puts billboards across the border in Mexico"—a statement that brought smiles to Californians when it was originally published. Less whimsical was the Pearson accusation that an anonymous "editor of a newspaper on the outskirts of Los Angeles tells how he was offered $1,000 in Nixon advertising if he would come out editorially for Nixon. He refused . . ." and then, man of principle that he undoubtedly was, wrote not a word of the proffered bribe in his paper.

The Brashear method in dealing with Nixon relied heavily on red-flag words and ideas. Mrs. Douglas, he said, had favored Federal ownership of offshore oil lands. (Most Californians favored state control of these invaluable reservoirs.) But "Nixon favored the oilmen's stand for state ownership, a stand *based on the simple truth that a state legislature is far easier and cheaper to bribe than the Federal government.*" Mrs. Douglas believed in government ownership of the power utilities. "Nixon, *and the big utilities,* preferred the private distribution of power *and the higher, profit-compounding rates.*" (Emphasis added in both quotations.) It would have been enough to say that Mrs. Douglas leaned toward a socialist approach, that Nixon was a private enterpriser. But a record was being made, and it was necessary to show that Nixon was "a tool" of the fat cats.

To "prove" this point, Brashear cited an instance in which Nixon "was welcomed at the home of Kyle Palmer, Political Editor of the tory Los Angeles *Times*." Among the guests were a banker, several industrialists, *Times* Publisher Norman Chandler, and a group of film executives. The average reader would never know from this list that Darryl Zanuck was a battling liberal and ardent admirer of Franklin D. Roosevelt or that the movie colony, with few exceptions, was consistently left of center. Brashear was interested only in the bank accounts of the guests, and in the kind of "guilt by association" that *The New Republic* deplored at other times.

To belabor two articles in a magazine of limited circulation might seem like an exercise in futility. But if *The New Republic* series was a seedbed for future and widespread attitudes about Nixon, then it assumes an importance of far greater magnitude. And it can be stated incontrovertibly that the material *The New Republic* unveiled turned up in news stories, magazine articles, books, and pamphlets in all the years that followed. In the 1956 campaign, when it was open season on Nixon, Democratic speech writers seized on the anti-Nixon mythology, now widely disseminated, further etching their version of the Nixon image on the minds of voters. *Collier's*, the Washington *Post*, *Harper's*, *Life*— to name but a few—absorbed the fabrications and misrepresentations of *The New Republic* series by a kind of unconscious osmosis.

In the 1956 campaign, for example, Senator Kefauver's speech writers leaned heavily on this material. "Kefauver said Nixon showed in his 1946 race against Jerry Voorhis that 'he played hooky the day they read the Constitution' in his school," Richard L. Lyons reported in the October 18 Washington *Post*. "He said the voters in Voorhis' district received phone calls saying he was a communist and that businessmen favorable to Voorhis were warned their bank credit would be canceled if they backed him openly." But even the more moderate, the "reasoned," criticism of Nixon picked up the old slurs, perhaps unconsciously, from the butcher-paper pages of *The New Republic*. Richard Rovere, in *Harper's* of September 1955, tried to sustain the point that Nixon was interested in strategy rather than policy by referring to the alleged remark that "he guessed" he was a Republican. Americans for Democratic Action, in a widely circulated pamphlet, drew heavily from the series.

The cumulative effect of the attacks on Nixon was to diminish him even in the eyes of politicians who did not accept the validity of the charges against him. That these things could be said about Nixon made people wonder; it made them say, "I don't know why I don't like him, but . . ." And this, in turn, encouraged his opponents to say things about him that they would never have said about other men in public life, thereby diminishing him further. "In 1956," Stewart Alsop wrote for the July 12, 1958, *Saturday Evening Post*, "it was an essential part of Adlai Stevenson's campaign strategy to drive Nixon to extremes by brutal attacks on his integrity." Had this been his strategy in the case of any other politician, with the exception of Joe McCarthy, he would have had a chilly reception at his club and some pointed words from editorial writers. The debasement of Nixon, in newspapers and magazines, was a precondition for Stevenson's 1956 rhetoric.

In this ambience Stevenson could tell a laughing audience the story of the girl who "climbed the ladder of success, wrong by wrong. Well, Mr. Nixon has, too, by slyness, slickness, and slander" —and add, in another speech, that "this man's very political existence is a satire that mocks the aspirations of a democratic government in America." Yet it was Nixon, not Stevenson, who was called by the St. Louis *Post-Dispatch* a "Past Master of Innuendo." Stevenson could state flatly that "Nixon voted to deprive nearly a million workers of the protection of the minimum wage law," though no bill to do this had ever been introduced in the Congress, and cast aspersions on Nixon's integrity. Stevenson could, though he had just misrepresented the Pope's position on atomic testing, accuse Nixon of using "the poison pen, the anonymous phone call, and hustling, pushing and shoving." He could praise Senator Kefauver, "our Vice Presidential candidate," for "not having to turn over any new leaf"—an obvious reference to fatuous press talk about the "new Nixon"—and boast that "with him honor and truth are not tactics but characteristics," yet remain silent on Kefauver's record of opposition to anti-lynching legislation and other civil rights measures.

Kefauver himself could say that Nixon had "displayed a magnificent disregard of the Bill of Rights" and find justification for this in the fact that the Vice President had presided over the Senate when Joe McCarthy held the floor. He could also, presumably in the interests of ethical debate, charge that "Dick Nixon is trying to get into the White House on false premises, a false front, and a false face . . . the man who has voted against everything liberal . . . [with] a minstrel's disregard for the facts." He could mockingly welcome back the "new Nixon" to "the community of civilized men, of men who believe that it is possible in this democracy of ours to differ politically without assassinating each other"—and a month later describe his opponent as "the chosen instrument of the worst reactionaries in the United States." Harry S. Truman, always bigger than life and more irrepressible, could say grandiosely that Nixon "voted wrong every time, and it's the votes that count, not the talk—especially with a fellow who treats the truth as lightly as Mr. Nixon does." And Governor George Leader of Pennsylvania could suggest, when speaking in Oakland within sight of Alcatraz, that Nixon be sent to an "offshore island"—then make his point more obvious by wondering what there was about the Vice President that made people "think of Alcatraz as a retirement home for him."

These expressions of political animosity, however, only sketch in part of the picture. For the role of the press in Nixon's case was not solely in giving currency to the mythology of his past. Newspapermen contributed perhaps even more by cleaving to a double standard. Whatever Nixon said or did, it was examined carefully for rebuttal. The Vice President was, in fact, bird-dogged by eager reporters whose "interpretive" stories were often not much more than a polemic. If there was the slightest hint of a possible derogatory angle, the press was on the scent immediately. And whatever it dug up was never allowed to be forgotten. It became an endless process.

This might have been in the great tradition of American journalism, had it applied to all comers. But when Truman said that Nixon "voted wrong every time," there was no rash of stories twitting the former President by listing the number of votes Nixon had cast for Truman legislation. Nixon's opponents were spared this kind of scrutiny. Their words were reported, but the factual background was never cited to show that they might have been

somewhat cavalier with the facts. During the "secret fund" episode, a host of reporters tracked down every lead, no matter how
inconsequential, in the hope that they would discover a disreputa-
ble angle. But the newspapers yawned when Stevenson's *two* funds
—one of them of $100,000, contributed by contractors doing busi-
ness with the State of Illinois at the time Stevenson was Governor
—were discovered. A handful of newspapers printed the $100,000
fund story, but Stevenson's refusal to comment on it was not
challenged.

Method and treatment were the difference in the press approach
to Nixon and to his opponents. Nixon was kept perpetually on the
firing line, but the Stevensons and the Kefauvers could lash out
with impunity in what approximated certainty that the press would
not call them to task. Among his friends Nixon could hold forth
in controlled anger at his persecution. But he had learned from
Murray Chotiner, many years before, that complaining about the
press was self-defeating, complaining to publishers suicidal. Nixon
could only grin and bear it. He did not even make a little list of
those reporters who tried so hard to undercut him. Today, some
of them are still working the White House—and are treated with
the same courtesy as that handful of pro-Nixon newspapermen
still on the beat.

14

The Second Term

IN 1957 Richard Nixon could look back at his combative period and forward to the remaining years of the Eisenhower Administration with the realization that he had crossed a great divide in his career. Though he evaded all discussion of his possible candidacy in the 1960 Presidential election, he knew that substantial elements within the Republican Party—and President Eisenhower himself—considered him the heir apparent.

His every word and act was scrutinized by the organized punditry of the Washington press corps in this light. His past qualms about continuing in public life were dissipated by a change in Eisenhower's attitude to him, and by the President's obvious determination to invest in him more and greater responsibility in what could only be taken as part of a "grooming" for the Presidency. The somewhat condescending "You're my boy" of Eisenhower's accolade after the "secret fund" controversy had changed to the point at which, by December of 1957, the President could attest "the intimacy of our friendship" in a personal letter to Nixon.

Far more concrete was the memo written to Nixon by the President on September 3, 1957, urging his greater participation in the policy-making process. "My basic thought is that you might find it possible—and intriguing—to be of even more help in our whole governmental program dealing with affairs abroad than you have been in the past," Eisenhower said. "By your extensive travels, you have been of inestimable assistance to the Secretary of State and to me. In addition, you have gained an understanding of our foreign problems that is both unusual and comprehensive." But Eisenhower went beyond a call for Nixon's expertise in foreign affairs. "My belief is that this knowledge and comprehension, supplemented by your special position with one foot in the Executive branch and one foot in the Legislative branch, can be advantageously used to lay out advanced programs and schedules" in such important fields as monetary policy, defense policy, technical and financial foreign aid, trade, diplomacy, and the means to blunt a communist offensive that was to culminate in the Cuban Missile Crisis under President John F. Kennedy.

Nixon's entry into the foreign policy field had been heralded by a speech delivered in the waning days of the first Eisenhower term, on December 6, 1956, in New York. The Vice President used this occasion to put forward one of his own ideas—frequently iterated in the relative privacy of National Security Council meetings—that the time was ripe for a strong diplomatic offensive against the Soviet Union. The brutality of Soviet countermeasures against Hungary's freedom fighters in the 1956 revolt had badly damaged Kremlin prestige, and Nixon was convinced that the United States should exploit this situation fully. Without divorcing himself from the hasty and ill-conceived Dulles policy of forcing an Israeli withdrawal from Suez, the Vice President sought to place in context the words dictated by the Secretary of State, calling for "a declaration of independence" from the British and French. In effect holding out an olive branch, Nixon called for balance in United States relations with Western Europe and with the two allies who had intervened on the Israeli side.

"Americans are traditionally and justly against colonialism," he told me at the time. "But it would be suicidal to forget that in many areas of the world, the choice is not between colonialism and something better, but colonialism and something worse—namely communism." This was a theme that worked its way into public utterances. He wanted to remind the world that however successful the Soviets may have been in crushing Hungary, all the returns were not yet in. "Revolutions," he said, "acquire a certain dynamism. Before the 1917 revolution in Russia, there was the 'failure' of 1905—and one led to the other."

Though Nixon appreciated the President's suggestion that he be entrusted with a wider scope in foreign policy deliberations, he very carefully shunned any kind of titular authority in the field. To accept it would have put him in competition with the Secretary of State, an uncomfortable, self-defeating, and vulnerable position for any Vice President. And since final decisions would never be his, it might hang on his record policies to which he could give support only as a member of the Eisenhower team.

When Eisenhower offered him the Chairmanship of the Operations Coordinating Board, the core of the National Security Council, Nixon refused it. Such a post for him, he told the President, would create more problems than it would settle. As Chairman of the OCB, moreover, he would find himself in the impossible position of reporting to Under Secretaries. And, as he told Eisenhower, his effectiveness to the President, paradoxically, was a function of his anomalous position as Vice President—a position that made it possible for him to confer, advise, and press for action without violating protocol or pulling rank. At the suggestion of Secretary Dulles, therefore, Eisenhower authorized Nixon to "ride herd" on the OCB whenever necessary, but from the privileged sanctuary of his unofficial status.

In his newly assigned role Nixon went to bat for the Foreign Service, much to the surprise of those who remembered his preachments against the State Department during his days as a Representative and a Senator. Every time the department's request for funds came before the Congress there were attempts by the "economy bloc" to reduce the "representation allowance" for the Foreign Service. Called by its critics the "drinking allowance," it provided money for the entertainment that diplomats insisted was a part of their job in dealing with foreign dignitaries. "You don't get anywhere just by sitting in an office and writing handouts," Nixon argued. "In foreign countries you've got to cultivate people—

by having them to dinner, by entertaining. Under present allowance restrictions this is impossible, unless the Ambassador or the
Foreign Service officer has lots of money of his own."

But Nixon also attacked State Department policy in his urgent
calls for sending the best-equipped, best-trained, and most experienced people to the underdeveloped countries—what the department calls "hardship posts"—instead of to the far more pleasant
duty in London, Paris, or Rome. Nixon was convinced, and repeated his views whenever possible, that despite all the anti-
American propaganda, there was a great residue of pro-American
feeling in Asia and Africa. "One of our problems," he told me, "is
that we think in terms of winning over large masses of people.
But in all of North Africa, there are no more than several thousand
people who set the tone of thought and make government policy.
These are the people we must reach by the personal contact of
our best Foreign Service officers."

Late in May of 1957 the Vice President found himself in what
some would have considered the pleasant situation of giving
Harold Stassen, leader of the "dump Nixon" movement in 1956,
his comeuppance. As "Secretary of Peace," Stassen was pushing
for "disarmament" agreements with the Soviet Union. The Stassen
formula for peace was to offer concessions to the Kremlin, and to
pay any price for Kremlin approval. At White House deliberations
discussions were energetic and, in some cases, bitter—and as usual,
Stassen tried to win the day by taking his battle to the press.

Nixon opposed the Stassen proposals, but publicly he tried to
remain on the sidelines so as not to make it seem that he was after
revenge. Behind the scenes, however, he gave strong support to
Deputy Defense Secretary Donald Quarles, leading the Pentagon
opposition to Stassen, Admiral Arthur Radford (Chairman of
the Joint Chiefs of Staff), and Secretary Dulles. The Radford-
Quarles-Nixon-Dulles group within the National Security Council
contended that the Soviets needed disarmament for economic
reasons, that they were far more anxious for negotiation than was
the United States—Ambassador to Russia Charles E. ("Chip")
Bohlen gave unexpected support to this point—and that instead
of supinely offering any and all concessions, we should drive a

227

hard bargain. This, the NSC and the President decided, made more sense than what Stassen was proposing.

Domestically, civil rights was becoming an increasingly important issue, and on this question the Vice President ran into one of the typical reverse plays that make political life so hazardous in Washington. Despite resistance from Minority Leader Knowland and the President's low-key approach, Nixon had committed himself vigorously and at an early date to the enactment of a civil rights bill. Working with Deputy Attorney General Rogers, House Republican Leader Joe Martin, and Representative Kenneth B. Keating of New York, the Vice President pressed for a measure that would give the Justice Department the right to intervene in cases in which the aggrieved parties were too intimidated to initiate civil rights suits. Title III of the Civil Rights Act of 1956, which embodied this principle, seemed destined to pass. At the last moment, however, Lyndon Johnson threw his considerable legislative weight to the side of a "compromise" bill eliminating the clause. A coalition of Southern Senators, Hubert Humphrey, Wayne Morse, and United Auto Workers President Walter Reuther (who actively lobbied against the clause) defeated Title III—and only a rearguard action by the Nixon forces prevented further emasculation of the civil rights law.

While domestic policy wars continued at a "business as usual" pace, new developments in the Soviet Union were occupying an increasing measure of the Vice President's attention. Stalin's death and the slow emergence of Nikita Khrushchev as the most powerful of his successors were beginning to create new problems for the West, without solving any old ones. The change from the cold and calculated depradations of Stalin to the more bland manner of the Kremlin's "collective leadership" was beginning to lure many people into the belief that the Cold War was over and that the Soviet Union was entering into an era of conciliation with the West. This Nixon saw as "far more dangerous in the long run than the Stalin line of bluster and brute force." In opposition to State Department Kremlinologists, who felt that the "collective leadership" would hold together, Nixon believed that the real power lay in the hands of the Communist Party's First Secretary, Comrade Khrushchev.

Nixon also differed with some of his Administration colleagues on the why, the how, and the whither of the then-current convulsions in Soviet Russia. At National Security Council meetings he asserted that sudden humanitarianism in the Kremlin was not responsible for its seeming shift of policy, but rather the internal contradictions of communism were.

"The Soviet system is already overextended," he said to me in July 1957, recapitulating the views he had expressed before the NSC. "Whatever aid they give the neutral nations, they must take from their own people. A sound American policy would keep crowding the communists, would keep them off balance. And we need not fear the effect of any 'easing of tensions' between the East and the West. The death of Stalin has unleashed the power of public opinion in Russia. There is a clamor for consumer goods, for an easier life than communism prescribes for its people. Let's take advantage of this. But I'll never forget, and I hope no one in this country forgets either, that Khrushchev, Molotov, or Stalin may differ in tactics, but the strategy remains the same—to destroy us."

On October 4, 1957, a new dimension was added to the debate over the Soviet Union. On that day Moscow announced that it had sent a satellite into orbit around the earth. The popular American reaction was one of chagrin and apprehension. The scientific community, hag-ridden by its antagonism to American society and still scarred by its opposition to the enterprise that had led to the development of the hydrogen bomb, saw in the Soviet achievement proof positive of American inadequacies in education, of Soviet superiority. By a wrench of logical thought they used the Soviet Sputnik as Exhibit A in their brief against the halfhearted security imposed on scientific work in the area of national defense.

With equal obtuseness the Administration family—from Sherman Adams down—belittled the Soviet advance. The military, zealous as always in its demands for increased appropriations, seized the opportunity to clamor for more money. The newspaper Monday-morning quarterbacks cried havoc and placed the blame on President Eisenhower's doorstep. This made it a political issue, and politics was Nixon's major field of competence in the Administration.

Convinced that Sputnik was not a gauge of Soviet capabilities, compared with those of the United States, Nixon began digging into the subject. In Pentagon Intelligence reports he discovered that the Soviets had been working on space technology since 1946. The United States, on the other hand, had starved the space program, allocating a handful of millions to it, until well into 1953—the first year of the Eisenhower Administration. The first Sputnik, therefore, had been on the drawing boards eight years earlier, while the United States frittered away its money on the clumsy B-36 bomber, the crowning defense achievement of the Truman Administration, which was eventually scrapped. The Soviets, moreover, had focused all their efforts on one heavy-thrust rocket, whereas the Pentagon had experimented with a large variety of highly sophisticated—and therefore highly temperamental—ballistic missiles. Simultaneously, the military had tackled and licked three problems corollary to scientific achievement—problems not then solved by the Soviets—production, deployment, and phasing in. The difference between putting a military weapon on the production line, which the Soviets had not done with Sputnik, and making it operational was a giant stride.

As a practical politician, however, Nixon knew that to make these points would seem like alibiing Administration failures. Sputnik, he fully realized, was a major propaganda victory for the communists. But though it was as foolish to overrate the Russians as to underestimate their strength, he warned the nation that "we could make no greater mistake than to brush off this event as a scientific stunt of more significance to the man in the moon than to men on earth." Not knowing the attrition on America's defenses that the Sixties would bring, he told his associates that in the years to come the United States would hold the edge in deterrent power, through its manned aircraft, its nuclear submarines, and the IRBMs, which it could fire from bases throughout the world. (Those bases would be shut down by the Kennedy Administration in return for the Soviet Union's token withdrawal of its missiles from Cuba.) The hydrogen bomb, he noted, had made temporary leads by this or that group of powers an illusory advantage. In nuclear warfare no side could win unless the odds were preponderant.

The outcry over Sputnik gave Nixon a chance to propose once more a stepping-up of economic pressures against the communist bloc. His views, which came into conflict with the traditional approaches of the Treasury and the Budget Bureau, were neither novel nor politically expedient. He urged at Cabinet meetings that the taxing power be used to further the interests of the country, and not, as the Treasury insisted, merely to raise revenue. Therefore, he said, if a spectacular increase in American private investment abroad were necessary to counter the communists, the government should use that taxing power to bring this about. Specifically, he urged, there should be tax advantages to encourage investors to risk their capital in foreign countries. The operative words for Nixon during this period were suggest, urge, assert—not act. He was, after all, only the Vice President.

The situation changed abruptly, and with the drama that seems to mark every phase of Nixon's life, on November 25, 1957, seventeen months after Eisenhower's ileitis operation. Returning to his office late that afternoon, Nixon was told by Rose Mary Woods that Sherman Adams was trying to reach him. "I think it's something serious," she said. When Adams called again, he was his usual abrupt self.

"Dick," he said with no preliminary greeting, "could you come down to the White House right away?"

Ten minutes later, in the West Wing office of the Executive Mansion, Adams told Nixon that the President had suffered a "chill" at Washington's National Airport, waiting the previous day for the arrival of King Mohammed V of Morocco. He had been put to bed, but had gotten up to dictate some letters to his secretary, Ann Whitman. In the midst of this routine work, his speech had become jumbled and he could not express himself clearly.

"How serious is his condition?" Nixon asked.

Adams said that Eisenhower's physician thought that he had suffered a stroke. "We'll know more in the morning," Adams said. "This is a terribly, terribly difficult thing to handle. You may be President in the next twenty-four hours."

Adams had another problem. The President had scheduled a state dinner for King Mohammed. If it were called off, the press would realize that something very serious had befallen the President. Nixon decided that the newspapers should be told only of the President's "chill"—with a brief announcement that he would not be able to attend the dinner or make a television speech in Cleveland the following day. The medical report that evening confirmed the first diagnosis: Eisenhower had suffered an occlusion of a small branch of the middle cerebral artery. It affected his ability to speak, but his reasoning powers were not affected.

Once again, Nixon had been thrust into that limbo of potential power and little authority. In *Six Crises* he would write:

"The tension seemed even greater than at the time of the heart attack. In contrast to the period in 1955, this was the worst time possible, short of outright war, for the President to be incapacitated. It was a time of international tensions. Only a month before, the Soviet Union had put its first Sputnik in orbit, and the whole structure of American military might and scientific technology was under suspicion here and throughout the world. The most immediate problem was a scheduled meeting of the North Atlantic Treaty Organization in Paris on December 16, only three weeks away—a meeting of the NATO heads of State at which President Eisenhower was being counted on to rally our allies. . . .

"On the domestic front, the first signs of the 1958 economic recession were becoming obvious. At the same time, it was equally apparent that we would have to find more money to bolster our missile program. We were having serious budget problems: the fiscal 1958 budget was $71.8 billion, the highest in peacetime history, the government had borrowed up to its legal debt limit, and we had to prepare the fiscal 1959 budget with still higher defense spending. The Administration had also to complete its legislative program, the State of the Union message, the budget and economic messages for the opening of Congress in January. . . . The doctors prescribed sixty days of complete rest from the pressure of his job, if possible, or an extreme lightening of the work load." And they warned that though Eisenhower's stroke was "mild," it might be the first in a series of more damaging attacks.

The nation was far more disturbed by Eisenhower's stroke than it had been by his heart attack. For the issue now was not life or death, but possible mental incapacity even though the President recovered. Friendly newspapers called on Eisenhower to resign, and the New York *Post*, perhaps the most intransigently anti-Nixon daily, editorialized that "the issue is whether the U.S. is to have Richard Nixon as President or no President. We choose Nixon." More seemly papers and columnists—the Washington *Post*, the Providence *Journal*, and Walter Lippmann among them —suggested that Eisenhower delegate his Presidential powers temporarily to Nixon. But Eisenhower was not buying this. Belligerently, in the two weeks following the seizure, he drove himself to carry on as usual. "Either I run this damn show," he said, "or I'll resign." When, because of the blockage in communication patterns, the wrong word would come out, Eisenhower would become furious at himself. Press criticism and editorial suggestions that he was not up to the job hurt him deeply, but he persisted in following through.

During this Presidential crisis, there was no real thought of delegating powers to the Vice President, at least not in the White House. Nixon's main effort was to reassure the President that he had not been incapacitated by the stroke, that his speech was improving and his slips of the tongue were neither important nor noticeable. But both the President and his advisers knew that, after three serious illnesses, the country expected some provision to implement the vague prescriptions of the Constitution. The President therefore set William Rogers, now Attorney General, to work on legislation clarifying and codifying the steps to be taken, should there be need for them. Congress, however, refused to act.

In early February, therefore, Eisenhower called in Nixon and Attorney General Rogers and handed each of them a copy of a four-page letter he had drafted to "Dear Dick." Some minor changes were made and then Ann Whitman typed out the PERSONAL AND SECRET communication, one copy of which went to Nixon, one to Rogers, and one to Dulles. The full text has never been released. The operative paragraphs spelled out Eisenhower's wishes, should he be struck down once more:

"The President and the Vice President have agreed that the

following procedures are in accord with the purpose and provisions of Article II, Section 1, of the Constitution, dealing with Presidential inability. They believe that these procedures, which are intended to apply to themselves only, are in no sense outside or contrary to the Constitution but are consistent with its present provisions and implement its clear intent.

"(1) In the event of inability the President would—if able—so inform the Vice President, and the Vice President would serve as Acting President, exercising the powers and duties of the office until the inability ended.

"(2) In the event of an inability which would prevent the President from communicating with the Vice President, the Vice President, after such consultation as seems to him appropriate under the circumstances, would decide upon the devolution of the powers and duties of the Office and would serve as Acting President until the inability had ended.

"(3) The President, in either event, would determine when the inability had ended and at that time would resume the full exercise of the powers and duties of the Office."

The letter set a historical precedent. It also marked a new high in the relations between a President and his possible successor. And, as Nixon would later remark, "When you read it, you realize President Eisenhower would have made a very fine lawyer. He has a mind that sees all alternatives, all possibilities of a problem. He doesn't have what usually gets a poor lawyer into trouble— the one-track mind. . . . One of the interesting things about the President is that, like many great men in the nation's past, he is a very fine letter writer. He likes to write letters and dictates them fast and well. As far as I am concerned, I can write a good letter if I must, but I dislike to do it. To me it is such a time-consuming job. The chit-chat has to flow smoothly and easily and that is my great difficulty."

If he was not an easy letter writer, Nixon could command a situation by speech. In the shocked and worried moments when it was necessary to tell the nation of the President's condition and to offer reassurance as well, the Vice President had walked into the jaws of the television cameras and the crowd of reporters clustered outside the Executive offices. Speaking calmly, in marked contrast to other members of the Administration, Nixon had stressed that Eisenhower was "fully capable" of making important decisions, that there was "no thought of delegation of any of the President's authority," that the activities of government were continuing "smoothly and on schedule," and that he was confident that "the President will fully recover and that he will resume the duties of his office."

For nearly an hour he answered every question put to him, his jacket whipping in the cold wind, giving a detailed account of what had been done since the President's stroke. "The result," reported *Newsweek* White House correspondent Charles Roberts, "was that by late evening, instead of a picture of fright and confusion, Americans had a picture of government carrying on during a temporary Presidential disability. In the forefront of that picture was Dick Nixon."

Nixon's comportment after the President's occlusion cemented his friendship with Eisenhower. And it further projected the Vice President into the ranks of those who might seek the Presidency when a Constitutional limitation of two terms barred Eisenhower from running again in 1960. There were still hurdles to be negotiated, among them the 1958 congressional campaign. For all his personal popularity, the President had not been able to get Republican Congresses elected in 1954 and 1956. And, as always, Eisenhower left it up to Nixon to carry the brunt of the election campaign. At every turn, however, luck ran against the Republicans.

In July of 1958, for example, as the political cauldron began to bubble, scandal struck the Administration. A House investigating committee discovered that Sherman Adams, the most puritanical of Eisenhower's assistants and the guardian of the Presidential door, had accepted various gifts, including a vicuña overcoat, from Bernard Goldfine, a somewhat shady operator in New England textile mills and real estate. To compound the embarrassment for the White House, Goldfine had listed the cost of these gifts as tax-deductible business expenses. It was further disclosed that Adams had made a number of phone calls from the White House to Executive agencies poking into Goldfine's activities. Appearing before the committee, Adams had admitted the allegations made against him but argued strenuously that he had done nothing illegal. This, of course, missed the point, for it had been Adams among others who had called for Nixon's resignation during the "secret fund" battle, on the ground that a public official must be above the suspicion of suspicion.

Though Nixon's advice was neither requested nor offered during the early days of the Adams disclosure, he watched with concern as the Democrats—happy to see the morality issue, and the talk about Truman Administration scandals, destroyed—made full and justifiable political capital of the White House's discomfiture. He knew that antagonistic newspapers, hoping to compound the Adams scandal, had begun to search for incriminating facts to be used against himself. His association with Adams had been "not close, not friendly, but just correct . . . solely a business relationship." But he took it on himself to lecture a private meeting of Republican State Chairmen. They should stand together instead of acting like "cannibals" by their panic-stricken demands for the resignation of Adams, he told them. "It doesn't take much guts to kick a man when he is down."

In the weeks that followed, as the Democrats gleefully pointed fingers at Adams, paying no mind to Eisenhower's plea that he needed his "chief of staff," the President sought Nixon's advice. Through the early part of August, Eisenhower brought up the subject on three occasions with Nixon, asking him to find a way to resolve it. Late in August, and at the President's prompting, Nixon spoke to Adams. "I indicated," he said, "that while I doubted that it would have a decisive effect on the November election, Republican candidates would feel compelled to turn on him simply to protect themselves. This could only make his position with the President impossible. I also told him that, after the election, he would not be able to carry out his duties as liaison with members of Congress as he had in the past." This advice may have impressed him, but it was not until September 22 that Adams resigned.

The 1958 campaign had begun long before the Adams disclosures had shaken the Republican Party, however. And Nixon had been pondering on the issues and the answers for many months. Early in January of 1958 he had sat with me, summing up his views of the world situation and of his party's chances, amplifying opinions stated in fragmentary fashion in the past, and plotting some new ground.

Did he feel that in its overtures to the free world, then coming fast and furious, the Soviet Union was leading from strength or weakness?

"It would be foolhardy to say that the Russians are leading from weakness," Nixon answered. "But these overtures, the endless letters to the President, indicate that the Russians are less strong than many would have us believe. These moves are carefully planned to reduce the impact of United States actions. . . . If Russia were as strong as she pretends, Mr. Khrushchev would not be pleading for summit meetings. He would be dictating to us."

What difficulties did Nixon believe were afflicting the Soviets?

"The Soviets face political and economic difficulties," Nixon said. "Khrushchev's internal strength stems from the post he holds, First Secretary of the party. But he can hold that post only by showing extraordinary flexibility, anticipating the opposition, and when necessary taking over its program. He deposed Malenkov, then became a Malenkovite on consumer goods. He downgraded Stalin, and became a Stalinist. He is shifting again, as the cross-currents of internal Soviet dissatisfaction indicate. And we must never forget that, though he was able to flatten Hungary, the next satellite explosion may have deep and irreparable effects in Russia itself. The students in Leningrad rioted during the Hungarian crisis. It could be worse next time.

"Economically, the Soviet Union still faces great problems in agriculture and production. All our Intelligence estimates show that this has the Soviet leadership very worried. Some 50 per cent of the Soviet labor force is tied down to the farms and produces less than the country needs. Here in America 10 per cent of the labor force produces far more than we can consume. The push in rocketry and space technology demonstrates a high degree of scientific knowhow and an intensification of scientific effort. We mustn't sell the Russians short on this. But the effort has robbed the Soviet economy of consumer and heavy goods, of the very means of extending the Soviet Union's economic base. In the long run this is dangerous. We are bombarded with statistics of the Soviet rate of economic growth—but these are always revised downward, and they remain percentage figures.

"Popular pressure in Russia can be more of a factor, as Khrushchev himself has shown, than a mechanical analysis of Soviet power would grant. Foreign aid, though more promise than performance in the Soviet Union, is still a considerable drain—and so are the increasing demands from Iron Curtain countries."

How did he think the United States should respond to Soviet pressures?

"Broadly stated, our policy should be double-pronged," Nixon said. "First, we must wage peace in the United Nations, at NATO and other conferences, and in our relations with the Afro-Asian countries. But we must also make it clear that we will not tolerate Soviet expansionism. If we bore in, as we have done, it will joggle the propaganda arm of the Soviet leaders. Whatever the Russians have done to us propagandistically, however, they do not menace the United States in the here and now of world politics. They have done us a service, with their great claims of space prowess, by making the country aware of future pitfalls.

"This Administration is developing a carefully considered strategy, not an improvised program, to prevent the communists from parlaying their temporary propaganda successes into a permanent military breakthrough. Arms and missiles are an essential part of the President's strategic thinking. Putting the powerful American economy to work for us, and keeping it in gear, is another phase of that strategy. To achieve this, we may have to lay away for the time being the hope of a balanced budget. We may also have to relinquish the luxury of interservice rivalries.

"In the foreign policy field, we have already begun to beef up our operations in one of the touchy areas of the world, the Afro-Asian complex, and we must continue to give considerable thought to Latin America. It would be wise to increase development funds and to offer government incentives in the form of tax benefits to private investment in less well-developed areas. Aid by our government, even when there are no strings attached, often has the psychological drawback of seeming like a handout to the rest of the world."

It was being said that the Administration and Secretary Dulles had reversed the Theodore Roosevelt dictum "Speak softly and carry a big stick." Did the Vice President consider this a valid criticism?

"No, I do not," he answered. "The President, Foster Dulles, and this Administration feel that we should carry the big stick of adequate defense, but we have tried to pitch our voices to the size of the room."

Feet up on the desk of his Capitol hideaway, Nixon could hold forth on general issues. But he was also confronted by the very specific problems that he was forced to cope with as *de facto* leader of the Republican Party at Eisenhower's express wish. Recession was creeping across the country, born of bad times in the automobile industry. Six months earlier he had told a meeting of Young Republicans that there were "three sure-fire issues against an Administration in power—failure in foreign policy, leading to war; failure in domestic policy, leading to depression; failure in administration, resulting in corruption." Two Sputniks had raised the spector of the first issue. Corruption would become a factor when the Goldfine case broke through to the nation's front pages. And the recession could well develop into depression, reminding the voters of 1929.

Even as the campaign's fireworks approached, Nixon still resisted treating the current recession as a political issue. "I think I ought to speak out on the recession," he told me. "You see, I know what it means to be born poor." This sense of what the threat of unemployment can mean to a low-income family had led Nixon to alter his role in the Administration. Where he had once been a spokesman for official policy, he now struck out on his own in an effort to influence that policy. Within the official family, a battle was raging. On the one hand, there were those who called on the President to stem the rising tide of unemployment by initiating a vast emergency program of public works. On the other hand, a group headed by Treasury Secretary Anderson counseled a wait-and-see policy.

President Eisenhower tended to side with Anderson, whose arguments were cogent: years of "pump priming" and other Federal projects had failed to pull the nation out of the Great Depression of the 1930s. In the tugging and hauling within the Administration, Republican members of Congress were threatening to jump on the "massive public works" bandwagon. But Nixon rejected both positions. Instead he espoused a cut in consumer taxes, and he took the unusual step of calling a press conference to express his views. "A tax cut," he told reporters, "would be the fastest and surest and best method of providing jobs and stimulating production."* He noted that "WPA, PWA, and what have you" had been tried in the past by Roosevelt, but "after years of emphasis primarily on government spending rather than private enterprise, there were still 10 million unemployed in the early months of 1940." An across-the-board tax cut—"one that will put money in the hands of consumers and purchasers"—was a flexible measure. "If the recession tapers off," he said after the press conference, "we can always restore taxes. But we can't stop work on a billion dollars' worth of half-finished post offices."

When Nixon's remarks appeared in the newspapers the following day, congressional Republicans called Nixon by the dozen to ask if he had been speaking for the White House. Nixon confessed that the idea of a tax cut was his own. Eisenhower, however, believed that either a tax cut or a public works program was premature. And Treasury Secretary Anderson, a former Democrat and a Texan, quickly entered into an agreement with Senator Lyndon Johnson and Speaker Sam Rayburn, binding them and the Administration to bipartisanship on any tax cut. Opposed by the President and outflanked by Anderson, Nixon was forced to retreat. But he had made his point, and the public-works proposals, which had been winning support in the Congress, were blocked. To this extent, Nixon had won—and so had the taxpayer. But

---

* The Kennedy-Johnson Administration would resort to a tax cut, with outstanding success, to avert a recession of its own.

without the tax cut, the country did not pull out of the slump in time to help the Republicans running for office that fall.

As the 1958 campaign hit its stride the absence of Sherman Adams from the White House was a positive help to Nixon. When he struck out on his own, no little voice whispered into Eisenhower's ear. This new state of affairs was best exemplified when the Democratic Advisory Committee—Harry S. Truman, Adlai Stevenson, and Dean Acheson leading—issued a blast at the United States for supporting the Free Chinese in their defense of the strategic offshore islands of Quemoy and Matsu. The committee also called for a plebiscite on Taiwan and accused Dulles of pushing the United States to the "brink of nuclear war." Nixon, campaigning hard in the Midwest, struck back on his own. "In a nutshell, the Acheson foreign policy resulted in war, and the Eisenhower-Dulles policy resulted in peace," he said, referring to Korea. "I challenge every Democratic candidate . . . to state unequivocally whether he favors a continuation of the Eisenhower foreign policy . . . military strength and diplomatic firmness . . . or a return to the Acheson policy of retreat and appeasement." It was a loaded question, but effective.

At his press conference that week the President was asked if he went along with Nixon's attack on the Democrats. "I believe in the long term America's best interests will be best served if we do not indulge in this kind of thing," Eisenhower answered. For the first time Nixon made public answer to what seemed like a Presidential rebuke—and an inexplicable one. "For those of us who have the responsibility of carrying the weight of this campaign," Nixon said with unexpected sternness, "to stand by and allow our policies to be attacked with impunity by our opponents without a reply would lead to inevitable defeat. . . . That is a mistake. I don't intend to make that mistake in this campaign."

The press waited in anticipation for fireworks from the White House—and they seemed to be forthcoming when a Presidential aide said condescendingly, "Dick is so tired he must be punch-drunk." Instead, the President was delighted by Nixon's show of independence, and with no Adams to restrain him fired off a telegram: "CRITICISMS HAVE INVOLVED LEBANON . . . QUEMOY AND

241

MATSU. . . . THESE ACTIONS, WHEN CRITICIZED, SHOULD BE SUPPORTED BY OUR SIDE. NO ONE CAN DO THIS MORE EFFECTIVELY THAN YOU. ALL THE BEST TO YOU. D.D.E." Nixon wound up the controversy by restating his thesis: "There has developed in recent years the unsound idea that hard-hitting debate on the issues which confront the country is somehow wrong." Truman answered him with two words: "Character assassination."

But in a sense Nixon was shadow-boxing. Sputnik, a mild recession, and the Sherman Adams case had changed the national mood. Ineptitude in the Administration, the Adams practice of isolating Republicans from the kind of patronage that keeps a party on its feet, and the Republican propensity for cutting its own throat rather than the opposition's were too big an albatross for the poor organization, lacking of Presidential guidance, to carry. The year 1958 was one of Republican defeat. But among the State and County Chairmen—the men Nixon would need in 1960—the consensus was that he had saved the party from debacle. This was so reflected in the attitude of Republican professionals that *Newsweek*, in its December 22, 1958, issue, could report: "Within the Administration last week the word was 'Clear it with Dick.' "

Perhaps this word reached the Soviet Union. Certainly, the special importance of Nixon within the Eisenhower Administration was not lost on the Kremlin. Neither was the possibility that he might be the next President, with whom it would have to deal. When Soviet Deputy Premier Anastas Mikoyan visited the United States early in 1959, he asked particularly to see the Vice President.* At 4:30 P.M. on January 6 Mikoyan walked into Nixon's formal office in the Capitol. Both men sat down under the tinkling Jefferson chandelier—installed there by Teddy Roosevelt to keep his Vice President awake—warily sizing each other up. For the first few minutes the two men sparred. Mikoyan remarked that Nixon's office was half the size of his own. Nixon replied that people in this country didn't think too much of Vice Presidents. "You are more democratic here," Mikoyan observed. After

---

* This account is based on the official transcript, which I was allowed to see.

some chatter about the difficulties arising out of the two-party system, Mikoyan quipped that Americans like to argue.

"You can do this among your friends," he said. "But how can the two of us work out our problems?" Both men agreed that more could be accomplished by talking than by fighting. Nixon's first thrust was in the form of a remark citing Soviet talk of "peaceful competition" and Soviet boasts that they would overthrow the free governments of the West. Mikoyan then displayed a flexibility that Nixon had never found among other communist officials.

"The Soviet leadership may have made mistakes," Mikoyan said, "but it is intelligent." How could the Soviet Union hope to overthrow the United States? Only a "Don Quixote" would suggest this. There was no cause for American worry, he said softly, though De Gaulle might have some cause for concern, given the big French Communist Party. When Nixon raised the issue of Hungary, Mikoyan gave the stock answer. The Soviet Union had an alliance with the Hungarian government. It was "forced" to act in its own interests. How would the United States feel if a communist government took over in Mexico or Canada?

Mikoyan then shifted to a plea for an end to anti-Soviet propaganda by United States agencies—presumably the Voice of America and the quasi-official Radio Free Europe. This country was spending $100 million annually on propaganda against the communist world. "It is all wasted," he said. The Soviet Union was too strong, and since Stalin's death it had been further strengthened by internal reforms. "Stalin's methods did not help," Mikoyan said. "He was too inflexible in foreign policy." Stalin, moreover, did not read much and isolated himself from people in his later years. "The decisions he made, therefore, had no proper basis." The new leadership was different. It had learned from Stalin's mistakes, and the Soviet people who had suffered much in the past had a right now to a better life.

"The Soviet Union is spending too much on armaments," Mikoyan told Nixon. "This is money lost." But he added, with an implied threat, that the United States was increasing its military budget—and the Soviet Union would be forced to follow suit. At this point Nixon interrupted the flow by returning to the question

243

of propaganda. Did Mikoyan mean to imply that the Soviet Union did not support the Communist Parties of other countries?

Of course the Soviet Union did not support other Communist Parties, Mikoyan replied. "The Cominform was detrimental," and the Kremlin's present policy was one of "non-interference." It gave advice when asked, but usually this advice was rejected by the world's Communist Parties. The events in Hungary were not the fault of the Russians but could be attributed to the "mistakes of communist leaders there," Mikoyan argued. "What we did in Hungary was bad, but necessary."

Whatever differences existed between the United States and the Soviet Union, Mikoyan asserted, relations were improving. The Soviets did not want war—"not because we are weak or cowards," but because they wanted to improve their country. Nixon told him that it would be good for both countries if Latin America, Asia, and the Near East could embark on programs to improve their lot. No one in the United States, he added, believed in a preventive war.

"This may be true," Mikoyan answered, "but I do not believe that this has always been so."

There was a lengthy discussion of the Berlin situation and of Khrushchev's ultimatum to the West. Mikoyan then proposed that the world's two greatest powers should settle all their differences bilaterally. Nixon replied that the United States could not betray its allies or sanction actions that eliminated them from the world's councils. But Mikoyan brushed that aside by charging that the United Nations was "unfair" to the Soviet Union—and the fault was America's. Then he startled Nixon by suggesting that "your country and mine postpone agreement on such matters as outer space until we arrive at a *modus vivendi*."

Nixon once more stated that no settlement could be based on American surrenders—and then they switched to lighter matters. Mikoyan was bothered by the picketing by anti-Soviet groups, he said. "I'm not exactly a stranger to picketing," Nixon commented wryly. Mikoyan praised him for his courage in facing hostile crowds in Latin America. Then he invited Nixon to visit Russia. "Someday," Nixon said vaguely.

Then, to wind up the meeting, he remarked that Armenians had settled in California, and that they were industrious citizens. "We think very highly of Armenians in California," Nixon said to his Armenian-born guest.

Mikoyan smiled. "That's more than you can say for Russia," he said.

When the two men parted, Nixon, in Mark Twain's phrase, "counted the spoons," convinced that this was the cleverest Soviet official he had ever met, and glad that he was not Premier Khrushchev. With a man like Mikoyan prowling the Kremlin corridors, he later said to me, "no ruler in the Soviet Union can sleep peacefully."

Not many months later he was walking those corridors in the company of a man far tougher and far more determined than Anastas Mikoyan.

15

Journeys and Missions

AS Vice President, Richard Nixon discarded all tradition. Instead of being a Throttlebottom so unknown that he could not get a library card, he was the center of news from the beginning of his tenure. Instead of spending his days dozing in a Capitol Hill office or attending ceremonial functions, he became an important and functioning participant in the affairs of the Administration. This was due, in part, to his nature. From boyhood he had always projected himself into the action. President Eisenhower's idea of the Presidency and his reluctance to overextend himself made him rely on Nixon. But Nixon's greatest break with the Vice Presidential past was in the role he played as a spokesman for America and an ambassador of goodwill. This role was the gift of a President who realized that Nixon was at his best when meeting the leaders of the world and its so-called "little people." From the start of his journeyings he combined successfully the postures of stateman and man-in-the-street, with benefits accruing to the country and to himself.

The early trips, for all their success, had been ceremonial. He had toured the Far East, visited the Caribbean, attended the inauguration of President Juscelino Kubitschek of Brazil, represented Eisenhower at the tenth anniversary celebration of Philippine independence, and made a whirlwind swing through South Vietnam, Thailand, India, and Pakistan. It was not until his visit to the Hungarian border that the traveling Vice President was thrust into an assignment fraught with peril and international implications.

As of December 6, 1956, Nixon had no knowledge that the President was choosing him to "show the flag" to the captive peoples behind the Iron Curtain and to demonstrate American sympathy for those who had fallen under the fire of Soviet tanks, as well as to the refugees who had escaped from the terror in Budapest. On that day Dick and Pat Nixon were in New York, relaxing from the rigors of the 1956 election campaign and planning to see a few plays. His hard-working staff had been looking forward to short vacations in the pre-Inaugural lull. Then came a request from the President—Eisenhower always put it in the form of a request—and a White House announcement.

Nixon cut short his New York jaunt to return for the briefing, strategy, and planning sessions that always preceded his trips abroad. An official explanation of his mission—to survey the refugee situation in Austria—deceived no one. The real reasons, Nixon confided, were these: "It will be a dramatic gesture of American support for the embattled Hungarians, caught between Soviet Mongolian troops and their own communist quislings. And it will allow me to reassure Austrian leaders that the United States stands behind them, should the Russians decide that Austria has violated her neutrality in giving asylum to the Hungarian freedom fighters who are pouring over the border in great numbers." The Austrian government, he added, was deeply concerned over possible repercussions.

In the days in which Nixon prepared for his trip Soviet forces in Hungary worked strenuously to stem the flow of refugees. By night the winter mist was punctuated by magnesium flares. Machine guns and the shouts of pursuing soldiers could be heard on the Austrian side of the border. But the refugees continued to cross the line. On the day when Nixon arrived in Vienna for conferences with Austrian officials and Embassy personnel more than a thousand refugees evaded their Soviet captors. Two days later, on the morning when he visited the border, Soviet blood-hounds—both human and canine—had cut the number to two hundred.

Wherever he went—to visit Austrian refugee camps, to thank the Austrian President for that small country's generous aid to the Hungarians, to act as Santa Claus at a Christmas party for refugee children—Nixon received a warm but sober welcome. The trip to the border, one of the few well-kept secrets of that or any other trip, was one of Nixon's most moving experiences. Accompanied by Bill Rogers and Representative Bob Wilson of California, and by a group of jittery Austrian police officials, he arrived at the Austro-Hungarian line at 3:30 A.M. On the way he stopped to talk to one refugee who had hobbled fifteen miles on the stumps of amputated legs to reach safety.

At the border Nixon surveyed the bleak and terrible terrain where men and women, the halt and the healthy, the young and the old crawled through underbrush, dashed across open ground, and dodged bullets—gasping as they reached the straw-colored peasant huts that were their shelter until transport was found to carry them to the camps. This sight—and the rhythmic cries of "Russki hasza—Russians go home" from recent arrivals—touched Nixon deeply. "This is an object lesson I will never forget," he said quietly to a security official.

Returning to New York, the Vice President stopped off at the Waldorf Towers to discuss his impressions with former President Herbert Hoover, who had headed the American relief program in Europe and Russia after World War I. In Washington, Nixon reported to the President. His recommendations were for greater aid to the Austrians, who were struggling to manage the tremendous financial burden of feeding and housing thousands of Hungarians. He also urged that a larger number of refugees be admitted to this country than the Administration had pledged itself to accept. On a long-range basis he suggested drastic changes in the repressive McCarran-Walter Immigration Act and in its system of quotas, which set up categories of immigrants according to their race and national origin.

Three months later Nixon was traveling again—a twenty-thousand-mile trip to the independent nations of Africa. Morocco, Ghana, Liberia, Uganda, Ethiopia, Sudan, Libya, and Tunis were on the itinerary, with a side trip to Rome to have an audience with Pope Pius XII. It was work all the way, with attendant discomforts. In Liberia protocol demanded that he wear top hat and cutaway. Sweat rolling down his face, he transferred from his DC-6B to an air-conditioned Cadillac for the forty-mile drive to Monrovia— and the equipment broke down, leaving the Nixons and their hosts in a hermetically sealed, ambulant Turkish bath. In Accra the Vice President represented Eisenhower at ceremonies marking the official birth of Ghana, giving Prime Minister Kwame Nkrumah a ballpoint pen, a two-thousand-volume technical library, and a Steuben glass cup from the President. He chatted with native chiefs and took a long, critical look at United States Information Agency activities.

A year later Roy Rubottom, Jr., the Assistant Secretary of State for Latin American Affairs, called on Nixon at his office. The State Department wanted the Vice President to represent the President at the inauguration of President Arturo Frondizi of Argentina. It was important, Rubottom said, that the highest possible American official be present, in order to counter hostile propaganda which charged that the United States supported the deposed dictator, Juan Perón. Nixon was preparing for the 1958 election campaign and struggling, along with other members of the Administration, to find ways to end the recession that had hit the country. He therefore told Rubottom that he could not make the trip. To get Nixon to change his mind, Rubottom enlisted the aid of Secretary Dulles, who in turn spoke to the President. As Nixon put it, he was now "boxed in." Reluctantly accepting, he told Rubottom that he would go only on the condition that the trip would last no more than one week, from takeoff to touchdown at National Airport.

When the announcement of the trip was made, Washington correspondents wondered whether it was worth the effort. It seemed, on the face of it, ceremonial and lacking in real news— and the Vice President agreed with them. When invitations from other South American countries filled the diplomatic pouches, Nixon agreed resignedly to extend his visit to eight Latin American countries over a period of two and a-half weeks.

"This was to be my seventh major trip abroad as Vice President and by this time I had convinced the career men in the State Department that I should use such visits not only to talk to government leaders but also to meet the opinion makers and people in all walks of life . . . university students, labor leaders, editors," Nixon has written. "I wanted to do more than simply mouth prepared platitudes designed to avoid trouble. I was determined to meet and answer head-on some of the attacks which were currently being made against the United States in Latin America."

As usual, Nixon went through Central Intelligence Agency reports, briefings from the desk man of the State Department, research papers, and volumes of memoranda prepared especially for him. He was informed by Allen Dulles, the CIA chief, that there was a possibility of some anti-American demonstrations, but no hint of possible violence.

But trouble was being carefully brewed. Following the announcement, a series of secret and extraordinary planning sessions began at 3 Vocelova Street in Prague. Behind the façade of the International Union of Students a general staff of political activists started drafting the directives and writing the slogans that would be used against Richard Nixon in Latin America. Propaganda broadcasters from the communist world, beaming their Spanish-language programs 102 hours a week, began spewing an incendiary line. In Mexico City, Lima, and Caracas orders were issued to men trained in riot and insurrection. Instructions were prepared for the manufacture of Molotov cocktails. Communist-led unions of the dwindling Confederation of Latin American Workers were given their marching orders. Communist Party members—eighty-five thousand in Argentina, five thousand in Bolivia, and eighty thousand in Venezuela—were assigned their roles. Fellow-traveling organizations and newspapermen close to the party were tipped off to beat the drums of hatred.

The Soviet Union had a variety of motives for its plot against Nixon. From still-secret Intelligence reports and from accounts of communist operatives who have since defected to the West, the Kremlin's reasoning can be reconstructed. First, the communists believed that the public humiliation of America's second-highest elected official would make the United States look ridiculous, adding disdain to the perennial anti-Americanism of many Latin Americans. (This is why the instigators of the attacks on Nixon resorted so much to spitting, not a typical act south of the border.) Second, the communists felt they had a score to settle with Nixon himself. If they could drive the mobs into a high enough pitch of frenzy, it might lead to assassination—another blow to American prestige since it seemed certain that there would be no retaliation. Third, whatever the outcome of the planned riots, they would "radicalize" a certain percentage of the participants who would be confronted by police counter-violence.

There was one factor helpful to their purposes on which the communists had not counted—the predisposition of the world press to ignore the routine aspects of the trip and emphasize every little incident of conflict. In Montevideo, for example, the crowds that met Nixon were uniformly friendly and sometimes enthusiastic. The exception was a handful of pickets, who, as the motorcade passed the University of the Republic, waved signs demanding "*Fuera Nixon*" ("Get out, Nixon"). The news reports of Nixon's arrival, however, played up the pickets and came close to ignoring the friendliness of the reception as a whole.

To counteract this, Nixon insisted on an unscheduled visit to the university's law school, where, for an hour, he answered questions, many hostile but all searching, from students eager to hear what he had to say about United States "exploitation" of Latin America and the support this country gave to some dictatorships. Caught unprepared, the communists could not pack the meeting, and they were limited to asking a few loaded questions and distributing leaflets. When they shouted anti-American slogans as Nixon was leaving, they were drowned out by the students and the cry of "*Vivan los Estados Unidos*" ("Long live the United States").

In Argentina, a country still suffering from the depredations of the Perón dictatorship, Nixon gave as much encouragement as he could to the Frondizi government. He surprised some of his critics by a series of meetings with labor leaders, set up by Serafino Romualdi, the AFL-CIO's Latin American expert, who had been invited to travel with the Vice President. He also had intensive conversations with government and business leaders on the severe economic problems facing Argentina.

The next stop, in Paraguay, was a brief one. The country was a dictatorship, and it was official American policy to be no more than correct in any relations. When Nixon addressed its National Congress, he praised its stand against communism, but he also added that the best way to fight leftist totalitarianism was not by imposing one of the right but by setting up a system based on political freedom and economic democracy. That part of his speech, however, was not reported in the controlled Paraguayan press. (When Nixon returned to the United States, he recommended that though this country continue to abide by the non-intervention clauses of the Montevideo Pact of 1933, it demonstrate its dedication to a free society with "a formal handshake for dictators, an *abrazo* [embrace] for leaders in freedom.") In Bogatá, Colombia, a country whose mass starvation was being alleviated by $50 million of American surplus food and $40 million in monetary aid, there was relatively little trouble from the communists or from dissident political elements.

As Nixon flew to Peru he was assured by Assistant Secretary Rubottom that Lima would give him his friendliest welcome. Relations with the United States had been consistently friendly. True, the country was suffering from the recession that gripped the United States, with copper, its principal mineral export, down in price and cotton depressed by Washington's policy of "dumping" its vast surpluses on the world market. This was giving the Peruvian government some bad moments, but Nixon had no premonition that the fireworks made in Prague would begin in Lima.

Riding from the airport to the center of the city, he noticed that there were few people on the streets to welcome him. Those who paid attention to the motorcade were either apathetic or hostile. When Nixon was told by a Peruvian official that the route of the motorcade had not been publicized in order to prevent "incidents," the Vice President was "somewhat disquieted." That evening Nixon was called from a reception at the United States Embassy by his military aide, Major Don Hughes, and his assistant on national security affairs, Colonel Robert Cushman, Jr. They had bad news. The communists had organized a mass demonstration at the University of San Marcos, where Nixon was to speak the following day. The Rector had told an Embassy official that he hoped the visit would be canceled, in order to avoid the possibility of real danger. The Lima Chief of Police had concurred.

"My visit to San Marcos had been widely publicized," Nixon said afterward. "I didn't want to cancel it because of threats from the communists. On the other hand, I didn't feel that I should rely on my judgment alone. But I did say that if the Rector of the university should publicly withdraw his invitation, I would bow out."

This the Rector would not do. Nixon knew why. In many Latin American countries university officials were—and are—under the thumb of the students and their professional leaders. By strikes or other forms of violent "persuasion" they were able to compel the dismissal of those they did not like, for whatever reason. Had the Rector withdrawn the invitation to Nixon, he might have found himself out of a job, or worse. The communists wanted Nixon there in order to stage a riot. The Chief of Police also refused to warn Nixon publicly to stay away. Though the Communist Party was illegal in Peru, it still operated openly, wielding considerable power. The Chief of Police had no desire to tangle with it. After conferring with his staff, with Embassy officials, and with Peruvian officials, Nixon took the American Ambassador, Theodore Achilles, aside to ask his advice.

"I believe from a personal standpoint you should make a decision not to go," Achilles said. "But from the standpoint of the United States, I will have to say that your failing to go may lead to some very detrimental publicity reactions throughout the hemisphere."

"I gave little thought to the possibility of personal injury to myself," Nixon has written, "not because I was 'being brave' but because such considerations just were not important in view of the larger issues involved. A man is not afraid at a time like this because he blocks out any thought of fear by a conscious act of will. He concentrates entirely on the problem which faces him. . . . It would not be simply a case of Nixon being bluffed out by a group of students but of the United States itself putting its tail between its legs and running away from a bunch of communist thugs.

"In a larger sense, this was another round in the contest which has been waged from the beginning of time between those who believe in the right of freedom of expression and those who advocate and practice mob rule to deny that right. . . . While it is pleasant to be popular and liked, I have always thought that our country in its leadership should never lose sight of [its] goals, objectives, and aspirations. Thus, while I could understand why the Peruvian leaders shrank from this crisis, I thought that my actions should not be inhibited by their fears. . . ."

Nixon's estimate of the situation was correct. The press corps accompanying him had been arguing the pros and cons, and it was evenly divided as to whether he would face the communists at San Marcos or take the easier course of appearing at Catholic University, which had not been infiltrated. A thousand people had waited for hours outside his hotel with the same thought. Nixon made the decision almost at the H-hour. He had given instructions the night before that only he, Jack Sherwood, his Secret Service aide, and one other were to leave the car at San Marcos—should he go— and that the police were not to use weapons of any kind. If there were violence, it would have to be initiated by the students. "San Marcos," he said to Sherwood after a wreath-laying ceremony at the tomb of General José de San Martín, Peru's liberator—and stepped into his car.

As the motorcade approached the university Nixon could hear what he later described as the "frenzied howls of the mob." "*Fuera Nixon*" had now become "*Muera Nixon*" ("Death to Nixon"). "I had faced communist mobs before, though nothing like this," he said later. "The only way to handle it was to take the offensive, show no fear, do the unexpected, do nothing rash, remain flexible, and trust to luck." Fifty yards from the university gates Nixon and his two aides got out of the car and advanced on a tense mob of several thousand students. There was an uneasy stir, and the students began to retreat slowly. The shouting began to die down, and Nixon called to them—his words translated into Spanish—"I would like to talk to you. If you have any complaints against the United States, tell me what they are and I'll answer them. That's the democratic way to discuss our differences."

"For a few moments," he would write, "I thought I might get the situation under control. Those in front of me continued to give way and I walked directly into the mob. But the older ones in the rear, the ringleaders, saw what was happening. They tried to whip up a frenzy again, egging the younger students on, just as if they were driving them with whips. They shouted insults at those who shook hands with me. There were only a few leaders— the usual case-hardened, cold-eyed communist operatives. The great majority were teenage students. And what struck me about them was not the hate in their eyes, but the fear. We had no weapons; the police, following my instructions, were not with me. And yet the very fact that we dared to walk toward them seemed to strike fear in their hearts."

When the communist leaders saw that Nixon was beginning to control the situation, they began throwing stones. One hit Jack Sherwood in the mouth, breaking a tooth. Others hit Nixon's shoulder. "All right," he said, "let's get out of here. But move slowly. Keep facing them." Back in his open car, he stood up on the rear seat to call the students "the worst kind of cowards, afraid to face the truth." But who had won? The press was almost unanimous in its praise of Nixon, there had been no violence— and the communists had been convicted of having attempted violence to silence him.

At Catholic University, the next and unannounced stop, the students were willing to listen to what he said. The communists, unprepared, plugged their loudspeaker into the public-address system and tried to drown Nixon out, but other students ripped out the wires and ejected the hecklers from the building. By this time word had reached San Marcos that Nixon was at Catholic University and winning over his audience. "We'd better cut this off," Sherwood told him. "We'd better get out of here. The mob from

San Marcos is marching here." To cries of "*Viva Nixon*," he left the hall. But there was another mob at his hotel. A block away Nixon and his party got out of the cars and advanced on foot. When he was recognized, there were shouts of "*Viva Nixon*." This alerted the ringleaders, who began pushing toward the Vice President.

"Just as I reached the hotel door," Nixon wrote, "I came face to face with a man I later learned was one of the most notorious communist agitators in Lima. . . . He let fly a wad of spit which hit me full in the face. I went through in that instant a terrible test of temper control. One must experience the sensation to realize why spitting in a person's face is the most infuriating insult ever conceived by man. I felt an almost uncontrollable urge to tear the face in front of me to pieces. Sherwood deserves the credit for keeping me from handling the man personally. He grabbed him by the arm and whirled him out of my path, but as I saw the legs go by, I at least had the satisfaction of planting a healthy kick on his shins. Nothing I did all day made me feel better."

Back in his hotel room Nixon showered and changed, pondering on what the rest of the day would bring. As he sat relaxing, Major Hughes entered the room and stood at attention, to Nixon's surprise. "Sir, could I say something personal?" he asked.

"Sure," said Nixon.

"Sir," said the jet fighter pilot, a Purple Heart veteran of Korea, "I have never been so proud to be an American as I was today. I am honored to be serving under you."

The rest of Nixon's stay in Peru was a triumphal tour as the reaction against the outrages of the communists set in. An anti-American demonstration that had been set for that afternoon was hastily called off as its communist instigators realized that they might be dealt with as they had intended to deal with Nixon. He was dressing for a state dinner when Colonel Cushman presented himself to give him a report on the day's events, and on the general response. It had all been favorable, Cushman said to him. However, Assistant Secretary Rubottom was worried that the riots might have embarrassed the Peruvian government and negated the goodwill that Nixon's trip was to have generated.

As Nixon put it, "I blew my stack." In a rare show of real anger the Vice President sent word that he wanted to see Rubottom immediately. But Rubottom was also changing for the state dinner and said he would see Nixon later. "I want him to come at once, and just as he is," Nixon demanded. A half-dressed Rubottom presented himself, only to get both barrels. Before the decision was made to go to San Marcos, Nixon said, it was not only proper but vital for them to state their case against it. Once the decision had been made, it was their duty as members of his staff to support him—as he did at National Security Council meetings when his viewpoint was rejected. Then he laced into the Foreign Service, of which Rubottom was a part. Too many Foreign Service officers, Nixon lectured, tended to compromise, to play it safe, to avoid conflict. This might seem like the safe or smart way to do things when the communists threatened or bullied. But the United States was doomed to defeat if its representatives ran from danger or pussyfooted.

"I am not suggesting that our representatives be rash," Nixon stormed, "that they should go looking for trouble, that they should not exhaust every possible means for honorable compromise of differences. But I do know that we are up against opponents who are out to beat us, not just to hold their own. We, too, must play to win. What we must do is act like Americans and not put our tails between our legs and run every time some communist bully tries to bluff us."

He would later write: "What I said in the heat of anger, I still believe to be basically true."

But Nixon's anger might well have been directed at Peruvian officialdom as well. For, as a secret report now in State Department files shows, there had been some tacit complicity between the rioters and a government that thought it would be smart policy to have "mild anti-Nixon demonstrations." An outburst of communist rioting might frighten the United States into increasing military and economic aid to Peru. The President's nose, moreover, was out of joint because he had not been invited to Washington by Eisenhower, the Prime Minister because he was not given the amount of time with Nixon that he felt was merited. There was also official annoyance because Nixon insisted on meeting opposition leaders, labor officials, and students. There had been no idea that the demonstrations would get out of hand or that the attacks would boomerang, making a hero of Nixon and publicizing the weaknesses of the Peruvian government.

The rioting in Lima may have saved Nixon's life. On the day of the San Marcos confrontation twenty-four activists had met in Bogotá to plan the assassination of Nixon. The communists who had convened the meeting believed that the Vice President's death would create such chaos that a "revolutionary situation" would inevitably follow. In that chaos they hoped to overthrow existing government and perhaps take power. But they proposed to leave nothing to chance. The following day, May 9, there was a series of meetings to organize a paramilitary campaign against Nixon. The precise deployment of activists was worked out, the movement of demonstrators mapped, and provisions made for roadblocks to halt the Nixon motorcade. The logistics of supplying overripe fruit and stones for throwing were also taken up. The Colombian Communist Party and the Frente Liberál del Pueblo supplied the money for slingshots and other supplies, as well as for fifty-five thousand leaflets denouncing Nixon and urging the people into the streets.

The events in Lima alerted the police of Colombia and Ecuador, and they took firm steps, rounding up the thirty-four leading conspirators and seizing "military" supplies just before Nixon arrived. Maximum security precautions were also taken. In Quito, Ecuador, the government—which had issued a special airmail stamp in Nixon's honor—made sure that all demonstrations would be peaceful. But far more important in discouraging violence was the response of Latin Americans to what they saw as the shame that had befallen them. To Spaniards and *Latinos* a guest has a special status. A man who does not treat his guests well is beyond the pale —and this is where Lima found itself. Even the communists were forced to issue statements that they had no part in the rioting.

Caracas was something else again. The communists all along had seen the Venezuela visit as a culmination of their efforts. The party there was strong and the ruling junta weak. Ever since the announcement on March 14 of Nixon's visit, they had been preparing. Communist newspapers pounded away at the theme of

"Yankee imperialism," of United States support for the overthrown dictator, Perez Jiménez. Resolutions were rubber-stamped for use by anti-American organizations, demanding that the invitation to Nixon be withdrawn. Late in April the Venezuelan government had called together the leaders of all student organizations, communist and otherwise, and they had agreed "to cooperate in not disgracing Venezuela by doing dishonor to a distinguished guest"— but this had been immediately ignored.

On May 3 the communist newspaper *Tribuna Populár* announced that the demonstrations in Caracas would be more "vigorous" than anything yet seen. The Vice President was accused of being a "racist," a "lyncher." On May 10 the *Tribuna Populár* published a twenty-four page supplement, a compendium of vicious stories, half-truths, and categorical inventions. On its front page it ran a picture of Nixon—a bloody beast with wolf's fangs, captioned "Tricky Dick." *"Fuera Nixon"* signs were carefully altered to read *"Muera Nixon."* Young street gangs roamed the city, breaking streetlights and store windows.

Two days before Nixon's scheduled arrival in Venezuela, Jack Sherwood handed him a message from U. E. Baughman, Chief of the United States Secret Service. It read: "The Central Intelligence Agency advises the Secret Service in Washington that information has been received relating to rumors of a plot to assassinate the VP in Venezuela." Far more serious was the report from Frank M. Berry, a former Secret Service agent then advising the Nicaraguan government on security procedures. His sources disclosed that a tremendous anti-American demonstration had been organized by the communists in Caracas, with the murder of the Vice President its aim.

Nevertheless, the Venezuelan government continued to protest that there was no real danger. The night before Nixon's arrival the American Embassy in Caracas had sent a message to Nixon: "Venezuelan government security agencies are confident of their ability to handle the situation but are increasing security measures to such an extent that the advance representatives feel the Vice President might believe he is being over-guarded," it read. This was followed by another message: "Everything under control."

It was an unlucky May 13, 1958, when the Vice President's

259

plane put down at Maiquetia Airport, outside of Caracas. A huge and ugly crowd had been permitted to collect, waving hate slogans and screaming at the top of its lungs. The mob had been brought to the airport in an organized caravan of buses, and the police had let them in. Nixon realized that it would be ridiculous to attempt the usual formalities and exchanges of greetings, and he so informed Foreign Minister Oscar Garcia Velutini. But the Nixon motorcade, instead of being lined up on the ramp according to the usual custom, was parked on the other side of the terminal building, exposing Pat and the Vice President to the crushing, screeching mob. The Police Chief refused to clear a path for the Vice President and his party. "They are harmless," he said. "They have a right to demonstrate."

As Pat and Dick reached the terminal door they were brought to a halt by the playing of the Venezuelan national anthem. Standing at attention, they felt themselves drenched by the spit that came from the mob on the observation deck. "What a really lousy thing this is," Nixon thought. But he would not budge. As the band played the organizers of the mob were redeploying it on the street outside, where they blocked Nixon's access to the waiting limousines, rented from a local undertaker. There were soldiers with fixed bayonets, but they did nothing. A handful of Secret Service agents cleared a path through the spitting, garbage-throwing crowd.

Caracas was twelve miles away, most of them on the broad *Autopista* that Perez Jiménez had cut through solid mountain. As the Nixon motorcade sped toward the city, agitators in automobiles zigzagged on the road, cutting off the official cars, and throwing stones and garbage. Nixon, in a closed car, perspired and fumed. The Foreign Minister, a well-intentioned man, apologized profusely and tried to wipe the spittle off Nixon's clothes with his handkerchief. "Don't bother," Nixon snapped. "I'm going to burn these clothes as soon as I can get out of them."

"The Venezuelan people have been without freedom for so long that they tend now to express themselves more vigorously perhaps than they should," the Foreign Minister said, adding to Nixon's irritation. "In our new government we do not want to do anything which would be interpreted as a suppression of freedom."

"If your new government doesn't have the guts and the good sense to control a mob like the one at the airport, there soon will be no freedom for anyone in Venezuela," Nixon answered. "Freedom doesn't mean the right to engage in mob action. Don't you realize that the mob was communist-led? Didn't the mob at the airport deny free speech to you and me? Didn't they shout and spit during the playing of their own national anthem?" These were words he would ponder years later when he was President and similar mobs were rampaging America's major universities.

The Foreign Minister agreed with Nixon. "But I hope you won't say that publicly because our government is fearful of doing anything which will embarrass or anger the Venezuelan communists. They helped us overthrow Perez Jiménez and we are trying to find a way to work with them."

Nixon said nothing. He might have been angrier had he known that the communists had prepared a series of ambushes for his motorcade. An advance party, already in the city, had tried to give warning, but three messages that the Caracas police presumably sent by radio never reached the motorcade. Just as the Nixon party left the *Autopista* it was stopped by a roadblock of cars and buses. As the motorcade stopped rioters poured out of houses and into the street, spitting, throwing rocks, and shouting obscenities. The next ambush, within the city limits, stopped the motorcade briefly, but six Secret Service men were able to open a way through the attackers, again with no help from the police. Four blocks from the Pantheon Plaza, where Nixon was to lay a wreath, three banks of buses, cars, and trucks blocked the road. Out of an alley poured some five hundred people, many of them armed with iron pipes and clubs. The leaders of the attack rode piggyback so that they could direct operations.

For twelve terrible minutes stones flew and spit drenched the Nixon car. (In order to see, the driver had to turn on his windshield wiper.) A large rock smashed against a car window, spraying glass on the Foreign Minister's face. "It's my eye," he moaned. "This is terrible." The frenzy was such that Earl Mazo, one of the reporters on the trip, would later liken it to "a scene from the French Revolution." To Nixon, it was obvious that this was where the communists planned to stage their assassination. "If we were to survive," he said later, "I knew that I had to control my emotions. I had to remain cool, not to give way to anger.

"But there was one emotion I could not restrain. That was hatred for those who would use teenagers, just a little older than my daughter Tricia, to do their dirty and fanatical work. The immediate problem, however, was to get out alive. One of the ring-leaders had begun to bash in the window next to me with a big pipe. The shatterproof glass began to splatter, and my interpreter got a mouthful. I could look right at the man bashing in my window. His expression was one of pure hate. He hit the window ten times before it began to give way. Then I heard him shout a command and our car began to rock. That was a common mob tactic—to rock a car, turn it over, and set it on fire. For an instant, the realization passed through my mind—we might be killed—and then it was gone."

"Sherwood must have had the same thought," Nixon would write. "He pulled his revolver and said, 'Let's get some of these sons-of-bitches.' I could see Rodham [another Secret Service agent] in the front seat with sweat pouring down his neck as he pulled his revolver and faced the attackers on my side of the car. 'I figured we were goners and I was going to get six of those bastards before they got us,' he was to tell me later. . . . I reached forward, put my hand on Sherwood's arm, and told him to hold his fire."

By this time almost the entire police escort had slipped away, leaving the motorcade to what seemed like certain death. In the car behind Pat Nixon sat steely cold, watching the attack on her husband, with no thought of the danger to her. In another car Rose Mary Woods was injured by flying glass.

This could have been the end. Then a small group of Venezuelan soldiers showed up. They forced an opening through the roadblock big enough for the Nixon car to slip through, with Pat Nixon's car right behind. But as the remnants of the motorcade sped toward the Pantheon Plaza, Nixon made a quick decision—and one that saved his life and those of many others, American and Venezuelan. He ordered his car to turn into a side street and drive in the opposite direction. For it was at the wreath-laying ceremony that the communists planned to deliver their most lethal blow. Venezuelan authorities investigating the riots subsequently discovered that at the plaza a hundred trained activists were to follow the usual rock-throwing with bombs. Near the plaza, in the house of a communist woman functionary, they found an arsenal of four hundred Molotov cocktails, primed and ready to go.

"We can't leave our protection," the Foreign Minister shouted hysterically.

"If that's the kind of protection we're going to get," Nixon told him, "we're better off going it alone."

Nixon's second quick decision was to stay away from the Circulo Militár, the $35 million officer's club, at which the Nixon party was to stay. Instead, he ordered the driver to take him to the American Embassy. "I felt as though I had come as close as anyone could get, and still remain alive, to a first-hand demonstration of the ruthlessness, fanaticism, and determination of the enemy we face in the world struggle"—a demonstration that had begun minutes after the Venezuelan Foreign Minister had reassured him that his country's communists were different, that they were "harmless radicals" and nationalists.

At the Embassy the Nixons could relax. All available men from various United States military missions had been mobilized to protect the Vice President. But Nixon did not know at the time that other steps were being taken. After consultation with the President, Secretary of State Dulles had communicated with the Venezuelan government to inform them that unless they gave Nixon adequate protection, American troops would be sent in. ("Mince no words," Eisenhower had said to Dulles. "We want to know whether they can guarantee Mr. Nixon's safety, and we want to know damn soon.") At the same time the Defense Department announced that "two companies of airborne infantry and two companies of Marines are being moved to certain U. S. bases in the Caribbean. The movement is being undertaken so these troops will be in a position to cooperate with the Venezuelan government if assistance is requested. . . ." President Eisenhower was widely criticized for this troop movement, but the junta ruling Venezuela got the point. From that moment on Nixon was adequately guarded by units of the Venezuelan army—the police were obviously useless—and there were no more incidents.

The next day there were official meetings and an elaborate luncheon at the Circulo Militár. Then, under heavy guard, the Nixon motorcade moved down the same streets they had traveled the day before—streets now empty of people—to a deserted airport.

The next stop was San Juan, and Nixon was met by cheering crowds and a warm welcome from Puerto Rico's Governor, Luis Muñoz Marin. Back home fifteen thousand people were at National Airport when Nixon's Air Force DC-6B put down, and Eisenhower made it a point to greet him personally, in a show of support and affection. The entire Cabinet, the bipartisan leadership of the Congress, and a large group of Latin American students from the Washington area also joined the official welcomers. And eighty-five thousand people lined Washington's streets—the biggest crowd in its history. "The ordeal of the trip was over, the trip I did not want to take because I thought it would be dull," Nixon would write of his homecoming mood. He also took some grim pleasure from the fact that, once more, an attack on him had badly boomeranged. For a period of time he was a national hero, and few denied him his badge of courage.

The expressions of admiration were not, however, universal. Senator Wayne Morse demanded an investigation of the Nixon trip. And William V. Shannon of *The New York Times*, then with the New York *Post*, found words of understanding and praise for the Caracas rioters! "Because North Americans tolerate Nixon's behavior is no reason why South Americans must also accept it," he wrote. "South Americans have more self-respect than we do."

This appraisal, as Nixon knew, was a substitute for facing some of the tough, perhaps insoluble problems of hemisphere relations. "The riots were a symptom," he told a press conference. "The real, basic question is why it happened." To me, he pointed out that the United States, as a world power, could not hope to be loved. Many of the attacks were hardly logical. "We're damned if we do and damned if we don't," he said, recalling that the United States had been criticized by Latin Americans when it condemned Argentina's dictator Juan Perón in 1945, and equally criticized for not condemning Venezuela's dictator Marcos Perez Jiménez in the 1950s.

Nixon believed that the "good neighbor policy"—a term coined by President Herbert Hoover when he inaugurated it—had now become merely an empty phrase. The United States was so busy with other matters that it tended to ignore its next-door neighbors. Some American diplomats shied away from contacts with pro-United States groups and pro-democratic labor leaders and moved only in the rarefied atmosphere of the diplomatic and social world. "If we want the people of Latin America to remain anti-communist," Nixon added, "we have to show them that we are interested in them as people and not just as pawns in the Cold War, that we are willing to help them as they move toward political and economic progress." In considerably greater detail Nixon outlined his views to the National Security Council.

While the horrors of the Latin American trip were still fresh in Nixon's mind he could say, "I hope there won't be another for a long time." And he agreed when J. Edgar Hoover told him, "Don't try to top this trip, Dick. It can't be done."

Six months and six dates later he was in London, on a ceremonial visit to participate in the dedication at St. Paul's Cathedral of a memorial chapel to the American dead of World War II. The trip marked a turning point in the attitude of the British toward the Vice President. British intellectuals, whose opinions of Nixon had been derived from the generally hostile stories sent by English correspondents in America, were prepared for the unsavory character of the Herblock cartoons. He had gone, even though some among his friends advised him to beg off. Violence, they argued, won sympathy—but sneers would not. He rejected the advice, though with some qualms.

Even before his arrival the British press had laid down a barrage of criticism. "Plastic politician," said London's *Observer*. "Organization man," said the *News Chronicle*. "Superb political gamesmanship," said the Manchester *Guardian*. "In one of the odd situations of modern diplomacy," *Time* remarked, "Nixon was personally on trial and double-dared to make a mistake." This was the tenor of British thinking when he arrived on November 25, still marked by the scars of the 1958 election campaign.

His speech at the Pilgrim Society, on the day of his arrival, paid tribute to the British system ("Every time an American acts politically within the democratic context, he reflects his British heritage"), but it also defended American policies not much to the liking of his hosts. "The American government and people want peace," said Nixon. "But we believe that we in the free world could render no greater disservice to the cause of peace than to fail to stand firm in the Formosa Strait"—the British had been irritated by Eisenhower's defense of Quemoy and Matsu—"against the use of aggressive force to settle the differences between nations. I realize that there are many well-intentioned critics of this firm policy both in the United States and in the United Kingdom. Our disagreement is not on ends but on means. . . . Let us resolve that because of transcendent need for unity in the face of continuing threats to world peace, no issue should be allowed to divide us."

The following evening he spoke again—this time in the half-century-old Guildhall of London, where in 1945 General Eisenhower had greeted the victory of Allied arms. Recalling Khrushchev's economic challenge to the West, he ticked off two key points: (1) "Let us adopt as our primary objective not the defeat of communism but the victory of plenty over want, of health over disease, of freedom over tyranny"; and (2) "British colonialism had had its faults, but it also . . . brought the great ideas which provided the basis for progress in the future." Nixon told me that he thought the Guildhall speech "the best I ever wrote"—and Foreign Secretary Selwyn Lloyd called it "the most eloquent defense of the Western position that I have ever heard." In conferences with Conservative and Labour Party leaders, however, Nixon made his major breakthrough. Charles Hill, a member of the British Cabinet, asserted that Nixon had "completely disspelled any impressions" that he was "just a smart operator." And Alf Robens, formerly of the Labour Government, noted that "of course, there was much with which we disagreed, but all of us were struck by his sincerity." Even Richard Crossman, a left-wing socialist M. P., confessed that he had been impressed.

Before a group of Oxford students he goodnaturedly answered a ribbing question: What did he think of Nelson Rockefeller? "I think he will make a good Governor," Nixon answered. Before the laughter had subsided, he added, "If he should get the nomination for the Presidency in 1960, he will make an excellent campaigner and a fine candidate."* But the real test came when, in the gold and crystal-chandeliered ballroom of Claridge's, he stood before TV cameras and answered the questions of 350 correspondents for an hour and five minutes. When he had finished, the usually undemonstrative British stood up and applauded, and some even tried to get his autograph. Britain's mass-circulation Sunday papers, which had sneered at Nixon before the conference, said, "Jolly good, isn't he?"

This should have been the climax of his journeys for the most traveling of America's Vice Presidents. But history, and Dwight David Eisenhower, had one more mission for Nixon—one that would bring him his greatest acclaim.

---

* Nixon had cause to be piqued. Rockefeller, who sent him an adulatory cable after the San Marcos crisis, had a fortnight before the Oxford appearance answered questions about Nixon from the press in Caracas with "No tengo nada que ver con Nixon—I have nothing to do with Nixon.

16

Into the Bear's Cave

THE announcement in June 1959 that Vice President Nixon
would open the United States National Exhibition at Sokolniki
Park in Moscow created a commotion from one end of Washington to another. For here was America's number-one anti-communist paying a courtesy visit to the core of the communist world.
That he was merely reciprocating a visit by Deputy Premier Frol
Kozlov to the Soviet Fair in New York did not lessen the excitement. It was not, however, the first time that a Nixon visit to the
Soviet Union had been considered. In my files there is a confidential memorandum noting that the President had suggested a similar
journey to Nixon in 1955, but that he had been persuaded by
Secretary Dulles to drop the project. In the four intervening years
the situation had changed. Negotiations between East and West
over a Soviet-provoked Berlin crisis had reached their usual impasse,
and it was widely believed that Nixon would bear a message from
Eisenhower to Khrushchev. Actually, the idea for Nixon's Soviet
trip had come from Abbott Washburn, Deputy Director of the
United States Information Agency, who carried it up the chain
of command to Secretary Dulles and the President after Nixon
had agreed.

In preparing for the trip, Nixon received what he later described as "the most intensive series of briefings" of any he had been subjected to prior to other of his state visits. No one knew which way Premier Khrushchev would jump or what he would consider an important topic for discussion. Nixon, therefore, had to be knowledgeable in such matters as the Berlin problem, atomic testing, East-West trade, the long-missing American airmen whose C-130 transport had been shot down by Soviet fighters, the relaxation of travel restrictions, press censorship, the opening of new consular establishments in the Soviet Union and the United States, communist jamming of American broadcasts, permission for a list of over a hundred Soviet relatives of American citizens to migrate to the United States, and a host of other major and minor topics.

Nixon sought out men who had met Khrushchev—Senator Hubert Humphrey; Ambassador Averell Harriman; newspapermen like Bob Considine, William Randolph Hearst, Jr., and Turner Catledge, all of whom had interviewed the Soviet Premier; commentators like Walter Lippmann; Soviet experts like Professor William Yandell Elliott of Harvard; Chancellor Konrad Adenauer of Germany; and, "most memorable" of all, John Foster Dulles, who was dying of cancer at Walter Reed Hospital. "What above everything else should I try to get across to Khrushchev?" Nixon asked Dulles. The former Secretary of State, in deep pain, thought for several minutes. Then he said:

"Khrushchev does not need to be convinced of our good intentions. He knows that we are not aggressors and do not threaten the security of the Soviet Union. He understands us. But what he needs to know is that we also understand him. In saying that he is for 'peaceful competition,' he really means competition between his system and ours only in our world, not in his. He says he is for 'peaceful coexistence.' What he means, as he has shown in Hungary, is that while a revolution against a non-communist government is proper and should be supported, a revolution against a communist government is invariably wrong and must be suppressed. Thus, the 'peaceful coexistence' which he advocates represents peace for the communist world and constant strife and conflict for the non-communist world.

"He must be made to understand that he cannot have it both ways. If we are to have peaceful competition of economic systems and political ideas, it must take place in the communist world as well as in ours. He will deny, of course, that he and his government are connected in any way with communist activities in other countries—and he will say that those activities are simply spontaneous expressions of a people's resentment against capitalistic regimes. Point the record out to him, chapter and verse. Show him that we are not taken in at all by the mock innocence of Soviet leaders, that we have concrete proof of the Kremlin's activities around the world. He should be told that until he puts a stop to these activities, his call for reducing tensions and for 'peaceful coexistence' will have a completely false and hollow ring."

While Nixon absorbed the advice and counsel he received from those who had known Khrushchev; while he took a crash course in Russian from Alexander Barmine, a onetime Soviet general in Intelligence who had escaped Stalin's purge; and while he worked on the speeches he would deliver in the Soviet Union, a team of State Department experts—led by Assistant Secretary Foy Kohler—was preparing the material on which Nixon would in due time base his unscheduled "great debate" with Nikita Khrushchev. This team included the most knowledgeable of State Department experts on United States-Soviet relations, and it systematically examined all points of conflict, all areas in which the United States could put its best foot forward, all the weaknesses of Khrushchev as blusterer-in-chief. Representing the Vice President at these sessions, I summed them up at the time in an office memo:

The material presented has been kicked back and forth, "brainstormed" at several conferences to which outside experts have been invited, and refined to its most useful form. A baker's dozen of topics have been chosen, position papers written, and briefs prepared for the Vice President's study in the next days and on the trip to Moscow.

The brainstorming sessions have taken place in the office of Foy Kohler—a corner room on the sixth floor of DOS, walnut-paneled, one wall covered with bookshelves. At a conference table the experts have read from top secret documents, accepted and rejected ideas. The end product of their work will be packed in a small portable safe that will accompany the Vice President.

Nixon has attended only one of these brainstorming sessions. But one of his aides is present at all of them, taking full notes.

The most important point of the briefings is to make certain that the Vice President will be able to dish out as much as he receives from the Soviet Premier. State Department officials believe that Nixon is capable of stopping the flow of Khrushchevian rhetoric. And those who observed him in his dealings with Deputy Premier Frol Kozlov, who patterns his public manner on that of his boss, are convinced that this is so. For, without entering into acrimonious exchanges, Nixon was able repeatedly to bring Kozlov up short.

A second memorandum—the question-and-answer account of an interview with Nixon by Kenneth Crawford, then *Newsweek's* Washington Bureau Chief, and me—gives an insight into Nixon's aims:

Q. What do you hope to achieve in this trip?

A. First, it will give me an opportunity to meet and talk with large numbers of Russian people. I shall make two radio and television addresses as Mr. Kozlov did in this country. . . . I shall talk with as many Russians as I possibly can face to face. I don't expect my talks to change the immediate course of events but I hope I can help clear up some misconceptions by speaking simply and clearly, not in diplomatese.

Q. What misconceptions do you have in mind?

A. The idea, for example, that the American people have warlike or aggressive intentions, or that their leaders have such intentions if the people don't—that there is a difference between the American people and their leaders. Perhaps I can make a dent in this kind of false notion.

Q. You put this opportunity to speak to the Russian people, as distinct from their leaders, first because you consider it the most important part of your mission?

A. Not necessarily. I also want to learn as much as I can about the spirit of the Russian people, their strengths and weaknesses.

271

I have no illusions about how much one can learn in a ten-day trip. I have read reams of Intelligence material, reports on conversations between Americans and Khrushchev. The contain much more information than I'll gather. Still, I have learned from experience that there is no substitute for seeing. I like to get the feel of a place for myself.

Q. What about your meeting with Khrushchev and the other Soviet leaders?

A. These talks can, of course, prove to be the most important opportunity afforded by this trip. I don't expect them to produce any new agreements or any breakthrough on Berlin or any other issue between East and West. I take with me no new offers, no new program. I mean to present the American attitude firmly and clearly on all major issues.

Q. Recent accounts of talks between Americans and Khrushchev suggest that he has done most of the talking and they have done most of the listening. How do you get away from that?

A. All the Americans who have talked with Khrushchev since President Eisenhower and Secretary Dulles saw him in Geneva have talked with him more or less in the capacity of reporters. My status will be somewhat different. I shall be talking as a representative of the U. S. government.

Q. It has been said that this trip will be crucial in your own career—that it can make or break you. What do you think about that?

A. I regard this as a very important trip, but there have been others. I don't feel that my personal fortunes are more or less involved than they have been in others. I do not mean to press for spectacular results. I shall present the American case as best I can and let the chips fall where they may. I mean to be courteous and proper but not soft and gullible. I don't believe the communists respect people who let them get away with statements and charges that should be answered. Events will have to determine the outcome.

Events, of course, did determine the outcome. But the Vice President, soberly preparing for a serious mission into unknown

terrain, had no idea that some of his "negotiations" with Khrushchev would be more like a three-ring circus than a green-table
dialogue. As he would later say, "I've made hundreds of calls on
high officials in all parts of the world. But no head of government
ever threw such a collection of four-letter words at me that the
interpreter blushed. Khrushchev is an insulting man, but I never
expected to be insulted on TV. He had rattled his missiles before,
but never in a model American kitchen, with a hundred reporters
taking notes." And in *Six Crises:* "Meeting with Khrushchev,
after talking with [Kozlov and Anastas Mikoyan], was like going
from minor to major league pitching. He throws a bewildering
assortment of stuff—blinding speed, a wicked curve, plus knucklers,
spitters, sliders, fork balls—all delivered with a deceptive change
of pace."

The day before Nixon was to take off for Moscow he was called
to the White House to receive an important and secret addition to
his general instructions. The President had decided to invite
Khrushchev to visit the United States, and Nixon was authorized
to discuss it during his Moscow conferences. This was a touchy
assignment, politically perilous for Nixon. Though the Eisenhower
Administration was convinced that a first-hand look at the size,
spirit, strength, and prosperity of this country would condition the
Soviet dictator's thinking, there were other who considered it an
act of appeasement that would also give him much-needed respectability in the councils of the world. Nixon knew that he would be
criticized for his part in the protocol of officially tendering that
invitation, even though he was merely carrying out the orders of
the President.

On the night of July 22 two giant jets took off for Moscow—
Nixon in a United States Air Force Boeing 707 from Friendship
Airport near Baltimore, and a press contingent numbering sixty-
five in a Pan American Intercontinental Boeing 707-321, a larger
plane of longer range, making its first commercial flight, from New
York's Idlewild Airport. The press flew non-stop, setting a record of
eight hours and forty-five minutes point to point.

It was cool and sunny at Vnukovo Airport when the Vice
President's plane put down. As it taxied past the line of already

obsolescent two-engine Soviet TU-104 jet transports, the American plane looked sleek and powerful and solid. A scattering of Soviet officials and members of the diplomatic corps were present to greet Nixon. But the airport had been cleared by the secret police and all spirit of festivity had been dampened. "As I stepped down from the plane," Nixon recalls, "I knew that they were giving me the cool treatment—correct but cool." There was no playing of national anthems and no band. But right outside the airport gates a crowd of three hundred people was waiting patiently for a sight of the Vice President. Nixon ordered the motorcade to stop, climbed out of his car, and greeted the people. "*Druzhba*," the crowd shouted. "Friendship." And a man in overalls said to Nixon, "The whole Soviet people welcomes you. I am a worker."

These two encounters set the tone for the entire visit: coolness and occasioned hostility from the government; friendliness from the average man. Nixon observed the difference and drew his conclusion. Knowing that the negotiations for an Eisenhower-Khrushchev meeting were virtually completed, he had expected something a little less crude than the elbow he got from Soviet officialdom during the first hours in Moscow. But these were personal reactions, and he was under strict orders from Eisenhower to observe but not to criticize, to listen but not to argue. Having accepted these conditions, however, he had informed the President that he would not sit quietly by if attacks on the United States were made. Ironically, at the time of his arrival, Khrushchev was addressing a mass meeting at the Moscow Sports Arena, lashing out at the United States, at Nixon, and at a resolution offering moral support to the captive nations passed the week before by Congress. (He had landed just ninety minutes before Nixon from a visit to Poland during which he had been coldly treated by Polish crowds ordered to greet him.)

At 5:30 the next morning Nixon, who had slept badly, decided that he would go for a walk to see the city unofficially. Waking up Jack Sherwood and the Soviet security policeman who also acted as their driver, Nixon asked to be taken to a market. "I wanted to see how differently they ran things from the way it used to be when I was a boy, driving a pickup truck to the produce market in Los Angeles," he said. Once again the friendliness of the Russian people became manifest. Nixon was greeted enthusiastically and loaded down with fruits and vegetables that the customers at the market insisted on buying for him. He was asked questions about life in the United States, about which they knew only what they read in the controlled press. And he was learning, too. "At each stall or counter," he would write, "there were two sets of scales: one used by the stallkeeper, and the other by the customer to re-weigh his purchase as a check against any cheating!"

As Nixon was about to leave, some of the people in the Danilov-sky Market asked him for tickets to the American Exhibit. Accord-ing to the terms of the agreement between the Soviet government and the United States, these tickets were supposed to be available to anyone. But the Kremlin had been making it next to impossible for the average Russian to buy them. Nixon explained that he had no tickets and not realizing that people were being deliberately kept away, he offered to pay for tickets in reciprocity for the gifts he had received. At Nixon's prompting Jack Sherwood gave a 100-ruble bill to one of the men in the market, but it was handed back with thanks and a laugh. It wasn't the cost but the unavailability, Nixon was told.

This caused the first "incident" of the trip. *Pravda, Izvestia,* and *Trud*—all official papers, of course—promptly attacked Nixon for trying to "bribe" and "degrade" the Soviet people. The Vice President was also accused of seeking publicity by offering money to a Soviet citizen while the photographers of the "Wall Street press" took pictures. The Soviet propaganda machine pounded away at this, though no photographers had been present, making whatever unpleasantness they could for their country's guest.

At 10 A.M. Nixon got his second taste of Soviet manners when he paid what was scheduled as a courtesy call on Khrushchev. This normally would have meant an exchange of polite words, but it was not to be so. Khrushchev was in a testy mood, perhaps because of his discomfiture over Poland. He stared at Nixon, looking him up and down for what seemed like minutes. Then he asked the Vice President to sit down—and launched into a diatribe against the United States, his voice shrill and his big fist pounding the table. The putative cause of his anger was the Captive Nations Resolution, which, Nixon knew—and knew that Khrushchev knew —was merely an excuse for the fireworks.*

It was, however, Khrushchev's way to put Nixon on the defensive, to rattle him, and perhaps to get him to lose his temper. But Khrushchev, as Nixon would later remark, "never loses his temper —he uses it"—a capability that Nixon shared. "Khrushchev was putting on an act," Nixon said afterward. "If he hadn't had the Captive Nations Resolution to use for taking the offensive against me, he would have found something else." As his host's language became more violent and as obscenities filled his speech, Nixon tried to answer factually. But the answers were ignored. Finally, Khrushchev realized that he was not going to make Nixon lose his temper, and the "courtesy call" ended abruptly.

From Khrushchev's luxurious Kremlin offices the two men drove to Sokolniki Park and the American Exhibit, for a guided tour and preview. Russian workmen were still at work—"some of them don't even know what a claw hammer is," an American supervisor told me. Other Russians had crawled under the fence to see Nixon and Khrushchev and to get their own preview. The moment Khrushchev appeared, they converged on him enthusiastically. As the secret police began to drive them back, Khrushchev held up his hand. Reporters were swept aside by the surging crowd, but Khrushchev laughed and joked with the people. In gutter Russian

---

* The resolution, Public Law 86-90, simply reflected the feeling of the Congress and said nothing that Khrushchev had not heard before. It stated, in part, that ". . . Whereas the enslavement of a substantial part of the world's population by communist imperialism makes a mockery of the idea of peaceful coexistence . . . and / Whereas the imperialistic policies of Communist Russia have led, through direct and indirect aggression, to the subjugation of the national independence of [twenty-four nations and peoples] and others; and / Whereas these submerged nations look to the United States, as the citadel of human freedom, for leadership in bringing about their liberation and independence . . . and / Whereas it is vital to the national security of the United States that [this] desire . . . should be steadfastly kept alive . . . Now, therefore, be it / Resolved by the Senate and House of Representatives . . . that the President is authorized and requested to issue a Proclamation designating this third week of July, 1959, as 'Captive Nations Week' and inviting the people of the United States to observe such week with appropriate ceremonies and activities. . . ."

—this according to Harrison Salisbury of *The New York Times*— he played up to them, throwing his arms around an oil-stained workman and ecstatically hugging an old woman in a *babushka*.

It was at the RCA exhibit that the first public confrontation took place. On view was a new color videotape process, and an Ampex engineer ushered the two men into the "studio" so that they could be recorded, the tape to be used for greeting visitors to the exhibition. Khrushchev, however, was suspicious. He thought the telecast was going out live to the United States and wanted to say little. But he could not resist the temptation to play up to the Russian workmen in an overhead gallery or to the newspapermen present. Boasting that the Soviet Union would catch up economically with the United States in seven years, Khrushchev said:

"When we catch up with you, in passing you by, we will wave to you. Then, if you wish, we can stop and say, 'Please follow us.' Plainly speaking, if you want capitalism, you can live that way. . . . We can still feel sorry for you but since you don't understand us, live as you do understand." Then he returned to the Captive Nations Resolution, living up to the threat he had made that morning that it would be used to plague Nixon throughout his entire visit. Nixon again wondered why Khrushchev was trying to goad him. But he refused to show any annoyance. "Your remarks are in the tradition of what we have come to expect—sweeping and extemporaneous," he said. "Later on we will have an opportunity to speak, and consequently I will not comment on the various points you raised. . . . I can only say that if this competition in which you plan to outstrip us is to do the best for both of our peoples and for peoples everywhere, there must be a free exchange of ideas. After all, you don't know everything—"

"If I don't know everything," Khrushchev broke in, "you don't know anything about communism except fear of it." There was more picayune debate, with Khrushchev constantly interruping, constantly boasting that he would never concede a point. "You are a lawyer for capitalism and I am a lawyer for communism," he said. "Let's compete."

To which Nixon answered, "The way you dominate the conversation you would make a good lawyer yourself. If you were in the United States Senate, you would be accused of filibustering."

It was all froth, but as Nixon watched the playback with Khrushchev, he wondered what the American reaction would be. Khrushchev, he felt, had come out ahead, though his bluster and rudeness would make a negative impression. Khrushchev, however, was watching himself with schoolboy delight. But this did not temper his rudeness. On the way to the model home, a $14,000 cottage that was a major target of Soviet press attack (because of the chronic Soviet housing shortage), the two men passed a model American grocery store. "You may be interested to know," Nixon said, "that my father owned a small general store in California, and all the Nixon boys worked there while going to school."

Khrushchev turned to Nixon and said maliciously, "Oh, all shop-keepers are thieves."

"There is thievery everywhere," Nixon said quietly. "Even in the store I visited this morning I saw people weighing food after they had bought it from the state." Khrushchev turned away.

At the model house the "kitchen debate," as it came to be known, contributed little in the way of enlightenment or agreement. It was valuable to Nixon because it gave him a chance to observe the Khrushchev method and taught him how to cope with it. But it had its moments of drama. In the great press of people reporters were jostled and forced back so that no single correspondent was able to take notes on the entire argument. By comparing notes later, we were able to reconstruct the dialogue— a debate unique in the annals of diplomacy. It ranged from a discussion of American and Soviet construction techniques to peace, war, and leisure for women. Throughout, Khrushchev moved from heavy-handed humor to loud outbursts, and at one point, as he gesticulated, he poked Nixon angrily in the chest with a stubby finger. His inability to accept the model house, no more than average by American standards, betrayed the woefully low Soviet standard of living, and his own parochialism.

N. This type of house cost fourteen thousand dollars. It would be paid for over a period of twenty-five to thirty years. Most of the veterans of World War II purchased houses in the fifteen-thousand-dollar range. Anyone who makes a hundred dollars a week could afford this house. Any steelworker in the United States could buy this house. They make three dollars an hour. . . .

K. We can find steelworkers and peasants who can pay fourteen thousand dollars cash for a flat. . . . The fact is that all the newly built Russian houses will have this equipment. You need dollars in the United States to get this house, but here all you need is to be born a citizen.

Nixon had already seen the poor quality of Russian construction, and in the days ahead he would visit new apartment houses equipped with crude coal stoves. Except to high government officials and the pampered "artist" class—the ballerinas, film stars, top writers—modern refrigerators, dishwashers, and the other electric equipment of the model house were unreachable luxuries for the vast majority of Russians, but Nixon did not say this, either then or later.

By a series of detours the two men arrived at the endless Berlin crisis and the current Soviet ultimatum to the West to get out of Germany.

N. The moment we place either one of these powerful nations, or any other powerful nation, in a position through ultimatum where they have no choice but to accept dictation or fight, then you are playing with the most destructive force in the world. And this is very serious in the present world context. When we sit down at the conference table, it can't be all one way. One side can't put the other in an impossible situation through ultimatum. . . .

K. That sounds like a threat to us. We, too, are a giant. You can threaten us indirectly. We will answer threat with threat.

N. Who wants to threaten? We will never engage in threats.

K. We also have means at our disposal.

N. We are well aware of that. (Quietly.) We have, too.

The debate continued for the rest of the day. At the formal

opening of the Exhibit, Khrushchev took umbrage when Nixon tried to show him a voting machine. "We have no need for those in the Soviet Union," he said brusquely.

That night Nixon delivered a major address at the Exhibition which was, by prior agreement, published in *Pravda* and *Izvestia*. It was, as *Time* reported, "a ringing retort to Soviet internal propaganda that the Exhibition was not typical of U. S. life." For Nixon used the occasion to describe American life and the American standard of living to an audience that for four decades had heard just the opposite. "The 67 million American wage earners," Nixon said, "are not the downtrodden masses depicted by the critics of capitalism." And he quoted facts and figures—44 million American familes owned 56 million cars, 50 million TV sets, and 143 million radios; 32 million families owned their own homes. "What these statistics dramatically demonstrate is this: that the United States, the world's largest capitalist country, has from the standpoint of distribution of wealth, come closest to the ideal of prosperity for all in a classless society."

As Nixon moved about Moscow, Leningrad, Novosibirsk, and Sverdlovsk—the last two were cities that had been closed to Americans—the crowds grew bigger and friendlier. Obviously, the unremitting attacks in the Soviet press were not having the desired effect. The Soviets, therefore, introduced a new technique—the "spontaneous" heckler. The first of the breed appeared in Moscow, and the Soviet officials accompanying Nixon expected him to demand that the heckler be ousted. Instead, Nixon insisted that he be heard. At the Ob River dam, in Siberia, near Novosibirsk, a "worker" whose name and background were known in great detail to Nixon's hosts, asked, "Why do you encircle us with bases?"

N. When we both agree on disarmament proposals with adequate inspection, then we can take up the question of bases. Now, I'd like to ask you a question.

Heckler. I'm not satisfied with your answer.

N. Tell me where the troops of the Red Army are. The Soviet Union also has bases in foreign countries.

Heckler. That's a lie.

N. What about East Germany? What about Hungary? What about Poland? Why do you keep troops there?

Heckler. We have no troops there.

N. Is Poland your country? Is Hungary your country? Why do you keep troops there?

Heckler. There are American and Western troops in Germany, and the Soviet has to maintain forces for that reason.

N. You always have a reason. . . . Workers of all countries must look carefully at the policies of their governments as well as the policies of others.

The heckling became one of the major irritants to Nixon. In the Uralmash factory near Sverdlovsk he was interrupted in his inspection trip at least twenty times. He was also annoyed by police efforts to discourage the enthusiasm of the crowd. Outside the Uralmash plant Nixon saw a policeman manhandling a woman, one of the several thousand people who had waited for hours to see him. Breaking away from Georgi Zhukov, the Soviet Minister of Information, who was accompanying him, Nixon pushed into the crowd, seized the officer by the shoulder and shook him. "Don't ever do that again," he said sharply. "When the people are happy and want to express themselves, leave them alone."

In the limousine Nixon spoke his piece. "Mr. Zhukov," he said, "this little game you've been playing with me through your planted hecklers for the past few days has not been going well with the press, and in my opinion it is backfiring even among your own people. You underestimate their intelligence. They aren't dumb. They know when somebody is acting and when it's the real thing —particularly when the acts have been so amateurish. Now, I just want to put you on notice that I will continue to answer your hecklers without protest. But the next time I see one of your policemen trying to keep a crowd from indicating its friendship to the United States, I am going to blast the whole bunch of you publicly in a way you'll never forget. We have our differences and I believe in discussing them honestly and candidly. But we don't have to make a joke out of the whole business."

The "kitchen debate" and 'the staged heckling were window dressing. The real debate took place at Khrushchev's *dacha*, a luxurious country estate built in the days of the Tsars. After a pleasant lunch, and with the wives present, Khrushchev abruptly turned off the table talk and brought up the question of Soviet missile power. Just the day before, he told Nixon, he had been briefed on plans to shoot a rocket into space orbit with a payload of one hundred tons. Though Soviet missiles were the best in the world, he added, their mechanisms sometimes failed to work properly. Recently, a malfunction in an unarmed ICBM had caused it to miss the target area, and for a while it was feared that it would hit Alaska. "No doubt, you monitored that shot," he said. "In fact, I know you did." It was very difficult, given the present state of technology, for a great nation to keep anything like that secret, Nixon replied. Then he complained that though the United States had allowed Andrei Tupolev, the leading Soviet aircraft designer, to visit American missile plants, the Kremlin had not reciprocated. Khrushchev said that the time "is not ripe" for that kind of exchange.

Nixon then asked Khrushchev about a statement that he had made to Averell Harriman, admitting that missiles had been supplied to Red China for use against the Nationalist-held offshore islands of Quemoy and Matsu. This was a lie, Khrushchev said blandly. All he had said was that the Soviet Union would supply missiles if the United States attacked mainland China.

After some discussion of the cost of missiles Khrushchev informed Nixon that the Soviets could flatten the United States with 30 billion rubles invested in ICBMs. "Does that mean," Nixon asked, "that you already have produced those missiles?" Khrushchev conceded that his country merely had the capability. "Certainly you must know this," he said. "You must have our operational plans for war, just as we have your secret war plans." Ranging the field of military hardware, he then told Nixon that the Soviet Union had drastically reduced bomber production. "Missiles are more accurate, and they feel no revulsion at hitting a target, no matter what it is," he said jovially. He also volunteered that modern warfare had made big navies obsolete, that the Soviet

Union was building no more aircraft carriers or cruisers. "But what about submarines?" Nixon pressed. "We are building as many as we can," Khrushchev answered. "They are very good for launching missiles." Looking mockingly at Nixon, he added, "I want to whisper another secret. We will use our submarines to destroy ports, military areas, and our enemy's navy. Any potential enemy will be highly dependent on sea power, we will paralyze him. Our submarines will carry ballistic missiles and antiballistic missiles [ABMs] with a range of five hundred kilometers, and eventually a thousand kilometers."

In a revealing commentary on Soviet psychological warfare Khrushchev disclosed another "secret," that an "interview" for *Pravda* with the Soviet Air Force chief of staff in which he boasted that the USSR could obliterate the United States in a nuclear war had been dictated by Khrushchev himself—in answer to purported statements made by "American generals" of their country's retaliatory power. He also accused the United States of planning to set up missile bases in Iran. ("You may think your treaty with the Iranians is secret, but I can give you a true copy of it.") Khrushchev admitted, however, that the text of the treaty contained no provisions for missile bases. Nixon countered by informing Khrushchev that the United States, too, knew what was going on—and he cited as an example the directions for subversive activities issued to representatives of Communist Parties at a Moscow meeting. Khrushchev's reply was the old chestnut that communists have "always been against subversion and individual terror—but when the bourgeoisie does not surrender power peacefully, then mass uprisings are justified, and favored by communists."

Nixon, of course, immediately cited the terrorism directed against him in Latin America. Piously, Khrushchev said, "You are my guest, but truth is my mother, so I will not evade that"—and proceeded to do so immediately. The Soviets had favored the anti-Nixon riots, but this was the product of "righteous Russian indignation" over American policy, and not against Nixon specifically. The violence was directed at the American "imperialistic" approach. "What about the Soviet Union's approach to Hungary, Poland, and East Germany?" Nixon asked. Ah, said Khrushchev, that was an entirely different matter—and changed the subject. When he advocated free elections in Vietnam, Nixon interjected that he was glad Khrushchev agreed with the principle of free elections. "If you are for free elections in Vietnam, why are you against elections in East Germany?" But again Khrushchev changed the subject, shifting to the presence of Western troops in West Berlin and making an opening for Nixon to remark that the Soviets had eight divisions in East Germany.

For two hours they debated the German question, as Khrushchev tried to get Nixon to state *his* position rather than that of the United States. Then he reverted to the theme song of the visit—that the United States and/or Nixon were threatening him with war. On the nuclear test ban Khrushchev was evasive. Nixon asked him why, if he could not agree to inspection as a means of preventing underground testing, he refused to accept a ban on tests in the atmosphere. Khrushchev said it was "all or nothing at all." Nixon then brought up the question of a summit meeting with Eisenhower. About what was the Premier ready to negotiate? Surely he did not want a meeting at which he had already foreclosed all options. Khrushchev had no answer to that.

As Nixon would write, "We had ended up [after five and a half hours] where we had started. On each controversial point, Khrushchev had insisted that he was right and that we were wrong. He did not give an inch. He yielded perhaps half an inch on only one point I made: that he could not expect President Eisenhower to go to a summit conference merely to sign his name to Soviet proposals. But he added that the same was true for him: he would not go to a summit conference to sign U.S. proposals. 'I would much rather go hunting and shoot ducks,' he said."

The official meetings, the visit to the *Lenin*, the Soviet Union's untested but propaganda-rich atomic icebreaker, the inspection trips—these made the news. Far more significant were Nixon's own observations of the Soviet empire. When he started out for Moscow, he had been predisposed to be impressed by evidences of Soviet strength. He began to see, almost from his first hours there, that many American policy-makers had overrated Soviet industrial and military might. This did not mean that he considered the Soviet Union a pushover, and he realized that by maximum expenditures of effort and resources the Soviets could make spectacular achievements—sometimes at a cost hardly commensurate with the results. But Soviet productive capacity, methods, and technology were not impressive in American terms, even when the Russians were putting their best foot forward.

The heavy-machine-tool plant in Novosibirsk, which was proudly shown him, was years behind its American equivalent, and about one third of its equipment was obsolescent American machinery of the Lend-Lease days. Automation was nonexistent, although the Russians used the term for any remote-control device. The cities that had been billed as the "Chicago of Siberia" or the "Pittsburgh of Siberia" were primitive aggregations of buildings, unpaved streets, and many "blueprints" of things always to come. Communications between Siberia and European Russia were limited to the two-track Trans-Siberian Railroad. Motor roads—seas of mud in the spring and fall, blocked by snow in the winter—could be used only in the dry summer season. (The need was perhaps not great in a country whose automotive industry produced only a hundred thousand cars a year.) Construction, a desperate Soviet need, was fast but sloppy. Bricks crumbled and were badly laid. The houses cracked and chipped within months. The slums of Moscow were among the worst he had seen in any so-called modern state. Even the side shown to tourists was drab, ugly, and cheerless. The secret police were still very much in evidence. The midnight arrests of the Stalin era had ended, some of the pressure was off—but no one knew how long this would last. The capabilities of the *Lenin* were not impressive even as described by Russian engineers, and Admiral Hyman Rickover, who accompanied the Vice President on board, had found its atomic plant less efficient than he had been led to believe. In short, the industrial knowhow to match Khrushchev's post-Sputnik boasts was nowhere discernible.

But Nixon had learned much from his encounters with Khrushchev—lessons that would accrue to the advantage of the United States in its dealings with the masters of the Kremlin. In *Six Crises* he touched more than casually on this:

Khrushchev has often been called a chess player in conducting his international policies—I suppose because chess is a favorite

Russian game. I do not know chess, but I do know poker; and there is no doubt that Khrushchev would have made a superb poker player. First, he is out to win. Second, like any good poker player, he plans ahead so that he can win the big pots. He likes to bluff, but he knows that if you bluff on small pots and fail consistently to produce the cards, you must expect your opponent to call your bluff on the big pots. . . . Khrushchev has caught us bluffing on some small pots. He assumes, therefore, that we may be bluffing on Berlin—the big pot—and he may be tempted to call us on that one. There is nothing more dangerous in dealing with a man like Khrushchev than to talk bigger than we are prepared to act. . . .

The Eisenhower-Dulles foreign policy was formulated on the principle that we should stand ready to call international Communism's bluff on any pot, large or small. If we let them know that we will defend freedom when the stakes are small, the Soviets are not encouraged to threaten freedom where the stakes are higher. That is why the two small islands of Quemoy and Matsu, and all the other peripheral areas, are so important in the poker game of world politics.

Finally, I had seen a striking example of Khrushchev's diplomatic tactics.

First, he demands something to which he is not entitled. Second, he threatens war if he does not get what he demands. Third, he charges that we will be endangering the peace unless we negotiate on his demands. And fourth, the price of peace is giving him half or more of what he was not entitled to in the first place.

These thoughts, perhaps, were on Nixon's mind when he faced a mass press conference at Spaso House, the American Embassy, on August 2, his last day in the Soviet Union. Given the limited goals he had set for himself, the Soviet trip had been a success. Reports from Washington reflected the President's pleasure over the way he had comported himself under pressure from Khrushchev. American diplomats in Moscow were unanimous in their praise of his "kitchen debate," which they considered a triumph for the American cause. His TV-radio address to the Russian people the night before, spelling out in calm detail the American position, had been well received by everyone except the Soviet press. He had gotten a positive response from Khrushchev to Eisenhower's invitation. In short, he was content that the assignment was completed. But he did not know what was in store for him in Warsaw.

The Polish Government did not tell the people of Warsaw when the Vice President was arriving. It did not announce the route he would take into the city. But the people had their grapevine, and they knew. A quarter of a million strong they lined the highway from Warsaw's military airport to the city itself. When the open limousine came into view, they cheered, applauded, shouted, sang, and pressed forward. Here and there among the laughing faces women wept. Flowers were thrown into Nixon's car—so many flowers that the driver repeatedly had to stop to clear the windshield. When he did, men and women surrounded the car, seizing Nixon's hand and kissing it.

The contrast between the smiling excited faces of the crowd and the devastated streets of the Polish capital added a poignancy to the scene. The Poles had done much with their limited means, and in spite of the drain of the Soviet occupation, to rebuild Warsaw. It was all solid, in contrast to the ramsackle Soviet buildings, and in good taste. The "Old Town" with its lovely medieval square had been leveled by the Nazis; it was now completely restored, using the paintings of Canaletto as a guide to structure and embellishment. But there were still whole blocks piled with rubble, one building standing solitary, the shell-scarred façades in visual obbligato.

The Poles, however, seemed used to living in a city-that-was. The Nixon visit was more important at the moment, and they were ready to say it. They did not merely shout "Long live Nixon." They also called out, "Long live America! We love America! We love Poland!" It was a patriotic demonstration to show that whatever their government might do or say, they themselves belonged to the West. All the next day, whenever Nixon made an appearance, the crowds had mysteriously learned of it and gathered in large numbers to cheer or to sing "Stolat—*May You Live To Be a Hundred Years.*"

The Vice President's party learned quickly that there was some free speech in Poland. A Polish woman proclaimed emphatically, "When Khrushchev was here, they brought us in trucks and buses to welcome him. The government gave us flowers to throw. For Mr. Nixon we bought the flowers ourselves." Another Pole said to me, "The thing you Americans must learn is never to turn your back on the Russians." Within the government, moreover, the pro-American demonstrations were welcomed. A representative of the Foreign Ministry said to me obliquely that the Soviets would not be able to overlook the significance of the popular feeling. "Khrushchev will be annoyed when he learns that two and a half times as many people turned out for the Vice President of the United States than we could muster for him." Nixon, who found the country's Premier, Wladislaw Gomulka, tough, shrewd, and resourceful, was told that this was almost the official view.

On Monday, August 3, Warsaw made public a communiqué from Moscow and Washington, announcing the Eisenhower-Khrushchev meeting. The official Polish reaction was guarded, almost worried, but the meeting was hailed for the lessening of East-West tension it might herald. One Foreign Office official felt constrained to say, "I cannot help remembering another occasion when the Russians offered friendship to one of their enemies. It resulted in the Stalin-Hitler Pact and the partition of Poland." Then he smiled. "Like Khrushchev, we can speak in old sayings. 'When the cat fights, a mouse can steal the cheese.'" But the man in the street cheered all the louder for the Vice President and for America. "This is a great day for Poland," a college instructor said. "There may be some dangers, but it's better than war over Berlin."

The Vice President was back in Washington on August 5. The MATS terminal was crowded with dignitaries. A tired but exhilarated Richard Nixon stood at the head of the plane's ramp, with Pat at his side, waving and smiling. He had completed a tough assignment, crossing swords with Khrushchev yet not endangering the American position. His personal popularity was at its highest. But a long hard road stretched before him—the toughest road any American can travel. At its end was Chicago and the Republican

National Convention. And beyond that, perhaps, lay the Presidency—another assignment as fraught with perils as Caracas, as touchy as the debate with Khrushchev. Then Nixon slowly descended to the cheering crowd. Like all seasoned travelers, he knew that a man walks a step at a time. And he also knew that even as men make history, history makes men. It had plucked him up, and it could cast him down again.

17

The Two Defeats

"MAKE me a promise. Don't get fat and don't lose your zeal. You can be President some day." Those words were said to Richard Nixon on May 8, 1952, by Governor Thomas E. Dewey. It was not the first time that Nixon had been told that the Presidency might be his. In 1950, after the victory that elected him to the United States Senate, I said to him, "Dick, if you play your cards right, you'll be President," and it was typical of similar sentiments he had heard from other friends.

There was really no overwhelming reason for this belief, except for the tradition which says that the White House door is open to any American. But there was a political intensity about him which made it seem likely that he would never stop until he had reached the top. Nixon, of course, received the accolades with a deprecating smile. His rocketing rise to the Vice Presidency, however, turned a long-shot possibility into a realizable dream, and Dwight Eisenhower's illnesses had three times brought the Presidency briefly within the realm of probability. During the second Eisenhower Administration, moreover, it was apparent to those privy to White House thinking that the President was deliberately grooming Nixon to be his successor. Nixon had been, in fact, the first

Vice President in the nation's history who could legitimately wear the title of Assistant President, so consistent was his participation in the affairs of state.

He had been, however, as detached as any man can be who comes so close to the eventuality of high office. He could observe at first hand the burdens and strains of the Presidency. He knew too well the fickleness of public favor. And he was also touchily cognizant that the very factors which had projected him onto the national scene also worked against his candidacy. Twice in his career, after feeling the rage that he provoked among his adversaries, he had seriously contemplated retiring from politics. On the second occasion, just before the New Hampshire primary of March 1956, he had been so close to it that those few friends aware of his state of mind were convinced the step was imminent. On March 2, 1956—ten days before the voters changed his mind by their well-timed endorsement—I had said in a personal and confidential letter:

> I have been thinking about our conversation, and I still believe it would be a calamity if you quit now. . . Many, many people have pinned their hopes on you. If you back down, you will be letting them down. Can I urge you to do one thing? Let the matter ride for several weeks before you make up your mind. The furor will die down. Once you have acted, you cannot retrace your steps.

As he began his second Vice Presidential term, ambition had overcome the knowledge of what the Presidency would cost. But he also knew that if he gave the slightest hint of Presidential designs, it would expose him and his family to the kind of nagging attack that so troubled them all. Pat Nixon had never liked the world of politics. She had urged him repeatedly to remove himself from the rough-and-dirty of the political world. And she had no desire to see him plunging into the maelstrom of a Presidential contest. When, in an informal moment in 1959 at his house, a close friend had asked, "Dick, why does anyone want to be President of the United States?" Pat had sighed and said with real feeling, "You can say *that* again!" But by that time it was too late. Too many people had committed themselves to his candidacy, and he in turn had accepted their encouragement and quietly joined in their plans. To a man so engrossed by affairs of state, a bill of divorcement from politics have been impossible—a psychological factor in his decision more important than the normal ambition of every public figure to take his place in history.

Characteristically, Richard Nixon decided to run at a time when his personal fortunes and those of the Republican Party were pathetically low—right after the by-election of 1958. An economic decline, and President Eisenhower's refusal to use the White House and its prestige for building up the GOP, had convinced many that the party was in the process of rapid disintegration, much as the Whigs had been in the early 1850s. There were 35 Republican Senators out of 100, 135 Republicans in the 437-member House of Representatives, 14 Republican governors, and only 7 state legislatures in which the GOP controlled both houses. To win in 1960, Nixon knew, he would have to get the full vote of his party and add to it 50 per cent of the independent vote and 5 to 6 million Democrats. A Gallup poll, taken after the 1958 election, pitting him against Senator John F. Kennedy, showed Nixon trailing 41 to 59 per cent.

It was on a bleak and cold November 7, 1958, as Nixon recalls, that he met with Leonard Hall, former Republican National Chairman, and Clifford Folger, then Ambassador to Belgium, who had served as Republican Finance Chairman under Hall. The meeting had been suggested by Hall, and he opened the discussion with "It's time for you to decide what you're going to do in 1960. If you *are* going to be a candidate, you've got to start now."

Hall's statement came as no surprise to Nixon. But before answering, he outlined the situation as he saw it, presenting all the arguments against running. Then he asked Hall, "What are my chances for getting the nomination and winning the election?" As of that moment, Hall said candidly, Nelson Rockefeller, who had just taken the New York Governorship by more than half a million votes, would have a slight edge. But this advantage would be dissipated as he became enmeshed in the duties of the office. He was sure that Nixon would have no difficulty in winning the nomination. As to election, the odds were 5 to 1 against him, but with hard work and a few breaks there was a fighting chance.

These were not the most encouraging words to hear. Len Hall, once the ruler of New York politics, had his own reasons for urging Nixon: he had been brusquely pushed aside by Rockefeller. The Governor-elect, with the ballots hardly settled in their boxes, was saying that he was not certain whether he would "spend the next four winters in Albany"—as open a bid for the Republican Presidential nomination as he could make. If Hall was to stop the Rockefeller bandwagon, he would need a candidate without delay.

The time had come for Nixon to make an unequivocal decision—and he agreed to run. Hall, of course, had expected this. But he was close enough to Nixon to realize that the Vice President would have preferred to slip into the nomination without categorically declaring his candidacy, relying on his leadership of the Republican Party which he held as a result of Eisenhower's default, to turn the trick for him at the last minute. At another time, this would have been possible, but it could no longer work against a man as determined, direct, and powerful as Nelson Rockefeller. When the meeting broke up, Hall agreed to line up delegates for the 1960 convention, and Folger to become Finance Chairman once he resigned his Ambassadorship.

The first real strategy conference was held in Key Biscayne, in December, at the home of C. B. ("Bebe") Rebozo, a Florida real estate man whose friendship with the Vice President was based in part on his total lack of involvement in the incestuous and demanding world of politics. The others present were, for the most part, old personal friends and political supporters dating back to the early California days—Jack Drown, a regional magazine distributor, and Ray Arbuthnot, a good farmer with no experience in national politics. The professionalism was supplied by Len Hall and Robert Finch. Finch, unknown nationally, had gone through his baptism of fire in the unorthodox political battles of California. He was shrewd, attractive, easy of manner, able, and lacking the introversion that made Nixon such an enigma to the average politician.

This typically Nixonian mix of friends and pros arrived at a sound estimate of the Vice President's situation and worked out a *modus operandi* for the months to come. With Rockefeller obviously in the race the first question to be answered was: "Would he be able to make any sizable inroads into Nixon strength among regular Republicans?" Of this there seemed little likelihood. In three national campaigns Nixon had put most of the Republican Party machinery in his debt. He was known and respected by County and State Chairmen, by the congressional contingent, and by those whose contributions had kept the GOP alive in its leanest days. A minimal effort would keep the regulars safe for Nixon, and Nixon could go about his duties as Vice President and Eisenhower's anointed without having to grub for party support. From this privileged sanctuary, moreover, Nixon could quietly woo the so-called Republican "liberals"—those who had given the nomination in 1940 to Wendell Willkie and snatched it from Robert A. Taft in 1952.

But at this and other early meetings of the inner circle the question of Nixon's probable Democratic opponent was also discussed. The Vice President was certain that Jack Kennedy would be the most difficult man to defeat in a general election, and that he was also the most likely to be nominated. Nixon had served with Kennedy in the House of Representatives and had seen him in action in the Senate. Though their backgrounds differed wildly, Nixon liked Kennedy and never underestimated his political punch. He had, Nixon would write, "high intelligence, great energy, and a particularly effective television personality. He also had unlimited money which already had enabled him to employ a large, skilled staff of organizers, speech-writers, pollsters and others essential for a successful campaign. He had a head start with a personal staff who had begun their drive back in 1956, soon after he had come so close to winning the Democratic nomination for Vice President."

To those who argued that Kennedy was weak because of his youth, inexperience, and wealth, Nixon pointed out that he himself was only four years older, that Kennedy had begun his national political career in 1946—Nixon's year—that experience is fine but makes enemies for you, that wealth was no longer a minus factor, and that Kennedy's Catholicism would help rather than hurt. On this last point he was saying only what a careful study made for Kennedy had demonstrated.

Among Nixon and his advisers the consensus was that Nixon should travel the high road until the convention—a statesmanlike Vice President to the most popular President in living memory—unless and until Nelson Rockefeller decided openly to contest the nomination in the Republic primaries that would begin in March of 1960. There were some who faulted this decision, but it proved to be a good one.

By mid-1959 the professionals were conceding that the Nixon strategy was the only one for him. Governor Rockefeller's stock fell drastically when, to straighten out his inherited financial mess in New York, he was forced to raise taxes. By mid-1959 the Republican honeymoon with Rockefeller had ended, as Len Hall predicted it would, and Nixon's star was on the ascendant. In a memorandum to *Newsweek*, I summed up the situation as it then stood:

> Though Vice President Nixon is today's front-runner in the Republican Presidential stakes, he is under no illusion that the road to the Chicago Convention will be an easy one. He has always viewed the polls with a jaundiced eye—and he continues to do so despite the seemingly commanding lead given to him by Gallup and Trendex. Recent surveys have shown that both the GOP leadership and the rank-and-file are strongly for Nixon.
>
> But by nature, Nixon has always run scared—a form of practical pessimism. . . . However well Nixon may show up in the current trial heats, he and his aides are well aware that his chief rival, Governor Nelson Rockefeller of New York, can muster the muscle of part of the Eastern banking interests, of his great personal fortune, and of the impact on members of the mass communications of the Rockefeller Foundation beneficence. Nixon operates with a very small budget and a minuscule staff—one man to handle the calls and demands which pour into the Vice President's office daily, and to carry the political ball with

state chairmen, national committeemen, party workers, etc. In the Nixon organization there is one chief and very few Indians. The lights burn in Nixon's office long after others in the building have blinked out—but the staff is always desperately trying to hold its own against the pyramiding work.

Part of the difficulty stems from the multiplicity of Nixon's chores as "Assistant President." . . . In recent weeks, advisers have urged him to drop some of his activities in order to put in more time at the job of furthering his chances for the nomination. . . .

The Vice President believes, however, that the soundest and most effective course for him at this time is to concentrate on his duties. He is fully aware that he cannot run against the Eisenhower record, but he is slowly building up a body of views which support the President, yet indicate differences of degree or emphasis. A study of Nixon's speeches shows that he has been striking out for himself with increasing frequency ever since he differed with the Administration by urging tax cuts during the late recession. This is a delicate operation, for Nixon must at the same time create a separate public identity yet not antagonize Mr. Eisenhower. . . .

The issues of the coming campaign are, of course, very much on Nixon's mind. For one thing, they are also the daily problems with which he must deal. Often, however, what is big in the newspapers now will be dead by convention time or election day. At the time the first Soviet Sputnik went up, Nixon predicted flatly that this would not be an issue in 1960— the pundits notwithstanding.

He can, on occasion, fail to spot what seems like a simple fact of life. During one of the periodic Democratic outcries against Administration cuts in defense and the lowering of draft calls, Nixon wondered out loud (though privately) about the possible political effect. I asked him: "Dick, did you ever hear of a mother who voted *against* a man who kept her son out of the Army?" Nixon looked up, a little startled, then nodded his agreement.

What the issues will be in 1960 can change overnight—in

diplomatic crisis or economic depression. But given the indicated course of current history, it is Nixon's belief that the issues will depend in part on the candidates. A contest between Nixon and Senator Lyndon Johnson would differ radically from one between Nixon and Adlai Stevenson, Nixon and Kennedy— or Rockefeller and Senator Hubert Humphrey. On the very limited area of personal attack, for example, a Lyndon Johnson would be deprived of an issue against Nixon by the many flattering comments he has made about the Vice President in the past. . . .

What could lose the 1960 Presidential election for a Republican candidate? Nixon shrugs. "There could be many reasons— new issues that come out of left field, not working hard enough, thinking about how we can lose instead of planning on how to win."

Again, on November 27, 1959, I summed up the Nixon strategy:

Vice President Nixon plans to "mind the store" for the next six months. However energetically Governor Rockefeller ranges the nation, Nixon intends to remain close to Washington. With Mr. Eisenhower on a goodwill tour, the Vice President feels that his duty will be to sit as head of the National Security Council and the Cabinet, to preside over the Senate, and to work directly with such groups as the President's Committee on Government Contracts (which fights discrimination in hiring) and the Cabinet Committee on Economic Growth. He heads both these committees.

"No matter how much I might want to," Nixon says, "I would be unable to devote much time to extensive trips."

While Nixon was "minding the store" the more perceptive national reporters were beginning to turn away from the Herblock figure of Nixon climbing out of the sewer, and with some sympathy were attempting to analyze the loner who was making his bid for the Presidency. Theodore H. White, in *The Making of a President, 1960*, would offer the most serious evaluation:

Having made it on his own, he has had to learn to court people whom he has necessarily disliked. He has had to realize how vulnerable a naked man, without money or family prestige, can be in a hostile world that over and over savages him for no reason he can define. . . . A brooding, moody man, given to long stretches of introspection, he trusts only himself and his wife—and after that his confidence, in any given situation, is yielded only to the smallest possible number of people. . . . No other candidate [operated] with fewer personnel or kept more of the critical decisions in his own hands. Richard Nixon is a man of major talent—but a man of solitary, uncertain impulse.

As the 1960 campaign developed it was this solitary impulse that, without a Murray Chotiner to control or circumvent it, led to grave decisions that may have cost him the election. It was this solitary impulse, too, that made him insist on being his own campaign manager—a course as dangerous as being one's own lawyer in a major litigation. The two men he opposed—Rockefeller in the battle for the nomination and Kennedy in the general election—were as different from Nixon as they could conceivably be, certain of their money and position, never finding it necessary to defy the world because at their smile the world would happily defer, always assured that their play for power would be regarded as gracious and altruistic.

"I hate the thought of Dick being President of the United States," Rockefeller had said—a wounding remark to Nixon, and yet one which may have led him to treat the Governor in ways that eventually contributed to costing him the election. He did not know that the financial community, so important to him if he were to have the sinews of political war, had rejected Rockefeller from the very start because they considered him a *parvenu* in politics, a man who had not served his party in the days of defeat, a leader who thought that riches could buy those who were not as rich—but rich enough to count.

By late December of 1959 Rockefeller had read the handwriting on the wall. He could not take over the financial community, woo away from Nixon the regular Republicans, or stand the pressures and the strains of day-by-day campaigning in the boondocks. The Eisenhower Republicans suspected, and rightly so, that he was ready to repudiate him. On December 25, 1959, therefore, Rockefeller announced prematurely that he was out of the race—a mistake he would make again in 1968—and would not run in the primaries. He refused, however, to endorse Nixon. Privately, he said, "The more I campaign, the more I put Nixon on the front pages and the better I make the party look in general."

Rockefeller's withdrawal, paradoxically, was a blow to the Nixon forces. He wanted these contests to generate some excitement, to take some of the play away from the Democrats whose struggle for the nomination kept him in the public eye. "We've just been kicked in the groin," one of Nixon's close advisers said. On the other hand, there was a feeling of relief for Nixon. He had always deplored the way Republicans cannibalized each other. With no primaries there would be none of the bitter and destructive intraparty warfare that had in the past destroyed its electoral chances. The mistakes to be made, sadly enough, would come from Nixon himself. To compound the misfortune, Nixon would also have a run of bad luck.

At the turn of the year, however, Nixon's chances looked excellent. The Soviet trip had boosted his stock mightily—and the polls reflected it, with Kennedy now trailing 47 to 53. With the President away Nixon interceded in the steel strike, which for 116 days had crippled the economy. With a Taft-Hartley injunction due to expire late in January 1960, Nixon stepped in—bringing union and management together for eight days of arduous negotiation in which he participated. The settlement was the first steel contract since World War II that did not bring higher steel prices, yet gave labor an increase in pay commensurable with the rise in productivity. Neither the Soviet trip nor the steel settlement could have been predicted, but they gave Nixon enough national approbation to put him ahead of Kennedy.

No one could foresee, however, that having "withdrawn" from the race, Rockefeller would seek the nomination by indirection. Through "position papers" on the issues and in speeches around the country, he attacked the Eisenhower Administration, giving the Democrats the kind of ammunition they happily accepted. Only to a minor degree did he differ with the Eisenhower Administration, but these differences were made to seem like major criticisms of policy. None of this could be reflected in the primaries since Nixon was running unopposed. But Nixon knew in the long run this bracketing fire, which he could not answer since Rockefeller was not an avowed candidate, would hurt after the convention.

Early in March, Nixon was given some far more serious bad news. Dr. Arthur Burns, former Chairman of the President's Council of Economic Advisers, warned Nixon that the economy was slowing down. Unless the White House moved decisively, this slide would reach its low point in October, when it would have the most impact on the election. Nixon had seen this happen in 1954 and 1958, with disastrous consequences for the Republican Party. But neither Eisenhower nor the Cabinet agreed with the Burns prognosis, and it was further argued by the President that it would be improper for him to act simply on political grounds. Nixon pressed as hard as he could, but with no effect. A month before Election Day, the marked dip in the economy that Burns had predicted was an incontrovertible fact, and this hurt Nixon.

On the international scene the Administration suffered a serious setback. On the eve of a summit conference in Paris between Eisenhower and Khrushchev the Soviets shot down a CIA U-2 "spy" plane over Soviet territory. Instead of issuing a bland denial that the plane had been on a routine weather mission, the President admitted its espionage role. There was a furor at home over his ineptness and a great flailing of arms in Moscow. Khrushchev arrived at the conference his boorish best, insulted the President, demanded an apology, and broke up the meeting. Though there was considerable sympathy at home for Eisenhower, Khrushchev's bluster had created an international incident and, as Nixon put it, "the peace issue was tarnished."

This was bad luck and bad timing. But before the convention had officially convened, Nixon himself acted with incredibly bad judgment. He was obsessed with the idea that the Republican Convention must be dignified and harmonious, in contrast to the noisy spectacle put on by the Democrats two weeks earlier. But he knew that the Rockefeller forces were determined to create as much dissension as possible in the hope of so dividing the convention that their candidate could take the nomination away from Nixon. The Vice President knew that there was no danger of a Rockefeller blitz. What worried him was the thought that a battling convention would give the Democrats invaluable ammunition against him, and that a split party might deny him the Republican votes he so urgently needed. At issue was the platform.

For months a small group of Republicans, chairmaned by Charles Percy, head of Bell & Howell, had worked on a draft of the 1960 Republican platform. They had consulted with both wings of the party in an effort to keep the regulars and the Rockefeller delegates happy. From Albany and from his personal headquarters on West 55th Street in Manhattan, however, Rockefeller had shown his displeasure. He wanted a platform that would cry havoc, that would proclaim a national emergency, and that would be critical of the Eisenhower Administration. This, of course, neither the President nor Nixon could tolerate.

When the Rockefeller forces would accept no compromise on two planks, national defense and civil rights—threatening the floor fight that Nixon so feared—the Vice President decided to take matters into his own hands. From Washington he called former Attorney General Herbert Brownell, still influential in New York politics, asking him to arrange a meeting with Rockefeller. The place suggested for this meeting was Brownell's home, representing neutral territory. But Rockefeller would not have it so. After consulting his strategists in Chicago, he told Brownell that he would meet Nixon in his Fifth Avenue apartment—and insisted that after the secret conference the communiqué issued to the press must state that it had taken place at Nixon's initiative. Whatever policy statement resulted, moreover, would come from Rockefeller and not Nixon. It was, of course, a calculated slap in the face, but Nixon accepted—without informing any of his lieutenants in Chicago of the impending meeting or the terms under which it had been negotiated.

For seven hours, until early on July 23, Nixon and Rockefeller debated the wording of the planks in controversy. The result was the fourteen-point "Compact of Fifth Avenue." In effect, little of the language in the platform had been changed. The national defense plank, on which Rockefeller had been so adamant, saw an addition of 62 words to the original 540 and a slight pointing-up in emphasis. Only in one instance did Nixon accede to anything new—a plank calling for a thorough reorganization of the Executive Branch of government. It was not so much the changes that hurt Nixon as the secrecy of his meeting, and what many at the convention saw as a cap-in-hand approach to the man who had done the most to combat the conservatives in the Republican Party. The terms of the compact, moreover, caught the Nixon staff in Chicago completely by surprise. Herbert Klein, Nixon's press secretary in the 1956 campaign and on some of his journeyings, was denying its existence to the press almost at the very time it was announced. He had been speaking the truth as he knew it, but the press accused him of deception.

Among the party regulars—few of whom had compared the texts of the platform as drafted and as "revised" in the Compact—there was a feeling that Nixon had doublecrossed them. Senator Barry Goldwater, who was trying to quiet a Young Republican organization clamoring for his candidacy, called the "Compact of Fifth Avenue" a "surrender" to the liberals and "the Munich of the Republican Party." The platform committee was in open revolt. In Newport, Rhode Island, the President was furious because of the proposal to reorganize the Executive Branch. (He had planned to outline such a reorganization in his farewell message to Congress.) When the platform committee met the next night, it refused to change a word of its draft. The convention seemed out of control—which was just what Nixon had feared and Rockefeller had wanted.

At this point Nixon made a second mistake. Arriving in Chicago on Monday morning, he decided to make his fight with the platform committee on the civil rights plank. The original draft had been moderate in tone, avoiding any overt support of Federal intervention in the South or condoning of the sit-ins that were exaxerbating white Southern tempers. The Rockefeller draft outbid the Democrats for the Negro vote and incidentally reflected Nixon's personal feelings. But plumping for the Rockefeller language, Nixon guaranteed for himself the loss of the Southern states, steadily swinging into the Republican column since 1952, without any commensurate gain in the Northern Negro vote. And this loss in turn meant the loss of the election, as more than one delegate predicted. (Had Nixon carried the South, an analysis of the returns that November proved, he would have overcome the tiny popular plurality that gave the election to Kennedy.)

Only one other decision at the convention hurt Nixon as badly —and he would not know this until the campaign began: the selection of Henry Cabot Lodge as the Vice Presidential candidate. For Lodge proved to be both lazy and unpredictable. While Nixon ranged all fifty states, Lodge insisted on an afternoon nap each day. He also took it upon himself to make policy for the top of the ticket, his major excursion in that field being the announcement that Nixon would appoint a Negro to his Cabinet if elected. But this was all in the future. As Nixon stood before the cheering delegates to accept the nomination, there were storm clouds ahead, but no signs of the deluge. The rhetoric of his speech was of a piece with the occasion, full of exhortations and warnings of the peril ahead for the nation, yet confident of victory. It ended quietly, with an anecdote about the man who had been nominated in the same city by the same party a hundred years earlier.

"A hundred years ago," Nixon said, "Abraham Lincoln was asked during the dark days of the tragic War Between the States whether he thought God was on his side. His answer was 'My concern is not whether God is on our side but whether we are on God's side.' My fellow Americans, may that ever be our prayer for our country. . . ."

And in the early stages of the campaign it seemed that God was on Nixon's side. The Gallup poll showed him leading Kennedy 53 to 47 ten days after the Republican convention. His staff, headed by the experienced Len Hall, the campaign chairman, and Bob Finch, the campaign director, had been planning every step of the days and weeks to come. Herb Klein's slow-spoken understatement had softened the hostility of reporters and columnists, and in many instances their copy showed it. A fiercely loyal Rose Mary Woods shielded Nixon from those who felt that their minor needs were of major importance to the candidate. It would be some time before it became apparent that having two campaign chiefs, no matter how compatible, was a mistake. Sometimes their activities overlapped, and at other times important decisions were not made because of the gap between them. Reporters calling Len Hall would occasionally be told, "That's Bob Finch's department," and on calling Finch they learned that it was "Hall's department." James Bassett, the Planning Director, was too often overcome by the sense of his own martyrdom, the heaviness of his burden, and the unfair size of his salary.

But what the campaign needed more than anything was the iron hand and cold eye of Murray Chotiner, *hors de combat* as a result of the going-over he had received at the hands of the Senate Permanent Investigating subcommittee and its counsel, Bobby Kennedy, brother of the Democratic nominee. Lacking Chotiner, Nixon tried to be both candidate and campaign manager—a job beyond the energies or the scope of a single individual. Nixon's instincts were good. Had he not been personally involved, his understanding of the rhythm of public opinion, the ebb and flow of popular enthusiasm, the timing that is so essential in politics would have been operative. But as a man keeping up with a murderous schedule and making routine tactical decisions in moments of deadening fatigue, he could not be the judge of the day-to-day strategy that makes up a political campaign. As Theodore H. White would point out, "Richard M. Nixon was running for President, and it was his instinct as solitary leader that governed his campaign from beginning to end."

For a while that instinct seemed to be speaking loud and clear. Late in August, in Atlanta, Georgia, he was welcomed by 150,000 people, primed for him by their own enthusiasm, standing five and six deep along the street as his motorcade went by. In the fourteen years in which he had been campaigning Nixon had never received a reception of this warmth and magnitude—"the greatest thing in Atlanta since the premiere of *Gone With The*

Wind," Ralph McGill would remark. In spite of himself Nixon was impressed, and he was convinced that he had found the formula that would win him the election. It was in Atlanta that he tested the set speech which, with variants, would carry him through most of the campaign. His appeal to Democrats to turn to the Republican Party as the custodian of Jeffersonian principles cast aside by the latter-day Democrats struck home. So, too, did his plea for nonpartisanship, for freedom through local government rather than the behemoth state.

But there was one issue with which he could not contend, and he watched helplessly as the Democratic strategists pushed it for all it was worth—John F. Kennedy's Catholicism. He had instructed all Republican campaigners not to raise the religious issue. He had flatly warned that anyone who did would not be allowed to take part in the campaign. He had closed the book on Jack Kennedy's religion. But there were people beyond his control who openly plunged in—his friend Dr. Norman Vincent Peale being one—by questioning the fitness of any Catholic for public office and by suggesting that Kennedy's ties to the hierarchy of his Church would subject him to pressures and condition his acts. With justice the Kennedys could cry "Foul!" and they worried the point throughout the weeks leading to Election Day, ascribing anti-Catholic sentiments by innuendo to any who opposed the Democratic candidate. This ensured Kennedy's hold on the big-city Catholic bloc, which had been drifting away from the Democratic Party, but it also gave Protestants a twinge of conscience. Were they against Kennedy because they disapproved of his politics or his Catholicism?

The religious issue, however, was not the sole determinant in the outcome of the election. Bad luck and faulty instinct both contributed dramatically to the decline in Nixon's electoral fortunes.

The bad luck was physical. Weakened by an attack of the flu and a temperature of 103 that he had ignored in order to address a convention of the Machinists Union, Nixon was susceptible to infection. On his trip through the South, he had struck his knee on a car door. Hot compresses failed to relieve the pain, and on the advice of Dr. Walter Tkach, the White House physician, he had gone to Walter Reed Hospital for X-rays and a fluid tap. Over the weekend he ignored the pain and continued to work on the speeches he planned to deliver in the next two weeks.

On Monday, August 29, he received a call from Tkach, urging him to go back to the hospital. When Nixon protested that he had no time, Tkach said, "Look, I know what your schedule is, and I'm just as anxious as you are to keep it. But you'd better get to the hospital if you don't want to do the rest of the campaign on one leg." At Walter Reed Hospital the doctors told him that the infection in his knee was hemolytic staphylococcus aureus, and that he would have to be off his feet and immobilized for at least two weeks, with his leg in traction.

Nixon's schedule was already a tight one, but he insisted that he would not retreat from his promise to campaign in the fifty states, even though it would mean compressing his appearances into a period two weeks shorter than he had anticipated. Though friends and advisers pleaded with him, pointing out that massive shots of penicillin and other antibiotics had undermined his health, that he had lost weight, and that he needed rest, Nixon overruled them. From that point on he lived in a nightmare of activity.

This bad luck was compounded by his faulty judgment of accepting a challenge to debate Senator Kennedy on television. He knew that the televised debates could do him no good. "Kennedy has everything to gain and very little to lose," he said to me. "I'm better known than he is and I'm the front-runner. By appearing with me, he'll get far greater exposure than he would on paid television time and alone. And how do I handle him? If I hit him hard, he'll have the sympathy of the audience. If I don't, then I'll look weak." But the Republican National Chairman, Thruston B. Morton, had already accepted the principle of the televised debates and Nixon feared that he would seem to be running away from a confrontation with Kennedy if he refused the challenge.

Nixon reasoned that the campaign was going well—much better, in fact, than he had expected. The South seemed solidly his and a swing through the Midwest had been highly successful. But he had not fully recovered from the knee infection or regained the weight lost in the hospital. He could not suspect that the television cameras and the harsh lighting would so relentlessly emphasize what was only slightly apparent in the flesh. And he did not realize that against the Kennedy "charisma"—a word already worn by press usage—the classical style of debate, of making points, would not impress an audience seeking drama rather than logic. This failure to understand the nature of the television medium led him to veto suggestions that he set conditions on the format of the debate which neither Kennedy nor the networks could accept.

On September 26, the afternoon of the first debate, Nixon spent a solitary five hours digesting material prepared by his researchers and cramming his head "with facts and figures which my staff suggested might be raised" by the reporters who were to question him and Jack Kennedy. Nixon might better have spent the time relaxing, but the habits of a lifetime dictated that kind of intensive preparation. By the time he arrived at the studio he was in the grip of a great and rising tension, whereas Kennedy looked hale and fit and deeply tanned. When Ted Rogers suggested make-up, Nixon refused, allowing only an application of powder to cover the "five-o'clock shadow" that the cameras have always caught, even when he is freshly shaven. The powder only added to the wanness that so struck the television audience.

The rest is history. A reading of the text of that first debate shows that Nixon had the edge in the "facts and figures" he had ingested that afternoon. But on the television screen he looked sick, pale, and worried. Because he perspires easily, he seemed nervous every time he wiped the sweat from his face. Kennedy, who had spent the afternoon in a give-and-take session with intimates, exuded confidence; Nixon looked ill-at-ease. Kennedy held the offensive; Nixon, fearful of accusations that he had gone for the jugular, was defensive. Would the outcome have been different if he had "come out swinging," as one of his advisers urged? Would Nixon have been in better shape had he not struck his knee again that evening as he got out of his car to enter the studio?

The major disaster, however, was not in the audience reaction.

Nixon had been hurt, but not too badly. The effect on his advisers and his campaign staff were the major factors in what followed. Until the first debate, they had seen Nixon as the winner. After that they were thrown into a mood of depression that communicated itself to the candidate. And Republican leaders, disconcerted by what they considered to be Nixon's gentle treatment of his opponent and his "me too" approach, descended on him with angry criticism. He had, they said, thrown away the opportunity to let 120 million Americans know that there was a difference between the two parties.

One question, put to Nixon by Sander Vanocur of NBC, had also given tremendous currency to a thoughtless quip made by President Eisenhower. "What major decisions of your Administration has the Vice President participated in?" Eisenhower had been asked a month before. "If you give me a week," he had answered with a grin, "I might think of one." Now, at the height of the campaign and before what may have been the biggest television audience up to that time, this remark was dignified into a serious downgrading of Nixon's contribution to the Eisenhower Administration, thereby depriving him of his major claim to support—his experience in office.

From that point on there was gloom in the Nixon camp, a gloom he was too tired to fight. To pick up strength and the ten pounds he had lost, Nixon took to drinking chocolate milkshakes, four a day. He looked better and stronger in the next three debates, but the damage had been done and neither the impetus nor the enthusiasm of the early days of the campaign were ever regained. Reporters who covered him were certain that though he continued to fight, he had in his mind already lost the election. This was not true, but it had an effect on their stories and communicated itself to the public.

When the polls began to show slippage, the drive went out of the campaign effort. The issues no longer counted, though Nixon continued to stress them—he would devote pages of his account of the 1960 campaign to a painstaking analysis of his position and Kennedy's. The pendulum had swung because a significant segment of the American voting public had decided that they liked Kennedy better. His youth was an asset, his "style" entranced them, his wealth offered them glamor. The issues were for the politicians.

On Election Day the Nixons voted in Whittier, their home town. Then Nixon, weary though he was, decided that the drive to San Diego would do him good. He could not face the long hours of waiting for the polls to close. In 1946 he had taken off by himself, but this was impossible now. With Don Hughes, Jack Sherwood, and John DiBetta of the Los Angeles Police Department, their driver, they rolled south—recognized only once at an Oceanside gas station. When they reached San Diego, Nixon did not want to turn back, and they drove to Tijuana for a Mexican meal.

It was after five when they returned to Los Angeles and the results were already beginning to come in from the East Coast. There was no discernible pattern at first. Kennedy was ahead in some Southern States, Nixon in others. Connecticut had been conceded to the Democrats, but Kennedy's plurality was bigger than Nixon had expected. At 5:30 P.M. the network computers were giving Kennedy the victory. At 6:30 P.M. NBC set the odds at 15 to 1 for Kennedy. A reading of the votes showed a tight election. But as the night progressed Kennedy's lead in the popular vote began to dwindle. At 11 P.M. Len Hall told Nixon, "It's a real squeaker." At 12:20 A.M. Nixon said to the crowd at the Ambassador Hotel, "If the present trend continues, Senator Kennedy will be the next President of the United States."*

The next afternoon Nixon conceded the election formally in a telegram to Kennedy. But the vote remained close—so close that talk of vote fraud in Texas, Illinois, and Missouri stirred Republican hopes. President Eisenhower, in his first conversation with Nixon after the defeat, had himself raised the question and suggested that something be done about it. In the post-election days, however, Nixon was in no shape to give serious thought to anything. His nerves were too close to the skin, his emotions too much engaged. A word of kindness or encouragement brought tears to

---

* That announcement probably cost him Illinois. Hearing it, poll watchers there went home before all the votes had been counted.

his eyes. He found consolation in a message, sent to him by the national reporters who had covered him, ending with, "It was the majority opinion of the regulars in the press corps that we have toured with a champ. And we double it in spades for Pat."

Nixon was further jolted when President Hoover called from New York to Key Biscayne, where the Nixons were resting, relaying a message from Joseph Kennedy, the President-elect's father, asking that victor and vanquished meet. When Nixon asked for Hoover's advice, the former President told him, "We are in enough trouble in the world today. Some indications of national unity are not only desirable but essential." Nixon agreed, then called President Eisenhower to let him know of the impending meeting. Eisenhower, too, approved. "You would look like a sore-head if you didn't," he said. Within minutes Kennedy had called Nixon and the arrangements for the meeting had been made.

Nothing of great import was discussed. They talked of the campaign, of their fatigue now that it was over, of the problems inherent in the Presidency—but this in superficial terms—and of the Central Intelligence Agency. Nixon brought up the question of the admission of Red China to the United Nations, stressing his opposition, and Kennedy seemed to agree, though he admitted that some of his advisers counseled it. Kennedy then remarked that because of the closeness of the election, he might appoint some Republicans to diplomatic posts—Henry Cabot Lodge, perhaps. "I wonder, in fact, if after a few months you yourself might want to undertake an assignment abroad on a temporary basis," Kennedy said. The closeness of the election, Nixon demurred, made it "all the more imperative for me not to accept an assignment in the new Administration. Any other course of action," he said, "would be widely misinterpreted and could be a very damaging blow to the concept of the two-party system of party responsibility." It seemed to Nixon that Kennedy was considerably relieved by the refusal.

But for Nixon there was still the plaguing problem of what to do about the evidence of vote fraud that was piling up. The Kennedy plurality had been minuscule, roughly 113,000 votes. Nixon's percentage of the total vote had been 49.6. The electoral vote had divided 303 to 219. A shift of only 11,000 votes, if properly distributed, would have given Nixon the election. And those votes could be found in the areas where fraud was charged. Among them—and these were sworn to—were the following, tabulated by Nixon:

(1) *Fannin County, Texas, which went 3 to 1 for Kennedy*: there were 4,895 voters on the official "poll tax list" but 6,138 were counted.

(2) *Angela County, Texas, 27th Precinct*: 86 individuals were officially recorded as having voted—but the final tally was Kennedy 147, Nixon 24.

(3) *Fort Bend County, Texas, two adjoining precincts*: in one, which voted Nixon over Kennedy, 458 to 350, 182 ballots were declared void "at the discretion of the judges." But in the other, 68 to 1 for Kennedy, not a single ballot was declared void.

(4) *In Chicago, Mayor Richard Daley's 6th Ward, 38th Precinct*: after 43 voters had cast ballots (by machine), the machine tally read 121 total votes. This precinct returned a final count for Kennedy, 408 to 79.

(5) *In another Chicago precinct*: this one voted for Kennedy, 451 to 67. The initial registration of a husband and wife was challenged on grounds of "false address," but on Election Day both voted; on recanvass it was found that there were no such persons at the address listed.

(6) *Chicago, 2nd Ward, 50th Precinct*: there were only 22 voters on the official list but 77 individuals voted.

These were but a few of the reports that came to Nixon. A careful survey by Earl Mazo for the New York *Herald Tribune* was turning up substantial independent verification of what Nixon knew to be true. And there were large areas still to be explored, such as the Missouri vote in which a section of St. Louis, bulldozed flat for an urban renewal project, had "voted" solidly for Kennedy.

But to get a recount in Cook County, Illinois, Nixon discovered, would take well over a year. There was no assurance that under Texas law any legal action was possible. Nevertheless, Republican leaders felt that the effort involved would be worth it. Even if the election results were not reversed, the party would benefit in the 1962 and 1964 elections. And Kennedy's moral leadership of the nation would be undermined. The Nixon forces were therefore waiting for the go-ahead signal when they were told that no fight for an honest count would be made. It would create a Constitutional crisis, Nixon said, and undercut the new President in his dealings with foreign governments at a touchy time. The final decision, however, was Eisenhower's, though this was not widely known until after his death. He had first encouraged those who favored a legal battle, but he had second thoughts. Nixon concurred, and in *Six Crises* he took all the responsibility. At the time, however, many of those who had worked long and hard in the election were bitter in their reproach of the President. They felt that Eisenhower had once more pulled the rug out from under his Vice President.

All that remained for Nixon, then, was the sad chore of removing himself from public life—there were thousands of letters to be answered, hundreds of offers of employment to be considered, and the accumulation of fourteen years in Washington to be sorted and winnowed. There were dinners to be given for those who had aided him in the campaign or who had been at his side during the hours of trial. And on January 6, before a Joint Session of Congress, there was the prescribed ceremony of counting the electoral votes and announcing the victory of John F. Kennedy, the defeat of Richard Nixon.

"Only once had the defeated candidate had the responsibility of presiding over his own 'funeral' . . . and this had occurred exactly one hundred years before when John C. Breckenridge announced the election of Abraham Lincoln," Nixon would write. He memorialized the occasion by a brief speech to his colleagues of House and Senate. The ovation was long and heartfelt. Even Speaker Sam Rayburn, whose personal feelings toward Nixon had bordered on hatred, applauded, shook his hand, and said, "I'll miss you here, Dick."

There was one last official act, the Inauguration—and then Nixon was a private citizen. All the prerogatives and appurtenances of his office were stripped from him. He was free, and alone. After the ceremonies and a luncheon at the F Street Club, Dick, Pat, and their two girls left for the "long vacation" they had looked forward to ever since twelve years earlier, when he had been yanked off a cruise ship by an unexpected development in the Hiss Case. But this, too, was cut short. After two weeks Nixon became fidgety. He needed to be where things were happening, where he had a job to do. Returning to Washington, he worked out of a room in the law offices of Bill Rogers, maintaining contacts with Republican leaders and seeking an outlet for his energies.

A defeated Presidential candidate can write off his losses and retire permanently to private life. Or he can begin to plan for a comeback. Nixon did neither. That he thought in terms of 1964 was implicit in his conversation but never explicitly stated. It was as if he had put his political future on a back burner, allowing it to simmer until decisions could be made. Should he run for Governor of California, as friends and political associates were urging him to do? Should he accept the niche of "titular leader" of his party and try to build from there? These were the questions he asked himself—but at no time did he contemplate leaving politics forever. It was simply a question of how he could return.

No matter what his decision, it was clear that he could not continue to live in Washington, one of the many who remain to haunt the scenes of former glory after they have been removed from office. His political base was California, and though he could not move his family until the close of the school year, he began to re-establish himself there. Traveling back and forth, he tested the water in both places.

"Do you think I should run for Governor?" he asked me during one of his stays in Washington.

"Can you win?" I asked.

"They tell me I can,' Nixon said.

"If you are sure you can win, then run," I said. "But if you have any doubts, don't."

Nixon said nothing, but it was clear from his look that he had the same thought very much in mind. Others counseled him more eloquently. In February of 1961 he received one of his infrequent letters from an ailing Whittaker Chambers:

It seems possible that we may not meet again—I mean at all. So forgive me if I say here a few things which, otherwise, I should not presume to say.

You have decades ahead of you. Almost from the first day we met (think, it is already twelve years ago) I sensed in you some quality, deep-going, difficult to identify in the world's glib way, but good, and meaningful for you and multitudes of others. I do not believe for a moment that because you have been cruelly checked in the employment of what is best in you, what is most yourself, that that check is final. It cannot be.

. . . It does not change the nature of your journey. You have years in which to serve. Service is your life. You must serve. You must, therefore, have a base from which to serve.

Some tell me that there are reasons why you should not presently run for Governor of California. Others tell me that you would almost certainly carry the State. I simply do not know the facts. But if it is at all feasible, I, for what it is worth, strongly urge you to consider this. There would be a sense and an impression of political come-down? Great character always precludes a sense of come-down, greatly yielding to match the altered circumstances. The public impression will then take care of itself—may, indeed, become an asset. I believe you to be, rather uniquely, a man who can do this.

Nixon, however, was not ready to make any clearcut decision. It was enough to sell his $70,000, eleven-room house in Wesley Heights and to experience the pleasures of watching the construction of a new home in California. Adams, Duque & Hazeltine, a Los Angeles law firm with substantial corporate clients and an interest in politics, offered him a partnership, but Nixon refused it. Instead, he agreed to be "of counsel," which did not tie him down to legal routine and allowed him to keep loose. He was not happy, but he was active, which for Nixon is almost the same thing.

Friends and politicians continued to pressure him, however. Eisenhower told him it was his "duty" to run for the Governorship, and there were seconding votes from Len Hall, from Senator Thomas Kuchel, from Senator Barry Goldwater, from Senator Hugh Scott. Even Murray Chotiner joined the chorus, making his views known privately and publicly. If he did not declare himself as candidate for Governor, it was the consensus, he would fade away as other defeated Presidential candidates had done. There would be no contributions to keep a campaign organization together, no headlines, and no forum. In response to these importunings Nixon would go no further than to promise an answer by September of 1961. Meanwhile, he devoted himself to the law and to speechmaking.

In April he was summoned to the White House after President Kennedy's Bay of Pigs disaster. For more than an hour the two men discussed the tense Cuban situation.

"What would you do now?" Kennedy asked.

"I would find a proper legal cover and I would go in," Nixon answered. Then he suggested three justifications for open American intervention. "One, a new definition of aggression, based on the premise that Soviet-bloc equipment was used by the Castro forces, and that we had an obligation to see that the anti-Castro forces were at least equally supplied. Second, send American forces in under our treaty rights because of the potential threat to the Guantanamo Naval Base. Third, send American forces to protect the lives and property of the several thousand American citizens still in Cuba." Nixon argued that there might be an outcry from friendly and hostile governments, but that the national interest was the President's prime concern.

In May, Nixon continued to project himself as the leader of the loyal opposition by contracting with the Los Angeles Times-Mirror Syndicate for a series of newspaper articles, eleven in all, which were read with care by policymakers in the Kennedy Administration and by average citizens alarmed at the deteriorating state of

American prestige. He warned that the United States—meaning the White House—must not retreat on Berlin, still under threat from the Soviets and their East German puppets. He called for long-range foreign aid programs instead of ineffective year-by-year planning and funding. He criticized Kennedy for "a Hamlet-like psychosis," which paralyzed action in Cuba and in Laos. He argued that Red China had disqualified herself for membership in the United Nations by her own actions as an "unrepentant" aggressor nation. He charged that the John Birch Society and its "irresponsible tactics . . . hurt the fight against communism"—and this cost him dear in the gubernatorial election the following year.

In June the novelist Adela Rogers St. John, an old friend and supporter, persuaded him to write a book. Dictating from brief notes written on yellow legal-size pads, Nixon worked for seven months on *Six Crises*, an interesting but curious volume that combined homily, autobiography, political analysis, and his knowledge of the workings of government and diplomacy—all keyed to Nixon's personality and a style of writing that shifted from the moving and perceptive to the stilted expression of the non-writer. The format was artificial and so were Nixon's attempts at dissecting what he called the "crisis syndrome," but it offered insights into Nixon's character and motivation which, for the most part, the reviewers missed.

The excitement of writing, of examining his career, filled Nixon's life. For the first time, too, he was making money and could enjoy his now completed house near Beverly Hills, its swimming pool, and all the luxuries that sudden prosperity afforded him. He could be with his family again, glad that his daughters had been removed from a Washington political environment that had brought them tears and the malicious attacks of their schoolmates. California politics were not his bag—he was interested in international affairs, diplomacy, national issues—and he was not certain that Governor Edmund (Pat) Brown would be easy to beat, or that the state Republican Party, divided and discouraged after a series of defeats, could be revitalized.

On the other hand, the polls showed him leading Brown, 53 to 37. The politicians agreed that there was an element of risk should he run. But it seemed impossible that a Governor as lackluster as Brown could win against a national figure like Nixon. Finally, on September 27, 1961, after a family conference in which Pat had left the decision to him, Nixon announced his candidacy.

"I often hear it said that it is a sacrifice . . . to serve in public life," he stated. "For me, I have found it to be the other way around. On my return to private life, I have found that from a salary standpoint, the income has been beyond anything I could ever have dreamed. And I have found, of course, other things in private life that are very attractive. But . . . I find that my heart is not there—it is in public service. . . . As far as my present opportunities are concerned, the most challenging, the most exciting position that I can seek, and in which I could serve, next to being President of the United States, is to be Governor of what will be the first state in the nation."

The nomination, however, was not his for the asking. He had waited too long, or at least long enough for Joseph Shell, Republican leader of the State Assembly, to covet the governorship and to deploy his own forces. As a member in good standing of the California right-wing movement, he had the support of a strong John Birch organization and the backing of many conservative Republicans who felt that Nixon's years in the Eisenhower Administration had vitiated his anti-communism and infected him with Eastern liberalism.

In the bruising primary fight he found the "soft on communism" label pinned on him by Shell supporters—and though Nixon won easily with a 2-to-1 vote, the party was scarred. Since he needed most of the Republican vote if he was to win in November, he was faced by the dual task of mollifying those who had been for Shell and of winning over enough Democratic votes to compensate for the GOP's minority status. Polls showed that the communist issue was popular in California, and Nixon, for want of anything better, returned to the subject that had so dominated his public life. There were, in any case, no major issues. The Democrats could assail him for having been too long divorced from state problems, and he could counter only by pleading "guilty to my experience in national and international problems" and by demonstrating a comprehensive awareness of the local scene—neither of which had great political sex appeal. Even more damaging than these Democratic charges was the speculation that he was attempting to use the Governorship as a stepping stone to the White House in 1964. Try though he might to dispel this notion, he failed. It was, after all, a logical assumption with more than a little truth to it. A flat promise that he would not seek the Presidency and would refuse a draft did not convince the voters. Such promises are a ritual part of the electoral process in America.

The use by the Democrats of these arguments, and the renewal of the litany of accusations that had followed him through the years did not seem to hurt. The Nixon campaign seemed to be taking hold. The polls still showed Brown leading, but the gap was rapidly closing, and Nixon was reasonably confident that there was sufficient time for him to pull ahead. His hopes were dashed when President Kennedy announced that the Soviet Union was building IRBM bases in Cuba and beginning the deployment of missiles pointed at the United States. "I just lost the election," Nixon said when he heard the news. Then he issued a statement fully supporting the President. With the nation's attention focused on the tense confrontation between Kennedy and Khrushchev, the Nixon campaign slowed to a walk. And when worry turned to relief that war was not imminent, the national approbation for Kennedy worked locally against the man who had been his antagonist in 1960. Knowing he had lost, Nixon resorted to a stridency that contributed to the final outcome, a vote of 47.4 per cent.

At 10:20 A.M. on November 6, the day after the election, as Herb Klein, his press secretary, was conceding the election, Nixon walked abruptly into the ballroom of the Beverly Hilton Hotel and took over the microphone. "Good morning, gentlemen," he said. "Now that Mr. Klein has made his statement, and now that all the members of the press are so delighted that I have lost, I'd like to make a statement of my own." No one expected what followed. For in congratulating Governor Brown, Nixon also poured out the bitterness he had felt for many years against political opponents who felt no qualms about slandering him, and against the treatment he had received from the press:

I believe Governor Brown has a heart, even though he believes I do not.

I believe he is a good American, even though he believes I am not. . . .

I am proud of the fact that I defended my opponent's patriotism. You gentlemen didn't report it, but I am proud that I did that. I am proud also that I defended the fact that he was a man of good motive. . . .

I want that—for once, gentlemen—I would appreciate if you would write what I say, in that respect. I think it's very important that you write it in the lead, in the lead. . . .

One last thing. At the outset I said a couple of things with regard to the press that I noticed some of you looked a little irritated about. . . . Never in my sixteen years of campaigning have I complained to a publisher, to an editor, about the coverage of a reporter. I believe a reporter has got a right to write it as he feels it. . . . I will say to a reporter sometimes that I think, well, look, I wish you would give my opponent the same going over that you give me. . . .

I made a talk on television, a talk in which I made a flub. . . . I made a flub in which I said I was running for Governor of the United States. The Los Angeles *Times* dutifully reported that.

Mr. Brown the last day made a flub . . . in which he said, "I hope everybody wins. You vote the straight Democratic ticket, including Senator Kuchel"—a Republican. The Los Angeles *Times* did not report it.

I think that it's time that our great newspapers have at least the same objectivity, the same fullness of coverage, that television has. And I can only thank God for television and radio for keeping the newspapers a little more honest. . . .

As I leave you, I want you to know—just think how much you're going to be missing. You won't have Nixon to kick around any more, because, gentlemen, this is my last press conference. . . .

I hope that what I have said today will at least make television, radio, and the press first recognize the great responsibility they have to report all the news and, second, . . . if they're against a candidate, to give him the shaft, but also recognize, if they give him the shaft, put one lonely reporter on the campaign who will report what the candidate says now and then.

Thank you, gentlemen, and good day.

With this, everyone agreed, Nixon had rung down the curtain on his public life. He had been emotional, and this was considered damaging. He had attacked the press, which would never forgive him. He had shown his anger and disappointment before the nation—or that part of it which would see it on television. Four days later television's verdict was in. On the ABC network Howard K. Smith tastefully wrapped up Nixon's career with a half-hour presentation: "The Political Obituary of Richard Nixon." Among those invited to the festivities was Alger Hiss, convicted of perjury for denying espionage, and out of the Federal penitentiary into which Nixon had helped put him. The outcry against Smith, against James Hagerty, once President Eisenhower's press secretary and now an ABC Vice President, and against the network shook the industry. And the public, which had rejected him, came to his defense.

"What does an attack by one convicted perjurer mean when weighed on the scales against thousands of wires and letters from patriotic Americans?" Nixon said. There was sympathy for him, but few thought to see the Phoenix rise again, and Nixon himself was not among these few.

18

The Impossible
Return — I

IT can be said with 20-20 hindsight that if Richard Nixon had been elected Governor of California in 1962, he would not be President of the United States today. With the same kind of post-vision it can also be said that had he not run at all, he would have tried and failed to win the Presidential nomination in 1964, thereby counting himself out forever.

Victory in California would have boxed him in—for he would have been the Governor of a troublesome state who had solemnly sworn that he would not seek the Presidency in 1964. And had he remained a private citizen until the quadrennial stakes began, he would have been the wrong man for a Republican Party that had been absorbed by Barry Goldwater. The year 1964 would be Goldwater's because a majority of Republicans were convinced that Nixon's brand of politics—neither conservative or liberal—was not for them. They believed that Goldwater could win, but like the followers of the late Robert A. Taft, they preferred losing with Goldwater than winning with any candidate to his left.

For Nixon, vacationing in the Bahamas in mid-November of 1962, any contemplation of a future chance to unpack his bag in the White House—or even the thought that he would be allowed to attempt it—seemed like a ridiculous exercise. He had snapped his swan song at the press in Beverly Hills, and he had been universally assured that no one would forget the outburst or forgive it. The defeat had been his seventh crisis, and he was tired of being the whipping boy of American politics. His daughters, Tricia and Julia, were still combative, but Pat wanted no more of the stretched nerves, the emotional chaos, the sheer physical fatigue, or the high hopes that ended in abysmal disappointment. It had been no job at all for her to extract from Nixon a firm promise that there would be no more political tomorrows. His one reservation was that if the Republican Party wanted him as a campaigner, he would help. But beyond that he would not go.

Nixon's desire to cut the silver cord that kept him tied to politics caused him to leave the "gracious way" of California suburban life and the house he had built, and to move to the opposite end of the existential spectrum. Nothing could have been so removed from his past and from his instincts than to seek a new career in New York City's concrete canyons—Wall Street, corporate finance, and the rigid pursuit of place.

Political columnists like Joseph Alsop saw it otherwise, and they even found some obscure symbolism in Nixon's choice of a cooperative apartment in the Fifth Avenue building where Governor Nelson Rockefeller now hung his hat. The symbolism was otherwise, for in selecting Rockefeller's bailiwick he was depriving himself of the possibility of digging a new political base. His reasons were, to those who knew him, obvious: he needed the kind of life that would give him the emotional equivalent of political activity.

"New York is very cold and very ruthless and very exciting and, therefore, an interesting place to live," he said to Robert J. Donovan, Washington Bureau Chief of the Los Angeles *Times*. "It has many great disadvantages but also many advantages. The main thing, it is a place where you can't slow down—a fast track. Any person tends to vegetate unless he is moving on a fast track. New York is a very challenging place to live. You have to bone up to keep alive in the competition."

Finding an appropriate place for himself on the "fast track" was not difficult. Elmer Bobst, the self-made multimillionaire Board

Chairman of Warner-Lambert Pharmaceutical, a frequent golf partner in the Vice Presidential days who took an almost fatherly interest in Nixon, opened the doors of the law firm that handled his business—Mudge, Stern, Baldwin & Todd. The Pepsi-Cola Company offered to retain him if he took up law practice in the East and Nixon was set to seize opportunities that were "greater than [in] any place in the United States or the world." On May 2, 1963, therefore, Nixon announced that as of the beginning of June he would move to New York City.

As a practicing lawyer he did not have to take the New York State Bar examinations. Under the principle of reciprocity he was required only to write a five-hundred-word statement, outlining his views on what he believed American government ought to be. When he was sworn in at a ceremony in Albany, the Presiding Justice, Bernard Botein, broke all precedent by reading Nixon's statement to those participating. It was an almost matter-of-fact formulation, but it impressed those who had been charged with passing on his admission to the New York Bar:

> The principles underlying the government of the United States are decentralization of power, separation of power and maintaining a balance between freedom and order.
>
> Above all else, the framers of the Constitution were fearful of the concentration of power in either individual or government. The genius of their solution in this respect is that they were able to maintain a very definite but delicate balance between the federal government and the state government, on the one hand, and between the executive, legislative and judicial branches of the federal government on the other. . . .
>
> Throughout American history there have been times when one or the other of the branches of government would seem to have gained a dominant position, but the pendulum has always swung back and the balance over the long haul maintained.
>
> The concept of decentralization of power is maintained by what we call the federal ssytem. But the principle is much broader in practice. Putting it most simply, the American ideal is that private or individual enterprise should be allowed and

encouraged to undertake all functions which it is capable to perform. Only when private enterprise cannot or will not do what needs to be done should government step in. When government action is required, it should be undertaken if possible by that unit of government closest to the people. For example, the progression should be from local, to state, to federal government in that order. In other words, the federal government should step in only when the function to be performed is too big for the state or local government to undertake.

He had said this, in one form or another, many times before—and he would say it again, although perhaps with decreasing frequency, after he became the custodian of the Executive Branch.

But this essay into conservative political philosophy was not related to his work in his first years as a Wall Street lawyer. From his large and comfortable office at 20 Broad Street he conducted the legal affairs of such corporations and brokerage firms as Mutual of New York, General Cigar, the Irving Trust Company, Hornblower and Weeks, Eversharp-Schick, Investors Diversified Services, Matsui of Japan, several railroads, General Precision Equipment, and Pepsi-Cola. He served on the board of directors of several large corporations and succeeded Herbert Hoover as Board Chairman of Boys' Town. He joined all the right clubs—Metropolitan, Links, Blind Brook, among others. He lived in a $135,000 apartment, paying $10,000 a year for maintenance, and reported a gross annual income of some $200,000 from his legal work, his investments, his book, and his articles and speeches.

As a lawyer, moreover, he was ready to tackle cases with deep Constitutional involvement. His most famous was carried to the Supreme Court, where his adversary was Harold Medina, Jr., ironically, the lawyer who had advised and briefly represented Whittaker Chambers in the days of Alger Hiss's libel action. At issue was an individual's right to privacy as opposed to an unlimited freedom of the press—the "balance between freedom and order," perhaps, that Nixon had cited in his statement to the New York courts. Specifically, in *Time Inc. v. Hill* the James Hill family was suing *Life* magazine for violating its privacy in a picture story in which actors posed for scenes from a play then running on Broadway. The Hills had been held prisoner in their Philadelphia home for nineteen hours by escaped convicts. The play had taken liberties with the facts, and the Hills objected to the depiction of their ordeal in *Life*, charging that it was a false account and therefore damaging. The state had awarded the Hills $30,000 in compensatory damages. Time Inc. had appealed, and the Supreme Court had agreed to rule.

Nixon, representing the Hills, prepared almost as if the Constitution itself were on trial. He literally memorized scores of court decisions, legal works, and sociological commentaries. Before the high court, therefore, he put on a dazzling performance as the justices bore down on him with questions and disputations. Though the Washington *Post* described the case made by Nixon as "one of the better oral arguments of the year," the Supreme Court ruled five to four that the freedom of the press had precedence over the right to privacy. Justice Abe Fortas, destined to be replaced on the court by Nixon after disclosures of conflict of interest and unethical conduct, wrote a minority opinion sustaining the Nixon thesis: "For this court totally to immunize the press—whether forthrightly or by subtle indirection—in areas far beyond the need of news, comment on public persons and events, discussion of public issues and the like, would be no service to freedom of the press."

Nixon worked hard at his legal chores, as the senior partner of what had become Nixon, Mudge, Rose, Guthrie & Alexander. (In time the law firm of John Mitchell was absorbed and his name was added.) Every morning Nixon's chauffeur drove him through the New York traffic to spacious offices at 20 Broad Street, overlooking New York Harbor. The superabundance of energy that he had devoted to politics was now channeled into the making of a great law firm, and he and his associates prospered. Eventually, more than a hundred lawyers were working under Nixon's direction. Legal business took him to the foreign capitals he had visited as Vice President, and the reporters and photographers were at hand—but they were not after page-one-column-eight news. He was now a feature celebrity, not a newsmaker.

Perhaps for the first time in his life, be began to relax. Since he was not trying to make the political scene, the slings and arrows of outrageous newspapermen were elsewhere directed. Old opponents could now give him that small degree of friendliness and affection usually reserved for retired ball players and aging matinee idols. He was making money, and he could afford to be playful. In March of 1963 still another "new Nixon" appeared on the Jack Paar show. "Should you be called 'Dick' or 'Mr. Nixon'?" Paar asked him.

"I wouldn't worry about that," Nixon answered. "I've been called everything."

"Can Kennedy be defeated in '64?"

"Which one," was Nixon's riposte.

"Boy, I hate a smart-aleck Vice President," Paar said to the audience, and they loved it.

But for all of this Nixon's life was not full. His work in corporate law, his occasional exercises in forensic drama, and his pleadings before foreign governments in behalf of clients did not fully satisfy the former Vice President. Politics was in his blood—and though he tried to forget it, others would not. Though he had shown that he could run the "fast track," it was really not the emotional equivalent he had sought. And the political situation in the Republican Party made it imperative that he be portrayed as a man on the comeback trail.

As Barry Goldwater and Nelson Rockefeller began squaring off in 1963 for the Party's Presidential nomination, each needed to invoke that rare possibility, the deadlocked convention, to prod his followers to greater activity. Nixon, with a foot in each camp, was not deceived. "After California," he said, "the odds are a thousand to one against me that I could ever be the candidate. Who bets against those odds?" But he was a political man, and as such he could not help wondering, now and then. In spite of his prior resolution, he began positioning himself where lightning might strike. He would sum up his attitude in mid-1968 in a chat with a British correspondent:

"There was some talk in 1964, but I had no illusions about it. I mean, hell, my philosophy has always been that you do the job no matter how grubby or irrelevant it is or because of your personal ambitions. Inevitably, your mind will adopt a certain fatalism. . . . A man must be in the arena if he is going to fight. I stayed in that arena without the expectation of ever being the candidate again. But should the occasion arise, I would be there. It did, and I was."

There was another reason for staying in the arena. Nixon did not want to relinquish whatever contribution he might make to his party and to the government. And he was realist enough to know that as long as press and public considered him a contender, no matter what the odds against him might be, they would take him more seriously. Throughout the Spring of 1964, therefore, he played the game of hanging his clothes on a hickory limb but never going near the water. The newspapers and the commentators agonized hourly over Goldwater's presumably fluctuating fortunes. But Nixon knew, better than most people, that only a small act of God would be able to stop the Goldwater bandwagon. You can't stop somebody with nobody, the old political saw warns, and Nixon agreed. He was only half a candidate.

The tactics he devised required the utmost delicacy. To project himself too far forward would earn him the anger and distrust of the party regulars whose hearts belonged to Barry. Being too reticent would convince them that he was truly in retirement. During this period, he played his role consummately well, being all things and nothing to all men, making just enough noise to keep the pundits at their typewriters but antagonizing no one. Both wings of the Republican Party watched him warily, and wooed him in the hope that his considerable influence among rank-and-filers would be thrown to their side. He remained the parfit Republican knight, slipping only once.

In June of 1964 the Governors of the nation met for their annual conference in Cleveland. Normally, this meeting is no more than a back-slapping session in which the more ambitious sound off on the problems of the day, make a few headlines in their hometown papers, and act like provincial statesmen. In this instance, however, it was well past the eleventh hour for the Republicans present, if they wished to stop Barry Goldwater. Governor William Scranton of Pennsylvania had backed and filled, never committing himself. Governor George Romney of Michigan also played coy. Both were against Goldwater, but neither was quite ready to bell the cat. In Gettysburg, General Eisenhower watched with frustration the inept performance of the two men who might possibly spike Goldwater's guns. After a conversation with Romney the General told Nixon that if a Republican of some stature sounded the call, the Michigander would respond to a "draft." And only with Romney in the lists, Eisenhower asserted, could there be a deadlocked convention.

But when Nixon took Eisenhower's advice, speaking up for Romney, he found himself out in left field. Either Eisenhower had misunderstood Romney or he was trying to flank Goldwater. When Romney made a fast dive for the storm cellar, disavowing the resounding clarion, Nixon was left stranded. He had achieved nothing and won himself the enmity of Goldwater adherents who cried "Betrayal!" Nixon backed away as quickly as he could. And when intermediaries for Goldwater offered Nixon the Vice Presidency, he refused. He could not afford another defeat, and he was certain that in a general election Goldwater would lose.

After the Cleveland Governors' Conference, Nixon conferred with Bob Finch and others privy to his ambivalent attitude toward a Presidential candidacy. They agreed that any attempts between that time and the Republican Convention in July to stop Goldwater could be futile and counterproductive. If Nixon was to keep the loyalty of the Republican professionals, he would have to bow to Goldwater's predominance and reassert his role as the party's most dedicated campaigner. If Goldwater should win, then his reward would be the approbation of his colleagues. But a Goldwater defeat would reinstate Nixon as the bridge between the warring wings of Republicanism. No one would be able to say that, like Nelson Rockefeller, he had fouled the party's nest or given the Democrats the ammunition with which to shoot down the GOP standard-bearer.

Nixon's place in the Goldwater campaign of 1964, therefore, was summed up in the words he used to introduce Goldwater to the wildly cheering delegates who had nominated him: "Before this convention, we were Goldwater Republicans, Rockefeller

Republicans, Scranton Republicans, Lodge Republicans. But now that this convention has met and made its decision," he said, "we are Republicans, period, working for Barry Goldwater for President of the United States."

With this broadly conciliatory statement he paid a debt to the candidate who, in 1960, had done as much for Nixon at a divided convention. It was, moreover, the statement of a party man to party men—and it would not be forgotten. Neither would the six weeks of grueling campaigning for Goldwater which Nixon put in—covering fifty thousand miles and thirty-six states. None of it was waste motion. Goldwater lost the election—washed away in a Democratic sweep of mammoth proportions, but Nixon had re-established himself in the hearts and minds of the most important constituency in the world—the men who kept the Republican Party alive in triumph and adversity, who controlled its machinery, and who nominated its Presidential candidates. No one could have predicted it then, but this was his single most important move in his advance on 1968.

Nixon sets at late 1966 or early 1967 the time in which he "actively" decided to seek the Presidency once more. This is true if "actively" is the operative word. In every man's mind there is an area of semantic deception, and Nixon would have said that his gyrations before 1964 had been designed only to keep himself within reach of the lightning bolt. He was, it should be recalled, bound by a promise to Pat Nixon that he would never again expose either or both of them to the tribulations of a candidate's life. He had made that promise in good faith, but he now withdrew it in what intimates report was a tearful confrontation—though this has never been confirmed. But 1964 had given him once more the smell of the tanbark—the crowds that cheered or raptly listened, the challenge of a determined opposition, the movement, the excitement, and the sense of accomplishment. It had also proved that as of that time and place, the Republican Party was leaderless. Barry Goldwater had neither the taste nor the desire for party leadership, and this left Nixon as the one man who could gather up the pieces of the 1964 debacle.

The extent of his commitment became apparent long before

the operative date set by him as the time of his return to the Presidential fray. No man in retirement would have taken 1965, a national "off year," to involve himself in the Virginia gubernatorial campaign on behalf of a Republican candidate whose chances could hardly be called great. Yet Nixon covered eleven hundred miles in two days, speaking for A. Linwood Holton, saying to the Republican Party, in effect, "Here I am." When the 1966 congressional elections rolled around, Nixon was the major stellar attraction for a party that seemed on the ropes and ready for a TKO.

Until then he had not recruited any political staff. Rose Mary Woods, in an office next to his at 20 Broad Street, had handled his non-legal chores alone—as always dedicated, as always ready to put in long and tiring hours as his buffer against the world of politics. Now Nixon hired Patrick J. Buchanan, a young editorial writer from the St. Louis *Globe-Democrat*, to maintain contact with Republican and independent conservatives. His apartment on Fifth Avenue, until then sacrosanct, became the locus of meetings with political activists ranging from William F. Buckley, Jr., Editor of *National Review*, to the rotund and oracular journalist Victor Lasky. Charles McWhorter, a former head of the Young Republicans who had served Nixon faithfully in past campaigns, began to figure in the small print of news stories. And Bob Finch, though active in California politics, was once more on Nixon's most important consultative agenda.

The 1966 congressional campaign was the payoff. As he had in 1954 and 1958, Nixon made himself the quarterback for a Republican Party that desparately needed him. In that rising of the Phoenix, Nixon campaigned in thirty-five states, for eighty-six candidates, raising an estimated $5 million for the party. He infused new life into local races, and made national stories for the candidate. When the votes were counted, the statistics showed, as *The New York Times* reported, that "a G.O.P. House candidate for whom Nixon did not campaign stood only a 45 percent chance of winning, while a man he embraced stood a 67 percent chance. It is hard to knock a coach who raises the team average that much."

There were other statistics that made Nixon look even better.

For 1966 was the year in which Senator Robert F. Kennedy also tried to build a national political machine for the 1968 Presidential campaign. Despite the attraction of the Kennedy name and the adulation of many young people, the results of Bobby's campaigning that fall were in marked contrast to those of Nixon. He campaigned for eleven gubernatorial candidates, only three of whom won. He campaigned for ten senatorial candidates, and only four won. And in the House races, where he had pushed hard, the Democrats took a bad beating. Nixon, of course, could not and did not take all the credit for the victories. It was a Republican year in which the GOP picked up 47 seats in the House, 3 in the Senate, 8 governorships, and 540 seats in state legislatures.

The 1966 campaign projected Nixon into the Presidential scene in another way. Though he was fighting for local candidates, his attack was on Lyndon Johnson and therefore received far more attention than it normally would have. His campaign oratory, moreover, was of the "rocking, socking" variety that he had given up in 1964. "Every time a housewife goes into a supermarket today, she is faced with the High Cost of Johnson. . . . Every time a businessman tries to make a loan that would produce more jobs, he runs into interest rates that are really the High Cost of Johnson. . . . Every time a young couple tries to buy a home these days, the door is slammed in their faces by the High Cost of Johnson," he said in one of his basic speeches.

Though he abstained from any criticism of the President during the October conference of America's Vietnam allies in Manila, Nixon opened up with both barrels when Johnson returned. "How many more American troops . . . do we currently plan to send to fight in Vietnam in 1967? Will the draft quota, which reached a fifteen-year high in October, have to be raised again to meet our troop requirements?" Unexpectedly, Johnson gave Nixon the kind of boost that made him all the more an important contender for the Republican Presidential nomination. Boiling with anger, Johnson called Nixon a "chronic campaigner" and a man who "never did really recognize and realize what was going on when he had an official position in the government." And, he added with a violence that surprised the press, Nixon "doesn't serve his country very well" as a private citizen. The liberal press, seldom solicitous of Nixon's sensibilities but happy to take on the President, read in that last remark a challenge to Nixon's patriotism, and came to his defense.

Now only the very naïve could believe that Nixon was not grooming himself for the 1968 election. Nevertheless, in the old tradition of American politics Nixon continued to deny it. On November 6, 1966, when he was asked on a television program by William Lawrence of ABC, "Mr. Nixon, now that you have toured thirty-five states [and] renewed all your political due bills, when are you going to start running for President yourself?" Nixon replied, "After this election, I am going to take a holiday for at least six months with no political speeches scheduled whatsoever."

His political associates, already gearing up for the preliminaries of battle, were thrown into confusion by this disclosure of a decision they had not known was made. The fall election had raised up four possible challengers for 1968, Governor Romney in Michigan, Governor Ronald Reagan in California, Governor Rockefeller in New York, and Senator Charles Percy in Illinois—all from vote-heavy states and all seriously discussed by the press. The professionals in the party discounted Romney and Percy. But Rockefeller, hurt by personal scandal in 1960, had emerged again as a solid vote-getter. And Reagan's stunning victory by a million-vote plurality had immediately caught the imagination of the nation's conservatives who saw him as the one man in the Republican Party with the charisma and the television presence that had become the formula for political success since 1960.

Would Nixon's absence from the political arena give the new faces of 1966 an unchallengeable head start? There were some in Nixon's growing entourage who thought so and urged him to reconsider. But Nixon held to his belief in the rhythm of politics. There was a time to press forward and a time to draw back. In drawing back, he could still keep his name and his activities before the public without trying to edge out newly discovered political stars in their hour of acclaim. So Richard Nixon went traveling, perhaps remembering that much of his earlier popularity had been gained in this fashion.

In England he conferred with Prime Minister Harold Wilson and other British leaders; in France with the Foreign Minister Maurice Couve de Murville; in Germany with Chancellor Kurt Georg Kiesinger, Foreign Minister Willy Brandt, former Chancellor Konrad Adenauer; in Italy with President Giuseppe Saragat, Premier Aldo Moro, and Pope Paul VI. Going behind the now less-than-Iron Curtain, he talked to officials in Romania and Czechoslovakia, and visited the Soviet Union as a tourist when communist officials refused to see him. Vietnam had become a national preoccupation, and Nixon showed up there in April 1967 to discuss the military and political situation with Ambassador Henry Cabot Lodge. (When he was questioned on his return about this meeting, Nixon said evasively, "We had a very interesting discussion and actually we made a deal. He is going to put a Pepsi-Cola cooler in the Embassy in Saigon.")

In Saigon, however, Nixon laid down a foreign policy line that would echo in the months to come. The great debate in the 1968 campaign, he said, "will not be how to negotiate defeat [in Vietnam] but how to bring more pressure to bear for victory"—a direct slap at Senators Eugene McCarthy and Robert F. Kennedy, each in his own way positioning himself for the Democratic Presidential nomination. The Vietnam issue in 1967 was rapidly crowding every other problem and controversy from the national consciousness, and Nixon saw it as the door-opener to the White House. But of equal importance to his strategy considerations was the knowledge that foreign policy was his strong suit. His recognized qualifications in that field were far more impressive than those of any potential competitor—in or out of the Republican Party. The major thrust of his "non-campaigning" had to be in the field of international affairs, since any sustained venture into domestic controversy would jeopardize his announced removal from the political scene.

Nixon had laid the groundwork for this in a series of vigorous and incisive articles written for the *Reader's Digest* in 1964 and 1965. In the January 1964 issue Nixon took a categorical stand on the Captive Nations of Eastern Europe—one that ran directly counter to the Kennedy-Johnson policy of conciliating the Soviet

Union, of playing down differences with the communist world, of officially bolstering the theory that the men of the Kremlin had "matured." He wrote:

> Khrushchev knows that he is sitting on a powder keg. He knows that the overwhelming majority of the people of East Germany, Hungary, Czechoslovakia, Poland, Bulgaria, and Romania hate their communist governments and would rise against them if they thought they had a chance to succeed. . . . Khrushchev hopes to keep the lid on this Pandora's box of troubles for his communist empire by negotiating a non-aggression pact between the NATO nations and the communist Warsaw Pact group. . . .
>
> Yet there are strong pressures from within as well as from without the . . . Administration to make such a deal. I believe that only the mobilization of an aroused and informed American public opinion will prevent the sellout of the hope of 97 million enslaved people in Eastern Europe to be free. More and more we hear talk about "accommodation," "disengagement," and other devices which add up to our approval of Soviet domination of Eastern Europe. . . . I believe the time has come for a complete change of direction and emphasis in foreign policy toward that area. . . .
>
> The communist goal is to impose slavery on the free world. Our goal must be nothing less than to bring freedom to the communist world.

In the context of the 1968 campaign those words would have a tragic ring. Czechoslovakia, breaking loose from Soviet domination, began to press forward to comparative freedom, only to be strangled by Soviet invading forces. In the name of "accommodation" and "disengagement" President Johnson did no more than to protest lamely in public while he quietly let the Kremlin know that the United States would take no countermeasures in defense of the Czechs. In an August 1964 article for *Reader's Digest*, specifically devoted to Vietnam, Nixon again assailed the two-way stretch of American foreign policy. Its title told the whole story: "Needed in Vietnam: The Will to Win."

Time and again we have demonstrated that we have no real intention of winning this war. Instead, we are trying to achieve a precarious balance of not-quite-winning and not-quite-losing. . . . What we must do is to instill in ourselves and our allies a determination to win this crucial war—to win it decisively. We must recognize that we are in a life-and-death struggle that has repercussions far beyond Vietnam, and that victory is essential to the survival of freedom. . . . A victory for us in South Vietnam will shatter the myths of communist invincibility and of the inevitability of a Chinese take-over in Southeast Asia. It will restore all the prestige we have lost and give us more besides. . . . The crisis is not one of competence but of *confidence*. It is a test not of power but of our capacity to use our power correctly and with courage. All that is needed in short, is the will to win— and the courage to use our power—*now*.

In December 1965 Nixon returned to the Vietnam war, again for the *Digest*, updating his previous arguments and conclusions. "I am convinced that the major danger today is not military defeat on the battlefield, but diplomatic defeat at the conference table," he said. Advocating negotiation, he urged that only North Vietnam be included, not the Viet Cong. He set down "three minimum conditions" for any agreement with the communists: "North Vietnam must stop its aggression against South Vietnam; South Vietnam's independence and freedom from communist control must be guaranteed; there must be no reward for the aggressors." And he raised a moral question: "Has the United States the right— after pledging to support a small nation in its fight for freedom—to negotiate a settlement that would destroy that nation's freedom?"

But perhaps the strongest words in Nixon's series for the *Reader's Digest* sounded in a discussion of the Cold War, published in November 1964. In it he assailed those who argued that the time had come to put aside "old" concepts of Soviet intentions, to forget the record, and to substitute friendliness for wariness.

This is no time to be complacent about our position in the world. The last four years have seen the greatest series of foreign

335

policy failures of any comparable period in our history. In Europe, the Grand Alliance is in shambles, with several of our allies refusing to support the United States in our policy toward Latin America and Asia. In Germany, the Berlin Wall stands as a grim monument to American weakness and indecision in the face of a flagrant communist challenge. In Asia, Vietnam is only the most recent and most shocking of a series of foreign policy disasters that has reduced American prestige to an all-time low in that part of the world. . . . We have been humiliated, frustrated, outguessed and outmaneuvered at every turn. In the face of this record, how can anyone in a responsible policy-making position say that the cold war is thawing?

The cold war isn't thawing; it is burning with a deadly heat. Communism isn't changing; it isn't sleeping; it isn't relaxing; it is, as always, plotting, scheming, working, fighting. . . . While the danger of destruction by total war has gone down, the danger of defeat without total war has gone up. . . . We must understand that the communist threat is worldwide, and if communism takes over in one country the tremors are felt clear around the world. I completely reject the idea that there are so-called peripheral areas, collateral areas—like Cuba and Vietnam—that are not important.

In mid-1967, with his candidacy established though not announced, Nixon turned once more to the printed word to perpetuate his image as the American political figure most knowledgeable in international affairs. In so doing, however, he took into account the perils of setting words down on paper where they might furnish future ammunition to his critics and opponents. The manner and the approach of an article for *Foreign Affairs*, published in its October issue, differed dramatically from those of his *Reader's Digest* series. He discoursed more on what was than on what should be. This opened him to criticism for the nature of his analysis but presented little that could be quoted against him in the period ahead.

For example, he noted without comment that "If another friendly country should be faced with an externally supported communist insurrection . . . there is a serious question whether the American public or the American Congress would now support a unilateral American intervention, even at the request of a host country." This made it vital for nations in the path of potential aggressors to establish an indigenous "framework for their own future security."

In doing so, they need to fashion arrangements able to deal both with old-style wars and with new—with traditional wars, in which armies cross over national boundaries, and with the so-called "wars of national liberation," in which they burrow under national boundaries.

I am not arguing that the day is past when the United States would respond militarily to communist threats in the less stable parts of the world, or that a unilateral response to a unilateral request for help is out of the question. But other nations must recognize that the role of the United States as world policeman is likely to be limited in the future. To ensure that a U.S. response will be forthcoming, if needed, machinery must be created that is capable of meeting two conditions: (a) a collective effort by the nations of the region to contain the threat by themselves; and, if that effort fails, (b) a collective request to the United States for assistance.

Writing of Communist China, Nixon continued his opposition to its admission into the United Nations, but tempered it as well:

Any American policy toward Asia must come urgently to grips with the reality of China. This does not mean, as many would simplistically have it, rushing to grant recognition to Peking, to admit it to the United Nations and to ply it with offers of trade—all of which would serve to confirm its rulers in their present course. It does mean recognizing the present and potential danger from Communist China, and taking measures to meet that danger. It also means distinguishing carefully between long-range and short-range policies, and fashioning short-range programs to meet our goals. . . . The world cannot be safe until China changes. Thus our aim, to the extent that we can influence events, should be to induce change. The way to do this is to persuade China that it *must* change: that it cannot satisfy its imperial ambitions, and that its own national interest requires a turning away from foreign adventuring and a turning inward toward the solution of its own domestic problems. . . .

During the next decade the West faces two prospects which, together, could create a crisis of the first order: (1) that the Soviets may reach nuclear parity with the United States; and (2) that China, within three to five years, will have a significant deliverable nuclear capability—and that this same China will be outside any nonproliferation treaty that might be signed, free, if it chooses, to scatter its weapons among "liberation" forces anywhere in the world. This strengthens the urgency of building buffers that can keep the major nuclear powers apart in the case of "wars of national liberation," supported by Moscow or Peking but fought by proxy.

In summing up, Nixon took up a theme to which he returned in the early days of his Presidency—the "new isolationism":

Weary with war, disheartened with allies, disillusioned with aid, dismayed at domestic crises, many Americans are heeding the call of the new isolationism. And they are not alone; there is a tendency in the whole Western world to turn inward, to become parochial and isolationist—dangerously so. But there can be neither peace nor security a generation hence unless we recognize now the massiveness of the forces at work in Asia. . . . History has its rhythms, and now the focus of both crisis and change is shifting. Without turning our backs on Europe, we have now to reach out westward to the East, and to fashion the sinews of a Pacific community.

But the printed word and the statesmanlike posture, as Nixon well knew, did not win primaries, sweep conventions, or convince the electorate. Having decided once more to risk all in a race for the Presidency, he had to forge a political machine, call up his

political reserves, and devise his political strategy. Far more important, he had to present himself to the Republican Party's effectives
as the inevitable man, the only man who could bring together its
disparate elements and field a winning team in 1968. In 1967, even
among his staunchest supporters, there were many who felt that
he could not do it—even though he might be the best man for the
office.

19

The Impossible
Return — II

IN January of 1967 shrewd politicians in Washington were surmising that the strongest team the Republicans could field in 1968 would be Governor Ronald Reagan of California, with Senator Edward Brooke of Massachusetts as his running mate. This ticket, they asserted, had the proper geographical "spread," balanced conservative and liberal, and drove a wedge between responsible Negro leaders and extremist civil rights agitators. Governor Romney, getting the happy treatment from those in the press and proclaimed the St. George who would slay conservative dragons, never impressed the professionals. "Give him six months," one Capitol Hill wit said, "and he'll bore the American people to death." Nelson Rockefeller was a question mark, a moody and self-indulgent man whose political instincts usually faulted him.

And then there was Richard Nixon. The comment about him was almost a litany. "He's got the experience—more than any other Republican candidate—and he'd make a good President. But he just can't win." Not knowing his strategy, they could not decide whether he was running for the Presidency or merely jogging to keep himself in political trim—and this disturbed them.

The "can't win" syndrome, nurtured by a thousand political

pieces friendly and unfriendly, was an article of faith among those claiming the greatest wisdom in political matters. Logic seemed to be on their side, but politics is seldom logical. It deals more with emotional possibilities than with mathematical probabilities. But in spite of their certainty, the political analysts felt twinges of doubt about Nixon. He went about his business, writing his foreign policy pieces and avoiding stage center, with a sense of confidence and lack of tension that also-rans seldom exhibit. Though Nixon had tripped twice—in 1960 and in 1962—the professionals still respected his political acumen. Did he know something they didn't know? Had the harried and nervous man of his Presidential test, the strident and irascible loser of the California gubernatorial heat, discovered a new formula?

Perhaps he had. Unobtrusively, he was changing his style and his pace—and looking for a new team to match his new approach. In April of 1968, during his leisurely primary campaigns, he would say to the London *Daily Express* correspondent, "It is all in the pacing now. I must not stack it full. I want to do fewer things better. I want more time to think. Most politicians just get up and yak away, reading words they are not familiar with. With me it's a fetish to get into a subject, to feel it. And that requires time. There's so little of that. I have also surrounded myself with another generation, a younger generation. . . . Look at my small band. There's Leonard Garment. He's left of Nixon, a liberal. There's Pat Buchanan. He's right of Nixon."

In the early months of 1967 Nixon was taking the time to think, working out positions that would remain with him in the frenetics of the 1968 campaign year, studying the mistakes of 1960. He was carefully analyzing the accounts of that defeat and taking to heart the comment of a political writer like Theodore H. White that he was most impressive when he spoke and acted with deliberation, when there was a resonance to his manner that matched the resonance of his voice. It was not so much that he was creating a "new Nixon" but that he was distilling the better qualities of the "old Nixon." At the same time he was assiduously reminding the voters that of all the candidates he had more experience, knew more of the world's leaders, and had seen more of the earth's surface. By June of 1967 he had made his point. Writing then of a Nixon campaign that had begun to roll, I said in a syndicated column:

If foreign policy is the key to the 1968 election, then Dick Nixon's chances will be immeasurably enhanced. A private poll taken by the highly reliable Opinion Research Corporation of New Jersey demonstrates this with statistical clarity. Pitting Mr. Nixon against Governor Nelson Rockefeller of New York, Governor George Romney of Michigan, and Senator Charles Percy of Illinois—the men most mentioned as possible Republican candidates, though the absence of Governor Ronald Reagan of California from the list of contenders should raise some eyebrows—the ORC poll shows the following results:

Among Republicans, Mr. Nixon polled a preponderant 67 percent as the candidate strongest in foreign policy. The Messrs. Rockefeller, Romney, and Percy rated 7 percent, 8 percent, and 3 percent respectively. Among Democrats, Mr. Nixon led with 38 percent, against Mr. Rockefeller's 16 percent, Mr. Romney's 15 percent, and Mr. Percy's 3 percent. Interestingly enough, Mr. Nixon runs strongest among independents—the swing vote which, we are told, determines elections. . . .

What gives Nixon adherents their greatest satisfaction at this time, however, is a Gallup poll figure. The Gallup pollsters sent out inquiries to all Republican County Chairmen. This is not a poll in the usual sense of the word, being targeted at a specific group. The response to these queries was, in George Gallup's phrase, "an amazing 68 percent." Of the County Chairmen who answered, 1,272 expressed a preference for Dick Nixon. The second highest number, 348, went to Mr. Romney, with Mr. Rockefeller trailing at 71.

By absenting himself from the infelicities of politics, moreover, Nixon was allowing the past, present, and future of his Republican competitors to come to a confluence that would slow them down decisively. In September of 1967 George Romney had finished himself off by confessing that he had been "brainwashed" by the generals into support of the Vietnam war—an excuse that deprived his shift to opposition of any conviction and made him look ridiculous. His campaigning in New Hampshire, the first state to hold its primary election, was an unqualified disaster in which he showed himself to be a king of platitudes and a would-be President whose major approach to the country's problems was to shake the reluctant hands of annoyed voters. And regulars in the Republican Party would not forget his refusal to endorse the ticket in 1964. If they did not remember Nixon's remark right after the election— "Those who divided the party this year cannot unite it"—they felt it in their bones.

Reagan was parrying questions on his candidacy by saying that he was Governor of California and had no time, in a problem-ridden state, to spend on the arduous job of primary-winning. Privately, he believed that it would be impossible to divorce the party regulars—the State and County Chairmen—from their long marriage to Nixon. The place to make his fight, his advisers told him, was at the convention—if a deadlock developed between Nixon and Rockefeller. He was not experienced enough to know the odds against it, and his lieutenants failed to seize what few opportunities they had to lay the groundwork in the winter and spring of 1968.

Rockefeller seemed like the only contender with any real muscle and the wherewithal to exert it. He was Governor of an important state, he had a large but scattered following, the mass media welcomed him as the man who could arouse the electorate and stop the Nixon bandwagon. But his chances were blighted by his on-again-off-again tactics of 1960 and his defection in 1964. Republicans at the grass roots tended to distrust him, to see him as a man of unpredictable moods who could not be counted on in the stretch. He was respected for his vote-getting abilities in New York, a state that more often than not succumbed to the Democrats in gubernatorial contests, but this also raised the suspicion that in philosophy and politics he was not really a Republican. Rockefeller's major asset was the iterated and reiterated claim that "he can win"—but this had been tarnished by the 1967 polls that showed Nixon consistently ahead of all comers among Republicans and occasionally spurting to first place among independents. Those

343

who had seen Rockefeller in action over the years also wondered whether on the primary trail, where stamina, both physical and emotional, is of the essence, he would fall by the wayside.

This, then, was the situation on February 1, 1968, when Richard Nixon—rested and relaxed at the starting gun for the first time since 1952—invited the press to his Fifth Avenue apartment to hand them a letter "To the Citizens of New Hampshire," announcing his decision to enter the Republican Presidential primary.

. . . Peace and freedom in the world, and peace and progress here at home, will depend on the decisions of the next President of the United States.

For these critical years, America needs new leadership.

During fourteen years in Washington, I learned the awesome nature of the great decisions a President faces. During the past eight years, I have had a chance to reflect on the lessons of public office, to measure the nation's tasks and its problems from a fresh perspective. I have sought to apply those lessons to the needs of the present and to the entire sweep of this final third of the 20th century.

And I believe I have found some answers.

It was the kind of statement expected of the "new Nixon"—serious in tone and modest in manner. Neither the tone nor the manner was new, of course, but the context was. The press and public, perhaps for the first time in Nixon's post-senatorial career, were aware that the man they insisted on seeing in a different light might well be the next President of the United States, and so their eyes and ears reacted differently. They had been conditioned, too, by the Johnson years, and Nixon's very lack of flamboyance had appeal.

And now the long streak of bad luck that had plagued Nixon since the spring of 1960 suddenly ended. On February 26, Len Hall—who had taken over as Romney's campaign manager for reasons that defied analysis, unless, as rumor had it, he had done so at the urging of Nelson Rockefeller—presented his candidate with a poll of New Hampshire voters, taken by Market Opinion Research, a Romney-owned company. It showed that Nixon would carry the state with 70 per cent of the total Republican vote, leaving Romney to limp in with 10 per cent. News from other states where Romney planned to campaign was as gloomy. Two days later, more relieved than despairing, Romney told a press conference at the Washington Hilton Hotel that has candidacy had "not won the wide acceptance" he had expected and that he was withdrawing. With no competition Nixon polled 80,666 votes in New Hampshire, a record for the state. The focus now was on Rockefeller. At the time of his withdrawal, Romney had remarked, "Nelson is the only man in the party who can stop Nixon now." It was a dubious statement, for Rockefeller's thinking and ambition were ambivalent, and the pull in either direction was a serious handicap.

But the liberal wing of the Republican Party—the amateurs who had felt in 1964 that the defeat of Goldwater was more important than their party's future—honestly, almost passionately, believed that Rockefeller should and could bring Nixon down. They wanted a sign, a word, from the man they hoped would be their candidate. But all he would say was, "I am not going to create dissension . . . but I am ready and willing to serve the American people if called." In American politics that is not enough. General Douglas MacArthur had waited for the call in 1952, after he had been ousted by President Truman from command of the United Nations forces in Korea. The voters, then and always, wanted a candidate who would fight for the nomination and then press on for election. They felt, with some justice, that a man who had to be coaxed into running for the nation's highest office did not deserve it.

The pressure on Rockefeller was real enough—though how much of it was spontaneous and how much of it inspired by the incredibly wide-ranging machine of Rockefeller interests, no one will ever know. Certainly, the crescendo of encouragement that came from much of the nation's press could not have been prompted by Rockefeller, his brothers, or his aides. By March 21, when Rockefeller called a press conference in New York to announce his decision, a national Draft Rockefeller committee had been set up in Annapolis by Maryland's Governor Spiro Agnew. Others of equal importance had committed themselves to a Rockefeller candidacy. But Nixon's newfound luck prevailed. Rockefeller stepped before the television cameras and the newspaper and electronic reporters and said coldly that he was not a candidate.

"I find it clear at this time that a considerable majority of the party's leaders want the candidacy of former Vice President Richard Nixon," he said. "And it appears equally clear that they are keenly concerned and anxious to avoid any such divisive challenge within the party as marked the 1964 campaign."

Once again he had marched up the hill and marched down again. Those who had rallied to his cause were left in undignified political exposure, and they never forgave him. His reentry into the race, forty days later, stirred up some excitement but few believed that he could command the loyalty of those he had, in his own words, "let down."

It was now Nixon's ball game. In the Wisconsin primary Nixon polled 80 per cent of the vote. There was a record turnout for him in Indiana, Nebraska gave him 70 per cent of its Republican primary vote, Oregon 73 per cent. Shunning the primaries, "non-candidate" Rockefeller stumped the country and issued position papers on the issues, but the only real obstacle to the nomination for Richard Nixon was Ronald Reagan. Could he mount a blitz at the Republican Convention in Miami? There was a slim chance, and though Nixon felt certain that he had locked up the necessary delegates, he continued to campaign, though still in the low-key, slightly quizzical manner that had been his style since New Hampshire. If there was any cause for concern, it was the vote that Reagan got in Oregon and in Nebraska without visiting the states and at an expenditure by his eager supporters of less than one tenth of the money that the Nixon forces poured into those states. In terms of raw power, however, Reagan could take to Miami only the California delegation, of which he was the favorite son.

But this was a simplification, and it underestimated his main strength—the South. Had Reagan declared himself a candidate early in the scramble for delegates, he would have had the South at his feet. Since 1952, the Republicans had been whittling away at the base of Democratic electoral power, which the national party had taken for granted. "Where will it go?" was the attitude, "To the party of Lincoln?" But the South's horrendous memories of the Reconstruction had been eroded by the civil rights program of Harry S. Truman and by the Kennedy New Frontier. Although Nixon's record against segregation was clearcut, the South could accept him; in a Democrat the things he said and did would have been considered close to treason, perhaps because he paid more than lip service to the doctrine of states' rights and states' responsibilities. But the South had been Reagan's to take, if only he had declared himself.

While the actor-turned-politician had sat in Sacramento, denying his availability, Nixon gathered delegates. As William Rusher, the publisher of *National Review*, would say on the opening day of the convention—bemoaning the difficulty of bringing delegates into the Reagan camp—"How can we convince Southern delegates to come to our side when Barry Goldwater, [South Carolina industrialist] Roger Millikan, [Senator] John Tower [of Texas], and Strom Thurmond have committed themselves to Nixon?" The key to the Reagan strategy was Senator Thurmond, who towered above the other Southern delegates by the main force of his craggy personality and by the prestige he had gained below the Mason-Dixon Line, in his days before switching to the Republican Party, from his defiance of the Truman Administration and the national Democratic Party on the civil rights issue. As long as Thurmond was for Nixon the Reagan candidacy was a forlorn hope, nourished by Southern desires but frustrated by Southern practicality. If Thurmond could be made to defect, then Nixon's first-ballot victory might be denied him. And there was general agreement that if the convention went to a second or third ballot, Nixon's strength would be badly eroded.

To complicate the situation, the liberal forces were working hard to build up Reagan in the hope that he would puncture a hole in the Nixon fortress big enough to allow Nelson Rockefeller to march in. Taking its cue, perhaps unwittingly, from Rockefeller, *The New York Times* reported that Nixon was considering for his Vice Presidential choice Rockefeller, Mayor John Lindsay of New York, or Senator Charles Percy of Illinois. All three were anathema to the Southern delegates. But Nixon, who had arrived late at the convention—he had been on Long Island writing his acceptance speech—quickly covered that base.

347

He called Thurmond to his suite at the Hilton Hotel and assured him that the Vice Presidential nominee "will not be objectionable to the South"—in effect giving Thurmond veto power over the choice. This assurance not only mollified the Southern delegates but placed them in a position of power that they found highly gratifying. The belated efforts of Clifton White, the manager of the Reagan campaign, to pry loose any appreciable number of Southern delegates foundered on Thurmond. "We like Ronnie, we want Ronnie," the Southerners told him. "But we have to go along with Strom." And Strom would not budge.

That was how it stood on the night before the convention would choose the nominee. The Reagan forces—divided into an "official" camp led by White and a strong contingent from *National Review*, and a dissident group generaled by Wainwright Dawson of the United Republicans of America, Philip Brennan, Jr., a free-lance public relations counselor, and former Congressman Donald Bruce —muttered darkly that there would be some surprises, but real conviction was lacking in their predictions. And then a small drama of large import took place. Representative Melvin Laird, a power in Republican inner circles, was having dinner in one of the many plush restaurants off Collins Avenue, Miami's main street. A news-paperman, with friends and sympathies in both the Nixon and the Reagan camps, stopped at his table. "Who is the Vice Presidential candidate going to be?" the newspaperman asked. "It should be either Reagan or Rockefeller," Laird said, "but it's going to be Chucky-boy"—Senator Charles Percy, a man totally objectionable to the South.

Later that night, at one of the hotel bars, the newspaperman repeated the story to one of Reagan's adherents. At noon the next day a group of Reagan supporters met with Senator Thurmond. They repeated the newspaperman's account of Laird's remarks to him, and he was visibly shaken. "It can't be true," said Thurmond. "I have Nixon's word that the Vice Presidential nominee will not be objectionable to me."

"This is before Nixon has been nominated," the Reagan sup-porters said. How could he be certain that Nixon would not back away from his promise? "If he does choose Percy," Thurmond was asked, "what will you do?" "I'll get up on the floor of the convention and denounce him," Thurmond said, "and that will cost him the election." But Thurmond was obviously worried. When he left the Reagan delegates, he went immediately to Nixon. The promise was repeated, and Thurmond passed the word to the Southern delegates that he was standing firm.

The rest is history. When the convention was polled, Nixon's 692 votes gave him the nomination—and Reagan mounted the platform to move that it be made unanimous. For the Nixon organization there had been no surprises. The delegates had voted to a man exactly as Richard Kleindienst, one of Goldwater's lieutenants in 1964 and now a Nixon insider, had tallied them that afternoon. There were no defections from the South.

For Nixon, who had been counted out once in 1960 and again in 1962, it was the most incredible comeback in American Presidential politics. In his suite at the Hilton—surrounded by Pat, Tricia and Julie, and young David Eisenhower, the former President's grandson and Nixon's son-in-law-elect—the moment was one of exhilaration and quiet vindication. "It is a wonderful moment," he said, "but you know I am somewhat fatalistic about it. I feel the Presidency seeks the man. I was ready. I was willing. The events all fell together. About tonight I was confident. . . . Yes, I expected to win tonight."

But in truth, the Presidency seeks the man only when the man seeks the Presidency. Nixon had fought every step of the way, taking nothing for granted. He had made himself the servant of his party, and now the party was his. The first great obstacle had been overcome, and now there was the election. But there too he was confident. He did not know that the Democratic Party, already torn by its repudiation of President Johnson, in the grip of an internecine battle for the Presidential nomination, and shaken by the assassination of the one man in its ranks perhaps capable of galvanizing the country, would be convulsed by events and circumstance at its own convention over which it had no control.

The last act of the Republican Convention had still to be played, the nominal selection of the man hand-picked by Nixon to be his running mate. It would have to be a compromise candidate, one acceptable to the South and to the North. In a session that ran from 3:30 A.M. to 5:30 A.M., the names of Percy and Senator Mark Hatfield were mentioned. Percy did not have a prayer, and Hatfield had canceled out his own chances earlier in the convention by submitting a strongly doveish Vietnam speech for Nixon's approval. (The speech had been rewritten, but Hatfield had been scratched.) Robert Finch, Nixon's personal choice, had long since refused the honor. The compromise was Governor Spiro Agnew, unknown to the average voter, little known to most of the delegates, but acceptable to the South. When his name was announced, the press and the delegates were startled. There was talk of placing Reagan's name in nomination, but he would have no part of it. There were rumblings of a liberal revolt, but these subsided. Agnew was the one, nominated by the current liberal hero, John Lindsay. Only Romney, still nursing some faraway hope, was ready to submit to the humiliation of defeat. A handful of rebellious delegates placed his name in nomination—and were able to poll 186 votes to Agnew's 1,128; 26 delegates abstained.

When the press got to Nixon the following day, he had an explanation for his choice: "Agnew's one of the most underrated men in America, a man who can show poise under pressure. You can look him in the eye, and you know he's got it. He has a good heart. He's an old-fashioned patriot, highly controlled. If the guy's got it, he'll make it. If not, I've made a bad choice." There were two other reasons. First, Agnew had led a revolt against Nelson Rockefeller among the Republican Governors—and Nixon owed him something. Second, he was the only possible man who met all the requirements of the convention.

Ahead now was the campaign itself—once the Democrats had nominated their own candidates. The convention city was Chicago, with its complex of clustered hotels, its many restaurants, and a great arena that had seen so many nominees rise to the challenge of history. Few doubted that the accolade would go to Vice President Hubert Horatio Humphrey, selected by a President who had chosen not to run for reasons variously interpreted as pique or patriotism—annoyance at his rejection by the nation in a time of trial, or determination to take himself out of politics in order to be free to end the bloodletting in Vietnam.

The other contenders had been long out of the running by the time the gavel pounded to open the proceedings. Senator Eugene McCarthy, the first to take on Lyndon Johnson, had generated much heat but little light. His "children's crusade"—the young people who manned his primary barricades—had been colorful and heartwarming, but he had failed to make it against the power of the Democratic machine. The regulars were afraid of him, of his political whimsicality, of an independence that sometimes verged on the irresponsible. Senator Robert F. Kennedy had been galvanic, but in the days before an assassin's bullet brought him down he had shown weaknesses and a tendency to temporize. He had barely come through in the California primary where he needed it big, and had he lived the road ahead would have been badly mined.

In his pre-convention roadshow Humphrey played the clown, laughing and weeping in an abundance of uncontrolled emotion. His liberalism was badly tarnished by his role in a pragmatic, horse-trading administration. And the great national antipathy toward President Johnson had rubbed off on him. Humphrey had one asset that McCarthy, still battling, lacked—the votes of the delegates. Press and public, as the convention got under way, predicted a routine affair in which some excitement might be generated by the battle over a Vietnam plank in the platform, by the conflict in the Democratic Party over "law and order," and by the tactics of the New Politicians to substitute "confrontation" for parliamentary procedure. They did not expect the battle in the streets between the semi-organized New Left—predominantly Yippies and Hippies—and the Chicago police. It was this battle that became the major event of the convention—with Mayor Richard Daley, last of the oldtime machine bosses, cast as villain by some, as hero by others, but symbolizing the counter-brutality that shocked the nation.

If there was to be a revision of the scenario at the convention hall, it could be written only by Senator Edward M. Kennedy—Teddy to the delegates, as his brother had been Bobby. But Kennedy, borne down by the sorrow of his brother's death and feeling keenly his responsibilities as the last living son of old Joe Kennedy, would have no part of it. He did not want to run for President and he knew that the Vice Presidential nomination would only ensnare him in the politics of confusion which the party was busily generating. When the Chicago riots erupted, leaving an indelible stain on the Democratic Party, the wisdom of his decision became manifest. In a moment of inspiration Humphrey chose Senator Edmund Muskie of Maine as his running mate—and Muskie, rising to the challenge, brought what little style and content were to be found in the 1968 Democratic effort.

One other candidate was in the field, the self-anointed former Governor of Alabama, George Wallace—racist in the past, demagogic in the present—who believed that he could panic the electorate into descending on the White House like a French Revolution mob. He had set out to rob Nixon of the South and to smash the Democratic Party in the industrial North by appealing to the prejudices of the white ethnic minorities who saw the black revolution as a challenege to its livelihood and to its lower-middle-class homes.

It was these two candidates—Humphrey, the stand-in for an incumbent President, and Wallace, the spoiler—that the Nixon organization was geared to defeat. From the start, the polls showed Nixon far ahead and, to his delight, gave him a valuable bonus. The Gallup poll reported that 56 per cent of the voters believed the Republican Party more capable of coping with the problems then facing America. For the first time in decades the Republicans, a minority party, had the apparent support of the majority—and this meant much in assessing Nixon's chances of victory.

Of considerable significance was the caliber of the Nixon machine and the organization of his campaign—more significant, perhaps, than campaign strategy or the issues. Among those who watched the machine roll effortlessly, there was agreement that it was perhaps the best-oiled in living memory. Where the teamwork had been faulty in 1960, it was now superb, with John Mitchell, a Nixon law partner, and Bob Finch working in tandem. The United Citizens for Nixon-Agnew was mobilized into a coordinated force of 5 million members. At the Willard Hotel in Washington, reopened as headquarters for the Citizens, some seven hundred paid workers and an army of volunteers worked quietly and efficiently under the tutelage of Charles Rhyne, a former law school classmate of the candidate. The staff was young and non-political. This sometimes drove the politicians into a frenzy of accusation that the campaign was "not professional," but it was the results that counted.

Computerization was widely used. To test the temper of the country, seven hundred portable "listening posts"—portable record- ing booths—were shifted from spot to spot. Those who wished to express their views could do so, and the miles of tape were flown into Washington each day for encoding on punch cards. The men, women, and children who had expressed their views duly received an answer, prepared by a computer, "signed" by Nixon—at a cost of twenty cents a letter. From the tapes the staff at the Willard could prepare a daily digest of what the voters were thinking and charts of the shift in public interest in the issues. If concern over violence in the streets rose, or interest in Vietnam ebbed, the word was flashed to Nixon's personal staff and to his speech writers.

There was another difference between 1960 and 1968—and that was Nixon's doing. He had learned that a harried candidate such as he had been in his first Presidential campaign transmits his sense of worry to the voters. He also makes mistakes. Nixon was determined not to make mistakes this time. Though he would cover 50,000 miles and venture into 122 cities and 30 states, his schedule was well paced—and the deliberate tempo of his journey- ing spelled out to the public the feeling of confidence that he shared with his close advisers. When the politicians, fearful that it was all too deliberate, too uncontroversial, urged him to move faster and hit harder, Nixon's advisers pointed to the floundering Humphrey campaign and offered an aphorism from Woodrow Wilson: "Never murder a man who is about to commit suicide." When Senator Thruston Morton of Kentucky heatedly argued that "we can't let Nixon be like Dewey who was afraid to say that the sun is shining because it might be considered controversial," the candidate refused to be budged.

He developed instead a technique for handling the controversial which silenced some of his critics in the Republican Party. His speeches were bland, cast in generalities, and devoid of rancor- making rhetoric, which, he felt, was unnecessary for a front-runner.

353

He dealt with troublesome issues in statements and position papers that few read, but that he could cite when he was accused of ducking comment on the nation's major problems. Bound into a book that went to opinion-makers, contributors, and those who asked for it, Nixon's stands on policy matters were there for all to see—but the volume usually ended on a shelf.

With the Nixon pre-convention luck holding up, the first stop had been Chicago, still bruised and touchy over the national reaction to the handling by Mayor Daley's police of the convention riots. A half million Chicagoans were on the streets to cheer Nixon and to prove to the country that they were not Yahoos. In a television broadcast that night Nixon capitalized on the city's mood by approving "dissent" as well as the "need for control." Thruston Morton and Senator Edward Brooke felt that Nixon should have been more tolerant of the student demonstrations and harder on the police, but the statement they drafted for him to issue was ignored. They called a press conference to air their differences with the candidate, but Nixon refused to rob himself of the "law and order" issue, or to invite the sharp criticism of Republican conservatives.

And he remained unruffled. As the campaign progressed he moved easily from a Billy Graham rally to a high school appearance in the Midwest. He refused to debate with Humphrey and, in fact, was publicly solicitous of the goring his opponent was getting from the New Left, the first time since the Thirties that a Democratic candidate was the victim of radical ferment. Humphrey, Nixon knew, had much of the labor vote and a preponderance of Negro support. But he had little else. George Wallace was robbing the Republicans of their tenuous but vital base in the South—and Nixon made him the primary target.

But for the most part, he played the confident—though not too confident—statesman, easy in his manner, quick with quips that relaxed the audience but did not wound. As the campaign rolled toward its conclusion, Nixon's advisers worried about the shift of votes from Wallace to Humphrey, as the "white backlash" lost its cut, and as lifetime Democrats began returning to their party. Nixon's advisers worriedly called for more volume. But Nixon had thought it through for himself in his years out of office and he would not be pressed into changing his strategy. He was right, for to have done so would have been an indication that Humphrey had become a threat. Worse still, it would have brought down on his head the charge that the "New Nixon" had been a fraud, that he was still the alleged knife-fighter of an earlier mythology.

Bolstering Nixon's confidence was one activity of his campaign organization which few knew about until well after the election and inauguration. "Operation Integrity" was its code name, and it was headed by Louis B. Nichols, once J. Edgar Hoover's right-hand man in the FBI and now the recently retired Administrative Vice President of Schenley Industries. Nichols was part of an advisory committee of prominent Americans which had been formed prior to the convention to help Nixon. In August, Nixon had called Nichols in to ask him to put his organizational talents to the task of preventing the kind of vote fraud that, most observers agreed, had given the Presidency to John F. Kennedy in 1960. The man for this job, Nixon told Nichols, had to have an unques-tioned reputation for objectivity, accuracy, and fairness—and this Nichols had established for himself even in the politics-prone world of Washington.

"Never, during thirty-five years in the FBI and in industry, had I faced such a task," Nichols wrote for the July 1969 *Reader's Digest*. "I began by enlisting friends and former FBI colleagues in various states. Obviously, with 175,000 precincts and an estimated 86 million registered voters, we could cover only the most urgent targets." But cover them "Operation Integrity" did. Nichol's first step was to set up a 100,000-man volunteer army to check registra-tion of voters in those areas prone to vote fraud. There was oppo-sition in plenty from local Democratic machines; even the Demo-cratic National Committee made an abortive attempt to drive Nichols out by charging that the real purpose of "Operation Integ-rity" was to "obstruct" and intimidate. The record showed where the obstructionism was.

In Lake County, Indiana, solidly in the grip of a notorious politi-cal machine, "Operation Integrity" workers were thrown out of the polls, threatened by goons, and even arrested on trumped-up charges. But they nevertheless showed that the registration books were peopled by "ghosts"—non-existent voters. In Philadelphia,

Republican inspectors checked voting machines ten days before the election. They found that two-thirds of them lacked tamper-proof seals—and machines still in the warehouse had already recorded 1,083 "ghost" votes.

In St. Louis, scene of one of 1960's ballot robberies, "Operation Integrity" mailed letters to sixty-five hundred registered voters in the strongest Democratic districts. Fourteen per cent were returned because the voter had died or moved away. This prompted the St. Louis *Globe-Democrat* to suggest that there were "more haunted houses in St. Louis than there are in Disneyland." In Chicago, Mayor Richard Daley's boys were everywhere, resorting to attempted bribes and terror to keep six hundred "honest ballot" poll watchers from doing their job. With help from the courts, however, they were able to persist. The job they did saved the state for Nixon. In the 27th Ward, for example, "registration lists showed scores of voters living in burned-out buildings, vacant lots and houses where others resided," Nichols wrote. "About 170,000 of Chicago's 1.8 million registered voters were 'ghosts.'" Because of "Operation Integrity," the machine exercised restraint. The number of people who showed up to vote in suspect districts dropped 27 per cent, and the Democratic plurality fell by 52 per cent from what it had been in the primary.

"The theft of only 78,000 votes in St. Louis and Cook County (Chicago) would have deprived Richard Nixon of the required 270 electoral vote majority—and would have plunged us into a national crisis with Alabama's George Wallace holding the key," Louis Nichols says.

It was not until the last days of the campaign that Nixon's staff began to hear rumors of an impending blockbuster, courtesy of President Johnson. No one was quite certain what it would be, but they knew it had something to do with Vietnam. Then the White House announced that Johnson had ordered a halt in the bombing of North Vietnam, and the Nixon entourage quaked. For this single act, by calculation or happenstance, could have deprived the Republicans of the votes of millions of Americans who were fed up with the war and sharply dissatisfied with the way Johnson had been conducting it. Though Nixon was as hawkish as Humphrey, popular resentment had attached itself to the Democrat.

Would the voters now shift their sympathies to the Humphrey-Muskie ticket? Or would they see President Johnson's move as the political act of a desperate politician? This was what Robert Finch publicly charged, but he did not have to put the suspicion in voters' minds. They welcomed the bombing halt as a possible first step to peace, but they found the timing suspicious. Nixon could regret, again publicly, that the President's patriotism and integrity were being impugned, but the voters were no longer listening—and Nixon strategists returned to their earlier worry: Had Hubert Humphrey succeeded in uniting his fragmented party? The Harris poll, which in September had given Nixon 43 per cent to Humphrey's 28, now showed Humphrey leading with 43 per cent to Nixon's 40. (After consulting with George Gallup, Harris squared his final figures with those of his leading competitor: Nixon 42 per cent, Humphrey 40 per cent, Wallace 17 per cent.)

The campaign ended as it had begun—with Nixon cool and confident, the "instant smile" so irritating to the press flashing as he answered questions read to him by Bud Wilkinson, onetime football coach, defeated senatorial candidate from Oklahoma in the Goldwater election, and sports broadcaster, in a well-managed but pedestrian telethon. No one would know whether it won Nixon any votes, but it projected the image of a winner to the nationwide TV audience, which was the only purpose of the ritual. Then Nixon returned to his hotel, the Century Plaza, a gleaming new hostelry in the make-believe of Los Angeles. As he drank a glass of milk and munched on a sandwich, his feelings sagged and combat fatigue gripped him. The mask of confidence he had worn since September began to crack as he looked ahead to the long D-day of the actual election—the payoff for all candidates, small or large. It was an ordeal he had undergone many times, but now this was it.

His hotel bed was hardly a slit trench, but he would have slept well anywhere. That is the nature of professionals in any field. Nixon tumbled into it, and for a while there were no problems.

The next day, on the flight back to New York, he could look out as the country slipped by under his plane. There were no speeches to write, no strategy sessions to occupy him. He was a man alone, waiting for the nation's verdict, the votes of the jury being cast as he waited. It was a strange day, one of small obeisances to the gods of good fortune—a day in which the Nixon of the public prints seemed remote and unreal to those who watched him. At one point, he summoned Pat and the girls to his private compartment and handed his wife a pearl-and-diamond pin with matching earrings. As they were admired he gently warned that the next hours could bring defeat. Then he was all business again, conferring with those who had been at his side ever since he had declared his candidacy.

It was a few minutes after 7 P.M. when the Nixon party arrived at the Waldorf Towers and the twin suites on the thirty-second floor. Unlike the man he would succeed, he refused the intrusion of television, and all sets were turned off. For more than thirty minutes he soaked in a hot tub, put aside a suit freshly pressed for his appearance before the crowd waiting for a victory statement in the ballroom downstairs, and presented himself to his followers in the wrinkled clothes he had worn all day. And then, as the hours took their toll and his fortunes rose and fell, Nixon barricaded himself behind his yellow legal pads, noting results, receiving messages from his field men, and trying to make a pattern of what the network computers could not fathom.

It was past midnight when Nixon was informed that Governor Rockefeller was at the hotel and wanted to see him. The news looked bad at the time, and Nixon, smiling wanly at Rockefeller's lack of taste, refused to see him. The television commentators were already discussing the possibility of an election without a decision. The Wallace vote made it seem all too possible that neither Nixon nor Humphrey would have a majority of the electoral vote, thereby throwing the election into the House of Representatives. Talk of Constitutional crisis filled the airwaves and was reported to Nixon. California was the key. If he took California, then he could be reasonably certain of taking the country.

Then, shortly before 3 A.M., Richard Milhous Nixon, hard-nosed politician, indulged himself in a gesture at once sentimental and superstitious, acknowledging his weaknesses and challenging the gods. He asked Bob Finch, Murray Chotiner, John Mitchell, and Robert Haldeman to meet him in the living room of his suite at exactly three. It had been at this precise hour, eight years earlier, that he had been forced to admit defeat. When he walked in, he asked the same question that had brought him the crushing news: "How do we stand?" Now it was different. The states that he needed for victory were safe, he was told. "That's how I see it," he said—and suddenly the albatross that he had carried since 1960 was off his neck. Fifteen minutes later he called Spiro Agnew in Annapolis. "Ted," he said, "we've won."

The rest of the country, bleary-eyed at its television sets, relied on the computers and on the delayed returns from California and Illinois, key to a Nixon victory. It was not until 11 A.M. of the following day that NBC conceded that "Richard Nixon will be the thirty-seventh President of the United States." Three quarters of an hour later Vice President Humphrey called to offer his congratulations and to inform Nixon that he would concede in fifteen minutes. "You put up a great fight, a great fight," Nixon said. There was little more to be said, even though he knew what Humphrey's feelings must be.

Then, as he scribbled notes for his victory statement, the transformation began. He was now a President-elect, weeks away from the time when everyone but his wife and children—even the most intimate of his friends—would address him as "Mr. President." It would be many days before he would know the extent of his victory—302 electoral votes to Humphrey's 191, 32 states to Humphrey's 13, and a plurality that, in spite of George Wallace's Southern inroads, was several times that of John F. Kennedy's 113,000 in 1960.

At 12:32 Richard Nixon, President-elect of the United States, stepped before the television cameras in the Grand Ballroom of the Waldorf Astoria. The boy from Yorba Linda, the two-time loser who had been counted out by everyone but himself, the most controversial political figure the United States had known since the passing of Joe McCarthy, stood isolated under the glaring lights, a solitary man now doubly alone in the isolation of the highest office on earth.

"A great philosophy is never one without defeat, but always without fear," he said.

20

Postlude and Prologue

"INTEGRITY and firmness are all I can promise," said George Washington on assuming the Presidency. "Tomorrow I shall come into my office in my own right," said Theodore Roosevelt. "Then watch out for me." And Dwight David Eisenhower, writing of his feelings when he walked into the Oval Room as President, remarked, "The homely old saw had proved to be true: in the United States, any boy *can* grow up to be President." In a very real sense these words and thoughts were the reflection of each man's character and style—the reluctant squire answering the call of duty, the irrepressible and happy battler, the man for whom greatness was always a surprise.

History has yet to record what Richard Nixon's revealing words were and to whom they were spoken. Those words would have been welcomed by a nation which, in the interregnum between Election and Inauguration had speculated: What kind of a President will Nixon make? Press and public expected immediate and measurable action, and the emergence of a sharply etched public philosophy to be blazoned across its front pages. Each observer according to his own ideology had high hopes or dire misgivings. Both Left and Right were surprised as the scene unfolded. Neither was fully satisfied. There was undisguised distress among conservatives, a certain astonished elation among liberals, and in both camps these early responses were soon revised.

Until the Inaugural Address the only guide was a speech on the Presidency that Nixon had delivered during the campaign. Like most campaign utterances, it was long on theory and short on specifics. But what it said was, in the shibboleth of the late Sixties, relevant. "We stand at a great turning point," Nixon had said, "when the nation is groping for a new direction, unsure of its role and its purposes, caught in a tumult of change."

In this watershed year of 1968, America needs Presidential leadership that can establish a firm focus, and offer a way out of a time of towering uncertainties. Only the President can hold out a vision of the future and rally the people behind it. . . . He has to take *hold* of America before he can move it forward.

This requires leadership that believes in law, and has the courage to enforce it; leadership that believes in justice, and is determined to promote it; leadership that believes in progress, and knows how to inspire it. The days of a passive Presidency belong to a simpler past. Let me be very clear about this: The next President must take an activist view of his office. He must articulate the nation's values, define its goals and marshall its will. Under a Nixon Administration, the Presidency will be deeply involved in the entire sweep of America's public concerns. The first responsibility of leadership is to gain mastery over events, and to shape the future in the image of our hopes.

The President today . . . must bear in mind the distinction between forceful leadership and stubborn willfulness. And he should not delude himself into thinking that he can do everything himself. America today cannot afford vest-pocket government, no matter who wears the vest. . . .

There are occasions on which a President must take unpopular measures. But his responsibility does not stop there. The President has a duty to decide, but the people have a right to know why. The President has a responsibility to tell them—to lay

361

out all the facts, and to explain not only why he chose as he did but also what it means for the future. Only through an open, candid dialogue can a President maintain his trust and his leadership. . . .

In order to lead, a President today must listen. And in this time of searching and uncertainty, government must learn to listen in new ways. A President has to hear not only the clamorous voices of the organized, but also the quiet voices, the *inner voices*—the voices that speak through the silences, and that speak from the heart and the conscience. . . .

For years now, the trend has been to sweep more and more authority toward Washington. . . . I plan a streamlined Federal system, with a return to the states, cities and communities of decision-making powers rightfully theirs. The purpose of this is not only to make government more effective and more responsive, but also to concentrate Federal attention on those functions that can only be handled on the Federal level. . . .

We are living today in a time of great promise—but also of too many promises. . . . A President must tell the people what cannot be done immediately, as well as what can. . . . America needs charts of the possible, not excursions into the impossible. . . .

What has to be, has to be done by President and people, or it won't be done at all. In asking you to join this great effort, I am asking not that you give something *to* your country, but that you do something *with* your country; I am asking not for your gifts but your hands.

It was very much in this mood, though with the heightening that history gives to every Inaugural statement, that Richard Nixon stood on January 20, 1968, in the cold grayness, isolated among the dignitaries and facing an assembled press and public. Now he was President, and the speech he had delivered on the duties and responsibilities of the office was both relevant and irrelevant. Would his words now answer those who had always found a riddle in his personality and an enigma in his deeds? As in all Inaugural addresses, he invoked history's "summons to greatness." And he summarized the nation's ills:

We find ourselves rich in goods, but ragged in spirit; reaching with magnificent precision for the moon, but falling into raucous discord on earth. We are caught in war, wanting peace. We are torn by division, wanting unity. We see around us empty lives, wanting fulfillment. We see tasks that need doing, waiting for hands to do them.

To a crisis of the spirit, we need an answer of the spirit. And to find that answer, we need only look within ourselves. When we listen to the "better angels of our nature," we find that they celebrate the simple things, the basic things—such as goodness, decency, love, kindness.

Greatness comes in simple trappings.

The simple things are the ones most needed today if we are to surmount what divides us and cement what unites us. To lower our voices would be a simple thing. In these difficult years, America has suffered from a fever of words; from inflated rhetoric that promises more than it can deliver; from angry rhetoric that fans discontents into hatred; from bombastic rhetoric that postures instead of persuading.

We cannot learn from one another until we stop shouting at one another—until we speak quietly enough so that our words can be heard as well as our voices. . . .

We have endured a long night of the American spirit. But as our eyes catch the dimness of the first rays of dawn, let us not curse the remaining dark. Let us gather the light.

Our destiny offers not the cup of despair, but the chalice of opportunity. So let us seize it, not in fear but in gladness—and "riders on the earth together," let us go forward, firm in our faith, steadfast in our purpose, cautious of the dangers; but sustained by our confidence in the will of God and the promise of man.

The echoes were there—echoes of Lincoln, of Whittaker Chambers, of Walter Lippmann, of Woodrow Wilson, of Franklin Delano Roosevelt. They rang in the interstices of his phrases, at once disturbing and comforting. These men had been his heroes, for varying and conflicting reasons—each one to him a giant. Of Lincoln's claim to Richard Nixon's complicity there could be no question. Of all the men who had taken the Presidency in their grasp, Lincoln was the most eloquent, the least affected, the man whose existential humor exceeded his tragic sense of life. A little like God, Lincoln had so loved his country that he had given his life to mending its heart. To Nixon, perhaps, the Lincoln out of a log hut, grasping for knowledge and recognition, was not too unlike the small boy in a general store where California's lemon country tangled with the tentacles of a growing Los Angeles.

The other echoes bounced off his envy of the academicians who rejected him as they did not reject a Princeton President who had nevertheless mastered the forms of politics sufficiently to leave his confused mark on history. They bounced off his uncertainties in the world of place, a man never sure that the dust of small-town America had really been wiped from his shoes. In the years of his success the externals had changed, but he still walked warily in the drawing rooms of the mighty and of those who lived securely in the lee of social power. Alice Longworth repeated to her friends that she was "very fond of Dick"—and they made a buzz when he escorted her to St. Matthew's Cathedral for Senator Joe McCarthy's wedding—but there was always a gentle irony in her eye and her tone when she discussed him among the "cliff-dwellers" of Washington's inner society.

But with the Inaugural over and the festivities done, President Nixon was caught in the crunch of the here-and-now. Duties, powers, and responsibilities were no longer theoretical. And his major problem in allocating the prerogatives of the Presidency was that he had first to hold them in his hand. The 1968 election had left Nixon with a House and Senate controlled, for the first time since the days of James Buchanan, by a party in opposition to the Administration at the start of a new President's tenure.

He was, statistically, a minority President—though the argument was made with some persuasion that the vote which went to George Wallace would have otherwise been his. But Nixon knew the country and its temper well enough to realize that politically, it was in balance. The great liberal tide that had swept over the nation since the New Deal era was ebbing—and for the first time in decades the mood had changed. What for want of a better name would be called "conservatism" was growing more acceptable, less of a liability. There was, in fact, the beginning of a conservative counter-sweep in the local primaries and elections of early 1969. The old divisions of party and ideology were breaking down as a submerged middle class began to rise up in indignation at the excesses of past years and past Administrations. Taxes were high, cities were unsafe, and America's role in the community of nations was challenged at every point.

Nixon analyzed the new state of the nation in long periods of reflection during the weeks of the interregnum. Never a man to be rushed into quick decisions, he followed his own bent and relied on his own calculations. He had never foreseen the President's posture as that of a King Canute, ordering the tide to recede. In the changed circumstances that obtained at the time he took his oath of office, he could not see that posture as one of beckoning in the waves. As a student of history and of the men who make it he realized consciously and intuitively that the time had come to bring quiet and stability to government, to eschew the major experimentation that had marked the tenure of all his predecessors since Franklin Delano Roosevelt. "Social engineering" had been a seductive term in another day—but he had never seen it as more than organized busybodying, and he would have none of it.

Among those who professed astonishment at President Nixon's "style" or lack of it, his failure to mount his horse and charge, it was commonly held that the caution of his first months had been conditioned solely by the extraordinary circumstances of his tenure—the tightly contested election, the balky nature of Congress, the congeries of problems he inherited from the previous President. But even in the late Fifties, when the Presidency seemed reasonably in his grasp, he had thought through the nature of his first months, even years, in the White House. In discussions with me and with other friends he had almost categorically indicated that there would be no sudden upheaval, no 180-degree turn in policy. "The country can't take it, and shouldn't take it," he said. His first effort, he believed, would be directed toward establishing a dialogue with the real American majority, the great middle class from which he had sprung. The pressure groups, the official and unofficial lobbies, the promoters were as always at hand and ready to talk. But the middle class would be harder to approach, and it was essential to win its confidence before he could begin to establish any real contact.

During the campaign, Nixon had pledged himself to bring the Vietnam war to an honorable end, to halt the ballooning inflation, to bring some order into America's muddle-through foreign policy, to restore to Americans the safety of their homes and persons, to reinvigorate the Constitutional process. Considering the "domestic tranquility" promised by the Constitution, he thought in terms of Edmund Burke's "little platoon"—the society that worked upward from the community to the vast Federal establishment—rather than in terms of the "Great Society" of Lyndon Baines Johnson.

Richard Nixon had no false modesty about himself or the office he occupied. Those who saw him at work agreed that he enjoyed being President and that he took his new responsibilities in stride. Unlike John F. Kennedy, who had roamed the White House during his First Hundred Days in what Arthur Schlesinger, Jr., called "a crisis of identity," Nixon was relaxed—perhaps more so than at any time in his entire life. He was not going to be rushed, nor was he ready to fritter away his nervous substance by cataloguing the animadversions of political critics, as Johnson and Kennedy had done. He had a much greater catalogue to assemble—the needs, desires, and practical demands of an anguished people. From that catalogue he had first to draw up a list of priorities. To take up these priorities required time and patience, and the realization that the imperatives of thirty-five years had a life of their own. As James Jackson Kilpatrick pointed out in a lucid disquisition for *National Review*, "he inherited built-in billions in untouchable outlays. He inherited programs-in-being, treaties in force, contracts already let, local commitments irrevocably made . . . a bureaucracy entrenched beyond belief. . . . Even if Nixon's nature were different, no incoming President could have spun this ship around in a hurry."

In the period of the interregnum he had tried to substitute drama for substance, introducing his Cabinet in a television spectacular that impressed no one but the people. But even here he had been thwarted by the dialectics of the situation—a phrase he had heard in various contexts from his friend Whittaker Chambers. His original plan had been to seed that Cabinet with a cross-section of American society—Republicans and Democrats, Jews and Catholics and Protestants, white men and blacks, liberals and conservatives. But all too often the men he wanted did not want him. He was forced to settle for a Cabinet that was efficient, cautious, and unspectacular.

The men who stood out were Melvin Laird, pragmatic, non-ideological, and hardnosed, for Secretary of Defense; William Pierce Rogers, an administrator with no experience in foreign affairs, for his Secretary of State; Robert Finch, trustworthy, good-hearted, but ambitious in his own right, for the all-inclusive post of Secretary of Health, Education, and Welfare; John Mitchell, a lawyer's lawyer who did not know his way around the Washington jungle, as his Attorney General. These men were his, and the rest were window dressing—capable and loyal, but untested. His "liberals" were not in the Cabinet, and they were suspect for their honesty to the liberal community: Daniel Patrick Moynihan to deal with urban problems and the uncertainties of minority politics and Henry A. Kissinger (hardly a certified "liberal" and hawkish on Vietnam) to formulate a national security policy. The country had politely applauded his choices, but there had been no tumultuous approval to reassure him, no Cimarron stampede to a new frontier. They merely underscored his Inaugural premise that the time had come for quiet discourse rather than Roman candles.

He had promised an end to the Vietnam war by a "plan" he never disclosed. But his options were nonexistent. The military told him that by a sudden escalation in air and naval attack, knocking out the Red River dikes and blockading Haiphong Harbor, he could bring the North Vietnamese communists to their knees. But there were always Senators J. William Fulbright and Edward Kennedy lurking in the cloakrooms of the Capitol to bring him grief. He could offer only free elections, guaranteed by the United Nations or an international commission, but this was immediately interpreted as a willingness to accept a coalition government. Beyond the generous and face-saving terms he offered Hanoi, there was only patience and the reasonable belief that the communists had only one or two rounds left in their military fowling pieces. But would the American people match his patience, his refusal to trade space and time for a mess of diplomatic pottage? He was taking a calculated risk that firmness would pay off before the 1970 elections had been set in their mold.

He grasped what Eisenhower, Kennedy, and Johnson never understood, that the time had come for the United States to conciliate its friends before it made overtures to its enemies—and his eight-day trip to the capitals of Western Europe soon after assuming the Presidency had enhanced American prestige and reassured the leaders of the free and semifree world that he would not embark on diplomatic adventures that would weaken the patchwork of anti-communist alliances or play host to Soviet ambitions for world conquest.

In the expansiveness of the campaign Nixon had promised to "clean out" the State Department. This pledge he had made in 1952, when the Democrats were in office—but it had been tucked away in 1960. To have brought up the subject would have been an implied criticism of the Eisenhower Administration. But the State Department had gone its schizophrenic way, with a middle echelon that derailed the policies laid down by the men at the top, as the attempted frame-up and dismissal of Otto Otepka, a security officer who took his duties seriously, abundantly demonstrated. The appointment of William Rogers as Secretary of State had obviously not been calculated to prevent the clean-up—

but made it absolutely predictable that nothing would be done. Rogers was far too close, socially and in spirit, with the men who might have been purged. As for Otepka, he had been reassured that vindication would be his. Instead, he was appointed to a well-paid membership on the somnolent Subversive Activities Control Board, an agency whose teeth and claws were already removed by the Supreme Court with the blessings of the previous Attorney General.

John Mitchell, the new Attorney General, seemed to hold the key to some fulfillment of the Nixon program as it affected the "silent majority" of Americans. His views on the restoration of law and order to the national scene and his disdain for the permissiveness of American society and its judicial surrogates were strong. As Nixon's campaign manager he had shown himself to be a tough and determined man, untouched by any liberal frivolity of mind. Here, clearly, was a man who would seek the means to stop the rampaging of the New Left on the country's disintegrating campuses, who would bring safety to streets dark with menace, ending the mob violence that erupted so frequently and senselessly. Here was a man who could inspire respect in the law enforcement process, and who would find ways to cope with an invisible empire of organized crime that was reaching into the stronghold of legitimate commerce, even into the banks themselves. But other than his limited part in dislodging Justice Abe Fortas from the Supreme Court, Mitchell in the initial six months contributed nothing that indicated progress that was discernible to the naked eye of a peering press corps.

In the area of the economy—perhaps as dangerous to the national health as the Vietnam war—the President had been called upon to make impossible decisions. In attempting to arrive at solutions involving employment and unemployment, Nixon never failed to remind his listeners that "I was once poor." This was not a rhetorical device, but something that went to the root of his thinking on economics. To halt the accelerating inflation, he saw only one effective course of action—a drastic cutback in Federal spending.

There was waste in plenty, as the General Accounting Office

would confess—15 per cent of the $200 billion budget, or about $30 billion, was going down the drain. But to locate that waste and then to eliminate it was a full-time job that no President had yet attempted. And it was certainly not something that could be accomplished briefly. To reduce the Federal budget significantly, cuts would have to be made in programs and Cabinet departments restricted in their activities. Much of this would have been in consonance with Nixon's belief that governmental activity should move up from the "little platoon"—the community—rather than down from Washington. But it would also bring about an increase in unemployment, to which Nixon objected viscerally, and as a man who hoped to elect a Republican Congress in 1970. He relied, therefore, on fiscal and monetary devices. He had called for an end to the 10 per cent surtax during the campaign. Now he reversed himself, asking that it be continued for another six months and then reduced to 5 per cent. He supported the Federal Reserve Bank's credit crunch, though by one of those paradoxes of economics a shortage of money seemed to be as inflationary as, in another time, the shortage of goods had been. The country, emulating its government, continued to spend and spend, inflate and inflate.

The flurry of proposed legislation that many had expected in the first weeks and months never materialized. Long before he took the Inaugural oath, the President had decided that he would not be stampeded into action—that neither criticism nor adulation would lead him to act precipitously. He had too much respect for the office and for himself as its occupant to move before he had carefully made his estimate of the situation. He was, as a close observer at the White House noted, working hard at "his projection of what he conceives to be the symbolism of his Presidency." He was, moreover, too astute a politician to delude himself into believing that an opposition Congress would lightly give him what he sought. And in this he was correct. It took a careful marshaling of forces, a quiet and practical campaign, to get the Congress to approve by a minuscule margin his Safeguard system of anti-ballistic missiles to protect the nation from the Soviet Union's growing first-strike potential.

In the seventh month of his tenure that symbolism had begun to emerge. As *U.S. News & World Report* would sum it up: "Mr. Nixon, intimates say, wants his countrymen to see him as a self-possessed President, a fair-minded man ready to listen to every side, an unflappable, unharassed Executive. . . . Most congressional Republicans and a fair number of Democrats credit the President with having achieved the impression he wanted to create, despite some political flash fires"—the inevitable controversy over political appointments, the sparks that fly as a new White House team adjusts itself to the pressures and responsibilities of office. Yet even as the headline writers etched their bemusement on the nation's front pages, Nixon was carefully structuring a foreign policy posture that would bring him praise from the capitals of Europe and attention from those of Asia.

The touchy but necessary process of bringing balance to America's overseas preoccupations, of making the Vietnam war only one of the Administration's concerns in a complex and itchy world, had quietly begun almost from the moment when he moved into the Oval Room. NATO, almost collapsing in despair over Lyndon Johnson's inattention, assumed new importance with Nixon's determination to restore it as a political force. And a world weary of war and the threat of war responded hopefully to the President's carefully planned search for a *modus vivendi* with the Soviet colossus. Contrary to popular belief, the Nixonian insistence that relations with the Kremlin must be based on astute self-interest and hard bargaining elicited a welcome response from the communists who preferred solid though small advances to the bravura of large proposals that never descended from Cloud Nine.

The happenstance of history aided Nixon in his insistence on walking before he ran. Six hundred million people sat by their television sets to watch what Nixon would call the "greatest week in the history of the world since the Creation": the landing of man—of two Americans—on the moon. Nixon risked all to involve himself in this great scientific spectacular, for had the penetration of a new planet ended in failure, he would have been hurt by it even as he now shared its success. There was criticism because he spoke to Neil Armstrong and Edwin Aldrin, Jr., as they stared with mild surprise at the barren reaches of the moon. Had he abstained from this felicity, he would have been charged with playing down what had been begun by another President. But his enthusiasm was patently genuine as he lauded them from the White House—as genuine as his almost boyish reactions when he cheered the astronauts from the bridge of the *Hornet* on their return to earth.

"No one has seen him so exhilarated, confident, jubilant, full of pride," said an eyewitness to the scene on the *Hornet*. "Suddenly he had found an event to give him full confidence as a leader."

Yet this was a superficial appraisal. The success of the moon landing had once more projected the United States into a position compromised by the bitterness of the Vietnam war. Nixon was aware of this more than most men, and cognizant that it would make his task as the leader of the free world easier by far. The confidence had been there all along, but now he could show it openly. Not by happenstance he had gambled on this success, timing a round-the-world trip to coincide with the universal excitement over America's pioneering feat. At no other time could his continent-hopping—the Philippine Islands, Indonesia, Thailand, India, Pakistan, Vietnam, Rumania, and Great Britain—have been better received. At no other time could he have enunciated his new foreign policy "doctrine" more auspiciously.

In Asia he had told the leaders of troubled and assailed countries that the United States was not abandoning them. But he had also underscored words written in another day—that the Asians could no longer expect Washington to generate the policies that would guide them, that they could no longer count on automatic support from the United States, that the first moves toward their salvation would have to come from themselves. The idea that this country could commit itself in advance to an endless series of Vietnams still persisted. To those who clung to this belief the President offered a diplomatic paraphrase of the old American saying that God helps those who help themselves, substituting America for the deity. His trip to Bucharest, opposed by the State Department—as it had opposed most of his overseas missions for

President Eisenhower—had been equally successful. Ignoring the counsel of those who argued that diplomacy was not to be entrusted to him, the President had begun a new political dialogue in Rumania, affirming that the United States was not riveted to any single international dogma, that it would accept honest mutuality from any nation in pursuing peaceful negotiations. The Rumanians had as quietly responded by improving their relations with Israel, demonstrating to the Arabs that communist support was not monolithic.

As he moved from country to country, however, the cries from a do-nothing Congress that the President was doing nothing domestically increased in volume. On his return they had Nixon's answer. The man who, it was said, wanted to be known as the "practical President" dropped into the laps of his Democratic and Republican critics as revolutionary an answer to the problems of poverty as had been seen since the early days of Franklin Delano Roosevelt's New Deal. Nixon and his aides had worked on his plan for weeks and months, and it had received his final approval over the objections of most of his Cabinet and his economic advisers. It was in many ways his own, and would be judged as such. Its aim was to fulfill Nixon's campaign promise that he would begin to move families from relief rolls to payrolls, doing away with the patchwork of "welfare" programs that had been sewn together since the Thirties at great cost but with little success.

The Nixon program for "income support" was, in the President's first message, spelled out in generalities, with the specifics to come in the legislation he would send up to Congress. Critics noted that it would double the number of people receiving financial aid from the government and increase costs. But Nixon had incorporated into the plan two principles long sought by those who saw "relief" as an endless drain on Federal, state, and local resources, with no resultant rehabilitation of its recipients. He had tied it to a job-training program, and required unemployed men and women in welfare families to register for work and to accept proffered employment on pain of losing their share of family-assistance payments. This alone recommended it to taxpayers who had grimly, if not always accurately, protested that the

373

nation's substance—and theirs—was being spent to support those who could but would not work. But Nixon went beyond the complex arithmetic of welfare and poverty. He called for a revenue-sharing plan that would bail out states and municipalities now desperately attempting to cope with increasing demands, returning to them functions preempted by the Federal bureaucracy over almost four decades of expansionism. As a Congressman, a Senator, a Vice President, and a Presidential candidate, Nixon had preached a philosophy of decentralization—and this he now sought to implement.

But this was only a beginning. It did not silence those who saw his quiet practicality as hesitancy and a lack of grasp of the imperatives of government. For those who criticized would not accept the very simple fact that the Nixon they lamented was a paper man of their own construction.

The country as a whole, with no interest in labels and no doctrinaire commitments, reacted differently. If the polls accurately reflected the national sentiment, then Nixon had achieved his initial goal. In the first six months of his tenure 65 per cent of the people gave him their support and approved his approach to Presidential duties and responsibilities. This was twenty percentage points more than he had polled in the election—his first real majority. The prerequisite for the dialogue he had sought were here, and though a rising obduracy in Congress could whittle away that strength, it demonstrated the essential accuracy of his reading of the national mood.

When the war in Vietnam had been ended and economic troubles contained, then Richard Nixon could begin to give his Administration the style and the content the country had voted for. Then and only then would the chroniclers of these times be able to draw a line separating the past of the ideologists from the future of a man who saw the United States not as a test tube but as a place where people lived and worked and pursued a timeless happiness. At such a juncture the real measure of Nixon would be taken.

But if he failed, it would not be for want of trying. This was something the boy from Yorba Linda had learned and the man in the White House would never forget. At night, when the pressures grew too great or the problems too perplexing, the man alone retired to the Lincoln Room, seeking his own respite while the White House slept.

Index